Date Due

Feb 10 60	69²		
Ap 5 61	69⁵⁴		

1ˢᵗ

2ⁿᵈ

3ʳᵈ

grammar, ⌐

Dictionary, ⌐

Smith's smaller classical
dictionary. Everyman's Library
History of Greece.
Bury's Student's
Edition
Wright – Hist. of Greek Literature.
Am. Book Co. $1.50
R. Jebb's – Introduction to Grk. Lit,
Gulick – Life of the Greeks.
Appleton & co.

Galy – Mythology
Classic Myths. $1.50
Ginn & co.

A. Fairbanks Rel. of Greeks.

Grk. Archaeology & Art.

Fowler & Wheeler Am. Bk Co.

"

H.F. Tozer.

Geography

Kiepert $ —"— & Co.
Atlas. $1.00

"

The Grk. view of Life
Lowes Dickinson .

"

E. Gardiner Grk. Sculpture
macmillan & co

"

A.L. Frothingham

Greek Architecture

"

J.P. Rambles & Studies in Greece .
Mahaffy .

BUST OF LYSIAS

(See Introduction, § 25.)

COLLEGE SERIES OF GREEK AUTHORS

EDITED UNDER THE SUPERVISION OF

JOHN WILLIAMS WHITE AND THOMAS DAY SEYMOUR

EIGHT ORATIONS

OF

LYSIAS

EDITED

WITH INTRODUCTION, NOTES, AND APPENDICES

BY

MORRIS H. MORGAN, PH.D.

ASSISTANT PROFESSOR IN HARVARD UNIVERSITY

BOSTON, U.S.A., AND LONDON

GINN & COMPANY, PUBLISHERS

1900

885.2.
L93

VIRO · DOCTISSIMO

GEORGIO · MARTINO · LANE

MAGISTRO · OPTIMO · AMATO

PREFACE.

THIS volume of selected orations of Lysias is intended primarily for students who have never before read an Attic Orator. It is not based upon any single German edition. Yet the editor is far from laying claim to much originality. He has drawn freely from his many predecessors, and, in especial, he is indebted, on nearly every page of the notes and the appendix, to Rauchenstein and Frohberger, as will be clear to all who know the editions of these two scholars. In the Introduction, the present editor, like everyone who now writes on an Attic Orator, has found invaluable aid in the work of Blass. A list of the books to which reference is made by abbreviations will be found prefixed to the Index, and a list of editions of Lysias in Appendix B.

The eight orations here printed are arranged, for convenience of reference, in their numerical order, but this is not the order in which the editor would recommend that they be read. Judged by his experience, the speech *For Mantitheus* is the simplest to a beginner in Lysias, and it should be followed by the speech *Against Eratosthenes.* The notes to these two speeches are, therefore, somewhat elementary in nature, and matters of syntax are more fully treated in them than in the notes to the other speeches.

The editor is under great obligations to Professors White and Seymour for their careful reading of the proof-sheets, and for their many helpful and illuminating suggestions. He is grateful, also, to his colleagues and former masters, Professors Goodwin and Allen, for their kind assistance here and there throughout the book; and he thanks Professor Gildersleeve for encouragement in his work and for what he believes to be a certain emendation in VII. 14.

M. H. M.

HARVARD UNIVERSITY,
August, 1895.

INTRODUCTION.

PUBLIC SPEAKING IN ATHENS.

1. HOMER relates that Achilles, when he set out to join the army of Agamemnon, was but a boy, "as yet unskilled in war and in public speaking wherein men win preëminence." Therefore Phoenix went with him, "to teach him all these things, — to be both a speaker of words and also a doer of deeds." [1] Thus, ages before the written word was known, we find that the skill to speak and the power to fight were rated equally, each contributing to make up the hero. Such a hero was Odysseus, strong in council, as the Greeks before Troy found him when he showed that the fatal tenth year was at hand, and terrible in the combat, as when on the threshold of his house in Ithaca "he stripped him of his rags," and "among the suitors each man looked about him how he might escape his utter doom." [2]

2. It is a misfortune that, of the surviving Attic prose, the simplest is so full of descriptions of wars and so coloured by the dialect of campaigns that the young student of the Classics sees for a long time only one side of the character of the ideal Greek. In the heroic age, to be sure, men were more ready to settle their disputes by battle than by argument. Even in our own day the sword is still the final arbiter, although the appeal to its decision grows constantly rarer. In the Attic age, the Greeks highly appreciated the more

[1] *Il.* ix. 440 ff. [2] *Il.* ii. 284 ff.; *Od.* xxii. 1, 43.

rational method of arbitration, though they did not employ it so often as we do. In spite of this, it is in the arts of peace that they are our best teachers, and to the history of their mastery of those arts our interest and admiration should chiefly be given.

3. Not until after the Persian wars could the Hellenic cities, now secure against the barbarian, begin that active and open intercourse which proved so favourable to the progress of literature in general and to that branch of literature which is here briefly treated — Oratory. Even before these wars, the habit of wearing arms was declining. It is a significant fact that the Athenians, a people destined to carry the art of oratory to its perfection, should have been among the very first to abandon the habit of wearing arms.[3]

4. Oratory, to the modern mind, is hardly a practical matter. Even in a university, the study of the art of speaking is not generally made a part of the regular course. If in this practical age we find but few orators, few men who, being called upon to speak in public, can acquit themselves to admiration, the reason must be that a man who takes the trouble to acquire the art in its perfection seldom finds occasions upon which to exercise it. When, on the other hand, we see that oratory was an art highly esteemed and ardently cultivated by an intelligent and thoughtful people like the Athenians, it is obvious that there were causes which made the ability to speak in public a thing to be desired in the common life of men. The occasions upon which a man feels the greatest need of the power of speaking persuasively are, first, when he is one of the counsellors of his country; and, secondly, when some personal need of his own is upon him. The councils of modern states are limited in the number of their

[3] Thuc. i. 6.

members. In Athens, the principal council was the Assembly
of all the citizens. In its meetings the policy of the state
received its final shape, and every citizen had equal rights to
speak and to be heard. But political oratory, while often the
duty of the citizen, is a duty that may be shirked. When,
however, the citizen's own safety or the safety of his property
is at stake, the obligation to accuse or to defend becomes
peremptory, — when, in fact, recourse is had to legal procedure.
But in modern times we avoid the task of speaking in person
by putting our cases into the charge of those whose profession is to speak for us, — our attorneys. In Athens, a
very different state of things prevailed, for there were no
attorneys in Athens at all. Athenian procedure did not allow
plaintiff and defendant to sit idly by, while counsel learned
in the law fought out their battles for them. Each party was
obliged to take his place in the court, and to make accusation
and to defend himself with his own lips. This law applied
to every case which could be brought before a court, from the
most trifling misdemeanor punishable with a small fine, to the
highest crime for which the penalty was death.

5. This fundamental difference between Attic legal procedure and our own goes far to explain the view which
Athenians took of the art of oratory. This was a weapon which
any man might be called upon to use; upon its possession
might depend his enjoyment of his property and even the
preservation of his life. And the requirement that each man
should personally plead his own cause does not appear to have
acted as a preventive of lawsuits. The Athenian fondness for
litigation grew to be the passion which is so humorously
caricatured by Aristophanes in his comedy of the *Wasps*.
Athenians were never happier than when listening to a lively
controversy, and probably but few personages in Athens could

have made with truth the assertion of Socrates to his judges:
" I am over seventy years of age, and yet I have never come up
before a court until to-day." [4]   Athenian lawsuits were as
varied in their subjects as are our own. There is hardly a case
upon our records which is not foreshadowed in Athenian
experience. Even the problem of monopolies and trusts, which
still remains unsolved, is not without its Athenian parallel.
Lysias wrote one of his most interesting speeches against the
members of a 'corn-ring.' [5]   Those who see in the character
of the Greek people only the perfection which appears in their
works of art make a mistake that is fatal to any real appreciation of the facts of ancient life. If we thus exalt the
Greeks, our mere mortal vision cannot comprehend their
features nor our thoughts sympathize with theirs. They were
human ; therefore they often erred. If they had not, we could
not feel their experiences half so keenly, nor learn so many
lessons from their history.

6. In Athenian procedure, besides cases similar to our own,
there were two classes of suits, foreign to any which are known
to modern practice, which added a great mass of business to
the work of the courts, and which made the need of the
power of speaking in public more general among the citizens.
Participation in public affairs was a far commoner thing in
Athens than it is in our communities. The meetings of the
public Assembly (ἐκκλησία) of all the citizens were no mere
annual or semi-annual functions, like the American town-
meetings. There were forty stated meetings of the ἐκκλησία
every year, and additional meetings whenever occasion required.[6]
For the Assembly was the supreme power of the State, the
training-school in politics for the young Athenian, and at its

----

[4] Plat. *Apol.* 17 D.

[5] Oration XXII.   See below, p.
89 ff.

[6] On the ἐκκλησία in general, see
Gilbert, *Antiq.* p. 285 ff.; Gow, p. 118
ff.; Smith, *Dict. Antiq. s.v. Ecclesia.*

meetings the greatest statesmen first won the attention which raised them later to office. To hold an office in the gift of the people was felt to be the highest honour to which a citizen could aspire, and it was an honour open to all citizens and rarely shirked. In the annals of the best days of Athens we do not read of a class of persons who confined their share in the government to private criticism of its conduct and who refused to aid in remedying the evils of which they complained. Even Socrates thought it necessary to bring forward a divine mission as his excuse for not taking part in affairs of state.[7] Public station seems to have been generally sought, but the taking up and the laying down of office were attended with certain restrictions which are of interest to our subject.

7. At the end of his term of office, every magistrate was obliged to submit to a public accounting (εὔθυνα or εὐθύνη, frequently used also in the plural, εὔθυναι) for all his official acts. This law applied not only to the high officers of the State, such as archons, generals, senators, ambassadors, and trierarchs, but also to every one of the whole multitude of minor officials in every department of state, civil or military, whether elected by the lot or by a show of hands. At the end of each officer's term, he was obliged to submit his accounts to thirty magistrates called λογισταί. If their examination showed maladministration of the public funds, they reported the case to the ten συνήγοροι, who, after satisfying themselves of the justice of the charge, laid the matter before a Heliastic court[8] consisting of 501 δικασταί. But this was not all. For it was the privilege of even the humblest citizen to appear and bring forward any complaint which he might have to make against the retiring official. Such charges were not con-

---

[7] Plat. *Apol.* 31 C.   See below on   [8] See below, § 41 ff.
XVI. 21.

fined to the administration of public money, but might be made with regard to any acts committed while in office. If the charge was of a personal nature, it was settled by inferior magistrates; if it was made on public grounds, it was brought before a Heliastic court. An official undergoing εὔθυναι was not allowed to leave Athens or to transfer his property before the investigation was completed; and he was not permitted to retire into private life until every charge against him had been answered or every penalty inflicted had been paid.[9]

8. But not only at the end of official careers did the sovereign people inquire into the conduct of its officials. By another law, every person elected or chosen by lot to an office was required, before he entered upon it, to show his fitness to hold it. The candidate must first prove that he was an Athenian citizen; then he must show that he worshipped the tutelary gods Ἀπόλλων πατρῷος and Ζεὺς ἑρκεῖος; that he took care of his family tomb; that he had been dutiful to his parents; that he had performed all the required military duties; and that he was assessed in the property class to which he legally belonged.[10] These were the principal points; but, as in the εὔθυναι, so in this admission examination (called δοκιμασία), the inquiry might take a wider range and extend to an investigation of the candidate's whole life.[11] Any citizen might come forward against him and show facts in his public or

---

[9] On the εἴθυναι, see Gilbert, *Antiq.* p. 224 ff.; M. and S. p. 257 ff.; Smith, *Dict. Antiq. s.v. Euthyne.* Between the forms εὔθυνα and εὐθύνη there is not inscriptional evidence enough to decide. See Meisterhans, p. 94; Bl.-Kühn. *Gr.* I, p. 382.

[10] For the general requirement of a δοκιμασία, cf. Arist. *Resp. Ath.* 55. 2, πάντες γὰρ καὶ οἱ κληρωτοὶ καὶ οἱ χειρο-

τονητοὶ δοκιμασθέντες ἄρχουσιν. For the questions put, cf. Arist. *ibid.* 3; Dinarch. II. 17. In the case of a few offices there were special qualifications, as the archonship; see on XXIV. 13. On the δοκιμασία in general, see Gilbert, *Antiq.* p. 218 ff.; M. and S. p. 236 ff.; Smith, *Dict. Antiq. s.v. Dokimasia.*

[11] *Cf.* XVI. 9; XXIV. 15, 19; and p. 28, n. 29.

private life which might disqualify him for office. The general principle of the δοκιμασία applied to others than officials. For example, every youth, on coming of age, was required to show that he was legitimately entitled to the privileges of citizenship [12]; cripples in receipt of state allowances must annually prove that they needed the aid, and every cavalry man must offer himself and his horse for the test of fitness.[13] Though the different classes of δοκιμασίαι came in the first instance before different magistrates, yet in the last resort almost all cases arising from these examinations might be brought into a Heliastic court for settlement. The candidate, if rejected (ἀποδοκιμάζειν), seems in some cases, at least, to have suffered partial ἀτιμία (see § 51).

9. Evidently, an enormous increase of business in the courts must have been the result of the working of two such laws as these which have just been examined. Not only would the good citizen feel it to be his duty to appear either to protest against the entrance of unworthy persons into office or to expose the unfaithful official at the end of his term, but these two occasions would also afford opportunities to a man's political or personal enemies to bring vexatious, slanderous, or unfounded charges against him for his political ruin. More than one-fourth of the extant genuine orations of Lysias were written for such occasions.[14] Even the greatest statesmen might well have feared to submit to such a scrutiny of their lives; every Athenian knew that his enemies would spare no pains to search his record to the very bottom. And here again, as in every other suit, came into operation the law which required every citizen to plead his own cause personally.

[12] *Cf.* XXXII. 9; Arist. *Resp. Ath.* 42; M. and S. p. 255; Gilbert, *Antiq.* p. 197 ff.

[13] *Cf.* Or. XXIV; XVI. 13; Arist. *Resp. Ath.* 49.

[14] For δοκιμασίαι, XVI, XXIV, XXV, XXVI, XXXI. For εὔθυναι, XII, XXI, XXVII.

10. At first hearing, this requirement appears to be the veriest subversion of justice, and one asks in wonder wherein lay safety for the untrained against the skilful orator, and for the ignorant against the highly educated man. This just question may best be answered by asking and answering another. At the time when the requirement began, or, even later, at the time of the Persian wars, who were the skilful orators and the highly educated men in Athens? The answer is, — there were none of either class. Education,[15] in this early period, was very simple, and was the same for all alike. In the small territory of Attica, in area less than one-tenth of Massachusetts or of Wales, there were few citizens who had not acquired the branches which for a long time comprised the entire curriculum, — reading, writing, counting, singing and lyre-playing, and gymnastics. There was nothing to read but Homer and the lyric poets. There was no prose to read, because none had been written. Greek literature, like that of every other nation, begins with poetry. To be an educated man in the days when education meant so little was not difficult. To be an orator was an impossibility, except in the sense of that natural oratory in which the Homeric hero excelled. In such a community, therefore, the law which obliged every citizen to plead his own cause was not so unfair as it appears to us with our knowledge of rhetoric and of logic. But after the birth of these arts, the old law was no longer fair for all alike.

11. This is not the place in which to attempt a full account of the beginnings of rhetoric as an art.[16] It must here suffice

---

[15] On this subject, see Blümner's *Home Life of the Ancient Greeks*, translated by Zimmern, p. 102 ff. ; Becker's *Charicles*, Goll's edition, II, p. 19 ff., English edition, p. 217 ff.; Hermann, *Privatalt.* p. 311 ff.

[16] For accounts of early rhetoric and rhetoricians, see Blass, *Att. Bereds.* I, p. 1 ff.; Jebb, *Attic Orators*, I, p. cviii ff.

to observe that Athens, in which the art was destined to reach its perfection, was not the place which saw its birth. Its rules were founded upon the theories and principles of rhetoricians who lived, spoke, and wrote treatises in the Ionic East and in Sicily. In Ionia of Asia Minor correctness in speaking and writing was first made the object of study. The first rules for the arrangement of the narrative and argumentative parts of a speech were formulated in Sicily by Corax of Syracuse, who lived about 470 B.C. His system was developed and committed to writing by his pupil Tisias, likewise a Syracusan, and reputed the earliest master of Lysias.[17] In this book, the first *Art of Rhetoric* ever published (no longer extant), was explained the use of the famous "arguments from probability," the great weapon of early rhetoric. For example, if a physically weak man be accused of an assault, he is to ask the jury, "Is it *probable* that a weakling like me should have attacked anybody?" while if the accused is a strong man he is to claim that it is *improbable* that he should have committed an assault in a case where his strength was sure to be a presumption against him.[18] This "topic of general probability," as it was called, became the favourite of the early rhetoricians and orators, and allusion will frequently be made to it in the notes on the following orations of Lysias.

12. The simple principles laid down by the first teachers of rhetoric were soon improved and amplified by their Ionic and Sicilian successors. Athens herself took no part in the early development of the art. It is true that Pericles was a great orator. Suidas notes that he was the first Athenian who composed a forensic speech before delivering it; his predecessors

---

[17] See below, § 16. On Corax and Tisias, see Blass, *ibid.* p. 18 ff.; Jebb, *ibid.* p. cxxi ff.

[18] Jebb, *ibid.*; *cf.* Arist. *Rhet.* ii. 24. 11.

had never written out their speeches beforehand. But the successes of Pericles were due to the personal spell that hung about the man himself rather than to any rules of rhetoric. "Persuasion," says the comedian Eupolis,[19] "sat upon his lips, and, alone of the speakers, he always left his sting in his hearers." Not until two years after his death did the Athenians become acquainted with the power of artistic oratory. In 427 B.C., an embassy was sent to Athens from Leontini in Sicily. Gorgias, the most famous orator and rhetorician of his time, was at its head. He addressed the Assembly, and the effect of his speech upon the future of oratory cannot be overestimated. The Athenians, already fond of public speaking and quick to appreciate natural excellence in it, were astounded, says Diodorus,[20] at the strange new fashion of the Sicilian's language. They were enchanted by his cleverly-balanced clauses, his artistic use of antithesis, his employment of *homoeoteleuta* and of other figures of rhetoric then new to them. His style of eloquence became the fashion. From this time forward, the Athenians, long accustomed to recognize musical rhythm and finished expression in poetry, now began to demand these qualities in prose. Ability to speak in public had always been indispensable to the citizen who wished to distinguish himself in politics or who had to defend himself in the courts. It was henceforward cultivated as a fine art, and Greek audiences (as Jebb remarks) criticized the style of a speech as we criticize the style of a book. Schools of rhetoric were soon opened. In the courts, artistic oratory and rhetorical arguments so caught the fancy of the Athenians that (as we have too much reason to believe) a suitor, who could offer these to the jury, had a strong case even against the

---

[19] *Frag.* 94, Kock. On the oratory of Pericles, see Blass, *ibid.* p. 34 ff.; Jebb, *ibid.* p. cxxviii ff.

[20] xii. 53. On Gorgias, see Blass, *ibid.* p. 47 ff.; Jebb, *ibid.* p. cxxiii ff.

adverse testimony of eye-witnesses.[21] In the Assembly, the finished and (as he soon became) the professional orator over-shadowed his humbler competitor for the public favour.

13. The knowledge of the devices of rhetoric evidently must have led to a modification in the working of Athenian legal procedure. The law had always required the citizen to plead his own cause,[22] — it always obliged him to *deliver* his own plea, but the letter of the law had never obliged him to *compose* his speech himself. As soon as the suitor, or the aspirant for the honours of the ἐκκλησία, found that there were people who could write a better speech for him in his need than he could hope to compose for himself, he naturally turned to them for aid. Nothing in the law forbade it, and thus arose the profession of the λογογράφος or speech-writer, — a profession which the great Athenian orators all practised. The ordinary citizen had not the time or the will to devote himself to the careful study which had now become neces-sary for success in the art; he was quick to realize that an honest suitor with a good cause, but without the help of rhetoric, ran the risk of being defeated by an opponent whose cause, although it might be weaker, was made to appear the better by the rhetorical aid which he had purchased from a λογογράφος. The suitor, therefore, had recourse to the speech-writer just as we go to our lawyers, — but with this difference, that the speech-writer's duties ended with the beginning of the trial of the case in court. He only wrote the speeches neces-sary, and perhaps gave his client some instruction in delivery.[23]

---

[21] See below, p. 5 and n. 49.

[22] No actual ' law' survives, but the whole constitution of the Athenian procedure shows so clearly the exist-ence of such a provision that we hardly need the words of Quintilian, ii. 15. 30, tum maxime scribere litigato-ribus, quae illi pro se ipsi dice-rent, erat moris, atque ita iuri, quo non licebat pro altero agere, fraus adhibebatur.

[23] M. and S. p. 919 f. On the συνή-γορος, see below, § 36.

14. The first Athenian who wrote speeches for pay was the orator Antiphon,[24] who came into prominence during the revolution of the Four Hundred,[25] and who was condemned to death as one of the leaders of that movement. A λογογράφος, therefore, if he were a citizen, might be active in public affairs on his own account as well as for others. The greatest statesman who practised the profession was Demosthenes. It is true that his most famous speeches were both written and delivered by himself, but he wrote also for other men. Demosthenes was first led to become a master of oratory by the dishonesty of his guardians, who cheated him out of his patrimony during his minority, and it was pecuniary misfortune which led Lysias, another of the Ten Orators,[26] to adopt the profession of the λογογράφος.

LIFE OF LYSIAS.

[AUTHORITIES. *Ancient:* 1) His own oration *Against Eratosthenes* (XII); 2) Plato, *Republic, init.,* and *Phaedrus, passim;* 3) pseudo-Demosthenes, LIX. 21 ff.; 4) Athenaeus, p. 592 f.; 5) Dionysius of Halicarnassus, Περὶ Λυσίου, containing a biography as well as a critical estimate; 6) the pseudo-Plutarchian biography in the Βίοι τῶν δέκα Ῥητόρων (*Moralia,* p. 835 C, ff.); 7) the brief biographies in Photius, *Bibl.* 262, and 8) in Suidas, *s.v.* Λυσίας. *Modern:* Since Hoelscher's *De vita et scriptis Lysiae oratoris, Berolini,* 1837, there have been numerous pamphlets or articles on the subject. These are cited and their results summarized in Blass, *Attische Beredsamkeit,* I, p. 339 ff.; Jebb, *The Attic Orators,* I, p. 142 ff.; as well as in the histories of Greek literature by Christ, Sittl, and others. See also Mahaffy's *Classical Greek Literature,* II, 1, p. 136 ff.]

15. Lysias was born probably in Athens,[27] but the exact year of his birth is undetermined. The traditional date,

[24] Ps.-Plut. *Vit. X Oratt.* p. 832 C; Diod. apud Clem. Al., *Str.* i. 365 (II, 66 Dindorf). [25] *Cf.* Lys. XII. 67.

[26] On the 'Decade,' see Jebb, *Attic Orators,* I, p. lxv f.

[27] Cicero, *Brutus,* 63; Dion. H. § 1; Plut. § 2; Suidas. But Christ and others believe that he was born in Syracuse.

accepted by the ancients and by many modern scholars, is 459 B.C., but there are facts which point to a later year, — say about 444.[28] His father Cephalus, the son of Lysanias and grandson of Cephalus,[29] was a wealthy Syracusan, who came to settle in Athens at the invitation of Pericles.[30] It was the wish of that great statesman to bring to the city foreigners of wealth as well as of learning. As one of the former, Cephalus, probably a manufacturer of arms at Syracuse, was attracted

[28] The traditional date rests on a mere conjecture, as Dionysius, § 1, admits when he says that Lysias returned to Athens from Thurii at the age of forty-seven, ὡς ἄν τις εἰκάσειεν. The year 459 was fixed upon because it was believed (probably on the authority of Lysias himself in his speech On his own Services) that he went to Thurii at the age of fifteen, and because Thurii was founded in 444 B.C. But there is no evidence that he went in the very year of its foundation (unless it lie in the imperfect ἔστελλον used by Dionysius); and if he was born in 459, it follows that he did not begin his active career as a speech-writer until he was fifty-seven years old. This seems to many very doubtful, considering his high reputation in the profession and his great fertility of production. The tradition is, however, still followed by Rademacher, De Lysiae oratoris aetate, Berolini, 1865; A. Schöne, Die Biographien der zehn att. Redner, Jahrb. für Philol. 1871, p. 761 ff.; A. Weineck, Das Geburtsjahr des Lysias, Mitau, 1880; B. Pretzsch, De vitae Lysiae oratoris temporibus definiendis, Halis, 1881; and by Jebb, p. 143 f. Another date, first suggested by Vater (Jahrb.

für Philol., Suppl. Bd. IX, p. 165 ff.), is 432. But this would make Lysias younger than Isocrates (born 436), and all accounts agree that he was older (cf. Plat. Phaedr. 278 E; Ps.-Plut. § 16 f.; Dionysius, Vit. Isocr. § 1; Ps.-Plut. Isocr. p. 836 E). The year 444 was first set by K. F. Hermann (Gesammelte Abhandlungen, p. 15), and to this or 445 Blass and Christ incline. It depends chiefly on the Plutarchian statement, § 3 (which may or may not be based on Lysias in his speech On his own Services), that Lysias did not go to Thurii until after the death of Cephalus. Now Cephalus was invited to Athens by Pericles, and this could hardly have been before 460 B.C. Lysias says (XII. 4) that his father lived thirty years in Athens; hence Cephalus died not before 429, and Lysias, if he went to Thurii in 429 at the age of fifteen, was born in 444. For a full discussion of this unsolved problem, see Blass. Nothing decisive about the date can be based upon the assemblage of persons in the Republic, for it is clear from the Protagoras that Plato did not pretend to pedantic exactness in such matters.

[29] Plat. Rep. 330 B; Ps.-Plut. § 1.

[30] Lys. XII. 4.

thither, induced no doubt by the commercial advantages offered by the capital of the Hellenic world.[31] The State, while refusing to foreigners any participation in public affairs, gave them, under the title of metics,[32] all the protection of the laws on payment of a special tax, and on performance of certain public duties. A privileged class of metics, called ἰσοτελεῖς, to which Cephalus belonged, was relieved from the metics' tax and duties, and shared the taxes and liturgies of the citizens. They were (like ordinary metics) sometimes allowed, as a special privilege, to own land and houses.[33] Probably Cephalus was thus a householder ; certainly his sons owned houses. He lived in Athens for thirty years,[34] and his wealth[35] and the protection of Pericles, together with the personality of the man himself, made him influential in the city. He had the virtue of true hospitality, must have been of a genial, kindly temperament (for his son says that he never had a lawsuit), and was well read in the best literature. The whole picture which Plato draws in the beginning of the *Republic* shows that Cephalus was known as a man of sweet and noble disposition, gifted with the dignity and courtesy of the old school. He had three sons, Polemarchus, Lysias, and Euthydemus, and a daughter who was married to one Brachyllus.[36] The third son is mentioned

[31] The story in Ps.-Plut. § 1, that Cephalus was exiled from Syracuse when Gelon became tyrant (485 B.C.), probably belongs to the life of his grandfather Cephalus.

[32] On the metics and isoteleis and their patrons (προστάτης), see Gow, p. 102 f.; Smith, *Dict. Antiq. s.vv. Metoecus* and *Civitas;* Gilbert, *Antiq.* p. 176 ff.; Hermann, *Staatsalt.* pp. 419 ff., 428 ff. See on XXXI. 9 and 29.

[33] Gilbert, *Antiq.* pp. 178, 183; Hermann, *Staatsalt.* pp. 420, 428.

[34] Lys. XII. 4. This statement does not necessarily preclude the view that Cephalus himself may have gone to Thurii to settle his sons there; Susemihl, *Plat. Forschungen*, II, p. 109.

[35] Plut. § 1; Plat. *Rep.* 330 B.

[36] The Ps.-Plut. §§ 3 and 15, calls Brachyllus a brother of Lysias, but, as Westermann and Blass conclude, this was an error due to a misunderstanding of [Dem.] LIX. 22, where it is doubtless meant that he was a brother-in-law.

(besides in the biographies of Lysias) only in the *Republic*, where he appears as a mere youth. The eldest, Polemarchus, seems to have been fond of philosophical studies, for he was called 'the philosopher.' [37] During his father's life he lived in the Piraeus, for he appears in the *Republic* as the host of Socrates. He was killed by the Thirty Tyrants, under the circumstances described in Lysias's Twelfth oration.

16. Since Lysias belonged to such a family, it is not surprising to hear that his early life was passed among the most distinguished of the Athenians.[38] His boyhood fell in the golden age of art and literature. He might often have seen the great sculptor Phidias, who was at that time engaged in superintending the completion of the Parthenon and in the creation of his masterpieces of the plastic art. Aeschylus, indeed, was dead; but the tragic poets Sophocles and Euripides, the comedians Cratinus and Crates, and the philosopher Anaxagoras, were familiar figures in the city. Such surroundings could not have been without their influence upon the mind of the future orator. When Lysias was fifteen years old, he went with his brother Polemarchus to Thurii,[39] a colony founded, under the superintendence of Athens, in Magna Graecia on the site of the ancient Sybaris. Possibly Pericles had granted rights in the colony to their father and they went to take possession of these ; for, according to the tradition,[40] Cephalus was now dead. The place was well suited to them both. It was a flourishing colony, and there was doubtless a good demand for the arms and armour which it was their trade to manufacture. Then, too, Polemarchus could indulge his taste for philosophy in the society of the sophists who were gathered

[37] Plat. *Phaedr.* 257 B ; Plut. p. 998 B.

[38] Dion. H. § 1 ; Ps.-Plut. § 2.

[39] Dion. H. § 1 ; Ps.-Plut. § 3 ; Grote,

Hist. of Greece, XLVII ; Curtius, *Hist. of Greece*, II, p. 535.

[40] See notes 28 and 34.

there from the different parts of Hellas, and we have no reason
to doubt the story that it was in Thurii that Lysias first studied
the principles of rhetoric from the Sicilian masters of the art.[41]
It may be that one of his masters in Thurii was Tisias,[42] the
pupil of Corax.[43] There is a legend that among the rhetorical
exercises of Lysias, written at this period, was a speech in
which Nicias, the noble but unfortunate general, was represented
as suing for his life from his Sicilian captors; but, even aside
from the style of the only fragment which remains of this work,
it seems highly improbable that Lysias could have found time
for such a composition at the moment of the Athenian defeat.[44]

17. For the prosperous life of the two brothers in Thurii
was brought to a sudden end. In spite of Dorian and Locrian
influences which had always been at work in the colony, the
Athenian party, with its democratic ideas, managed to keep the
upper hand until the disaster to the Athenian arms in Syracuse.
This fatal event was naturally a great blow to Athenian power
in the West. There was a revolution in Thurii, and three
hundred Athenians, among them Lysias and Polemarchus, were
banished for 'Atticism.'[45] They returned to Athens and found
the Four Hundred in power there. Then followed the most
stirring part of the Peloponnesian war; but Lysias and his
brother, as metics, were shut out from taking any active part
in politics. Such duties as they owed the State (the εἰσφοραί,
χορηγία, and the more voluntary λύσις αἰχμαλώτων) were
generously performed,[46] but their main interests were business,

---

[41] On the beginnings of rhetoric and
of artistic oratory, see Jebb, *ibid.* I,
p. cxvii ff.; Blass, *ibid.* I, p. 1 ff.

[42] So Ps.-Plut. § 3. But possibly
Lysias first heard him later in life, in
Athens, where Tisias was the master
of Isocrates; see Dion. H. *Vit. Isocr.*
§ 1.

[43] On Tisias and Corax, see above,
§ 11.

[44] Blass, *ibid.* p. 347; Jebb, *ibid.*
p. 147.

[45] Dion. H. § 1; Ps.-Plut. § 4.

[46] XII. 20. On the duties and bur-
dens of metics, see Gilbert, *Antiq.* p.
178 ff.

study, and social life. In their financial position, they were prosperous. Inheriting the capital of their rich father, they were wealthy,[47] and to increase this wealth they carried on an arms factory (probably also inherited) in which were employed one hundred and twenty slaves.[48] They owned also three houses,[49] which were richly furnished with all the necessaries and luxuries of life.[50] We have the express statement of the pseudo-Plutarch, that Lysias was an *isoteles*[51] like his father.

18. While Cephalus was alive, his sons seem to have lived with him in the Piraeus.[52] After their return from Thurii, Polemarchus seems to have lived in Athens,[53] and Lysias in the Piraeus.[54] Their life was untroubled by that bane of Athens, the lawsuit,[55] and there is no evidence that, at this period, Lysias wrote speeches even for others to deliver in the courts.[56] Such employment was not necessary, for he was rich enough to live without the additional income which he might thus have gained. But his thoughts were not altogether occupied with his business, as his sophistic writings, later to be noticed, clearly show. There is also a story told by Aristotle (in Cicero's *Brutus*, § 48) that Lysias kept a school of oratory for a time, but soon closed it, owing to the successful rivalry of Theodorus. This story may be partly true. Lysias is called a sophist in the pseudo-Demosthenic oration against Neaera (§ 21) and he appears as such in his epideictic orations and in the erotic essay in Plato's *Phaedrus*.

[47] XII. 6, 9, 11.
[48] XII. 8, 19.
[49] XII. 18.   [50] XII. 18 f.
[51] Ps.-Plut. § 9. And so doubtless was his brother. Boeckh (*Staatsh.* I, p. 177) thought that the ownership of houses was in itself a proof of ἰσοτέ-λεια; but see above, note 33.
[52] Plat. *Rep.* 328 B.

[53] XII. 16.
[54] *Cf.* the story of Lysias's arrest, which seems to have been made in the Piraeus (XII. 8, 12, 16), with Plat. *Phaedr.* 227 B.
[55] XII. 3 f.
[56] Blass, *ibid.* p. 348. Neither oration xx nor xiv is the genuine production of Lysias.

19. Thus, for seven years, the brothers lived in apparent security, — the favourites of fortune, working only as the rich man who labours merely to increase his wealth. But the sure march of events was bringing disaster upon them in common with their adopted country. In swift sequence came the disaster at Aegos Potami, the siege and fall of Athens, and the brief but blood-stained episode of the Thirty Tyrants. The few months of their misgovernment was a perfect reign of terror. One day was enough to decide the fate of Lysias and his family. The morning saw him honoured and happy, beloved by a large circle of friends, the wealthy owner of houses, manu-factories, and slaves, — at noon he was the prisoner of the Thirty, — the darkness of the night covered his flight from Athens, — his brother lay murdered, and the bulk of his posses-sions were confiscated by the plundering tyrants. The excit-ing story of that day is preserved in his own words,[57] spoken when, after the restoration of the democracy, he returned to Athens and sought vengeance on his brother's murderers.

20. The calamity which thus befell Lysias, great though it was, cannot have amounted to utter financial ruin if there is anything in the stories of his generosity towards the cause of the patriots in exile. Late as these stories are, yet they doubt-less contain at least some grains of truth, and may have been drawn from his own speech *On his Services*.[58] It is said that he contributed 2000 drachmae to the funds of the exiles,[59] furnished from two hundred to five hundred shields,[60] and paid the wages of three hundred soldiers, who were hired from Aegina.[61] This

[57] xii. 8 ff. For the general history of the Thirty Tyrants, see Grote, *Hist. of Greece*, chap. lxv; Curtius, IV, chap. 1. See also the Chronological table, below, p. 209.

[58] See below, § 21. On the help given by the metics in general to the exiles, *cf.* xxxi. 29.

[59] Ps.-Plut. § 7; Phot.

[60] Ps.-Plut. § 7; Phot.; Schol. Aeschin. *Ctes.* § 105; Justin. v. 9. 9.

[61] Schol. Aeschin. *ibid.*

last item may be an exaggeration which grew out of his
mission with Hermon to hire these mercenaries.[62]　He is said
also to have persuaded his guest-friend Thrasydaeus of Elis
to contribute two talents.[63]　We hear nothing further of his
life during the months of exile.

21. For his patriotic services in this time of need, Lysias
enjoyed for a moment the highest reward which the Athenians
had the power to give, but it was snatched away almost before
he could have appreciated that it was his.　Immediately after
the return of the exiles, the Assembly passed a decree, proposed by Thrasybulus, under which full citizenship was
given to Lysias.　But this decree was clearly unconstitutional;
for, as the Senate was not yet re-established, the decree had
not been submitted to it, as the law of the democracy
required, before being proposed to the people.　Hence,
Archinus brought a γραφὴ παρανόμων against Thrasybulus,
carried his point, and Lysias fell back to his former status
as a metic.[64]　Such is the traditional account of this affair;
but it now appears from a passage in Aristotle's *Constitution
of Athens* that the decree of Thrasybulus did not concern
Lysias alone,[65] but that it gave the citizenship to all (even
to slaves) who had returned from the Piraeus with the exiles.
It was natural enough that such a wholesale act, even aside
from its illegality, should have excited indignation, and the
new light from Aristotle renders unnecessary the ingenious

[62] Ps.-Plut. § 7; Phot.

[63] Ps.-Plut. § 7; Phot.; *cf.* Xen.
Hellen. iii. 2. 27.

[64] On the whole story, *cf.* Ps.-Plut.
§ 8; Phot.; Schol. Aeschin. iii. § 195;
Schol. Hermog. in Walz, *Rhet. Graec.*
V, p. 343.　On the γραφὴ παρανόμων,
see Gilbert, *Antiq.* p. 299; M. and S.
p. 428 ff.

[65] Arist. *Resp. Ath.* 40. 2.　If the
scholiasts and late writers drew their
information from Lysias *On his own
Services*, the language of the speech
made it natural that they should suppose that the decree applied only to
him.

conjectures [66] which have been made in order to account for the apparently pointed injustice done to a man who had deserved so well of the State. At some stage of this affair, Lysias seems to have made a speech or published a pamphlet entitled *On his own Services*, a work which has survived only in a few words quoted here and there,[67] but which doubtless provided the ancient biographers with many facts for their accounts of his life.

22. Reduced once more to the status of a metic and to comparative, if not actual poverty, Lysias naturally turned for employment to a profession for which his favourite rhetorical studies had prepared him. He became a λογογράφος,[68] and the rest of his life was spent in this profession. The fact that all his known forensic works were composed after his misfortunes shows that loss of money was the cause of his activity. The speechwriter's was not a life which brought a man real glory, in the Athenian sense of the word ; for the speechwriter received pay for his services, and Athenian prejudice forbade a gentleman to receive pay except from the State. There was, too, a feeling in all circles, both high and low, against the man who had the art of 'making the worse cause appear the better.' Neither Lysias nor Demosthenes, therefore, won any great fame among their fellowcitizens in their chosen profession,[69] although each earned money by it. The industry of Lysias was great: in literary productiveness he far surpassed every other Attic orator.[70] His attack on Eratosthenes must have been an excellent advertisement for him, and so was that other speech called

---

[66] Such as, for instance, that he was distrusted as a sophist. See Blass, *ibid.* p. 349 ; Usener, *Rhein. Mus.* XXXV, p. 149. Scheibe (*Jahrb.* XXXI, p. 359) doubted the whole story.

[67] Harp. *s.vv.* Κεῖοι, μεταπύργιον,

Φηγαιεῦσι. *Cf.* Ps.-Plut. § 11, and see Blass, *ibid.* p. 359 ; Jebb, *ibid.* p. 151 f.

[68] On this profession, see above, § 13.

[69] Schaefer, *Demosthenes*[2], I, p. 342.

[70] See below, § 33.

a *Plea for the Constitution*, composed about 403 B.C.,[71] and showing the author's true democratic spirit.

23. Not much remains to be said about the events of his life. He was married (we know not when) to his sister's daughter,[72] but we do not hear that he had children. That he was a well-known personage in Athens must be clear from the nature of the allusions to him in Plato.[73] But the story that he was once sent upon an embassy to the elder Dionysius of Syracuse rests without doubt upon a corrupt reading in one of his own works.[74] It is not likely that a metic would have been selected to represent the State on such a mission. Yet there were occasions when even a metic might display his powers of oratory for the admiration of his fellowmen and to draw attention to his own attainments. Such occasions were offered by the great national gatherings of Greece, the Games. At the most famous of these, the Olympian, there were intellectual as well as athletic exhibitions. In the time of Lysias, an author's surest road to fame lay in the reading or reciting of his own works to the largest possible number of hearers. At Olympia, an orator was sure of an audience gathered from all parts of the Hellenic world. His choice of a subject was naturally influenced by the public events which at the time were most interesting to his hearers. Thus, when Gorgias spoke at Olympia, the Greek States were distracted by civil war and the orator exhorted them to put away their discords and to unite against their common enemy, the barbarian.[75] At the time of Lysias's Olympic oration,[76] a new enemy to

---

[71] Oration XXXIV. See below, § 39.

[72] [Dem.] LIX. 22, and see above, note 36 and on XXXII. 4. This marriage did not prevent him from having relations with one of the *demi-monde; cf.* [Dem.] *ibid.* 21 ff.; Ath. p. 592 f.; Ps.-Plut. § 15.

[73] Plat. *Phaedr.* 227 A–279 A; *Clitoph.* 406 A; *Rep.* 328 B.

[74] XIX. 19. See Blass, *ibid.* p. 352; Jebb, *ibid.* p. 154.

[75] Jebb, *ibid.* p. 203 ff.

[76] Dion. § 29; Ps.-Plut. § 20; Diod. XIV. 109.

Greek freedom had arisen in the west, and against Dionysius, tyrant of Syracuse, he lifted up his voice. Only the first part of the oration is now extant, but it is evidence enough that he was capable of giving wise advice at a grave national crisis.

24. The date of the death of Lysias can be fixed with no greater certainty than that of his birth. The tradition that he lived to be eighty years of age seems to be based on nothing better than conjecture.[77] His literary life, however, ends for us in 380 B.C., for we hear of no works of his that bear a later date, and it is probable that he died soon afterwards.[78] The Plutarchian biography preserves eight verses from an elegy upon Lysias, written by Philiscus, the pupil of Isocrates.[79]

25. The lineaments of the orator have been transmitted to us in three Roman replicas of an ancient Greek work, possibly executed in the lifetime of Lysias himself. A print of the finest of them, the bust now in the Museum of Naples, forms the frontispiece of this volume.[80] It represents Lysias when well past the prime of life. The strong head with its broad, bald forehead, its serious, earnest eyes and fine lips, mark the man successful in the fields alike of thought and of action.

[77] Dion. § 12. The gossiping Ps.-Plut. § 9 sets his age at seventy-six or eighty-three years, and adds that he saw the boy Demosthenes (born 383 B.C.).

[78] Blass, *ibid.* p. 344; Jebb, *ibid.* p. 155.

[79] Ps.-Plut. § 17 f., who calls it an epigram. But it is clearly part of a longer poem, of no special literary value. See Bergk, *Poet. Lyr. Graec.*[4] II, p. 327.

[80] Taken from Brunn and Arndt, *Griechische und Römische Porträts*, Lief. xiv, No. 131. Engraved also in Visconti, *Icon. Gr.* I, Tav. xxviii, p. 337, and in Christ, *Gr. Litteratur-Geschichte.* See also Bernouilli, *Die erhaltenen Bildnisse berühmter Griechen*, p. 15; Furtwängler, *Masterpieces of Greek Sculpture*, p. 81. For the Capitoline replica (in the Room of the Philosophers, No. 96), see Brunn and Arndt, *ibid.* No. 133, and for the replica at Holkham Hall, Michaelis, *Ancient Marbles in Great Britain*, p. 317.

STYLE OF LYSIAS.

[AUTHORITIES. *Ancient:* Dionysius of Halicarnassus, Περὶ Λυσίου. *Modern:* Blass, *Attische Beredsamkeit*, I, p. 381 ff.; Jebb, *Attic Orators*, I, p. 158 ff. The more special works of narrower scope are cited in Blass. See also the authorities named at the head of § 15.]

26. We may well imagine that a career of dependence, coming after independence, was at first irksome to Lysias. Yet the life of a successful Athenian speech-writer, in the sense in which Lysias understood the claims of his profession, was neither inactive nor uninteresting. It demanded not only acquaintance with the laws and with procedure in court, but also deep insight into the character of individuals, and wide knowledge of human nature as a whole. Modern lawyers are spared the problem which Lysias felt that he had to solve. He deemed it not sufficient that the speeches which he wrote should be as perfect as he could make them in the law and the facts of each case. For they were to be delivered not by himself, but by his client; they were written in the first person for that client's own lips ; and therefore he conceived that the style and the character of the speech should be in keeping with the station and nature of the man who was to speak it. Strange as it may seem to us, Lysias was the first speech-writer to appreciate the necessity of suiting the speech to the speaker. Before his day, speeches generally bore the same stamp ; they were struck out, so to speak, according to a set pattern, they conformed to certain fixed principles of argumentation, and they were decorated with all the finest flowers of rhetoric.[81] The law did not require that the speech should be the genuine composition of the speaker, and early juries did not expect that it would be in keeping with his character. But Lysias saw the intrinsic

---

[81] Jebb, *ibid.* p. 164.

absurdity of such a system of cut-and-dried speech-writing, and he abandoned it altogether. His method was to study his client's character quite as carefully as his client's case, and to bring out that character in the speech which he put into the client's mouth. He threw aside the mould in which the earlier speech-writers were accustomed to fashion all their productions, and by suiting the speech to the speaker he composed a work not only more admirable from the point of view of literary art, but also better calculated to bring before the judges the actual circumstances, needs and just claims of the individual who was addressing them. The judges seemed to see and to hear the same man, instead of seeing one man and hearing the words of another. Lysias, then, wrote for a client so that he should have, as Jebb puts it, the whole advantage of professional aid while he appeared to be entirely without such aid.[82] The speeches of Lysias differ from each other as much as did the natures of the men for whom he wrote, and yet they are still alike in one particular : they contain scarcely any of the earlier florid eloquence and poetical ornamentation, but are written in the sober prose of ordinary life. Hence Lysias is the type (and the best type) of the class of orators who composed in what is called the Plain Style ($\grave{\iota}\sigma\chi\nu\grave{o}\nu$ $\gamma\acute{e}\nu os$, genus tenue).[83]

27. This suiting of the speech to the speaker is the great discovery and distinction of Lysias, and it is the best evidence of his genius. In close connexion with it, and indeed growing out of his close study of the nature of his clients, stands another of his special points of excellence. This is his success in the *delineation of character* ($\mathring{\eta}\theta o\pi o\iota\acute{\iota}a$), whether of the speaker or of

---

[82] Jebb, *ibid.* p. 164.

[83] On the Plain Style, see Blass, *ibid.* p. 388 ff.; Berbig, *Ueber das ge-* nus dicendi tenue des Redners Lysias; Jebb, *ibid.* p. 160 ff.

other parties in a suit. As Dionysius in substance says[84] : "Lysias proved himself the superior of all other orators in perception of human nature, and in assigning to each individual his appropriate emotions, characteristics, and actions. And therefore I accord to him the highest praise for his talent and skill in the employment of *ethopoiia*, as I can find no character in his works poorly delineated or lifeless. Excelling in the treatment of those features in which *ethopoiia* appears, namely, in thought, language and style, he not only lends to his clients the sentiments which are proper and useful and moderate, so that their speeches seem to be portraits of their characters, but also places in their mouths language which is both appropriate and clear, literal and popular. For lofty, strange, and studied terms ill befit true character-painting. Furthermore, his style of composition is plain and simple, for he recognized that the natural home of *ethos* is not in the periodic or rhythmic style, but ἐν τῇ διαλελυμένῃ λέξει. In every respect, Lysias' style is pleasing and persuasive, and it is so natural and easy, without any appearance of effort or of art, that I should not be surprised if laymen — yes, and even many scholars themselves — thought the result to have been reached without study and without the use of rhetorical methods."[85]   And in another chapter[86] Dionysius says in effect : "Of *ethos*, Lysias made most skilful use ; for frequently by reference to his client's past life and actions, to his character and habits, he portrays him as worthy of confidence and respect. When his life affords no opportunity for this method of treatment, Lysias himself makes up such a character for his client that he is deemed entirely trustworthy. For he represents his conduct

[84] I use (with a few slight changes) the paraphrase by Devries in his interesting and scholarly *Ethopoiia: A Rhetorical Study of the Types of Char-* *acter in the Orations of Lysias.* Baltimore, 1892. From this treatise I have derived much assistance.

[85] Dion. H. § 7 f.   [86] § 19.

as polite and graceful and modest, and makes him use language befitting such conduct. His client is always distressed at injustice and is always endeavouring to act with justice. The orator does not fail to introduce every detail that will serve these ends."

28. Such are the views of the Greek critic on Lysias' skill in *ethopoiia*. Even from the few orations contained in this volume we can see what his power was in this direction. How different are the pictures and how each stands out distinct from its own canvas! What a contrast between Mantitheus,[87] the brilliant, open-hearted, ambitious young patriot, and Philon,[88] the cowardly selfish miscreant who sacrifices his family and his country alike to his own interests! Compare the honest, straight-forward yeoman of the Olive Tree case[89] and the affected, over-clever Cripple[90] with his impudent wit. The accuser of Philon is a dignified senator, coming forward, like the prosecutor of the Grain-Dealers,[91] from a sense of the duty which he owes to the State ; and if his language is somewhat more rhetorical than that of other clients of Lysias, this is only natural to his position.[92] On the other hand, the defendant in the Twenty-third oration is represented as a mere adventurer, posing as a citizen, but really belonging to the lowest class in the commonwealth.[93] Finally, in the Thirty-second oration we find three characters so clearly and successfully drawn that they are as real to the reader as are any of the personages in the pages of the great masters of English fiction. There is the speaker, naïve and full of kindly sympathy for the widow and orphans, but animated by a just bitterness against the dishonest guardian[94] ; the widow, a noble and pathetic creature, who, like a

[87] Or. xvi. See Devries, p. 18 ff.
[88] Or. xxxi. See Devries, p. 28.
[89] Or. vii. See Devries, p. 33.
[90] Or. xxiv. See Devries, p. 34 ff.

[91] Or. xxii.
[92] See below, p. 135, and Devries, p. 26 f.
[93] See Devries, p. 42.
[94] *Ibid.* p. 34.

true woman, breaks down (for her children's sake, not for her own) all the barriers of convention behind which the women of her day were wont to live [95]; and Diogiton himself, unnatural father, cruel guardian, gibbeted forever on the page of Lysias as one of the meanest and most heartless men of that or any other day.[96]

29. Besides this excellence in ἠθοποιία, Dionysius selects and praises seven other characteristics of the style of Lysias, which may here be summarized. They are Purity, Simplicity, Clearness, Brevity, Vividness, Propriety, and Charm. The ancient critic calls Lysias pure in diction (καθαρὸς τὴν ἑρμη-νείαν),[97] and the best model of Attic Greek in this respect ; not, he adds, of the older Attic used by Plato and Thucydides, but of the Attic in common use in Lysias's own time. By the term ' Purity,' Dionysius means that Lysias does not use obsolete, strange or poetical words, and that he employs no constructions foreign to the idiom of his day.[98] Dionysius pronounces that no orator surpassed Lysias in Purity, and that only Isocrates even approached him. The second quality, Simplicity,[99] consists in the expression of the thought by means of ordinary words used in their ordinary sense. Lysias avoids all but the commonest figures of speech, and his metaphors are such as come unconsciously to the lips of the most uninstructed speaker. This literary attitude is perfectly suited, as Fuhr remarks,[100] to the circle in which his orations are confined. Unusual

[95] *Ibid.* p. 47 f.

[96] *Ibid.* p. 28.　　　[97] § 2.

[98] Blass, *ibid.* p. 407 f.; Jebb, *ibid.* p. 168. About the only instance of older syntax noted in Lysias is the use of τέ as a simple conjunction ; see on xxxi. 2. The somewhat rare and poetical words noted in Or. xxiv are perfectly in keeping with the tone of

mock elevation there. A few others are noted in Jebb, p. 169 ; Blass, p. 408 f.

[99] ἡ διὰ τῶν κυρίων τε καὶ κοινῶν καὶ ἐν μέσῳ κειμένων ὀνομάτων ἐκφέρουσα τὰ νοούμενα, Dion. H. § 3. See Blass, *ibid.* p. 409 f.; Jebb, *ibid.* p. 169 f.

[100] In the introduction to his revision of Rauchenstein's edition, p. 8.

metaphors and, in general, figures of speech belong to the higher style of public oratory, although even here the great master Demosthenes is sparing in his use of them. They are entirely out of place in everyday lawsuits, the parties to which are ordinary citizens.[101] The earlier orators, in their choice of words, had recourse, in search of the sublime, to the language of poetry; Lysias found the way to a greater effect through the use of the commonest words, so combined, however, that often, when he seems to speak like the plainest citizen, he is in reality most artistic.

30. No writer, Dionysius goes on, has ever surpassed Lysias in Clearness (σαφήνεια).[102] Even those to whom his matter is strangest rarely find his expression obscure. In this he differs from Thucydides and even from Demosthenes; for in their writings it may often happen that we understand the subject with which they are dealing and yet find difficulties in apprehending their language. On the subject of the Brevity (βραχύτης) of Lysias, which is the fourth of the qualities selected by Dionysius,[103] we have a dictum of the Roman critic Favorinus,[104] who used to say: "if you take away or alter a single word in a passage of Lysias, no matter how carefully you go about it, you spoil the meaning of the passage."[105] There are of course exceptions to this, as to all other generalizations, and some of them (due for instance to Lysias's fondness for parallelism, symmetry, and synonymous expressions) are noted as they occur in the speeches.

---

[101] On Lysias's use of figures, see Blass, *ibid.* p. 409 ff.; Jebb, *ibid.* p. 170 ff. For *paronomasia* and *homoeoteleuton*, see on XII. 78, and p. 135, note 19; *antithesis*, XXIV. 16, and p. 135, note 19; *chiasm*, XVI. 18, XXXI. 5, 12, 32; *synonymous phrases*, XVI. 13.

[102] § 4. See Jebb, *ibid.* p. 171.
[103] § 5. See Jebb, *ibid.* p. 171; Blass, *ibid.* p. 411.
[104] Second century A.D., the master of Gellius.
[105] Gell. ii. 5.

31. The fifth quality, Vividness (ἐνάργεια), Dionysius [106] defines as the power of making one's hearers see what is being described. He truly adds that nobody can be so dull of apprehension as not to believe that he has almost under his very eyes the scenes of Lysias's narratives and that he is associating with the personages introduced in them. A good test of the truth of this saying is the description of Lysias's own arrest by the Thirty and his escape from their clutches [107]; or the scene in the oration against Diogiton where the mother of the boys upbraids her father for his heartlessness.[108] The quality of Propriety (τὸ πρέπον)[109] differs from ἠθοποιία in that the latter is the delineation of the character proper to the speaker or to a personage in his speech ; while Propriety is a wider term, denoting the proper adaptation of the speech to all the circumstances. These of course differ with every case, and in the different parts of a speech Propriety will call for a change of tone to accord with the station of the different persons addressed, whether judges, opponent, audience, bystanders, friends or foes in general. In this quality Dionysius is of opinion that Lysias was never excelled.

32. There remains finally the quality which Dionysius [110] calls the best and the most characteristic of the style of Lysias, — a crowning excellence wherein he surpassed all the other great orators. This is a kind of Charm which lies efflorescent upon all his language (χάρις τις πᾶσιν ἐπανθοῦσα τοῖς ὀνόμασι). It cannot be analyzed, says Dionysius, any more than one can analyze the true essence of physical beauty, the delight of harmony, or the delicacy of rhythm. These are all qualities to be appreciated by the aesthetic sensibilities, not to be explained

---

[106] § 7.   See Jebb, *ibid.* p. 172 f.

[107] *Cf.* XII. 8–16.

[108] *Cf.* XXXII. 12–18.

[109] § 9.   See Jebb, *ibid.* p. 176.

[110] § 10–12.   See Blass, *ibid.* p. 397 f.; Jebb, *ibid.* p. 176 ff.

by rational analysis. The ancient critic does not attempt to define more closely the Charm of Lysias. He only tells us that when all other means fail in determining the authenticity of a speech attributed to this orator, he applies to it the test of this surpassing distinction. If the Charm is there, the speech is genuine ; but if the language has not the distinctive mark of sweetness and loveliness (ἐὰν δὲ μηδεμίαν ἡδονὴν μηδὲ ἀφροδίτην ὁ τῆς λέξεως χαρακτὴρ ἔχῃ), the work is to be rejected. It is evident that such a fleeting quality as this can hardly be felt in its fulness by the modern scholar who has not at hand, for purposes of study and comparison, the countless ancient works which, familiar to Dionysius, are now altogether lost. We can feel that Lysias is simple and clear, brief, vigorous and active ; seldom dry or monotonous ; almost always alive and sprightly. We can see in his language the speech of everyday life and the literary idiom most happily combined. But not any one nor all of these qualities were what Dionysius meant by the Charm. We must take the word of the great critic that it is there, and endeavour by constant reading and re-reading to gain some appreciation of its nature.

WORKS OF LYSIAS.

[AUTHORITIES. Blass, *Attische Beredsamkeit*, I, p. 353 ff.; Sittl, *Geschichte der Griechischen Litteratur*, II, p. 143 ff.; Jebb, *Attic Orators*, I, p. 199 ff.; Mahaffy, *History of Classical Greek Literature*, II, i. p. 143 ff. See also above, at the head of § 15.]

33. The career of Lysias as a speech-writer lies, as has been said, between the years 403 and 380 B.C. In these twenty-three years, his industry and reputation in his profession must have been of the greatest; for he wrote at least double the number of

speeches attributed to any other Attic orator.[111] In explanation
of his fertility, Blass observes that Lysias, being a métic, was
debarred from the public business which demanded much of
the time of men like Demosthenes and Hyperides; and that in
his day there were fewer men engaged in his profession than in
the time of the later orators; further, that his younger contemporary and principal rival, Isocrates, was much occupied in
teaching rhetoric in his school. This is all true enough. But
it would be unfair to the fame of Lysias to suppose that such
negative reasons for his preëminence in production are the only
ones that existed. It is far more natural to believe that
his speeches had the reputation of being the best that could be
had; and the remarkable art with which he suited the speech
to the character of the speaker must have been as highly appreciated by his contemporaries as it is by us. His misfortunes
under the Thirty, the generous part which he had played during the exile of the patriots, and his public appearance against
Eratosthenes, all no doubt commended him to the people at
large ; while his relations with a certain class of men of education and literary tastes, so evident from the allusions to him in
Plato, may naturally have led them to apply to him in case of
need. And the tradition that he failed in but one suit,[112]
exaggerated though it may be, is yet exactly the sort of story
that one expects to find told of the favourite counsel of the day.

34. As time went on, it was only natural that many speeches
were attributed to Lysias which were not his genuine works.
Any good speech which bore the stamp of the Plain Style was,
in a loose way, supposed to be his. Nothing, apparently, was
done to sift out his real works from the spurious before the
recensions of Caecilius and of Dionysius of Halicarnassus,

---

[111] See Blass, *ibid.* p. 353; Jebb,　　[112] Ps.-Plut. § 10.
ibid. p. 152.

rhetoricians of the Augustan age.[113]   They found 425 works
attributed to him, but they threw out 192 as spurious, retain-
ing 233 as genuine.[114]   Of the 425, we know 172 by title or
from fragments, or by the preservation of them entire.[115]   Of
these 172, there are extant 31 complete orations in the Palatine
manuscript,[116] large fragments of three other orations which
were quoted by Dionysius as examples of the art of Lysias, and
the *Eroticus* or speech on Love, found in the *Phaedrus* of Plato.
Of the remaining 137, we have only fragments or merely the
titles, but even these show marvellously well the varied business which occupied Athenian speech-writers.

35. The thirty-one orations preserved in the Palatine manuscript seem to have been selected from a complete edition of the
works of Lysias.   They fall into three divisions.[117]   The first
consists of the first oration, spoken in a murder trial, and the
second, the spurious funeral oration.   The latter and the
Olympiacus are the only two *epideictic* or 'show' pieces which
we have under the name of Lysias.   The orations in the second
division (III to XI inclusive) seem to be arranged with reference to the kind of case for which they were written.   Thus,
the third and fourth orations are on wounding with murderous
intent ; the fifth, sixth and seventh are on sacrilege ; the
eighth to the eleventh inclusive (except the eighth which has
found its way here accidentally) were written for libel suits.
The orations in the third division (XII to XXXI inclusive)

[113] On them, see Jebb, *ibid.* p. lxiv. ff.

[114] It is not known whether Dionysius or Caecilius first fixed upon this
number.   The ancient followers of
both critics seem to have adopted it.
Cf. Ps.-Plut. § 10; Phot.; Dion. H.
§§ 17 and 12; Suidas (in whom the
number 300 may be due to an error in
writing the numeral τ' for σ'); Blass,

ibid. p. 355 ; Jebb, *ibid.* p. 199.   Among
the most famous of the spurious works
was the *Defence of Socrates;* see Blass,
p. 351; Jebb, p. 153.

[115] For a complete list, see Blass,
ibid. pp. 357–375.

[116] See Appendix I A, MANUSCRIPTS.

[117] See Blass, *ibid.* p. 377 ff.; Jebb,
ibid. p. 201.

cannot be classified, but may have been selected by the com-
piler each for its individual interest. Of these thirty-one
speeches, six certainly seem to be spurious, namely, orations II,
VI, VIII, IX, XI, XX ; and orations XIV and XV probably
fall under this category.[118] Hence there are twenty-six orations
(twenty-three in the manuscript and three in Dionysius) which
are now commonly received as genuine works of Lysias. The
subjects of these speeches call for brief consideration here.

36. Twenty-four of the twenty-six speeches were written for
delivery in court (λόγοι δικανικοί) and fall into two classes :
speeches intended for public and speeches for private causes.
This classification depends upon the ground of complaint
(ἔγκλημα). If this ground was an offence against the State, the
action was a public action (ἀγὼν δημόσιος or δίκη δημοσία, or
simply γραφή); if it lay in an offence against an individual, the
action was a private action (ἀγὼν ἴδιος or δίκη ἰδία, or simply
δίκη).[119] The term public action naturally covers a wide field,
for the interests of the State are widespreading. The speeches
of Lysias which fall under this head were written for the actual
litigants or for public prosecutors (συνήγοροι).[120] This συνήγορος
was a person chosen by the State to defend its interests, and
he might of course engage the services of a speech-writer. As
for private individuals, we have seen above that the law required
them to plead their own causes ; but there were natural exceptions to this rule. Such was the case of Miltiades, who was
accused of treason when wounded and unable to speak for
himself. He was brought into court on a litter and his brother
was allowed to speak for him.[121] A similar case was that of

[118] For the grounds of rejection, see
the treatment of each speech in Blass
and Jebb.

[119] On this division, see Gilbert,
Antiq. p. 404 ; M. and S. p. 191 ff.

[120] On συνήγοροι, public and private,
see Smith, *Dict. Antiq. s.v. Synegorus.*

[121] Nepos, *Milt.* 7. His *friends* were
his advocates, according to Hdt. vi,
136.

Isocrates, who was unable from illness to appear in court and was represented by his son. But even when a suitor was able to speak and had introduced his case himself, custom allowed a second or even a third speech to follow on the same side. The person who spoke such an additional speech was also called συνήγορος, and out of him, rather than out of the λογογράφος, developed the modern lawyer. For the actual suitor, after the briefest introduction, might practically disappear from the case, leaving the real speech to be made by his συνήγορος. According to the law, this private συνήγορος or advocate could receive no pay from the suitor : he was supposed to be no more than a kinsman or friend who spoke simply out of sympathy, and his speech usually began with an explanation of the personal interest which led him to appear.[122] In the generation after Lysias, such private advocacy was often paid for,[123] — under the rose indeed, and subject to the risk of legal penalties.[124]

37. The public orations of Lysias, therefore, were written for the real suitors, or for συνήγοροι, public or private. Among them we find cases in which the alleged offence was committed directly against the State, such as embezzlement of the public funds [125] or such misconduct in office as would be made the subject of inquiry at the εὔθυναι.[126] An offence against the people as a whole was the attempt of the Corn-Ring to buy up a large quantity of grain at a low price, to hold it until the supply in the market was small, and then to sell it at a large advance. There were stringent laws against such speculation.[127] Other public causes related to claims for moneys due the Treasury or to confiscations [128]; another class consisted of cases

---

[122] *Cf.* Or. xxxii.

[123] *Cf.* Lycurg. *Leocr.* 138.

[124] *Cf.* [Dem.] xlvi. 26. For the similar law in Rome, see Smith, *Dict. Antiq. s.v. Lex Cincia.*

[125] Or. xxviii, xxix.

[126] Or. xii, xxi, xxvii ; *cf.* xxx, an εἰσαγγελία for neglect to come up for the εὔθυναι. [127] See on Or. xxii.

[128] Or. xviii, xix.

against persons accused of sacrilege or impiety against the State religion.[129]   We have also five speeches either for or against candidates undergoing examination for office, the δοκιμασία.[130] Again, in murder cases and in assaults with intent to wound, the State was the offended party, as it is to-day.   We have already noticed the speech against Eratosthenes [131] at his εὔθυναι. Closely connected with this case is that of the villainous informer Agoratus, who had lived five years in Athens, plying his infamous trade.[132]   A case of a different sort is the charge brought against a man of the middle class who had killed his wife's lover.[133]   This speech is very valuable to us because it vividly illustrates the manner of life in a small Athenian household where only one servant was kept.   We have a full description of the house and the housekeeping.   The accused, for whom Lysias wrote the speech in question, gives an interesting picture of the position of a woman of the *bourgeois* class.   Speaking as though he considered himself a pattern for all husbands to follow, he says :

" The way I treated my wife was this : I tried not to disoblige her when she wanted to do anything, and not to be under her thumb, either.   I kept my eye on her all I could, and gave all reasonable attention to her.   When she had borne me a child, I gave her my confidence and all my household to look after.   This was my notion of matrimony.   Now at first, Athenians, she was just the best wife that ever lived ; she was a mighty good provider, didn't waste things, and kept house very shrewdly.   But my mother died, more's the pity, and her death was the beginning of all my troubles.   My wife went to the funeral, and there that man caught sight of her." [134]

---

[129] Or. v, vii.

[130] Or. xvi, xxiv, xxv, xxvi, xxxi.

[131] See § 19.

[132] Or. xiii.

[133] Or. i.

[134] *Cf.* i. 6 f.

38. We have only four speeches written by Lysias for private actions, but the suits, fortunately, were all different in subject. One was an action for libel, brought by a man who had been publicly called a parricide.[135] Another was laid by a ward against his guardian, for mal-administration of the trust estate.[136] The third was written for the trial of a disputed claim to property,[137] and in the fourth a man is accused of claiming, unlawfully, the right to citizenship.[138]

39. Twenty-four of the twenty-six speeches of Lysias have now been considered. Two remain, his only extant works which were not written for the law-courts. One of them was composed for a citizen to deliver in the Assembly (λόγος δημηγορικός), at a time shortly after the fall of the Thirty, when there was a question of changing the constitution of Athens by restricting the franchise to owners of real estate.[139] The other was the Olympic oration, a 'show piece' (λόγος ἐπιδεικτικός), which we have already examined.[140]

40. Among the fragments of Lysias's works are the remains of a few letters, which are, all except one, of an erotic nature. Indeed, he first gave the letter its place among the forms of literature.[141] Further, the youthful Phaedrus, in Plato's dialogue of that name, reads to Socrates a discourse on Love, which is, he says, the composition of Lysias. Socrates proceeds to criticise the discourse, much to its discredit. Although the ancient critics accepted the work as the genuine production of Lysias, the question of its authenticity has been much debated by modern scholars; still, the prevailing view now ascribes it to the orator.[142] With such sophistic writings, however, the young student of Attic Oratory is but little

---

[135] Or. x. [136] Or. xxxii. [141] See Sittl, *Gr. Litteraturgeschichte*,
[137] Or. xvii. [138] Or. xxiii. II, p. 144.
[139] Or. xxxiv. See above, § 22. [142] Blass, *ibid.* p. 424 ff.; Jebb, *ibid.*
[140] See above, § 23. p. 305 ff.

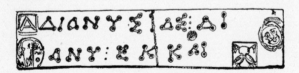

Fig. 1.

Fig. 2.

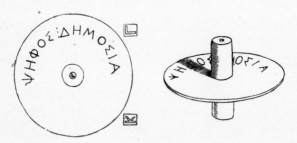

Fig. 3.

concerned. The object of these pages has been to present
Lysias as a man of action and as an exponent of Athenian life.
Our brief examination of the contents of his works may have
sufficed to show what a great treasure-house of facts we have in
them. One might almost say that the writings of no other
Greek author, except Aristophanes, are so rich in material
for the fascinating study of the everyday manners and cus-
toms of Athenian antiquity.

PROCEDURE IN HELIASTIC COURTS.

[AUTHORITIES. *Ancient :* Aristotle, *Resp. Ath.* 63 ff.   *Modern :* Meier and
Schoemann, *Der Attische Process*, p. 769 ff.; Gilbert, *Constitutional Antiquities
of Athens and Sparta*, English translation, p. 376 f.; Hermann, *Staatsaltertümer*, p. 538 ff.]

41. Almost all Athenian law cases of any importance,[143]
except those concerning murder and homicide,[144] were, unless
settled by arbitration,[145] tried in the Heliastic courts. For these
courts, jurors (ἡλιασταί or δικασταί), frequently called in
English *judges* or *dicasts*, were selected annually and formed
a body known as the ἡλιαία, which was presided over by the
thesmothetae or six junior archons. In the fifth century B.C.,
the whole number of the jurors chosen each year was six
thousand. But after the archonship of Euclides (403 B.C.),
when the judicature was reorganized, the number did not
exceed five thousand. Any Athenian citizen over thirty years
of age and in full possession of civil rights (*i.e.* not suffering

---

[143] The judges of the demes (see on
XXIII. 2) decided cases involving sums
of less than ten drachmae.

[144] These crimes were tried in special
courts, not here described, as none of
the orations in this volume have to do
with such cases. For an account of
such courts, see Gilbert, *Antiq.* p. 379
ff.; M. and S. p. 11 ff.

[145] See on XXXII. 2.

ἀτιμία[146]) might be enrolled as a juror. On entrance into this office he took an oath, the exact form of which is unknown, though it probably ran somewhat as follows : —

ψηφιοῦμαι κατὰ τοὺς νόμους καὶ τὰ ψηφίσματα τοῦ δήμου τοῦ Ἀθηναίων καὶ τῆς βουλῆς τῶν πεντακοσίων, περὶ δ᾽ ὧν ἂν νόμοι μὴ ὦσι, γνώμῃ τῇ δικαιοτάτῃ καὶ οὔτε χάριτος ἕνεκ᾽ οὔτ᾽ ἔχθρας. καὶ ψηφιοῦμαι περὶ αὐτῶν ὧν ἂν ἡ δίωξις ᾖ (I will give my verdict on the actual facts concerned in the prosecution). καὶ ἀκροάσομαι τῶν τε κατηγορούντων καὶ τῶν ἀπολογουμένων ὁμοίως ἀμφοῖν. ὄμνυμι ταῦτα νὴ τὸν Δία, νὴ τὸν Ἀπόλλω, νὴ τὴν Δήμητρα, καὶ εἴη μέν μοι εὐορκοῦντι πολλὰ καὶ ἀγαθά, ἐπιορκοῦντι δ᾽ἐξώλεια αὐτῷ τε καὶ γένει.[147]

42. The whole number of six or five thousand jurymen rarely, if ever, sat together in any one case. The number employed varied according to the importance of the suit or the value of the property involved. No case is known to us on which less than 200 jurors sat, and we find courts consisting of 400, 500, 1000, 2000,[148] and 2500 jurymen mentioned in the authors. In order to avoid a tie, an extra man seems generally to have been added to these round numbers. The whole body of jurors was divided for the year into ten sections, designated by the letters of the alphabet from A to K, each section, in the fourth century, containing members from all the tribes. Each juror was given a ticket or token (πινάκιον) made of boxwood or of bronze, inscribed with his own name, the name of his father, the name of his deme and the letter denoting his section.[149] There were ten different court-rooms, and the ten

---

[146] See below, § 51.

[147] As reconstituted by Fränkel, *Hermes*, XIII, p. 452 ff. See also Gilbert, *Antiq.* p. 392; M. and S. p. 152 ff.; and below, on XXII. 7.

[148] *Cf.* Lys. XIII. 35.

[149] On the πινάκια in general, with references to special writings, see Gilbert, *Antiq.* p. 397, and Sandys on Arist. *Resp. Ath.* 63. 4. For the inscriptions on extant πινάκια, see *CIA.* II, 875-940. The bronze πινάκιον illus-

sections were allotted among these by lots drawn on the days of trials. This was the practice at least during the Peloponnesian War; but in the time of Aristotle, though the sections were retained, the jurors were allotted [150] individually, and not by sections, among the different court-rooms. We cannot determine which of these methods was followed in the time of Lysias's forensic activity.

43. Early in the morning of each day on which the courts were to be held [151] the Heliasts assembled, presented their πινάκια, and were assigned by lot (whether in sections or individually) to the different courts in which they were to sit in judgment on that day. Each court had its own name,[152] and was further distinguished by the colour of the lintel of its door. Each juryman, on being assigned to a court, was given a staff or bâton (βακτηρία) of the colour of the court into which he was to go. With this in hand he proceeded to his court, and on entering gave up his staff and received a sort of counter (σύμβολον [153]), which he was obliged to show at the end of the day in order to obtain his fee of three obols.

trated (actual size) in Fig. 1 (opp. p. xliii) is taken from *Annuaire de l'Association pour l'encouragement des Études Grecques*, XII (1878), p. 206, where it was first published. The inscription runs: Διονύσιος Διονυ (*sc.* σίου) ἐκ Κοί (*sc.* λης). The letter of the section, A, stands in the upper left-hand corner; below it is an owl between the letters A and Θ (for Ἀθηναίων). On the right is a gorgon's head, and below it the bodies of two owls with a single head between A and A.

[150] For the complicated method by which they were allotted, see Arist. *Resp. Ath.* 63 ff., and Gilbert, *Antiq.* p. 397 ff.

[151] Courts ordinarily sat daily except on festivals and unlucky days; Gilbert, *Antiq.* p. 403.

[152] For the names, see Gilbert, *ibid.* p. 396.

[153] For the σύμβολον, cf. Arist. *Resp. Ath.* col. 32, 13 ff., and see Benndorf in *Zeitschr. für österr. Gymnasialw.* XXVI, 1875, p. 601. Such a σύμβολον is illustrated (actual size) in Fig. 2 (opp. p. xliii), taken from the *Monumenti Inediti*, VIII, tav. 32. The original is of lead, and has on one side the owl and olive-branch (as represented on the three-obol piece) and the abbreviation ΑΘΗ, on the other the letter of the section.

44. The furniture of the courts was simple. In each stood a
statue of the hero Lycus, of whom little is known save that he
was, so to speak, the patron saint of the dicasts. The court
was enclosed by railings (δρύφακτος), which the public were
allowed to approach unless cases involving the religious Myste-
ries were being 'tried. Within the railings were wooden
benches for the jury. In the fourth century there was a
platform or tribune (βῆμα [154]) for the presiding magistrate, as
well as one for each of the parties to the suit, and one for
speakers and witnesses. A water-clock (κλεψύδρα) also stood
in the court; for, in certain kinds of cases, the time allowed for
speeches was limited.[155] There was, too, a table on which stood
the voting-urns, to be described below.[156]

45. The general division of law-suits (δίκαι, the generic term)
into public (γραφαί) and private (δίκαι, in the narrower sense)
has already been mentioned.[157] Suits were also classed as δίκαι
κατά τινος or πρός τινα. In the former, the court was asked to
punish a defendant for some personal infraction of the laws; in
the latter, to decide a question of legal right or title as between
two parties. Further, every suit was either an ἀγὼν ἀτίμητος
or an ἀγὼν τιμητός. In an ἀγὼν ἀτίμητος the proper penalty
(τίμημα) was known beforehand, being fixed by law.[158] In an
ἀγὼν τιμητός, the jury, if it found the defendant guilty, had
next to proceed to determine what penalty he ought to suffer
or to pay (ὅ τι χρὴ παθεῖν ἢ ἀποτεῖσαι [159]). In such a suit the
plaintiff (ὁ διώκων or κατήγορος) proposed a penalty (τιμᾶσθαι
τῷ φεύγοντι), the defendant (ὁ φεύγων) another (ἀντιτιμᾶσθαι),

---

[154] See on XII. 24.

[155] For the clock, see on XXIII. 4,
and M. and S. p. 927 ff.; Sandys on
Arist. *Resp. Ath.* col. 34 f.

[156] See p. li.

[157] See above, § 36.

[158] As in the Olive-Tree and Corn-
law cases; see pp. 4 and 92.

[159] *Cf.* Plat. *Apol.* 36 B; Arist. *Resp.
Ath.* col. 35, 21 f.

and the jury appear to have been obliged to choose between these two.[160]

46. The actual course of an ordinary law-suit, whether public or private, may now be considered.[161] First the plaintiff summoned (προσκαλεῖσθαι [162]) the defendant to appear before that magistrate whose duty it was to receive a charge of the sort which was to be made. Thus, Diogiton was summoned before the first archon [163]; the defendant in the Olive-Tree case, before the archon βασιλεύς [164]; Pancleon, before the third archon, the Polemarch.[165] The magistrate entitled to receive the charges was said to have ἡγεμονία δικαστηρίου,[166] — that is, the direction of all the proceedings which followed, including the duty of presiding in the court on the day of the trial. The summons (πρόσκλησις) before the magistrate had to be made in the presence of witnesses, generally two, called κλητῆρες.[167] At the same time the plaintiff named the day on which he wished the defendant to appear. On or before this day,[168] the plaintiff presented to the magistrate his written indictment (λῆξις or ἔγκλημα [169]), thus lodging his suit (δίκην λαχεῖν [170]).

[160] It has been thought that the jury were not thus bound, but that they might inflict a punishment of their own choosing. But *cf.* Arist. *Resp. Ath.* col. 36, 35 ff.; and see M. and S. p. 216 ff.; Gilbert, *ibid.* pp. 405, 413.

[161] In general, see M. and S. p. 769 ff.; Gilbert, *ibid.* p. 406 ff.

[162] *Cf.* XXIII. 2.

[163] See p. 152.   [164] See p. 4.

[165] See p. 105.

[166] See Gilbert, *ibid.* p. 376, and below, p. 75, note 12. This magistrate was sometimes termed εἰσαγωγεύς, as he brought the case into court (εἰσάγειν) after the preliminary investigation; see M. and S. p. 45.

[167] See on XXIII. 2. In certain cases no summons was required, as in the ἐφήγησις (see on VII. 22) and the εἰσαγγελία (*cf.* XVI. 12, XXXI. 26, and see p. 92). The latter was a denunciation made before the Senate or the Assembly, and it might result in a trial before a Heliastic court.

[168] See M. and S. p. 794, note 111.

[169] In public suits the term ἀπογραφή was sometimes used. See on VII. 2 and M. and S. p. 303.

[170] This phrase probably originated in the drawing of lots to determine the order in which suits should come up for investigation.

On the day appointed at the summons, the magistrate announced
to the parties whether the suit was or was not εἰσαγώγιμος,[171]
— that is, whether it was in his jurisdiction, and laid in the
proper form. Next, if he accepted the suit, he fixed a day for
the preliminary investigation (ἀνάκρισις), and the plaintiff or
both parties (according as the suit was public or private) were
required to pay the court fees (πρυτανεῖα[172]). The magistrate,
while awaiting the ἀνάκρισις, posted the charge in some public
place. The following is an example of a charge : —

Ἀπολλόδωρος Πασίωνος Ἀχαρνεὺς Στεφάνῳ Μενεκλέους
Ἀχαρνεῖ ψευδομαρτυριῶν, τίμημα τάλαντον. τὰ ψευδῆ μου
κατεμαρτύρησε Στέφανος μαρτυρήσας τὰ ἐν τῷ γραμματείῳ
γεγραμμένα.[173]

The defendant's answer (ἀντιγραφή[174]) had also to be in writing. To the particular charge just quoted it was as follows :—

τἀληθῆ ἐμαρτύρησα μαρτυρήσας τὰ ἐν τῷ γραμματείῳ γεγραμμένα.

47. At the ἀνάκρισις, the written statements of each party
were confirmed by them under oath (the διωμοσία or ἀντωμοσία[175]). Then the defendant might put in any objections
which he chose to raise to the admissibility of the suit. He
might do this, for instance, by a παραγραφή[176] or by the διαμαρτυρία.[177] If he raised no objection, the ἀνάκρισις proceeded.
Both sides brought forward all the evidence which they had to
offer, whether consisting of laws, decrees, documents of any
sort, witnesses with oral testimony or affidavits taken by com-
missioners, as well as the evidence of slaves, given under the
torture.[178] The whole body of evidence, reduced to writing,

---

[171] See p. 105 and on XXIII. 5.

[172] See Gilbert, *ibid.* p. 407; M. and
S. p. 799 ff.

[173] *Cf.* Dem. XLV. 46.

[174] See below, p. 104, and M. and S.
p. 830.

[175] See on XXIII. 13.

[176] See p. 104.

[177] See on XXIII. 13, and Gilbert,
ibid. p. 407.

[178] See on VII. 34.

was then sealed up by the magistrate in a box called the ἐχῖνος, to be kept safely until the day of the trial.

48. At the actual trial, therefore, little remained to complete the case except the speeches on each side and the decision of the jury. The magistrate, the jurors assigned by lot, and the parties to the suit took their places,[179] and the proceedings began with sacrifice and a prayer led by the herald (κῆρυξ). The clerk (γραμματεύς) then read the charge and the answer to it. Next came the plaintiff's speech, followed by that of the defendant. In many suits, two speeches were allowed to each party, and these entirely aside from such speeches as might always be made by the συνήγοροι, whose function has been considered above.[180] Either party might question[181] his opponent, who was obliged by law to answer; but there was no oral examination or cross-examination of witnesses at the actual trial. In this respect Athenian procedure was obviously very different from ours. The evidence of the witnesses, given and written down at the ἀνάκρισις, was merely read aloud by the clerk at the time of the trial, the witness meanwhile standing on the βῆμα used by the speakers. After the reading, the witness acknowledged the evidence as his. Each party to the suit used every effort to influence the jury in his favour, often departing widely from the business in hand (ἔξω τοῦ πράγματος λέγειν) to call attention to his past services or to enlarge upon his present misfortunes; sometimes the suitor came into court with the suppliant olive branch (ἱκετηρία) in his hand; frequently he brought with him his children or other dependent members of his family in order to enlist the sympathy of the jurors. Even tears and lamentations were common enough, for

---

[179] If the defendant did not appear, he lost his suit by default (see on XXXII. 2); if the accuser was absent, the defendant was acquitted.

[180] See § 36.

[181] *Cf.* XII. 24, XXII. 5.

these and all such appeals to pity as have been mentioned were
forbidden only in the Areopagus, where, too, the speaker was
expected to keep closely to the real subject.[182]

49. After the speeches, the case was committed to the jury,
who proceeded to vote. In the fifth century, the ballots used
were muscle shells (χοιρῖναι), which were cast into one of two
urns, according to the verdict which the juror wished to render.
But in the time of the great orators, the ballot (ψῆφος) was a
bronze disc, having an axis (called αὐλίσκος) running through
its centre and protruding on either side. The form is well
known from extant specimens.[183] Each juror was given two of
these ψῆφοι, exactly alike except that in one the axis was solid
(ἡ πλήρης ψῆφος), in the other perforated (ἡ τετρυπημένη
ψῆφος). At the time of voting the herald proclaimed: " ἡ
τετρυπημένη τοῦ πρότερον λέγοντος, ἡ δὲ πλήρης τοῦ ὕστερον
λέγοντος." [184] Hence (since the plaintiff spoke first), the perforated ballot denoted condemnation, and the solid ballot
denoted acquittal. At the herald's summons, the juror took
his ballots one in each hand, holding them [185] (probably with

---

[182] See on VII. 42.

[183] See Fig. 3 (opp. p. xliii). The
ψῆφος there represented (inscribed
ψῆφος δημοσία, with the letters K and Γ
on the reverse) was found on the Pnyx
in Athens in 1861, and was illustrated
and described in the *Annali dell' Inst.
Archeol.* for that year by Rousopoulos;
more fully by the same scholar in the
Ἀρχαιολογικὴ Ἐφημερίς, 1862, p. 305 ff.,
with an illustration of the actual size
of the original. From this illustration
Fig. 3 is taken, but is reduced one
half in size. Rousopoulos describes,
but does not illustrate, a second ψῆφος,
exactly like the first except that its
αὐλίσκος is solid. He also gives a description and an illustration of a third

ψῆφος made of clay, of rude late work-
manship, considerably different in appearance from the first two. It could
never have been used in the classical
period in Athens. Yet Daremberg and
Saglio, *Dict. Antiq.* III, Figs. 2515 and
2516, as well as Sandys, Arist. *Resp.
Ath.*, frontispiece, publish both the
first and the third ψῆφος without a
word of the distinction which Rousopoulos carefully drew between them.

[184] *Cf.* Arist. *Resp. Ath.* col. 36, 14 ff.

[185] Arist. *ibid.* 16 ff. says: ὁ δὲ δικαστὴς ... πιέζει τὸ μέσον τῆς ψήφου, καὶ
οὐ δεικνύων τοῖς ἀγωνιζομένοις οὔτε τὸ
τετρυπημένον οὔτε τὸ πλῆρες ἐμβάλλει
τὴν μὲν κυρίαν εἰς τὸν χαλκοῦν ἀμφορέα,
τὴν δὲ ἄκυρον εἰς τὸν ξύλινον.

finger and thumb pressing on the extremities of the axes) in
such a manner as to allow no bystander to distinguish the
πλήρης from the τετρυπημένη, and approached the voting-table.
Here stood two large urns (καδίσκοι or ἀμφορεῖς), the one of
bronze or copper, the other of wood. Into the former (called
ὁ κύριος) the juror cast the ballot with which he wished to
record his verdict; into the latter (ὁ ἄκυρος) he cast the other
ballot. In this way a secret vote was assured; for nobody save
the voter could tell which ballot was deposited in ὁ κύριος.
After all had voted, the ballots in ὁ κύριος were counted by the
presiding magistrate, and the verdict thus obtained was
announced by the herald.[186] In case of a tie, the defendant won
the suit. If the prosecutor in a public suit[187] did not receive
one fifth of the votes, he was fined 1000 drachmae and suffered
ἀτιμία to the extent of being debarred from ever again bringing
a suit of the kind which he had lost. In many private suits, if
the prosecutor did not obtain the required fifth (τὸ πέμπτον
μέρος), he was fined the ἐπωβελία, — that is, he had to pay the
defendant one obol in each drachma's worth (i.e. one-sixth of
the value) of the property in dispute.[188]

50. After the verdict had been announced,[189] it was necessary, if the suit was τιμητός, for the jury to decide what the
penalty should be (τιμᾶν τῷ φεύγοντι). In the fourth century,
they did this, after hearing the proposals of each side, by balloting
again in the manner just described. In the fifth century, each

---

[186] On the voting in general, cf.
Arist. *Resp. Ath.* col. 35, 27 ff., and
see M. and S. p. 934 ff.; Gilbert, *ibid.*
p. 410 ff.

[187] But not in Olive-Tree suits; see
on VII. 37.

[188] See pp. 104, 153, and M. and S.
p. 947 ff.; Gilbert, p. 414.

[189] There was no actual appeal, in

our sense of the word, from the verdict
of a Heliastic court. A sentence might
be annulled if the condemned proved
that he was the victim of false witness,
or if he showed that he had lost the
case by a default when he could not
have avoided absence at the fixed time
(see on XXXII. 2).

juryman was given a wax tablet on which he drew a long line
if he favoured the plaintiff's proposal, a short one if he favoured
that of the defendant. This second part of a trial was called
the τίμησις.

51. The ordinary punishment [190] in most suits consisted of a
money fine. Fines were levied far oftener in Athenian cases
than in ours, because imprisonment was rarely employed. In
fact, our favourite penalty of imprisonment for a fixed period
as a punishment for crime, was probably unknown in Athens. A
man might be kept in the prison (there was only one in
Athens [191]) until he had paid the fine fixed by a court; he might
be imprisoned, in certain cases, while awaiting trial unless he
could give the security of fellow-citizens; persons condemned
to death, like Socrates, were imprisoned until execution; but
all this is very different from our system. Even murderers
awaiting trial might be allowed to go at large; for if a murderer
was willing to leave the country and go into exile, the State
felt that it was rid of a pollution at the cheapest possible rate.
And it is to be noted that exile in antiquity meant far more
than it does now. A Greek, outside of his own State, had
practically no civil rights whatever; and unless he secured the
protection of a citizen of the State to which he fled (a difficult
matter for a criminal), the laws did not protect him and he was
at the mercy of the men among whom he took up his abode.
Such being the case, the Athenians naturally employed banish-
ment as one of the severest penalties which could be inflicted
upon criminals. The death penalty was also used. Besides
fines (extending up to confiscation of property), there was also
ἀτιμία. This word denoted the partial or total loss of the

---

[190] On punishments in general, see
Gilbert, *ibid.* p. 414; M. and S. p.
956 ff.

[191] See M. and S. p. 83; Smith, *Dict.
Antiq. s.v. Carcer.*

rights of citizenship.   One form of ἀτιμία has already been described,[192] and others are mentioned in the introduction to the Twelfth oration.[193]

[192] See above, § 49.

[193] See below, p. 30, and on ἀτιμία in general, cf. And. i. 73 ff.

ON THE SACRED OLIVE.

INTRODUCTION.

THE olive was pre-eminent over all the productions of the Attic soil for the variety of its uses and for the interesting parts which it played in many departments of public and private life. From the wood, which was so hard as to be all but proof against water, worms, and even time itself, were made joists, oars, handles of various tools, and implements of peace and war. This same quality, together with the ease with which the wood took on a polish, made it an excellent material for graven images.[1] From the sprays and leaves were woven garlands to be worn at festivals or to be the crowns of victors. The fruit, both fresh and preserved, was eaten then as now. But the most highly prized of all its products was the oil. This was used for anointing, both in the baths and the palaestra[2]; jars of it were given to victorious athletes; it was burnt in the lamps; and finally it was indispensable in cooking and was constantly used as we use butter and lard.[3]

While the olive was thus to the Greek a necessity of life, to the Athenian it was his country's pride and an emblem of her patron goddess.[4] For Athens was held to be the native place of the olive, at least so far as Greece was concerned.[5] There in the Pandroseum[6] was preserved the first of all olives, planted by Athena herself when she contended for the city against Poseidon.[7] Close

---

[1] On the uses of the wood, *cf.* Blümner, *Technologie*, II, p. 280. In much of the introduction to this speech I have closely followed Frohberger.

[2] Hermann, *Privatalterthümer*, pp. 213, 281, 350. [3] *Ibid.* p. 228.

[4] Curtius, *Stadtgeschichte von Athen*, p. 12.

[5] Hdt. v. 82. But the olive came originally from the Orient; see Hehn, *Kulturpflanzen*, p. 89 ff.

[6] Harrison, *Mythology and Monuments of Athens*, p. 512.

[7] Hdt. viii. 55, and on the myths connected with the olive, Bötticher, *Baumkultus*, p. 423 ff.

at hand in the Erechtheum was the ancient olivewood statue of
Athena Polias which fell from heaven.[8] As goddess of the olive,
Athena had a special name, Σκιράς,[9] and a special form of worship,[10]
and with her was associated Ζεὺς Μόριος,[11] who had an altar in the
Academy.[12] Here stood the group of twelve sacred olives[13] (μορίαι),
propagated from the first tree, and in their turn the progenitors of
the "olive grove of Academe" and of the numerous plantations
throughout the country.

The soil of Attica was particularly well suited to the growth of
the olive,[14] and the plain[15] of the Cephisus was the place in which
the tree did best. This plain is bounded on the north by Parnes
and Pentelicus, on the east by Hymettus, on the south by the
sea, and on the west by Aegaleüs. Here olive culture was most
remunerative.[16] The exportation of olives and oil, permitted by
Solon though he forbade the exportation of other products,[17] was a
most important part of Athenian trade and brought in a large
income to the State.[18] In the Roman period it was the chief
reliance of impoverished Athens,[19] and it is still among the valued
items of the Greek revenue.[20] The great statesmen Solon and
Pisistratus took pains to encourage the cultivation of the tree,[21]
which, in spite of its extraordinary productive power — for it keeps
spreading from scions springing from its own roots[22] — needed

[8] Harrison, *ibid.* p. 495.

[9] From γῆ σκιρράς, the soil in which
the tree thrives, Mommsen, *Heorto-
logie*, p. 54 f. Roscher, *Lexicon der
Mythologie*, I, p. 683.

[10] Σκιροφορία, *ibid.*

[11] Soph. *O. C.* 705.

[12] Schol. *ibid.*

[13] Suid. *s.v.* Paus. i. 30. 2. Ar. *Nub.*
1005.

[14] "For Greece the olive zone begins
south of the plains of Thessaly, as for
Italy it begins south of the plains of
Lombardy. The olive is found in
Phthiotis and Magnesia; in Epeirus,

only on the sea-coast." Jebb, Soph.
O. C. 700.

[15] Bursian, *Geographie von Griechenland*, I, 264.   [16] [Dem.] XLIII. 69.

[17] Plut. *Solon*, 24.

[18] Bötticher, *ibid.* p. 434.

[19] Hertzberg, *Griechenland unter
den Römern*, pp. 317 f.

[20] Oil to the value of twenty million
francs was made in Greece in 1875;
Baedeker's *Greece*, p. xlvi.

[21] Mommsen, *ibid.* p. 56. Bötticher,
ibid. p. 436.

[22] Bötticher, p. 423. Hence perhaps
Soph. *O. C.* 698, φύτευμ' ἀχείρωτον

constant watching to prevent degeneration into the wild olive (κότινος).[23]

Just as in well-governed modern countries there are laws to protect forests from ignorant or wanton destruction, so in Athens laws were made to preserve the olive trees which were so essential to the prosperity of the country. Even of his own private olive trees (ἴδιαι ἐλᾶαι) a man was not allowed to cut down more than two in a year for his own use, on penalty of a fine of 200 drachmae for each tree.[24] But the law was much stricter in regard to the sacred olives (μόριαι ἐλᾶαι, more commonly μορίαι[25] alone), which were under the protection of Athena and Zeus, and from which were made the crowns and the oil given to the victors at the Panathenaic contests.[26] To uproot them was utterly forbidden, and even the ground immediately about them could not be planted with anything else for fear of interference with the growth of the olive.[27] The Areopagus had charge of all matters relating to these trees, and its special committee of ἐπιγνώμονες[28] inspected each tree annually. The produce of the trees was, in the time of Lysias, farmed out to contractors,[29]

αὐτοποιόν, although the second adj. may refer to the miraculous self-renewal of the olive in the Pandroseum after its burning by the Persians, Hdt. viii. 55; so Jebb.

[23] Theophr. *H. P.* ii. 3.

[24] Law in [Dem.] XLIII. 71. The procedure against such an offender was by φάσις or some analogous process; M. and S. p. 299; Boeckh, *Staatshaushaltung der Athener*, I, p. 421.

[25] This word, originally an adj. and occurring as such in §§ 7 and 29, is accented throughout the speech as such by Frohberger and Thalheim. But it seems more likely that it was also used as a real subst., like ὑπερορία, XXXI. 8. This subst. we should write μορίαι (which indeed is the only accent found in codd. for it), not μόριαι. Hence in § 2

μορίων, but in § 29 μορίων. The etymology is very obscure. The ancients connected it with the death (μόρος) of Halirrhothius, son of Poseidon, who gave himself a mortal wound in trying to uproot Athena's sacred tree (Schol. Ar. *Nub.* 1005). Suidas connects it with μείρομαι, *share*, and explains that the trees were possessed in common by all Athenians. A modern idea, based on the same derivation, is that the μορίαι were all *parted*, or *propagated*, μεμορημέναι, from the original stock in the Acropolis. But the fact is that the origin of the name is lost in antiquity.

[26] Mommsen, *ibid.* p. 150 f. Arist. *Resp. Ath.* 60. Pind. *Nem.* x. 35.

[27] Lys. VII. 25.

[28] Lys. *ibid.* Harp. *s.v.* M. and S. p. 758.

[29] Lys. VII. 2.

but later this practice was abandoned and the State collected
annually about three-quarters of a pint[30] of oil for each tree from
the owners of land on which the μορίαι stood. The Areopagus, at
monthly sessions,[31] took cognisance of matters relating to these
trees. Any person who had destroyed one of them would be
brought before this court by the Archon Basileus[32] on a charge
of sacrilege (ἀσέβεια[33]). There was no statute of limitations
(προθεσμία[34]) to hinder the punishment of such an offender, no
matter how long after his crime he was arrested. The case was
ἀτίμητος, and the fixed punishment was confiscation of property
and exile.[35]

The Spartans seem to have spared the sacred olives during the
Peloponnesian war,[36] yet in the course of it and during the year of
anarchy numerous trees, both private and public, were injured or
destroyed.[37] After the restoration of the democracy the stumps
or trunks (στελέχη[38]) of the sacred trees were enclosed in fences
as a protection against wild animals, and to warn everybody that
the remains were as sacred as the trees themselves had been.
This precaution had a practical as well as a religious side. For
the olive was known to be so tenacious of life that even after a
stump had been given up for dead, it might send out shoots and

---

[30] τρι᾽ ἡμικοτύλια ἀπὸ τοῦ στελέχους
ἑκάστου, Arist. *Resp. Ath.* 60.

[31] Lys. VII. 25. So Rauchenstein.
It is commonly believed, however, that
a committee of ἐπιμεληταί (*cf.* §§ 7 and
29) visited the trees each month in
addition to the annual inspection of
the ἐπιγνώμονες.

[32] Dem. XXII. 27; XXXV. 48. See note
on § 22, and M. and S. p. 61 ff.

[33] M. and S. p. 368 f.

[34] § 17, and M. and S. p. 840.

[35] §§ 3, 25, 32, 41. M. and S. p. 375.
But Aristotle, *Resp. Ath.* 60, says that
formerly, when the state farmed out
the produce of the μορίαι, the penalty

was death; adding that since the oil
has been paid in by the owner of the
farm "the procedure has lapsed, though
the law remains." Here Aristotle is
thinking of the old punishment of death
inflicted in all cases of ἀσέβεια, and he
omits to note the modification in the
penalty which is clear from Lysias.

[36] Schol. Soph. *O. C.* 698–701.

[37] Lys. VII. 7, *cf.* 6 and 24; XIV. 33;
Isocr. XVI. 13.

[38] στέλεχος is kindred to στελεά,
shaft, στήλη (Curt. *Griech. Etym.* p.
212). It may denote also the entire
tree; *cf.* Hdt. viii. 55, [Dem.] XLIII. 69,
Arist. *Resp. Ath.* 60.

thrive once more.[39] The term σηκός,[40] properly signifying only the fence, in use included all that the fence enclosed, and hence in this speech it is applied to the stump of a μορία. Such a stump the speaker had been accused of removing contrary to the law.

This defendant was a rich owner of real estate,[41] who had held aloof from politics on principle,[42] but who had performed all his required public duties.[43] But in spite of this, he found himself accused by one Nicomachus, a young[44] man otherwise unknown to us, who seems to have been engaged by the speaker's enemies to worry him after the manner of a sycophant.[45] The original written charge was that the speaker had destroyed a μορία on one of his own farms. But when the trial began Nicomachus altered his accusation. He had found it impossible to prove by witnesses that there had been a μορία on this farm. He shifted his ground, therefore, and his charge, now verbal, not written, is that a σηκός, not a μορία, had been removed.[46] But he brings no witnesses to prove it, nor does he accept the defendant's offer of his slaves to be tortured.[47] On the other hand, the accused shows by witnesses that there had been neither μορία nor σηκός nor even a private olive tree on that piece of land since it came into his possession.[48] Here we might expect the defendant to rest his case, for it seems as if he had certainly said enough to make sure of an acquittal. That he goes on, however, shows that the judges in an Athenian court laid less stress upon the testimony of eyewitnesses[49] than we do, and preferred to hear argu-

---

[39] Hdt. viii. 55; Theophr. *H. P.* v. 9. 8; Verg. *G.* ii. 31, 181; Plin. *N. H.* xvi. 230, xvii. 241.

[40] σηκός is kindred to *saepire* (Curtius, *Griech. Etym.*, p. 161). But as 'enclosure' = all the ground enclosed and the plants and trees as well, the word stands also for the stump of the μορία (τῆς μορίας στέλεχος σηκὸς καλεῖται, Suid.); and conversely μορία may denote σηκός, *cf.* § 22, and Harp., σηκὸν ὡς ἔοικεν καὶ μορίαν ὀνομάζουσι τὴν αὐτήν.

[41] § 24.

[42] § 1.

[43] §§ 31, 41.

[44] § 29.

[45] § 38.

[46] § 2. For a similar manoeuvre, *cf.* Isocr. xviii. 7 and 53. Perhaps, however, the speaker exaggerates his difficulty. At least he had time to get Lysias to insert this section into his speech.

[47] § 20 ff. See on § 34 ff.

[48] §§ 5–10.

[49] Blass, *Attische Beredsamkeit*, I, p. 592.

ments. For in fact the accused begins again with what is in effect a new introduction,[50] and the last three-quarters of his speech is composed of 'arguments from probability.' He was no poor man to whom the slight gain from the sale of the wood might have been an object or who needed the ground upon which the σηκός was supposed to stand[51]; he had everything to lose by such a crime and nothing to gain[52]; his slaves, naturally against him,[53] and his neighbours, some of whom were unfriendly,[54] would have been likely to inform against him ; he owned fields on which stood many μορίαι which he might have cut down with less chance of detection than was possible in the case of this which the accuser calls the only one on the estate in question[55]; the accuser had brought no witnesses,[56] had neglected to arrest the accused in the very act,[57] and had even refused the offer of his slaves for torture[58]; the defendant is a good citizen,[59] the accuser is a miserable sycophant, the mere tool of the speaker's enemies.[60] So after a brief appeal to the pity of the court for his lonely state, the defendant sums up briefly,[61] and sits down.

The date of the speech cannot be fixed with exactness. The mention of the archon in § 11 shows that it must have been delivered later than B.C. 397–6. The words τοσούτῳ χρόνῳ ὕστερον in § 42 show that the suit was not brought for some time after the supposed crime had been committed. Probably the case was tried at the earliest in the year 395.[62]

---

[50] § 12.
[51] § 14.
[52] § 15.
[53] § 16 f.
[54] § 18 ff.
[55] §§ 24, 28.
[56] § 20 f.
[57] § 22.
[58] § 34.
[59] § 30 ff.
[60] § 38 ff.
[61] §§ 41–43.
[62] So Blass, *ibid.* p. 591, after Sauppe, *Philol.* XXV, p. 258.

ΑΡΕΟΠΑΓΙΤΙΚΟΣ

ΠΕΡΙ ΤΟΥ ΣΗΚΟΥ ΑΠΟΛΟΓΙΑ.

Πρότερον μέν, ὦ βουλή, ἐνόμιζον ἐξεῖναι τῷ βουλομένῳ,
ἡσυχίαν ἄγοντι, μήτε δίκας ἔχειν μήτε πράγματα · νυνὶ δὲ
οὕτως ἀπροσδοκήτοις αἰτίαις καὶ πονηροῖς συκοφάνταις
περιπέπτωκα, ὥστ᾽ εἴ πως οἷόν τε, δοκεῖ μοι δεῖν καὶ τοὺς
5 μὴ γεγονότας ἤδη δεδιέναι περὶ τῶν μελλόντων ἔσεσθαι ·
διὰ γὰρ τοὺς τοιούτους οἱ κίνδυνοι κοινοὶ γίγνονται καὶ
2 τοῖς μηδὲν ἀδικοῦσι καὶ τοῖς πολλὰ ἡμαρτηκόσιν. οὕτω
δ᾽ ἄπορος ὁ ἀγών μοι καθέστηκεν, ὥστε ἀπεγράφην τὸ
μὲν πρῶτον ἐλάαν ἐκ τῆς γῆς ἀφανίζειν, καὶ πρὸς τοὺς
10 ἐωνημένους τοὺς καρποὺς τῶν μορίων πυνθανόμενοι προσῆσαν · ἐπειδὴ δ᾽ ἐκ τούτου τοῦ τρόπου ἀδικοῦντά με
οὐδὲν εὑρεῖν ἐδυνήθησαν, νυνί με σηκόν φασιν ἀφανίζειν,
ἡγούμενοι ἐμοὶ μὲν ταύτην τὴν αἰτίαν ἀπορωτάτην εἶναι
ψευδῆ ἀποδεῖξαι, αὐτοῖς δὲ ἐξεῖναι μᾶλλον ὅ τι ἂν βούλων-

1. βουλή: the council of the Areopagus was addressed by the same term as the Senate; *cf.* xvi. i. — **δίκας**: as a general term, 'lawsuits.' — **πράγματα**: 'bothers,' not wholly in a legal sense as in xii. 3. — **περιπέπτωκα**: rarely (and never elsewhere in Lysias) used with persons in this sense ; *cf.* Dem. LIV. 25, οὐδεμί᾽ ἐστὶν ἐλπὶς σωτηρίας τῷ περιπίπτοντι τοῖς ἀσελγαίνουσιν. — **τοὺς μὴ γεγονότας** κτλ.: 'generations yet unborn'; the paradoxical turn lends a new zest to the well-worn charge of sycophancy ; see on xvi. i. — **ἀδικοῦσι** : perfect in sense. GMT. 27; H. 827.

2. ἄπορος: *difficult, perplexing*, rendered so by the change in the nature of the charge ; see p. 5. — **ὁ ἀγών**: *the case.* — **ἀπεγράφην** : the proceedings against him began with an *ἀπογραφή*. — **ἐλάαν**: = *μορίαν* here, but not so in § 10. — **τοὺς ἐωνημένους** : 'the contractors'; see p. 3.

3 ται λέγειν. καὶ δεῖ με, περὶ ὧν οὗτος ἐπιβεβουλευκὼς
ἥκει, ἅμ' ὑμῖν τοῖς διαγνωσομένοις περὶ τοῦ πράγματος
ἀκούσαντα, καὶ περὶ τῆς πατρίδος καὶ περὶ τῆς οὐσίας
ἀγωνίσασθαι. ὅμως δὲ πειράσομαι ἐξ ἀρχῆς ὑμᾶς διδάξαι.
4   Ἦν μὲν γὰρ τοῦτο Πεισάνδρου τὸ χωρίον, δημευθέν-
20 των δ' ἐκείνου τῶν ὄντων Ἀπολλόδωρος ὁ Μεγαρεὺς
δωρειὰν παρὰ τοῦ δήμου λαβὼν τὸν μὲν ἄλλον χρόνον
ἐγεώργει, ὀλίγῳ δὲ πρὸ τῶν τριάκοντα Ἀντικλῆς παρ'
αὐτοῦ πριάμενος ἐξεμίσθωσεν· ἐγὼ δὲ παρ' Ἀντικλέους
5 εἰρήνης οὔσης ὠνοῦμαι. ἡγοῦμαι τοίνυν, ὦ βουλή, ἐμὸν
25 ἔργον ἀποδεῖξαι ὡς, ἐπειδὴ τὸ χωρίον ἐκτησάμην, οὔτ'
ἐλάα οὔτε σηκὸς ἐνῆν ἐν αὐτῷ. νομίζω γὰρ τοῦ μὲν
προτέρου χρόνου, οὐδ' εἰ πάλαι ἐνῆσαν μυρίαι, οὐκ ἂν
δικαίως ζημιοῦσθαι· εἰ γὰρ μὴ δι' ἡμᾶς εἰσιν ἠφανισμέ-
ναι, οὐδὲν προσήκει περὶ τῶν ἀλλοτρίων ἁμαρτημάτων
6 ὡς ἀδικοῦντας κινδυνεύειν.   πάντες γὰρ ἐπίστασθε ὅτι

3. **ἐπιβεβουλευκώς**: cf. XIX. 3, οἱ μὲν
γὰρ (sc. plaintiffs) ἐκ πολλοῦ χρόνου ἐπι-
βουλεύοντες.—**ἅμ' ὑμῖν**: on the probable
exaggeration, see p. 5, note 46. On
ἅμα, see App.— **ἀκούσαντα**: concessive.— **περὶ τῆς πατρίδος** κτλ.: the
penalty was exile and confiscation of
property.

4. **Πεισάνδρου**: one of the leaders
of the Four Hundred; see on XII. 65.
After their fall his property was confiscated, and this estate formed part
of the reward of Apollodorus, one of
the murderers (XIII. 70 f.) of Phrynichus. He did not receive it until some
time after the murder, as the investigation (see App.) lasted long (cf.
πλεῖν ἢ τρία ἔτη, § 6).— **δωρειάν**: the
regular word used of a gift of honour

from the State.— **εἰρήνης οὔσης**: i.e.
after the surrender of Athens to
Lysander; for, according to § 9, the
speaker held the estate only five days
before letting it in the archonship of
Pythodorus, B.C. 404–3.— **ὠνοῦμαι**:
hist. present. The aor. of this verb
is not in classic use; ἐπριάμην is
generally used for it.

5. **μέν**: the adversative clause is
unexpressed, but is latent in the context; see on § 39 and XII. 8.— **τοῦ ...**
χρόνου: i.e. for an ἀφάνισις in the past.
The gen. is causal (G. 1126; H. 744),
although not found elsewhere with
ζημιοῦσθαι, but with κολάζειν, Ar.
Vesp. 244, τιμωρεῖν, Xen. *Cyr.* iv. 6. 8.
— **δι' ἡμᾶς**: cf. § 21 and see on XII.
58.

ὁ πόλεμος καὶ ἄλλων πολλῶν αἴτιος κακῶν γεγένηται, καὶ
τὰ μὲν πόρρω ὑπὸ Λακεδαιμονίων ἐτέμνετο, τὰ δ᾽ ἐγγὺς
ὑπὸ τῶν φίλων διηρπάζετο· ὥστε πῶς ἂν δικαίως ὑπὲρ
τῶν τότε τῇ πόλει γεγενημένων συμφορῶν ἐγὼ νυνὶ δίκην
35 διδοίην; ἄλλως τε καὶ ὅτι τοῦτο τὸ χωρίον ἐν τῷ πολέμῳ
7 δημευθὲν ἄπρατον ἦν πλεῖν ἢ τρία ἔτη. οὐ θαυμαστὸν
δ᾽ εἰ τότε τὰς μορίας ἐξέκοπτον, ἐν ᾧ οὐδὲ τὰ ἡμέτερ᾽
αὐτῶν φυλάττειν ἠδυνάμεθα. ἐπίστασθε δέ, ὦ βουλή,
ὅσῳ μάλιστα τῶν τοιούτων ἐπιμελεῖσθε, πολλὰ ἐν ἐκείνῳ
40 τῷ χρόνῳ δασέα ὄντα ἰδίαις καὶ μορίαις ἐλάαις, ὧν νῦν
τὰ πολλὰ ἐκκέκοπται καὶ ἡ γῆ ψιλὴ γεγένηται· καὶ τῶν
αὐτῶν καὶ ἐν τῇ εἰρήνῃ καὶ ἐν τῷ πολέμῳ κεκτημένων οὐκ
ἀξιοῦτε παρ᾽ αὐτῶν, ἑτέρων ἐκκοψάντων, δίκην λαμβάνειν.
8 καίτοι εἰ τοὺς διὰ παντὸς τοῦ χρόνου γεωργοῦντας τῆς
45 αἰτίας ἀφίετε, ἦ που χρὴ τούς γ᾽ ἐν τῇ εἰρήνῃ πριαμένους
ἀφ᾽ ὑμῶν ἀζημίους γενέσθαι.

6. ὁ πόλεμος: *i.e.* the Peloponnesian.
— **πόρρω:** *remote,* from the city. —
Λακεδαιμονίων: *i.e.* their garrison in
Decelea (but see p. 4). — **τῶν φίλων:**
'our own people.' Not a reference
to the party of Thrasybulus, for the
time (τοῦ προτέρου χρόνου, § 5) is too
far back, but either to the systematic
desertion and laying waste of their
own estates by the Athenians at the
beginning of the war to prevent the
Spartans from living on them (*cf.*
Thuc. ii. 14, and see p. 4, note 37),
or to the depredations of private and
public foraging parties from Athens.
— **ἄν:** on its position, see on XII. 37.
— **ἄλλως τε καί:** *particularly;* see
App. — **ἄπρατον:** no purchaser could
be found in the critical times when
the Spartans were in Decelea. — **πλεῖν**

κτλ.: *over three years.* On the form,
see App.

7. θαυμαστὸν εἰ: see on XII. 36. —
ὅσῳ μάλιστα: 'particularly as,' dat. of
degree of difference, here with a sup.
(G. 1185; H. 781 b); *cf.* § 39 (but with
comp. § 24), and Soph. *Trach.* 313,
ἐπεί νιν τῶνδε πλεῖστον ᾤκτισα βλέπουσ᾽,
ὅσῳπερ καὶ φρονεῖν οἶδεν μόνη. — **ὄντα:**
impf. in time; see on XVI. 5. — **κεκτημένων:** concessive.

8. ἦ που: see on XII. 35. — **ἀφ᾽ ὑμῶν:**
'on your part,' 'so far as you are
concerned,' belonging to ἀζημίους
γενέσθαι. *Cf.* Thuc. i. 39. 3, τῆς ἀφ᾽
ἡμῶν αἰτίας, Xen. *Hellen.* v. 1. 36,
αὐτονόμους δὲ ἀπὸ τῶν Θηβαίων τὰς
Βοιωτίδας πόλεις ἐποίησαν. With πριαμένους, we should have παρ᾽ ὑμῶν, as
in § 4.

9 Ἀλλὰ γάρ, ὦ βουλή, περὶ μὲν τῶν πρότερον γεγενημένων πολλὰ ἔχων εἰπεῖν ἱκανὰ νομίζω τὰ εἰρημένα·
ἐπειδὴ δ' ἐγὼ παρέλαβον τὸ χωρίον, πρὶν ἡμέρας πέντε
50 γενέσθαι ἀπεμίσθωσα Καλλιστράτῳ, ἐπὶ Πυθοδώρου ἄρ-
10 χοντος· ὃς δύο ἔτη ἐγεώργησεν, οὔτε ἰδίαν ἐλάαν οὔτε
μορίαν οὔτε σηκὸν παραλαβών. τρίτῳ δὲ ἔτει Δημήτριος
οὑτοσὶ εἰργάσατο· τῷ δὲ τετάρτῳ Ἀλκίᾳ Ἀντισθένους
ἀπελευθέρῳ ἐμίσθωσα, ὃς τέθνηκε· κᾆτα τρία ἔτη ὁμοίως
55 καὶ Πρωτέας ἐμισθώσατο. καί μοι δεῦρ' ἴτε μάρτυρες.

ΜΑΡΤΥΡΕΣ.

11 Ἐπειδὴ τοίνυν ὁ χρόνος οὗτος ἐξήκει, αὐτὸς γεωργῶ.
φησὶ δὲ ὁ κατήγορος ἐπὶ Σουνιάδου ἄρχοντος σηκὸν ὑπ'
ἐμοῦ ἐκκεκόφθαι. ὑμῖν δὲ μεμαρτυρήκασιν οἱ πρότερον
ἐργαζόμενοι καὶ πολλὰ ἔτη παρ' ἐμοῦ μεμισθωμένοι μὴ
60 εἶναι σηκὸν ἐν τῷ χωρίῳ. καίτοι πῶς ἄν τις φανερώτερον ἐξελέγξειε ψευδόμενον τὸν κατήγορον; οὐ γὰρ οἷόν
τε, ἃ πρότερον μὴ ἦν, ταῦτα τὸν ὕστερον ἐργαζόμενον
ἀφανίζειν.

9. ἀλλὰ γάρ: see on XII. 99. — γενέσθαι: had passed; cf. Xen. Hellen. ii.
4. 25, πρὶν ἡμέρας δέκα γενέσθαι. —
Πυθοδώρου: archon in the 'year of
anarchy,' B.C. 404–3.

10. οὑτοσί: shows that Demetrius
was present. — ὃς τέθνηκε: added to
show why he does not appear; cf.
XXXII. 26. — ὁμοίως: i.e. without ἐλάα,
μορία, or σηκός. — ἐμισθώσατο: cf. the
meaning of the active above. G. 1245;
H. 815.

11. ὁ χρόνος: the lease of Proteas.
The estate therefore had been let by
the speaker from B.C. 404–3 (§ 4)

through 398–7, a period of seven
years. — ἐπὶ Σουνιάδου: archon in
397–6, the first year after the period
of seven. — μὴ εἶναι: with μαρτυρέω
the inf. regularly takes μή. G. 1496;
GMT. 685. — ψευδόμενον: indir. discourse. G. 1588; H. 981. — ἃ μὴ ἦν:
an indef. rel. clause. G. 1426, 1428;
H. 912, 913. Cf. μηδείς, § 38.

12. The evidence being all in, the
speaker now makes use of 'arguments
from probability' (see Introd. § 11).
The thread is: 'People call me a keen
hand. Now what had I to gain by
destroying the tree, and what harm

12 Ἐγὼ τοίνυν, ὦ βουλή, ἐν μὲν τῷ τέως χρόνῳ, ὅσοι με
65 φάσκοιεν δεινὸν εἶναι καὶ ἀκριβῆ καὶ οὐδὲν ἂν εἰκῇ καὶ
ἀλογίστως ποιῆσαι, ἠγανάκτουν ἄν, αἱρούμενος μᾶλλον
λέγεσθαι ὥς μοι προσῆκε· νῦν δὲ πάντας ἂν ὑμᾶς βουλοίμην περὶ ἐμοῦ ταύτην τὴν γνώμην ἔχειν, ἵνα ἡγῆσθέ
με σκοπεῖν, εἴπερ τοιούτοις ἔργοις ἐπεχείρουν, καὶ ὅ τι
70 κέρδος ἐγίγνετό μοι ἀφανίσαντι καὶ ἥτις ζημία περιποιήσαντι, καὶ τί ἂν λαθὼν διεπραξάμην καὶ τί ἂν φανερὸς
13 γενόμενος ὑφ' ὑμῶν ἔπασχον. πάντες γὰρ ἄνθρωποι τὰ
τοιαῦτα οὐχ ὕβρεως ἀλλὰ κέρδους ἕνεκα ποιοῦσι· καὶ
ὑμᾶς εἰκὸς οὕτω σκοπεῖν, καὶ τοὺς ἀντιδίκους ἐκ τούτων
75 τὰς κατηγορίας ποιεῖσθαι, ἀποφαίνοντας ἥτις ὠφέλεια
14 τοῖς ἀδικήσασιν ἐγίγνετο. οὗτος μέντοι οὐκ ἂν ἔχοι ἀπο-

did its presence cause me?' — ὅσοι
φάσκοιεν: rel. general condition. G.
1431, 2; H. 914 b. — δεινόν: in a
bad sense, sharp, shrewd; so ἀκριβῆ.
— εἰκῇ: see App. to xii. 15. — ἂν
ποιῆσαι: representing a potential opt.
— ἠγανάκτουν ἄν: the iterative use.
G. 1296; GMT. 162; H. 835. — αἱρούμενος κτλ.: the thought is, 'in the
past I preferred people to speak of me
in appropriate terms; but now I should
rather have you all think of me as a
keen fellow, — one who would never
be guilty of such a foolish act.' — ἂν
ὑμᾶς βουλοίμην: I should like to have
you, Lat. velim. G. 1327; H. 903.
Cf. xii. 22. — ἡγῆσθε: after a potential
opt., a final clause as a rule takes the
subjv. in prose. G. 1270, 2; GMT.
180. — σκοπεῖν: represents the impf.
indicative. — ἐγίγνετο: the rare change
in indir. disc. to the impf. after a
secondary tense (σκοπεῖν). Cf. xii.
73. G. 1489; GMT. 674, 2; H. 936.

The direct question would be τί κέρδος
γίγνεται, where the pres. tense has
the force of μέλλει γενήσεσθαι, as in
Isaeus ix. 24. See on § 13 f., where
the impfs. themselves have this force.
— ζημία: material loss is meant, as
in xxxii. 21; cf. Plat. Hipparch. 226 E,
κέρδος δὲ λέγεις ἐναντίον τῇ ζημίᾳ;
— περιποιήσαντι: i.e. σώσαντι, cf. xiii.
63, ἡ δὲ τύχη καὶ ὁ δαίμων (αὐτοὺς)
περιεποίησε.

13. πάντες ἄνθρωποι: without the
art.; see on xvi. 15. — ὕβρεως: 'lawlessness.' — κέρδους ἕνεκα: cf. Isocr. xxi.
6, δῆλον γὰρ, ὅτι πάντες κέρδους ἕνεκ'
ἀδικοῦσιν. — οὕτω σκοπεῖν: 'look at it
in this light.' See on xvi. 18. — ἐκ τούτων: repeats the idea in οὕτω, and is
explained by ἀποφαίνοντας, denoting
means. One of the best 'arguments
from probability' lay in showing that
the accused had something to gain by
his alleged crime. — ἐγίγνετο: this
impf., unlike ἐγίγνετο in § 12, is the

δεῖξαι οὔθ' ὡς ὑπὸ πενίας ἠναγκάσθην τοιούτοις ἔργοις
ἐπιχειρεῖν, οὔθ' ὡς τὸ χωρίον μοι διαφθείρεται τοῦ σηκοῦ
ἐνόντος, οὔθ' ὡς ἀμπέλοις ἐμποδὼν ἦν, οὔθ' ὡς οἰκίας
80 ἐγγύς, οὔθ' ὡς ἐγὼ ἄπειρος τῶν παρ' ὑμῖν κινδύνων. ἐγὼ
δέ, εἴ τι τοιοῦτον ἔπραττον, πολλὰς ἂν καὶ μεγάλας
15 ἐμαυτῷ ζημίας γιγνομένας ἀποφήναιμι· ὃς πρῶτον μὲν
μεθ' ἡμέραν ἐξέκοπτον τὸν σηκόν, ὥσπερ οὐ πάντας
λαθεῖν δέον, ἀλλὰ πάντας Ἀθηναίους εἰδέναι. καὶ εἰ μὲν
85 αἰσχρὸν ἦν μόνον τὸ πρᾶγμα, ἴσως ἄν τις τῶν παριόντων
ἠμέλησε· νῦν δ' οὐ περὶ αἰσχύνης ἀλλὰ τῆς μεγίστης
16 ζημίας ἐκινδύνευον. πῶς δ' οὐκ ἂν ἦ ἀθλιώτατος ἀνθρώπων ἁπάντων, εἰ τοὺς ἐμαυτοῦ θεράποντας μηκέτι δούλους
ἔμελλον ἕξειν ἀλλὰ δεσπότας τὸν λοιπὸν βίον, τοιοῦτον
90 ἔργον συνειδότας; ὥστε εἰ καὶ τὰ μέγιστα εἰς ἐμὲ ἐξημάρτανον, οὐκ ἂν οἷόν τε ἦν δίκην με παρ' αὐτῶν λαμβά-
νειν· εὖ γάρ ἂν ἤδη ὅτι ἐπ' ἐκείνοις ἦν καὶ ἐμὲ τιμω-
ρήσασθαι καὶ αὐτοῖς μηνύσασιν ἐλευθέροις γενέσθαι.

direct thought unchanged. It has
the meaning of ἔμελλε γενήσεσθαι, like
the impf. partic. γιγνομένας in § 14; cf.
Andoc. I. 58, φονεὺς οὖν αὐτῶν ἐγιγνό-
μην ἐγώ, μὴ εἰπὼν ὑμῖν ἃ ἤκουσα, and
see Schoemann on Isaeus I. 44. Like
these is the use of ἐκέρδαινον, § 32,
denoting *likelihood;* see GMT. 38,
and cf. XII. 27, 88.

14. ὑπὸ πενίας: as, for instance, that
he wanted to make money by selling
the wood or using the ground occupied
by the σηκός. — παρ' ὑμῖν: the dat. on
the principle of παρὰ τῷ πολεμάρχῳ,
XXIII. 3; cf. XXI. 17, εἰ παρ' ἄλλοις ἐκινδύνευον. See App.— γιγνομένας: indir.
disc. (G. 1588; H. 981), representing
an impf. used like ἐγίγνετο, § 13. It

is the apod. of εἰ ἔπραττον, a prot. of
the simple first form: 'If I did any
such thing, many severe penalties
were bound to come upon me, as I
could show.' See App.

15. μεθ' ἡμέραν: 'in broad day.' —
ὥσπερ οὐ δέον: 'just as if it were not
important,' though the partic. is not
conditional as the neg. οὐ shows; see
App. to XII. 7, and for the acc. absol.,
G. 1569; H. 973. — αἰσχρόν: hence
not entailing a legal penalty. — τῶν
παριόντων: depends on ἠμέλησε. Cf.
§ 17, τῶν οἰκετῶν μηδὲν φροντίζειν.

16. δεσπότας: on the thought, cf.
Pub. Syrus, 194, fa m u l a t u r d o m i-
n u s u b i t i m e t q u i b u s i m p e r e t.
— ἐλευθέροις γενέσθαι: see on § 35;

17 ἔτι τοίνυν εἰ τῶν οἰκετῶν παρέστη μοι μηδὲν φροντίζειν,
95 πῶς ἂν ἐτόλμησα τοσούτων μεμισθωμένων καὶ ἁπάντων
συνειδότων ἀφανίσαι τὸν σηκὸν βραχέος μὲν κέρδους ἕνεκα;
προθεσμίας δὲ οὐδεμιᾶς οὔσης τῷ κινδύνῳ τοῖς εἰργασμένοις ἅπασι τὸ χωρίον ὁμοίως προσῆκον εἶναι σῶν τὸν
σηκόν, ἵν᾽ εἴ τις αὐτοὺς ᾐτιᾶτο, εἶχον ἀνενεγκεῖν ὅτῳ παρέ-
100 δοσαν; νῦν δὲ καὶ ἐμὲ ἀπολύσαντες φαίνονται καὶ σφᾶς
αὐτούς, εἴπερ ψεύδονται, μετόχους τῆς αἰτίας καθιστάντες.
18 εἰ τοίνυν καὶ ταῦτα παρεσκευασάμην, πῶς ἂν οἷός τ᾽ ἦ
πάντας πεῖσαι τοὺς παριόντας, ἢ τοὺς γείτονας, οἳ οὐ
μόνον ἀλλήλων ταῦτ᾽ ἴσασιν ἃ πᾶσιν ὁρᾶν ἔξεστιν, ἀλλὰ
105 καὶ περὶ ὧν ἀποκρυπτόμεθα μηδένα εἰδέναι, καὶ περὶ ἐκεί-

---

freedom, then, was the reward of a
slave who laid a μήνυσις against his
master. Death, however, was the
penalty for false information. On
the whole subject, see M. and S. pp.
330 f., 751.

17. οἰκετῶν: in this speech οἰκέτης,
θεράπων and δοῦλος are used as synonyms, although each really has a
special meaning of its own; see Hermann, *Privatalt.* p. 83. The gen.
depends on φροντίζειν, cf. XXXI. 31.—
παρέστη: 'occurred'; see on XII. 62.
— **προθεσμίας οὐδεμιᾶς**: see p. 4.—
οὔσης: causal and subord. to προσῆκον.
— **τοῖς εἰργασμένοις κτλ.**: the 'argument from improbability' falls into
two parts, 1) the insignificance of the
gain; 2) the fact that each lessee would
be concerned (προσῆκον) in seeing that
the estate lost no σηκός at any time,
as there was no statute of limitations
in such cases. — **προσῆκον**: on the
case, cf. δέον, § 15. — **σῶν**: on the
form, see G. 309; H. 227.— **εἶχον**: on

the mood, see G. 1371; H. 884. — **ἀνενεγκεῖν ὅτῳ**: for the phrase, see on
XII. 81.

18. παρεσκευασάμην: 'fixed,' 'put
up,' the means being well understood; so τοὺς συκοφάντας παρα-
σκευάζεσθαι, to '*fix*' the sycophants.
Bribing is not always meant by
the word, however; cf. XIII. 12,
δικαστήριον παρασκευάσαντες, *having
'packed' a court*, i.e. with their (the
oligarchs') creatures; XIII. 26, εἰ μή τί
σοι ἦν παρεσκευασμένον, 'if it hadn't
been a put-up job of yours'; also
XXIV. 1, and παρασκευήν, XII. 75.—
πεῖσαι: often used of bribing, cf. § 21.
— **γείτονας**: the omniscient neighbour
was as much of a pest then as he
often is now. *Cf.* such proverbs as
οὐδὲν γειτονίας χαλεπώτερον, Arist.
Rhet. ii. 21; ὀξύτερον οἱ γείτονες βλέ-
πουσι τῶν ἀλωπέκων, Macarius, vi. 40;
δυσμενὴς καὶ βάσκανος (*envious*) ὁ τῶν
γειτόνων ὀφθαλμός, φησὶν ἡ παροιμία,
Alciphron, i. 15. — **περὶ ὧν** and **περὶ**

νων πυνθάνονται; ἐμοὶ τοίνυν τούτων οἱ μὲν φίλοι, οἱ δὲ
19 διάφοροι περὶ τῶν ἐμῶν τυγχάνουσιν ὄντες. οὓς ἐχρῆν
τοῦτον παρασχέσθαι μάρτυρας, καὶ μὴ μόνον οὕτως τολ-
μηρὰς κατηγορίας ποιεῖσθαι· ὅς φησιν ὡς ἐγὼ μὲν παρει-
110 στήκη, οἱ δ' οἰκέται ἐξέτεμνον τὰ πρέμνα, ἀναθέμενος δὲ
20 ὁ βοηλάτης ᾤχετο ἀπάγων τὰ ξύλα. καίτοι, ὦ Νικόμαχε,
χρῆν σε τότε καὶ παρακαλεῖν τοὺς παριόντας μάρτυρας,
καὶ φανερὸν ποιεῖν τὸ πρᾶγμα· καὶ ἐμοὶ μὲν οὐδεμίαν ἂν
ἀπολογίαν ὑπέλιπες, αὐτὸς δέ, εἰ μέν σοι ἐχθρὸς ἦ, ἐν
115 τούτῳ τῷ τρόπῳ ἦσθα ἄν με τετιμωρημένος, εἰ δὲ τῆς
πόλεως ἕνεκα ἔπραττες, οὕτως ἐξελέγξας οὐκ ἂν ἐδόκεις
εἶναι συκοφάντης, εἰ δὲ κερδαίνειν ἐβούλου, τότ' ἂν πλεῖ-
21 στον ἔλαβες· φανεροῦ γὰρ ὄντος τοῦ πράγματος οὐδεμίαν

ἐκείνων : rare, instead of the usual
περὶ ὧν alone or περὶ ἐκείνων ἅ. The
καὶ περὶ ἐκείνων, *even on those very
points*, repeats and makes more emphatic the foregoing rel. clause. —
ἀποκρυπτόμεθα : denotes attempted
action, G. 1255; H. 825. — μηδένα
εἰδέναι : 'we conceal *from anybody's*
knowledge,' a construction on the
analogy of verbs of hindrance. G.
1549; H. 963. — τοίνυν : see on XVI.
12. — περὶ τῶν ἐμῶν : 'about what is
mine'; boundary disputes, and questions of trespass and damage result-
ing from it, like the case in Dem. LV,
are meant.

19. ἐχρῆν : see on XII. 32. — ὅς
φησιν ὡς : an almost unparalleled
construction. GMT. 753, 2. See App.
— ἀναθέμενος : *after loading up*, sc.
εἰς τὴν ἅμαξαν or a similar phrase.
The verb is extremely rare in this
literal sense ; cf. Plut. *Artox.* 11, τὸν

Κῦρον ἐπεχείρουν ἐπ' ἄλλον ἵππον ἀνα-
θέσθαι, Ar. *Eq.* 1056, καί κε γυνὴ φέροι
ἄχθος, ἐπεί κεν ἀνὴρ ἀναθείη (a quotation from the Little Iliad). — βοηλάτης : the Greeks used oxen as well as
horses and mules for draught purposes ; cf. Xen. *Oec.* 18. 4, καὶ ὑποζύγιά
γε καλούμενα πάντα ὁμοίως, βοῦς, ἡμιό-
νους, ἵππους. — ᾤχετο ἀπάγων : the
partic. expresses the leading idea
here. G. 1587.

20. τότε: 'then and there.' He might
then have taken the speaker in the very
act with witnesses ; cf. ἐπ' αὐτοφώρῳ
ἐλέγξαι, § 42. — ἐν τούτῳ τῷ τρόπῳ :
= eo pacto, denoting manner, cf.
Antiphon I. 8, τὰ γὰρ γενόμενα ἐν τούτῳ
ἀφανισθῆναι ᾠήθησαν. See on XXIV. 5.
— ἦσθα ἂν τετιμωρημένος : the rare
plupf. in the contrary-to-fact apod.,
expressing completion in pres. time.
G. 1397; H. 895. On the periphrastic
form, see GMT. 45.

ἄλλην ἡγούμην ἂν εἶναί μοι σωτηρίαν ἢ σὲ πεῖσαι. τού-
120 των τοίνυν οὐδὲν ποιήσας διὰ τοὺς σοὺς λόγους ἀξιοῖς με
ἀπολέσθαι, καὶ κατηγορεῖς ὡς ὑπὸ τῆς ἐμῆς δυνάμεως
καὶ τῶν ἐμῶν χρημάτων οὐδεὶς ἐθέλει σοι μαρτυρεῖν.
22 καίτοι εἰ ὡς φῄς μ᾽ ἰδὼν τὴν μορίαν ἀφανίζοντα τοὺς
ἐννέα ἄρχοντας ἐπήγαγες ἢ ἄλλους τινὰς τῶν ἐξ Ἀρείου
125 πάγου, οὐκ ἂν ἑτέρων ἔδει σοι μαρτύρων· οὗτοι γὰρ ἂν
σοι συνῄδεσαν ἀληθῆ λέγοντι, οἵπερ καὶ διαγιγνώσκειν
23 ἔμελλον περὶ τοῦ πράγματος. δεινότατα οὖν πάσχω ὅτ᾽
εἰ μὲν παρέσχετο μάρτυρας, τούτοις ἂν ἠξίου πιστεύειν,
ἐπειδὴ δὲ οὐκ εἰσὶν αὐτῷ, ἐμοὶ καὶ ταύτην ζημίαν οἴεται
130 χρῆναι γενέσθαι. καὶ τούτου μὲν οὐ θαυμάζω· οὐ γὰρ
δή που συκοφαντῶν ἅμα τοιούτων τε λόγων ἀπορήσει καὶ
μαρτύρων· ὑμᾶς δ᾽ οὐκ ἀξιῶ τὴν αὐτὴν τούτῳ γνώμην

---

21. **πεῖσαι**: see on § 18.—**ὑπό**: causal,
G. 1219, 1 c; *cf.* XXXI. 18, XXXII. 10,
18; Ar. *Vesp.* 1084, ὑπὸ δὲ τῶν τοξευ-
μάτων οὐκ ἦν ἰδεῖν τὸν ·οὐρανόν. For
ὑπό with impers. words, see on XII. 3.
— **δυνάμεως**: *influence;* see on § 27.

22. **ὡς φῄς**: *cf.* the scene described
by the accuser in § 19. — **τοὺς ἐννέα
ἄρχοντας**: a loose phrase, for certainly
not more than one would be needed.
This would be the βασιλεύς (with his
ὑπηρέται), M. and S. p. 293. See p. 4.
— **μορίαν**: here =σηκόν, *cf.* p. 5, note
40. — **ἐπήγαγες**: Lysias has in mind
the procedure called ἐφήγησις, wherein
a magistrate was brought to the very
spot to arrest a person who was com-
mitting a crime; still, M. and S., *l.c.*,
doubt whether the ἐφήγησις was ever
actually employed in olive-tree cases.
— **ἄλλους τινάς**: *or else some of the
members of the Areopagus.* Archons

did not become members of this
council until after their year of office
as archons. On this use of ἄλλος, see
on § 25. — **ἂν ἔδει**: on the use of ἄν,
see on XII. 48. — **οἵπερ**: 'the very
men who,' *cf.* ἅπερ, XXXII. 15.

23. **καὶ ταύτην**: *this also, i.e.* his
not having witnesses. The gender
is by assimilation (H. 632 a) with
ζημίαν, which means 'to my detri-
ment.'—**τούτου**: causal gen. (G. 1126;
H. 744); masculine as the following
clause shows as well as the μέν when
compared with ὑμᾶς δέ. — **οὐ γὰρ δή
που**: see on XII. 27. — **συκοφαντῶν**:
'playing the sycophant.' — **τοιούτων
λόγων κτλ.**: the thought is 'a sycophant may lack witnesses, but he will
never lack arguments.' The very
lack of witnesses Nicomachus seizes
upon as a proof that the speaker
had bought them off.

24 ἔχειν. ἐπίστασθε γὰρ ἐν τῷ πεδίῳ πολλὰς μορίας οὔσας
καὶ πυρκαϊὰς ἐν τοῖς ἄλλοις τοῖς ἐμοῖς χωρίοις, ἅς, εἴπερ
135 ἐπεθύμουν, πολὺ ἦν ἀσφαλέστερον καὶ ἀφανίσαι καὶ
ἐκκόψαι καὶ ἐπεργάσασθαι, ὅσῳπερ ἧττον τὸ ἀδίκημα
25 πολλῶν οὐσῶν ἔμελλε δῆλον ἔσεσθαι. νῦν δ᾽ οὕτως αὐτὰς
περὶ πολλοῦ ποιοῦμαι ὥσπερ καὶ τὴν πατρίδα καὶ τὴν
ἄλλην οὐσίαν, ἡγούμενος περὶ ἀμφοτέρων τούτων εἶναί
140 μοι τὸν κίνδυνον. αὐτοὺς τοίνυν ὑμᾶς τούτων μάρτυρας
παρέχομαι, ἐπιμελουμένους μὲν ἑκάστου μηνός, ἐπιγνώμονας δὲ πέμποντας καθ᾽ ἕκαστον ἐνιαυτόν· ὧν οὐδεὶς
πώποτ᾽ ἐζημίωσέ μ᾽ ὡς ἐργαζόμενον τὰ περὶ τὰς μορίας
26 χωρία. καίτοι οὐ δή που τὰς μὲν μικρὰς ζημίας οὕτω
145 περὶ πολλοῦ ποιοῦμαι, τοὺς δὲ περὶ τοῦ σώματος κινδύνους οὕτω περὶ οὐδενὸς ἡγοῦμαι· καὶ τὰς μὲν πολλὰς
ἐλάας, εἰς ἃς ἐξῆν μᾶλλον ἐξαμαρτάνειν, οὕτω θεραπεύων
φαίνομαι, τὴν δὲ μίαν μορίαν, ἣν οὐχ οἷόν τ᾽ ἦν λαθεῖν

---

24. πεδίῳ: the Athenian plain, see
p. 2. — **πυρκαϊάς**: *stumps of burnt
trees.* But see App. — **ἦν ἀσφαλέστερον**: apod. without ἄν, see on xii.
32.—**ἐπεργάσασθαι**: used of encroach-
ments or trespass by planting or building on ground where one has no right,
especially on sacred ground ; *cf.* § 29
and Thuc. i. 139. 2, ἐπικαλοῦντες ἐπερ-
γασίαν Μεγαρεῦσι τῆς γῆς τῆς ἱερᾶς. So
Aesch. iii. 113, ἄνδρες παρανομώτατοι,
ἐπειργάζοντο τὸ πεδίον (of Cirrha), Plat.
Legg. 843 C, ὃς δ᾽ ἂν ἐπεργάζηται τὰ
τοῦ γείτονος ὑπερβαίνων τοὺς ὅρους, τὸ μὲν
βλάβος ἀποτινέτω.—**ὅσῳπερ**: *inasmuch
as* (G. 1184 ; H. 781), *cf.* ὅσῳ, § 7. —
ἔμελλε: without ἄν, see on xii. 99.
25. τὴν ἄλλην οὐσίαν: *and my property besides.* Exile and confiscation
were the penalties. On this use of

ἄλλος, *cf.* §§ 22, 30, 32, and see G.
966, 2 ; H. 705. So Xen. *Anab.* i. 5.
5, οὐ γὰρ ἦν χόρτος οὐδὲ ἄλλο οὐδὲν δένδρον, Plat. *Phaed.* 110 E, καὶ λίθοις
καὶ γῇ καὶ τοῖς ἄλλοις ζῴοις τε καὶ φυτοῖς.
So in Lat., as Liv. v. 39. 3, explo-
ratoribus missis circa moenia
aliasque portas. — **παρέχομαι**:
see on xii. 74. — **ἑκάστου μηνός**: see
p. 4, note 31. — **ἐπιγνώμονας** : see
p. 3.

26. ζημίας: money fines are here
meant.— **σώματος**: he is thinking here
of his status as a citizen (*cf.* xxiii.
12), which he would lose if convicted ;
for a different sense see on xxii. 20.—
ποιοῦμαι and **ἡγοῦμαι**: see on xii. 7.—
ἐλάας: i.e. the μορίαι of § 24. — **εἰς ἄς**:
see App.— **ἐξῆν**: see on χρῆν, xii. 32 ;
so οἷόν τ᾽ ἦν and κρεῖττον ἦν below.

27 ἐξορύξαντα, ὡς ἀφανίζων νυνὶ κρίνομαι. πότερον δέ μοι
150 κρεῖττον ἦν, ὦ βουλή, δημοκρατίας οὔσης παρανομεῖν ἢ
ἐπὶ τῶν τριάκοντα; καὶ οὐ λέγω ὡς τότε δυνάμενος ἢ ὡς
νῦν διαβεβλημένος, ἀλλ' ὡς τῷ βουλομένῳ τότε μᾶλλον
ἐξῆν ἀδικεῖν ἢ νυνί. ἐγὼ τοίνυν οὐδ' ἐν ἐκείνῳ τῷ χρόνῳ
οὔτε τοιοῦτον οὔτε ἄλλο οὐδὲν κακὸν ποιήσας φανήσομαι.
28 πῶς δ' ἄν, εἰ μὴ πάντων ἀνθρώπων ἐμαυτῷ κακονούστατος
ἦ, ὑμῶν οὕτως ἐπιμελουμένων, ἐκ τούτου τὴν μορίαν
ἀφανίζειν ἐπεχείρησα τοῦ χωρίου, ἐν ᾧ δένδρον μὲν οὐδὲ
ἕν ἐστι, μιᾶς δὲ ἐλάας σηκός, ὡς οὗτός φησιν εἶναι,
κυκλόθεν δὲ ὁδὸς περιέχει, ἀμφοτέρωθεν δὲ γείτονες περι-
160 οικοῦσιν, ἄερκτον δὲ καὶ πανταχόθεν κάτοπτόν ἐστιν;
ὥστε τίς ἂν ἀπετόλμησε, τούτων οὕτως ἐχόντων, ἐπιχει-
29 ρῆσαι τοιούτῳ πράγματι; δεινὸν δέ μοι δοκεῖ εἶναι ὑμᾶς
μέν, οἷς ὑπὸ τῆς πόλεως τὸν ἅπαντα χρόνον προστέτακται
τῶν μορίων ἐλαῶν ἐπιμελεῖσθαι, μήθ' ὡς ἐπεργαζόμενον
165 πώποτε ζημιῶσαί με μήθ' ὡς ἀφανίσαντα εἰς κίνδυνον
καταστῆσαι, τοῦτον δ', ὃς οὔτε γεωργῶν ἐγγὺς τυγχάνει

---

27. δυνάμενος: 'a man of influence';
for this absolute use, cf. Dem. XXIII.
174, ὅπως ἂν ὑμᾶς δύνασθαι νομίζῃ. Cf.
δυνάμεως, § 21, and γενομένος ἐν δυνάμει, XXIV. 25. The orators always
eagerly disown any connexion with
the Thirty. — ἀλλ' ὡς ... ἐξῆν : we
should naturally have a participle
(ἐξόν, acc. abs.) after οὐ ... ὡς δυνάμενος. — μᾶλλον ἐξῆν : that time was
one of lawlessness (see on XII. 81) ;
cf. Isocr. XVIII. 16, νῦν δ' οὐδένα φανήσομαι τῶν πολιτῶν οὔτε χρήμασι ζημιώ-
σας οὔτε περὶ τοῦ σώματος εἰς κίνδυνον
καταστήσας ... 17, καίτοι πολλοὺς
ἐπῆρεν ἡ τῶν τριάκοντα πονηρία τοιαῦτα ποιεῖν. It has been thought that

the functions of the Areopagus were
utterly suspended during the rule of
the Thirty.

28. ὑμῶν ... ἐπιμελουμένων : said in
order to win the favour of the judges
by complimenting them on their
attention to duty. — οὐδὲ ἕν : see on
XXXI. 30. — εἶναι: impf., see on XVI.
6. — ἀπετόλμησε : here ἀπο- is inten-
sive in a bad sense, 'have the impu-
dence' ; cf. Aeschin. I. 64, ἀπετόλμων
ὑμῖν οὗτοι περὶ τῶν Ἑλληνικῶν συμ-
βουλεύειν.

29. μορίων : on the accent, see p. 3.
— ἐπεργαζόμενον : cf. § 24. — ἐπιμελη-
τής: curator. — ἡλικίαν ἔχων εἰδέναι :
cf. ἐπειδὴ οἱ παῖδες ὑμῖν ὀλίγου ...

οὔτ' ἐπιμελητὴς ᾑρημένος οὔθ' ἡλικίαν ἔχων εἰδέναι περὶ
τῶν τοιούτων, ἀπογράψαι με μορίαν ἀφανίζειν.

30 Ἐγὼ τοίνυν δέομαι ὑμῶν μὴ τοὺς τοιούτους λόγους
170 πιστοτέρους ἡγήσασθαι τῶν ἔργων, μηδὲ περὶ ὧν αὐτοὶ
σύνιστε, ταῦτ' ἀνασχέσθαι τῶν ἐμῶν ἐχθρῶν λεγόντων,
ἐνθυμουμένους καὶ ἐκ τῶν εἰρημένων καὶ ἐκ τῆς ἄλλης
31 πολιτείας. ἐγὼ γὰρ τὰ ἐμοὶ προστεταγμένα ἅπαντα προθυμότερον πεποίηκα ἢ ὡς ὑπὸ τῆς πόλεως ἠναγκαζόμην,
175 καὶ τριηραρχῶν καὶ εἰσφορὰς εἰσφέρων καὶ χορηγῶν καὶ
τἄλλα λῃτουργῶν οὐδενὸς ἧττον πολυτελῶς τῶν πολιτῶν.
32 καίτοι ταῦτα μὲν μετρίως ποιῶν ἀλλὰ μὴ προθύμως οὔτ'
ἂν περὶ φυγῆς οὔτ' ἂν περὶ τῆς ἄλλης οὐσίας ἠγωνιζόμην,

ἡλικίαν ἔχουσι παιδεύεσθαι, Plat. Lach.
187 C; see G. 1521. — ἀπογράψαι:
of a formal ἀπογραφή, cf. § 2.

30. On the thought, cf. XII. 33. —
τῶν ἔργων: the facts, i.e. the state of
things as he has described it. — αὐτοί:
'from personal observation,' as the
officials in charge of the trees. —
ταῦτα: object of λεγόντων. — λεγόντων: supplementary partic. as object
(G. 1580; H. 983); cf. Plat. Apol. 31 B,
ἀνέχεσθαι τῶν οἰκείων ἀμελουμένων.
For the causal gen., see Kühn. § 419,
1 d, but compare the nom. βασανιζόμενοι, § 35. — ἐνθυμουμένους: on the
case, not agreeing with that of ὑμῶν,
G. 928, 2; H. 941. But see on λέγοντι,
XII. 1. — πολιτείας: i.e. his standing
and conduct as a citizen; so, as contrasted with private life, in Andoc.
I. 10, ἦλθέ μοι ἐπιθυμία τῆς τε μεθ' ὑμῶν
πολιτείας ἐκείνης καὶ διαίτης.

31. προθυμότερον... ἠναγκαζόμην:
cf. XXV. 13, καίτοι διὰ τοῦτο (i.e. in
the expenses of liturgies) πλείω τῶν ὑπὸ

τῆς πόλεως προσταττομένων ἐδαπανώ-
μην, ἵνα καὶ βελτίων ὑφ' ὑμῶν νομιζοίμην.
This was a common boast; cf. Isocr.
XV. 145, τὰς δ' ἄλλας λῃτουργίας πολυτε-
λέστερον λελῃτουργήκατε καὶ κάλλιον ὧν
οἱ νόμοι προστάττουσιν. — τριηραρχῶν:
on the trierarchy, see Smith, Dict.
Antiq. s.v. trierarchia. — εἰσφορὰς and
χορηγῶν: see on XII. 20. — τἄλλα
λῃτουργῶν: such as the gymnasiarchy
and the lampadarchy, see Gow, § 77 c.
On the whole passage, cf. XXV. 12,
τετριηράρχηκα τε γὰρ πεντάκις καὶ
τετράκις νεναυμάχηκα καὶ εἰσφορὰς ἐν
τῷ πολέμῳ πολλὰς εἰσενήνοχα καὶ τἄλλα
λελῃτούργηκα οὐδενὸς χεῖρον τῶν πολιτῶν.

32. μετρίως: here not in a good
sense, as in XVI. 3, but like our 'only
moderately,' = mediocriter. The
thought is: 'I preferred to be generous
beyond what the law required though
I might merely have kept to its
letter and saved money without any
risk. Would such a man risk his all

πλείω δ' ἂν ἐκεκτήμην, οὐδὲν ἀδικῶν οὐδ' ἐπικίνδυνον
180 ἐμαυτῷ καταστήσας τὸν βίον· ταῦτα δὲ πράξας, ἃ οὗτός
μου κατηγορεῖ, ἐκέρδαινον μὲν οὐδέν, ἐμαυτὸν δ' εἰς
33 κίνδυνον καθίστην. καίτοι πάντες ἂν ὁμολογήσαιτε δικαιότερον εἶναι τοῖς μεγάλοις χρῆσθαι τεκμηρίοις περὶ τῶν
μεγάλων καὶ πιστότερα ἡγεῖσθαι περὶ ὧν ἅπασα ἡ πόλις
185 μαρτυρεῖ, μᾶλλον ἢ περὶ ὧν μόνος οὗτος κατηγορεῖ.
34 Ἔτι τοίνυν, ὦ βουλή, ἐκ τῶν ἄλλων σκέψασθε. μάρτυρας γὰρ ἔχων αὐτῷ προσῆλθον λέγων ὅτι μοι πάντες
ἔτι εἰσὶν οἱ θεράποντες, οὓς ἐκεκτήμην ἐπειδὴ παρέλαβον
τὸ χωρίον, καὶ ἕτοιμός εἰμι, εἴ τινα βούλοιτο, παραδοῦναι
190 βασανίζειν, ἡγούμενος οὕτως ἂν τὸν ἔλεγχον ἰσχυρότατον
γενέσθαι τῶν τούτου λόγων καὶ τῶν ἔργων τῶν ἐμῶν.

merely to be rid of the encumbrance of a trumpery olive stump?' — **πλείω ... ἐκεκτήμην**: 'I should be all the better off.' — **οὐδὲν ἀδικῶν**: 'without having broken the law.' — **ἐκέρδαινον**: 'I was to gain'; see on § 13.

33. τοῖς μεγάλοις τεκμηρίοις: *i.e.* as shown by his whole life and conduct rather than by the unsupported charge brought by Nicomachus. — **περὶ τῶν μεγάλων**: 'where the issues are great.' His citizenship and property were at stake. — **περὶ ὧν ... κατηγορεῖ**: ordinarily this verb takes the acc., but here the clause with περὶ is used for the sake of parallelism with the foregoing.

34. ἐκ τῶν ἄλλων: 'in another light,' see on XVI. 18. Evidence drawn from slaves under the torture is frequently spoken of as being the strongest sort of testimony; *cf.* Isocr. XVII. 54, ὁρῶ δὲ καὶ ὑμᾶς καὶ περὶ τῶν ἰδίων καὶ περὶ τῶν δημοσίων οὐδὲν πιστότερον οὐδ' ἀληθέστε-

ρον βασάνου νομίζοντας, and Lyc. *Leocr.* 29, τίς γὰρ ὑμῶν οὐκ οἶδεν ὅτι περὶ τῶν ἀμφισβητουμένων πολὺ δοκεῖ δικαιότατον καὶ δημοτικὸν εἶναι, ὅταν οἰκέται ἢ θεράπαιναι συνειδῶσιν ἃ δεῖ, τούτους ἐλέγχειν καὶ βασανίζειν. The owner of the slaves might offer them (παραδιδόναι) or his opponent demand them (ἐξαιτεῖν, § 36). Either offer or demand was called a πρόκλησις, always made in the presence of witnesses. If this challenge was accepted, a contract was drawn up specifying the method of torture and naming the torturer (βασανιστής). An offer was supposed to be a proof of a good conscience; refusal to accept (παραλαμβάνειν, § 36) it, as here, or to comply with a demand (*cf.* § 36), was used as a strong argument against the refuser. The evidence of slaves was accepted only on the application of torture. On the whole subject, see M. and S. p. 890 ff.; Smith, *Dict. Antiq. s.v. tormentum.* — **εἰμι**: see App.

35 οὗτος δ᾽ οὐκ ἤθελεν, οὐδὲν φάσκων πιστὸν εἶναι τοῖς
θεράπουσιν. ἐμοὶ δὲ δοκεῖ δεινὸν εἶναι, εἰ περὶ αὐτῶν
μὲν οἱ βασανιζόμενοι κατηγοροῦσιν εὖ εἰδότες ὅτι ἀπο-
195 θανοῦνται, περὶ δὲ τῶν δεσποτῶν, οἷς πεφύκασι κακονούστατοι, μᾶλλον ἂν ἕλοιντο ἀνέχεσθαι βασανιζόμενοι ἢ
36 κατειπόντες ἀπηλλάχθαι τῶν παρόντων κακῶν. καὶ μὲν
δή, ὦ βουλή, φανερὸν οἶμαι εἶναι ὅτι, εἰ Νικομάχου ἐξαι-
τοῦντος τοὺς ἀνθρώπους μὴ παρεδίδουν, ἐδόκουν ἂν ἐμαυ-
200 τῷ συνειδέναι· ἐπειδὴ τοίνυν ἐμοῦ παραδιδόντος οὗτος
παραλαβεῖν οὐκ ἤθελε, δίκαιον καὶ περὶ τούτου τὴν αὐτὴν γνώμην σχεῖν, ἄλλως τε καὶ τοῦ κινδύνου οὐκ ἴσου
37 ἀμφοτέροις ὄντος. περὶ ἐμοῦ μὲν γὰρ εἰ ἔλεγον ἃ οὗτος
ἐβούλετο, οὐδ᾽ ἂν ἀπολογήσασθαί μοι ἐξεγένετο· τούτῳ
205 δ᾽ εἰ μὴ ὡμολόγουν, οὐδεμιᾷ ζημίᾳ ἔνοχος ἦν. ὥστε πολὺ

---

35. οὐκ ἤθελεν: see on xii. 58.—
οὐδὲν...πιστόν: cf. v. 3, ὑμᾶς δὲ ἄξιον
μὴ τοὺς μὲν τῶν θεραπόντων λόγους πιστοὺς νομίζειν... § 4, ἴσασι γὰρ ὅτι, ἂν
ψευδόμενοι ἐλεγχθῶσιν, οὐδὲν μεῖζον τῶν
ὑπαρχόντων πείσονται, ἐὰν δὲ ὑμᾶς ἐξα-
πατήσωσι, τῶν παρόντων κακῶν ἔσονται
ἀπηλλαγμένοι. There Lysias holds a
brief against slave evidence; here he
must speak in its favour as he does in
what follows. Naturally it was easy
to argue on either side, and there is
much of this in both orators and
rhetoricians.—εἰ...μὲν...δέ: cf. xii.
36.—κακονούστατοι: in spite of the
comparative kindness with which
Athenian slaves were treated and
the close intimacy to which they were
often admitted by their masters (see
Becker's *Charicles*, Göll's edition, III,
p. 23 ff.; English, p. 365 ff.), such a
passage as this shows that the natural

antagonism would out; cf. Plat. *Legg.*
756 E, δοῦλοι γὰρ ἂν καὶ δεσπόται οὐκ ἄν
ποτε γένοιντο φίλοι. — βασανιζόμενοι:
supplementary partic. agreeing with
subject, for ἀνέχεσθαι here is intran-
sitive. But see on § 30.—κακῶν: generally here taken as referring to the
torture, but it may mean (as in v. 4
quoted above) their state of slavery;
see on § 16.

36. ἐμαυτῷ συνειδέναι: 'conscience
stricken,' 'conscious of guilt,' used
absolutely as in Lycurg. *Leocr.* 30,
οὑτοσὶ δὲ διὰ τὸ συνειδέναι ἑαυτῷ οὐκ
ὑπέμεινεν ἀλλ᾽ ἔφυγε (cf. conscii
sibi, Sall. *Jug.* 40. 2); generally with
an accompanying acc. or participle.
—σχεῖν: 'form.' On the tense, see
on ἐπεδήμησε, xii. 71.

37. εἰ ἔλεγον: i.e. 'if their testimony
had been such.' —ζημίᾳ: in olive-tree
cases, the accuser was not punished if

μᾶλλον τοῦτον παραλαμβάνειν ἐχρῆν ἢ ἐμὲ παραδοῦναι
προσῆκεν. ἐγὼ τοίνυν εἰς τοῦτο προθυμίας ἀφικόμην,
ἡγούμενος μετ᾽ ἐμοῦ εἶναι καὶ ἐκ βασάνων καὶ ἐκ μαρτύρων καὶ ἐκ τεκμηρίων ὑμᾶς περὶ τοῦ πράγματος τἀληθῆ
38 πυθέσθαι. ἐνθυμεῖσθαι δὲ χρή, ὦ βουλή, ποτέροις χρὴ
πιστεύειν μᾶλλον, οἷς πολλοὶ μεμαρτυρήκασιν ἢ ᾧ μηδεὶς
τετόλμηκε, καὶ πότερον εἰκὸς μᾶλλον τοῦτον ἀκινδύνως
ψεύδεσθαι ἢ μετὰ τοσούτου κινδύνου τοιοῦτον ἐμὲ ἔργον
ἐργάσασθαι, καὶ πότερον οἴεσθε αὐτὸν ὑπὲρ τῆς πόλεως
39 βοηθεῖν ἢ συκοφαντοῦντα αἰτιάσασθαι. ἐγὼ μὲν γὰρ
εἰδέναι ὑμᾶς ἡγοῦμαι ὅτι Νικόμαχος ὑπὸ τῶν ἐχθρῶν πεισθεὶς τῶν ἐμῶν τοῦτον τὸν ἀγῶνα ἀγωνίζεται, οὐχ ὡς ἀδικοῦντα ἐλπίζων ἀποδείξειν, ἀλλ᾽ ὡς ἀργύριον παρ᾽ ἐμοῦ
λήψεσθαι προσδοκῶν. ὅσῳ γὰρ οἱ τοιοῦτοί εἰσιν ἐπαι-

he did not get the usually required
one-fifth of the votes; see Introd. § 49,
and M. and S. p. 952. But he was
liable for any serious damage done to
the slaves under torture, *ibid.* p. 892.
— **ἔνοχος ἦν**: equiv. to a potential
indic. with ἄν, and hence an apod. of
an unreal condition. GMT. 431.—**μετ᾽
ἐμοῦ**: 'for my interest.' See App.

38.　οἷς ἤ . . . ᾧ: by the use of the
plur. οἷς, the speaker treats himself as
one of a class, and then draws particular attention to his opponent by the
sing. ᾧ. — **μηδείς**: indef.; see on § 11.
— **ἀκινδύνως**: see on ζημία, § 37. —
βοηθεῖν: *cf.* § 20, εἰ τῆς πόλεως ἕνεκα
ἔπραττες. — **συκοφαντοῦντα**: here the
charge of 'sycophancy' (already referred to in §§ 1 and 23) is more closely
pressed. It was a very common form
of invective in the courts. The speaker
in xxii. 1 protests against its applica-

tion to him; see also on xii. 2. On the
'sycophants,' see Smith, *Dict. Antiq.*
s.v. sycophantes.

39.　ἐγὼ μέν: 'I for my part,' frequently so used without a following δέ.
See note on § 5, and *cf.* Kr. *Spr.* 69,
35, 2. — **ἐχθρῶν**: perhaps he includes
γείτονες διάφοροι. — **ὡς**: belongs to
ἐλπίζων, as the following ὡς to προσδοκῶν. — **ἀργύριον**: the *chantage* or
blackmail form of sycophancy is
meant ; *cf.* the rich Crito's complaint
about the sycophants, νῦν γὰρ ἐμέ τινες
εἰς δίκας ἄγουσιν, οὐχ ὅτι ἀδικοῦνται ὑπ᾽
ἐμοῦ, ἀλλ᾽ ὅτι νομίζουσιν ἥδιον ἄν με
ἀργύριον τελέσαι ἢ πράγματα ἔχειν,
Xen. *Mem.* ii. 9. 1.— **ὅσῳ**: see on § 7.
— **ἐπαιτιώτατοι**: means with ὅσῳ, *the
more blame such suits* (κινδύνων) *cause,*
i.e. the more invidious they are. The
adj. is active and causal in sense, as
in Thuc. v. 65. 2, τῆς ἐξ Ἄργους ἐπαι-

220 τιώτατοι καὶ ἀπορώτατοι τῶν κινδύνων, τοσούτῳ πάντες
40 αὐτοὺς φεύγουσι μάλιστα. ἐγὼ δέ, ὦ βουλή, οὐκ ἠξίουν,
ἀλλ᾽ ἐπειδήπερ με ἠτιάσατο, παρέσχον ἐμαυτὸν ὅ τι βούλεσθε χρῆσθαι, καὶ τούτου ἕνεκα τοῦ κινδύνου οὐδενὶ ἐγὼ
τῶν ἐχθρῶν διηλλάγην, οἳ ἐμὲ ἥδιον κακῶς λέγουσιν ἢ
225 σφᾶς αὐτοὺς ἐπαινοῦσι, καὶ φανερῶς μὲν οὐδεὶς πώποτε
ἐμὲ αὐτῶν ἐπεχείρησε ποιῆσαι κακὸν οὐδέν, τοιούτους δὲ
ἐπιπέμπουσί μοι, οἷς ὑμεῖς οὐκ ἂν δικαίως πιστεύοιτε.
41 πάντων γὰρ ἀθλιώτατος ἂν γενοίμην, εἰ φυγὰς ἀδίκως
καταστήσομαι, ἄπαις μὲν ὢν καὶ μόνος, ἐρήμου δὲ τοῦ
230 οἴκου γενομένου, μητρὸς δὲ πάντων ἐνδεοῦς, πατρίδος δὲ
τοιαύτης ἐπ᾽ αἰσχίσταις στερηθεὶς αἰτίαις, πολλὰς μὲν
ναυμαχίας ὑπὲρ αὐτῆς νεναυμαχηκώς, πολλὰς δὲ μάχας
μεμαχημένος, κόσμιον δ᾽ ἐμαυτὸν καὶ ἐν δημοκρατίᾳ καὶ
ἐν ὀλιγαρχίᾳ παρασχών.
42 Ἀλλὰ γάρ, ὦ βουλή, ταῦτα μὲν ἐνθάδε οὐκ οἶδ᾽ ὅ τι
δεῖ λέγειν· ἀπέδειξα δ᾽ ὑμῖν ὡς οὐκ ἐνῆν σηκὸς ἐν τῷ
χωρίῳ καὶ μάρτυρας παρεσχόμην καὶ τεκμήρια. ἃ χρὴ
μεμνημένους διαγιγνώσκειν περὶ τοῦ πράγματος, καὶ

τίου ἀναχωρήσεως, the retreat which had
caused him (Agis) to be blamed.   See
App.—ἀπορώτατοι: cf. § 2.—φεύγουσι:
avoid, sc. by buying off their accusers.
40. αὐτῶν: instead of ὤν; see on
XXXII. 27. — ἐπιπέμπουσι: set on, let
loose; so of the Sphinx, ἂν ὁ κατὰ
χθονὸς Ἅιδας Καδμείοις ἐπιπέμπει, Eur.
Phoen. 810.
41. ἐρήμου: desolate, that is, with no
heirs to succeed. The adj. is common
in this sense in Isaeus, as in VI. 5,
ἔδοξεν αὐτῷ διαθέσθαι τὰ αὐτοῦ, μὴ
ἔρημον καταλίπῃ τὸν οἶκον, εἴ τι πάθοι.
— κόσμιον: a highly complimentary

epithet, cf. XII. 20, XVI. 18, XXII. 19,
and XXI. 19, ἡγουμένους ταύτην εἶναι τὴν
λῃτουργίαν ἐπιπονωτάτην, διὰ τέλους
τὸν πάντα χρόνον κόσμιον εἶναι καὶ
σώφρονα.
42. ἐνθάδε: i.e. before the Areopagus,
where speakers were expected to keep
more closely to the point than in other
courts; cf. III. 46, παρ᾽ ὑμῖν (the Areo-
pagites) οὐ νόμιμόν ἐστιν ἔξω τοῦ πράγματος λέγειν. See M. and S. p. 933. The
appeal to pity (§ 41) is therefore brief,
and so is the summary of the speech in
this epilogue.—πυθέσθαι ὅτου ἕνεκα:
three verbs depend on these words,

ἀξιοῦν παρὰ τούτου πυθέσθαι ὅτου ἕνεκα, ἐξὸν ἐπ᾽ αὐτο-
240 φώρῳ ἐλέγξαι, τοσούτῳ χρόνῳ ὕστερον εἰς τοσοῦτόν με
43 κατέστησεν ἀγῶνα, καὶ μάρτυρα οὐδένα παρασχόμενος ἐκ
τῶν λόγων ζητεῖ πιστὸς γενέσθαι, ἐξὸν αὐτοῖς τοῖς ἔργοις
ἀδικοῦντα ἀποδεῖξαι, καὶ ἐμοῦ ἅπαντας παραδιδόντος
τοὺς θεράποντας οὓς φησι παραγενέσθαι, παραλαβεῖν
245 οὐκ ἤθελεν.

κατέστησεν, ζητεῖ, ἤθελεν. — ἐπ᾽ αὐτο-   43. ἐκ : of ground for confidence,
φώρῳ : see on § 20.   frequent with πιστός and πιστεύειν.

AGAINST ERATOSTHENES.

INTRODUCTION.

THIS speech, as the Greek title shows, was delivered by Lysias himself, and it is unique among his extant forensic orations in this particular. Its subject-matter is of great biographical and historical value. In it Lysias gives some incidents in his own life up to the time of the Anarchy, and an account, from a thoroughly hostile point of view, of the government of the Thirty Tyrants. Both these matters have already been treated in a general way in the Introduction to this book, and specific points find mention in the notes and appendix to this speech. It remains, therefore, to deal here with Eratosthenes and with the occasion on which the speech was delivered.

Eratosthenes, here accused of the murder of Lysias's brother Polemarchus, first appears in history in the time of the Four Hundred. The oligarchs in Athens had sent out their emissaries to tamper with the Athenian forces on the coast of Asia Minor,[1] and such a mission seems to have been held by Eratosthenes at the naval station on the Hellespont. But the cause of the oligarchs failed on the Hellespont as completely as in the fleet at Samos, and Eratosthenes deserted the ship of which he was trierarch, and returned to Athens.[2] From the silence of Lysias it is evident that Eratosthenes was not one of the Four Hundred, although he is accused of favouring their designs. The orator can find nothing against him in his life for the next six years.[3] It is possible that he joined Theramenes and his friends in overthrowing the first oligarchy, but Lysias would naturally say nothing of such a democratic action.[4]

[1] See on § 42.　　　[3] § 43.
[2] § 42.　　　[4] § 67.

After Aegos Potami the oligarchs, whose clubs had probably never ceased their activity in secret, began to come forward more openly. They chose a 'central committee' of five called ephors,[5] and Eratosthenes was one of these. It cannot be said that he played an important part in the committee, for Lysias can prove only that he was a member of it.[6] He did, however, become one of the Thirty Tyrants. This is a fact mentioned by Xenophon,[7] the only ancient historian who names Eratosthenes. He may have been one of the ten persons nominated by Theramenes.[8] It comes out clearly from the account of his share in the arbitrary government of the Thirty that he belonged to the moderate faction, and that he obeyed the tyrannical majority only against his will. Even Lysias himself can make no serious answer to the defence brought forward by the advocates of Eratosthenes that he had done less wrong than any other member of the Thirty.[9] He joined Theramenes in opposing the measures against the metics which led to the death of Polemarchus, but he was no more able than his leader to induce the majority to take moderate views.[10] After the death of Theramenes the moderates seem to have been for a time completely at the mercy of the terrorists, and Eratosthenes, with the rest, had to choose between death and submission. In this crisis he was found wanting, and took part, to his shame, in the outrages in Eleusis and Salamis.[11]

But with the defeat of the Thirty at Munychia and the death of Critias, the moderate party raised its head once more. Eratosthenes, with Phidon and other opponents of the party of Critias,[12] stayed in Athens when the majority of the Thirty fled to Eleusis, and Phidon was chosen one of the First Ten who succeeded to the government. Eratosthenes was not one of these, but Lysias insin-

---

[5] § 43. Boerner (*De rebus a Graecis inde ab anno 410 usque ad annum 403 a. Chr. n. gestis*, Göttingen, 1894, p. 75 ff.) endeavours to prove that the ephors were regularly constituted magistrates who governed Athens from the beginning of the official year in which the Thirty were chosen until the Thirty were elected. But see Beloch, *Att. Polit. seit Perikles*, p. 93.

[6] § 46.   [7] *Hellen.* ii. 3. 2.
[8] § 76.   [9] § 89.
[10] §§ 25, 27, 50.   [11] § 52.
[12] § 55.

uates that he had such an evil influence[13] with Phidon and the others
that they disappointed the people and did not carry out the purpose
for which they had been chosen, the reconciliation of the democrats
and the oligarchs.[14] Of course he was not a member of the Second
Ten, a body not mentioned by Lysias,[15] for his past membership
in the Thirty would cut him off from being included among these
patriots. Apparently, however, he remained in Athens during the
five months of the First Ten's government, and until the trium-
phant entry of the followers of Thrasybulus.

Thus it was that Lysias on his return to Athens found there the
very man through whose agency Polemarchus had been delivered
over to the Thirty for execution. Eratosthenes had not gone to
Eleusis under the terms of the amnesty,[16] for, once there, he could
not have been brought back to answer such a charge as Lysias had
to make.[17] But remaining as he did in Athens, he must have
known that charges would be brought against him by his enemies,
and hence he must have availed himself as soon as possible of that
clause in the amnesty by which those of the Thirty who chose to
submit their accounts of office (εὔθυναι[18]) were no longer liable to

---

[13] § 58.

[14] Why was not Eratosthenes one of
the First Ten ? Was it because Phidon
and his associates were not really of the
party of Theramenes, but held a middle ground between them and Critias,
while Eratosthenes belonged to Theramenes out and out ? Or was it because
Phidon and his colleagues were real fa-
vourers of the Thirty, and were chosen
by a trick played on the people ? If
the latter is the true explanation, Eratosthenes, as a known opponent of the
Thirty, would not have been a member
of this Ten. [15] See App. to § 60.

[16] A general amnesty followed the
year of anarchy. From it were ex-
cepted the Thirty, the First Ten, the
Eleven, and the Ten who had governed

in the Piraeus, unless they were willing
to submit to εὔθυναι for their official
acts. Eleusis was recognized as an
asylum in which the Thirty and any
others who feared to return to Athens
might remain unmolested. See Xen.
Hellen. ii. 4. 38, and Arist. Resp. Ath. 39.

[17] If past murders are included under the provision in Arist. Resp. Ath.
39, τὰς δὲ δίκας τοῦ φόνου εἶναι κατὰ τὰ
πάτρια, εἴ τίς τινα αὐτόχειρ ἀπέκτεινεν ἢ
ἔτρωσεν, this would not apply to Eratosthenes, who had not killed Polemarchus with his own hand. However
doubtful the rest of the text is here
(I follow Sandys), still αὐτόχειρ or
something of similar meaning, like
αὐτοχειρὶ or αὐτοχειρίᾳ, must be read.

[18] See Introd. § 7.

attacks for the past.[19] This would be the easiest way once and for all to have done with those who had anything against him.[20] The solemn entry of the patriots from the Piraeus took place on the 12th of Boëdromion (September), B.C. 403.[21] Soon afterwards the regular magistracies were restored and the courts reopened. Among the first cases to come before the λογισταί[22] would be those of Eratosthenes, Phidon, or others among the Thirty, of the two Tens, of the Ten who had governed the Piraeus, and of the Eleven. As charges would naturally be brought against such men (except against the Second Ten[23]) by different accusers,[24] the courts prob-

---

[19] It has sometimes been thought (with Lübbert, *De amnestia anno CCCCIII decreta*, but against him see Grasser, *Amnestie des Jahres 403*) that the oaths of confirmation of the amnesty were not sworn until after the final overthrow of the Thirty in Eleusis. *Cf.* Xen. *Hellen*. ii. 4. 43. But Arist. *Resp. Ath.* 40, διελύθησαν δὲ καὶ πρὸς τοὺς ἐν Ἐλευσῖνι κατοικήσαντας ἔτει τρίτῳ μετὰ τὴν ἐξοίκησιν, ἐπὶ Ξεναινέτου ἄρχοντος (B.C. 401–0), shows that this final overthrow did not take place until two years after the democracy was restored. Hence Xenophon, unless absolutely at fault, can refer only to a reaffirmation of the oaths. It cannot be supposed that Eratosthenes's trial occurred so late as this.

[20] For further arguments in support of the view that the speech was delivered at an accounting, see Blass, *Att. Bereds.* I, p. 540 ff.; M. and S. p. 257 f.; Jebb, *Attic Orators*, I, p. 262; Weidner, in his edition of Lysias, p. 33; Wilamowitz, *Aristoteles und Athen*, II, p. 217 ff. (who notes that ἥκουσιν ἀπολογησόμενοι in § 22, *cf.* § 84, shows that Eratosthenes came voluntarily to the court). On the other hand, Fuhr and

Gebauer in their editions (p. 18, p. 17) hold that Eratosthenes was tried for murder in the court at the Palladium. Their strongest argument is that there is no direct mention of an εὔθυνα in the text. But the same sort of argument is equally strong against them; for Lysias in the first part of his speech makes almost as much of the pillage of his property as he does of the execution of his brother, and he does not even mention Polemarchus in his recapitulation at the end. Further, the action of Archinus (Arist. *Resp. Ath.* 40) in persuading the Senate to put to death without trial a person who had broken the oath μὴ μνησικακεῖν makes it very doubtful whether the partisans of the Thirty were at this time brought to court in any cases except those of εὔθυναι.

[21] Plut. *Moralia*, p. 349 F.

[22] See Introd. § 7.

[23] We have the express statement in Arist. *Resp. Ath.* 38 that no accuser appeared at the εὔθυναι of the Second Ten.

[24] So Weidner, *ibid.* See below on ἡμῶν, § 100.

ably sat a number of times in the cases that the λογισταί saw fit to bring forward, and these cases would follow in close succession, if some of them were not actually tried simultaneously in different Heliastic courts.[25]   Among the accusers at the εὔθυναι of Eratosthenes was Lysias. It was his moral duty, as next of kin to Polemarchus, to accuse the man who had been the agent in the murder, and he was entitled to do it in person either as an ordinary metic or as an isoteles.[26] For even metics had the right to bring either public or private suits in cases of injury committed against them personally, and, by all Greek moral law, Lysias had suffered such an injury in the murder of his brother. Perhaps as a metic[27] he needed a patron (προστάτης) at the preliminary hearing before the λογισταί, but before the Heliasts he could come forward and plead independently.[28]

According to the law, the accuser was bound in a γραφὴ περὶ τῶν εὐθυνῶν to state some specific act whereby the retiring official had injured him,[29] and not simply to bring sweeping charges. Hence Lysias specifies the murder of his brother. But Eratosthenes had not killed Polemarchus with his own hand, and he had several

[25] Hence one reason for the use of the pl. οὗτοι and the like in this speech. This use, where the pl. is not a mere rhetorical amplification behind which Eratosthenes stands as the representative of the whole Thirty (whose future punishment or acquittal is, according to Lysias, to depend on this test case), may refer to the εὔθυναι of Phidon and others going on at the same time. The principal passages are §§ 2, 22, 35, 36, 79, 80, 85, 86, 91, 100. But such places as Ἐρατοσθένους κινδυνεύοντος, § 62, and τούτου καταψηφιεῖσθε, § 90, show that Eratosthenes was the actual defendant in this particular trial.

[26] So Weidner, ibid.; Blass, Att. Bereds. I, p. 542; M. and S. p. 257, note 148, p. 266, note 182; Wilamowitz,

ibid. p. 221. This view is doubted by Fuhr, p. 12, and note 2. But to believe that metics had no right to appear as accusers at the εὔθυναι is virtually to suppose that officials were irresponsible for acts committed against them.

[27] See Introd. § 15 and note 32 upon it.

[28] M. and S. p. 753.

[29] M. and S. p. 266, and note 182. But just as in his δοκιμασία, Mantitheus thought it proper (XVI. 9), after answering the specific charge, to give an account of his whole life, so at his εὔθυνα Eratosthenes doubtless did the same; and hence probably the accusers were not held to the strict letter of the law in their attacks. On the general nature of the δοκιμασία, see Introd. § 8.

lines of defence, — such as that the Thirty had forced him to make the arrest, and that he had not been in favour of the killing of the metics, but, on the contrary, had opposed it. Lysias, therefore, does not confine himself to the specific charge. In fact he devotes to it only a little more than the first third of the speech (§§ 1–36). The remainder consists of an arraignment of the whole body of Tyrants and of the putting forth of the claim that Eratosthenes, as a member of the government, must bear the blame and be held responsible for all its acts. But Lysias does not rest even here. He goes back into the history of earlier attempts to establish an oligarchy in Athens, in order to show the part taken in these attempts by Eratosthenes and his friends and fellow-rulers, particularly Phidon and Theramenes (§§ 37–61). On his friendship with the latter Eratosthenes chiefly relied, because at the time of this trial the people of Athens had forgotten that Theramenes was ever their enemy, in their admiration of his stand against Critias. He had atoned for all his faults by a martyr's death. Hence it is Lysias's object to blacken the character of Theramenes as much as he can, and he devotes a good part of his speech to the attempt.[30] After this digression (§§ 62–78), he returns again to the general attack on the Thirty, calls for capital punishment on their representative (§§ 79–85, 90–91), sneers at the arguments of the advocates and witnesses of Eratosthenes (§§ 86–89), exhorts the democrats and the ex-oligarchs among the judges alike to do their duty in this test case (§§ 92–98), and closes with an appeal to the memory of the dead (§§ 99–100).

From the tone of the address to the judges one might think that Lysias felt that there could not be two opinions about the verdict that must follow. And yet he must have known how great were the chances against a conviction. The judges were composed of men of all parties, chosen by the lot. Many of them, who had

[30] On the truthfulness of the attack, see the notes and appendix to these sections (62–78); also *Der Athener Theramenes*, an exhaustive monograph by Dr. Carl Pöhlig in *Jahrbücher, Supplementb.* IX, 1877, p. 227 ff. The judicious view there taken is strongly confirmed by Aristotle, *Resp. Ath.* 28. 5.

belonged to the city party, hated the Thirty indeed, but still
they were not democrats. Some had belonged like Eratosthenes
himself to the faction of Theramenes, and the partisans of the
First Ten were probably represented. Even in the Piraeus party
there were men who wanted only a moderate, not a downright
democracy. All these different men knew that Eratosthenes had
never been prominent in the Thirty's crimes (§ 89); all would see
in a verdict against him a judgment passed on their own personal
and party views. There was in the minds of democrats and oligarchs alike an inclination to forget the past and not to increase
the list, already too long, of the victims of that year of blood.
It was only later that party feeling and party revenge were
manifested in all their bitterness.[31] Further, Eratosthenes had
defenders. Men of position were ready to be his advocates[32]; he
had plenty of witnesses.[33] But Lysias found it difficult to get
witnesses to support his main charge because the men he wanted
had been members of the oligarchical clubs.[34] The actual verdict
is not known. However, several years later, in 399–8, one of the
Thirty (probably either Phidon or Eratosthenes) was brought before
the Areopagus on a charge of wilful murder.[35] Hence, if not
actually acquitted at their εὔθυναι, Eratosthenes and Phidon may
have merely suffered ἀτιμία,[36] being prohibited from holding office,
voting in the Assembly, or from being present at sacrifices and
festivals. A fine may have been inflicted, so large that ἀτιμία was
the legal result of their inability to pay it. Whatever the verdict
was, the public appearance of Lysias and his brilliant speech must
have been of great assistance to him in his new profession of
λογογράφος.

[31] See Lys. xviii and xxv, and on
Archinus in note 20 above.
[32] §§ 86–88.
[33] § 87.
[34] § 46 f.

[35] Lys. x. 31. The speaker was born
in 417, so that his δοκιμασία εἰς ἄνδρας
could not have taken place before 399
B.C. (Weidner, ibid. p. 34).
[36] See Introd. § 51.

ΚΑΤ' ΕΡΑΤΟΣΘΕΝΟΥΣ

ΤΟΥ ΓΕΝΟΜΕΝΟΥ ΤΩΝ ΤΡΙΑΚΟΝΤΑ, ΟΝ ΑΥΤΟΣ ΕΙΠΕ ΛΥΣΙΑΣ.

1 Οὐκ ἄρξασθαί μοι δοκεῖ ἄπορον εἶναι, ὦ ἄνδρες δικασταί, τῆς κατηγορίας, ἀλλὰ παύσασθαι λέγοντι· τοιαῦτα
αὐτοῖς τὸ μέγεθος καὶ τοσαῦτα τὸ πλῆθος εἴργασται, ὥστε
μήτ᾽ ἂν ψευδόμενον δεινότερα τῶν ὑπαρχόντων κατηγορῆ-
5σαι, μήτε τἀληθῆ βουλόμενον εἰπεῖν ἅπαντα δύνασθαι,
ἀλλ᾽ ἀνάγκη ἢ τὸν κατήγορον ἀπειπεῖν ἢ τὸν χρόνον ἐπι-
2λιπεῖν. τοὐναντίον δέ μοι δοκοῦμεν πείσεσθαι ἢ ἐν τῷ
πρὸ τοῦ χρόνῳ. πρότερον μὲν γὰρ ἔδει τὴν ἔχθραν τοὺς

1. **ἄρξασθαι**: cf. Cic. de Imp.
Pomp. 3, huius orationis diffi-
cilius est exitum quam prin-
cipium invenire.—**λέγοντι**: partic.
with verb of ceasing; cf. § 100. G.
1580; H. 981. The dat. is assimilated to μοι (G. 928, 1; H. 941), cf.
XXII. 8. — **τοιαῦτα**: on the asyndeton, see App.—**αὐτοῖς**: Eratosthenes
and his colleagues. — **ἄν**: on its
position, see G. 1311; H. 862. With
δύνασθαι it forms the apod. to ψευδόμενον, *if one took to lying*, and to βουλόμενον. The inf. κατηγορῆσαι depends
on δύνασθαι, but εἰπεῖν belongs equally
to βουλόμενον and to δύνασθαι. On ὥστε
μήτ᾽ ἂν δύνασθαι, a potential expression, not in indir. disc., see GMT.

592. — **ἀνάγκη**: see App.— **ἐπιλιπεῖν**:
intrans., *fail, run out.*

2. **τοὐναντίον πείσεσθαι**: *our experience will be contrary.* — **πρὸ τοῦ**:
before this, former, the phrase serving
as adj. τοῦ is here demonstrative. G.
984; H. 655 d ; and see on XXIII. 8.—
ἔχθραν: *personal enmity.* In order
to avoid the suspicion of being a
sycophant (cf. XXII. 1) or a busybody, it was the custom to state one's
personal grievance in bringing a suit.
Cf. [Dem.] LIII. 1, οὐ συκοφαντῶν ἀλλ᾽
ἀδικούμενος καὶ ὑβριζόμενος ὑπὸ τούτων,
καὶ οἰόμενος δεῖν τιμωρεῖσθαι (for
in such circumstances Greek ethics
taught that revenge was a duty ; cf.
Lys. XII. 23 and 60; XXIV. 1; XXXII. 22)

κατηγοροῦντας ἐπιδεῖξαι, ἥτις εἴη πρὸς τοὺς φεύγοντας·
10 νυνὶ δὲ παρὰ τῶν φευγόντων χρὴ πυνθάνεσθαι ἥτις ἦν
αὐτοῖς πρὸς τὴν πόλιν ἔχθρα, ἀνθ᾽ ὅτου τοιαῦτα ἐτόλμησαν
εἰς αὐτὴν ἐξαμαρτάνειν. οὐ μέντοι ὡς οὐκ ἔχων οἰκείας
ἔχθρας καὶ συμφορὰς τοὺς λόγους ποιοῦμαι, ἀλλ᾽ ὡς ἅπασι
πολλῆς ἀφθονίας οὔσης ὑπὲρ τῶν ἰδίων ἢ ὑπὲρ τῶν δημο-
3 σίων ὀργίζεσθαι. ἐγὼ μὲν οὖν, ὦ ἄνδρες δικασταί, οὔτ᾽
ἐμαυτοῦ πώποτε οὔτε ἀλλότρια πράγματα πράξας νῦν
ἠνάγκασμαι ὑπὸ τῶν γεγενημένων τούτου κατηγορεῖν, ὥστε
πολλάκις εἰς πολλὴν ἀθυμίαν κατέστην, μὴ διὰ τὴν ἀπειρίαν ἀναξίως καὶ ἀδυνάτως ὑπὲρ τοῦ ἀδελφοῦ καὶ ἐμαυτοῦ
20 τὴν κατηγορίαν ποιήσομαι· ὅμως δὲ πειράσομαι ὑμᾶς ἐξ
ἀρχῆς ὡς ἂν δύνωμαι δι᾽ ἐλαχίστων διδάξαι.

4 Οὑμὸς πατὴρ Κέφαλος ἐπείσθη μὲν ὑπὸ Περικλέους εἰς
ταύτην τὴν γῆν ἀφικέσθαι, ἔτη δὲ τριάκοντα ᾤκησε, καὶ
οὐδενὶ πώποτε οὔτε ἡμεῖς οὔτε ἐκεῖνος δίκην οὔτε ἐδικασά-

τὴν ἀπογραφὴν ἐποιησάμην. —τοὺς φεύγοντας : φεύγων is the regular word
for *defendant* or *accused.* —ἀνθ᾽ ὅτου:
wherefore, that. The phrase is used
loosely as a conjunction. H. 999. —
ὡς οὐκ ἔχων : *as one who has no.* See
G. 1574; H. 978; and *cf.* § 13 and
XXXI. 24. —τοὺς λόγους ποιοῦμαι : a
phrase used either of accusation as
here and XXII. 1, or of defence as in
XXIV. 26. It simply equals λέγω.

3. πράγματα : business of any sort,
but freq. as here law business, *lawsuits.* —ὑπὸ τῶν γεγενημένων : "ὑπὸ
with a thing (*instead of a person*)
personifies it, setting it in a sort
of imaginative light," Gildersleeve,
A. J. P. VI, 488. *Cf.* XXIV. 6, 17;
and see on VII. 21. — κατέστην : with

πολλάκις this aor. forms a transition
from the common to the gnomic aorist. GMT. 156; *cf.* § 41; XXII. 16. —
ἀπειρίαν : the section reads like the
common plea for indulgence, but this
was really Lysias's *début.* — ποιήσομαι : fut. indic. after a clause denoting
fear, a rare usage. G. 1379; H. 887 b.
See App. — ὡς ἂν δύνωμαι : for the
mood, see on XVI. 9.—δι᾽ ἐλαχίστων:
for the usual διὰ βραχυτάτων of § 62,
XVI. 9. See App.

4. Κέφαλος : on the facts, see
Introd. § 15. —ἡμεῖς : *we brothers.* —
ἐδικασάμεθα : for the active meaning,
cf. § 100, and see G. 1245; H. 816, 8.
The word generally applied to the
plaintiff is διώκειν, esp. with φεύγειν.
Cf. XXXII. 2. — ᾤκουμεν : note the

25 μεθα οὔτε ἐφύγομεν, ἀλλ' οὕτως ᾠκοῦμεν δημοκρατούμενοι
ὥστε μήτε εἰς τοὺς ἄλλους ἐξαμαρτάνειν μήτε ὑπὸ τῶν
5 ἄλλων ἀδικεῖσθαι. ἐπειδὴ δ' οἱ τριάκοντα πονηροὶ καὶ
συκοφάνται ὄντες εἰς τὴν ἀρχὴν κατέστησαν, φάσκοντες
χρῆναι τῶν ἀδίκων καθαρὰν ποιῆσαι τὴν πόλιν καὶ τοὺς
30 λοιποὺς πολίτας ἐπ' ἀρετὴν καὶ δικαιοσύνην προτρέψαι,
τοιαῦτα λέγοντες οὐ τοιαῦτα ποιεῖν ἐτόλμων, ὡς ἐγὼ περὶ
τῶν ἐμαυτοῦ πρῶτον εἰπὼν καὶ περὶ τῶν ὑμετέρων ἀναμνή-
6 σαι πειράσομαι. Θέογνις γὰρ καὶ Πείσων ἔλεγον ἐν τοῖς
τριάκοντα περὶ τῶν μετοίκων, ὡς εἶέν τινες τῇ πολιτείᾳ
35 ἀχθόμενοι· καλλίστην οὖν εἶναι πρόφασιν τιμωρεῖσθαι
μὲν δοκεῖν, τῷ δ' ἔργῳ χρηματίζεσθαι· πάντως δὲ τὴν μὲν
7 πόλιν πένεσθαι, τὴν δ' ἀρχὴν δεῖσθαι χρημάτων. καὶ
τοὺς ἀκούοντας οὐ χαλεπῶς ἔπειθον· ἀποκτιννύναι μὲν γὰρ
ἀνθρώπους περὶ οὐδενὸς ἡγοῦντο, λαμβάνειν δὲ χρήματα
40 περὶ πολλοῦ ἐποιοῦντο. ἔδοξεν οὖν αὐτοῖς δέκα συλλαβεῖν, τούτων δὲ δύο πένητας, ἵνα αὐτοῖς ᾖ πρὸς τοὺς ἄλλους

tense, different from that of ἐφύγομεν.
G. 1259; H. 836.

5. ἐπειδὴ δ' οἱ τριάκοντα κτλ. : *cf.*
Xen. *Hellen.* ii. 3. 12, πρῶτον μὲν οὓς
πάντες ᾔδεσαν ἐν τῇ δημοκρατίᾳ ἀπὸ
συκοφαντίας ζῶντας καὶ τοῖς καλοῖς
κἀγαθοῖς βαρεῖς ὄντας, συλλαμβάνοντες
ὑπῆγον θανάτου. Lysias himself admits,
xxv. 19, that the Thirty began well ;
so Arist. *Resp. Ath.* 35.— φάσκοντες :
though pretending. — τῶν ἀδίκων κα-
θαράν: *cf.* sceleris purus. — οὐ
ἐτόλμων: very like ἤθελον with a neg.
(*cf.* § 58), 'could not bring themselves,'
cf. xxxii. 2. Without a neg. the verb
sometimes means 'have the heart to,'
cf. xxiv. 7 ; xxxii. 15, 20. For the
ordinary meaning, see above, § 2.

6. ἐν : *at meetings of, cf.* § 69. —

μετοίκων : see Introd. § 15. — πολιτείᾳ : this word, in the orators generally reserved for the democracy
(*cf.* xxxi. 32) is by Lysias applied
also to the Thirty's government. Here
and in § 77 it is put into the mouths
of members of the Thirty, but not so
in xvi. 3, 5. — τιμωρεῖσθαι . . . χρη-
ματίζεσθαι : note the chiastic order.
— πάντως : *at any rate.* — χρημάτων :
esp. as pay for the Spartan troops,
§ 94, *cf.* Xen. *Hellen.* ii. 3. 21.

7. περὶ οὐδενὸς ἡγοῦντο : 'they
cared not a whit.' See App. — ἡγοῦντο
and ἐποιοῦντο : on the synonymous
ending of the two members, see on
xvi. 13. — δέκα : Xenophon says
thirty, *Hellen.* ii. 3. 21, 40. — ᾖ : for
the mood, see on xvi. 6. — τοὺς

ἀπολογία, ὡς οὐ χρημάτων ἕνεκα ταῦτα πέπρακται, ἀλλὰ
συμφέροντα τῇ πολιτείᾳ γεγένηται, ὥσπερ τι τῶν ἄλλων
8 εὐλόγως πεποιηκότες. διαλαβόντες δὲ τὰς οἰκίας ἐβάδιζον·
45 καὶ ἐμὲ μὲν ξένους ἑστιῶντα κατέλαβον, οὓς ἐξελάσαντες
Πείσωνί με παραδιδόασιν· οἱ δὲ ἄλλοι εἰς τὸ ἐργαστήριον
ἐλθόντες τὰ ἀνδράποδα ἀπεγράφοντο. ἐγὼ δὲ Πείσωνα
μὲν ἠρώτων εἰ βούλοιτό με σῶσαι χρήματα λαβών· ὃ δ'
9 ἔφασκεν, εἰ πολλὰ εἴη. εἶπον οὖν ὅτι τάλαντον ἀργυρίου
50 ἕτοιμος εἴην δοῦναι· ὃ δ' ὡμολόγησε ταῦτα ποιήσειν.
ἠπιστάμην μὲν οὖν ὅτι οὔτε θεοὺς οὔτ' ἀνθρώπους νομίζει,
ὅμως δ' ἐκ τῶν παρόντων ἐδόκει μοι ἀναγκαιότατον εἶναι
10 πίστιν παρ' αὐτοῦ λαβεῖν. ἐπειδὴ δὲ ὤμοσεν, ἐξώλειαν
ἑαυτῷ καὶ τοῖς παισὶν ἐπαρώμενος, λαβὼν τὸ τάλαντόν με
55 σώσειν, εἰσελθὼν εἰς τὸ δωμάτιον τὴν κιβωτὸν ἀνοίγνυμι·
Πείσων δ' αἰσθόμενος εἰσέρχεται, καὶ ἰδὼν τὰ ἐνόντα καλεῖ

ἄλλους: the other eight. — ὥσπερ...
πεποιηκότες: 'just as on the adop-
tion, on good grounds, of any other
measure.' On this use of the partic.,
see G. 1576; H. 978 a; and App.
The partic. is pl. as if ἵνα ἀπολογίαν
ἔχωσιν had preceded. H. 633.

8. οἰκίας: it was illegal to enter a
man's house against his will (see on
XXIII. 2), but under the Thirty, said
Thrasybulus (Xen. Hellen. ii. 4. 14),
δειπνοῦντες συνελαμβανόμεθα καὶ καθεύ-
δοντες καὶ ἀγοράζοντες. — ἐμὲ μέν: in
μέν the thought of his brother is
latent; see on VII. 5. — ἀπεγράφοντο:
the usual word used of lists or inven-
tories; M. and S. p. 304. — ὃ δέ: on
the accent of the pronominal article,
see G. 139, 981¹; H. 272 b.

9. τάλαντον ἀργυρίου: see table of
money, p. 206. — ταῦτα: this pl. is

freq. in Greek where we use sing.;
cf. §§ 14 and 68. — ποιήσειν: for the
mood, cf. § 10 σώσειν, § 14 ποιήσειν, and
see on μεταμελήσειν, XVI. 2. — θεοὺς
... νομίζει: the use of ἀνθρώπους is
striking, for with θεοί this verb means
believe in. See App. On the mood, see
G. 1487; H. 933. — ἐκ τῶν παρόντων:
the prep. denotes ground or inference,
'judging from the present state of
things.' G. 1209 d; H. 798 d; see on
XVI. 18.

10. ὤμοσεν: for the tense, see on
κατήλθετε, XVI. 6. — ἐπαρώμενος: denotes manner. G. 1563, 3; H. 969 a.
On the form of oath, see on XXXII.
13. — λαβών: prot. of σώσειν (G. 1563,
5; H. 969 d), which depends on
ὤμοσεν (G. 1286; H. 948 a). — δωμάτιον: chamber, his bedroom, cubi-
culum.

τῶν ὑπηρετῶν δύο καὶ τὰ ἐν τῇ κιβωτῷ λαβεῖν ἐκέλευσεν.
11 ἐπειδὴ δὲ οὐχ ὅσον ὡμολόγητο εἶχεν, ὦ ἄνδρες δικασταί,
ἀλλὰ τρία τάλαντα ἀργυρίου καὶ τετρακοσίους κυζικηνοὺς
60 καὶ ἑκατὸν δαρεικοὺς καὶ φιάλας ἀργυρᾶς τέτταρας, ἐδεόμην αὐτοῦ ἐφόδιά μοι δοῦναι, ὃ δ' ἀγαπήσειν με ἔφασκεν,
12 εἰ τὸ σῶμα σώσω. ἐξιοῦσι δ' ἐμοὶ καὶ Πείσωνι ἐπιτυγχάνει Μηλόβιός τε καὶ Μνησιθείδης ἐκ τοῦ ἐργαστηρίου
ἀπιόντες καὶ καταλαμβάνουσι πρὸς αὐταῖς ταῖς θύραις καὶ
65 ἐρωτῶσιν ὅποι βαδίζοιμεν· ὁ δ' ἔφασκεν εἰς τἀδελφοῦ τοῦ
ἐμοῦ, ἵνα καὶ τὰ ἐν ἐκείνῃ τῇ οἰκίᾳ σκέψηται. ἐκεῖνον μὲν
οὖν ἐκέλευον βαδίζειν, ἐμὲ δὲ μεθ' αὑτῶν ἀκολουθεῖν εἰς
13 Δαμνίππου. Πείσων δὲ προσελθὼν σιγᾶν μοι παρεκελεύετο
καὶ θαρρεῖν, ὡς ἥξων ἐκεῖσε. καταλαμβάνομεν δὲ αὐτόθι

11. **οὐχ ὅσον**: emphatic, hence =
οὐ τοσοῦτον μόνον ὅσον, not only the
sum . . . but. Cf. Thuc. i. 51. 1, ὑπο-
τοπήσαντες (τὰς ναῦς) ἀπ' Ἀθηνῶν εἶναι,
οὐχ ὅσας ἑώρων ἀλλὰ πλείους, and
τοσαῦτα, § 95. — **ὦ ἄνδρες**: the invoca-
tion, as often, makes the statement
more emphatic; cf. xvi. 16, 19. —
τάλαντα: on the sum and on the
coins which follow, see p. 206. —
φιάλας: the φιάλη was a flat drinking cup, without handle or stem,
shaped like a deep saucer, and was
of earthenware or metal, often highly
ornamented. — **ἐφόδια**: travelling expenses, cf. xvi. 14. — **ἀγαπήσειν** . . .
σώσω: the dir. discourse was ἀγαπή-
σεις εἰ σώσεις, a cond. of the threaten-
ing or warning kind. G. 1405; cf.
§§ 35 and 90; xxxi. 29. The mood of
the prot. is unchanged from the dir.
discourse. On the meaning of ἀγαπήσειν, 'only too glad,' cf. xxii. 15,
and ἀγαπητῶς, xvi. 16.

12. **ἐξιοῦσι**: plural, though when a
partic. which belongs to two or more
substs. precedes the first, it is often
singular. Cf. § 72; so xiii. 17, γνοὺς δὲ
Θηραμένης καὶ οἱ ἄλλοι, ibid. 23, παραγενόμενος δὲ Νικίας καὶ Νικομένης καὶ ἄλλοι.
Cf. xii. 55, where it follows the first.
Likewise sometimes a finite verb, as
here ἐπιτυγχάνει, though ἀπιόντες follows; cf. Xen. Anab. ii. 4. 16, ἔπεμψέ
με Ἀριαῖος καὶ Ἀρτάοζος, πιστοὶ ὄντες
Κύρῳ. See G. 901; H. 607. — **Μηλόβιος**: all three men were of the
Thirty; see the list in Xen. Hellen.
ii. 3. 2. — **πρὸς** . . . **θύραις**: at the very
door. See App. — **βαδίζοιμεν**: opt.
because dependent on a historic present. G. 1268. — **εἰς Δαμνίππου**: on
the omission, see G. 953; H. 730 a.
Cf. τἀδελφοῦ above. Of Damnippus
we know nothing except from this
oration.

13. **ὡς**: see on § 2. — **ᾤχοντο**: they
were gone. G. 1256; H. 827; cf. § 75.

70 Θέογνιν ἑτέρους φυλάττοντα· ᾧ παραδόντες ἐμὲ πάλιν
ᾤχοντο. ἐν τοιούτῳ δ' ὄντι μοι κινδυνεύειν ἐδόκει, ὡς τοῦ
14 γε ἀποθανεῖν ὑπάρχοντος ἤδη. καλέσας δὲ Δάμνιππον
λέγω πρὸς αὐτὸν τάδε· "ἐπιτήδειος μέν μοι τυγχάνεις ὤν,
ἥκω δ' εἰς τὴν σὴν οἰκίαν, ἀδικῶ δ' οὐδέν, χρημάτων δ'
75 ἕνεκα ἀπόλλυμαι. σὺ οὖν ταῦτα πάσχοντί μοι πρόθυμον
παράσχου τὴν σεαυτοῦ δύναμιν εἰς τὴν ἐμὴν σωτηρίαν."
ὃ δ' ὑπέσχετο ταῦτα ποιήσειν. ἐδόκει δ' αὐτῷ βέλτιον
εἶναι πρὸς Θέογνιν μνησθῆναι· ἡγεῖτο γὰρ ἅπαν ποιήσειν
15 αὐτόν, εἴ τις ἀργύριον διδοίη. ἐκείνου δὲ διαλεγομένου
80 Θεόγνιδι (ἔμπειρος γὰρ ὢν ἐτύγχανον τῆς οἰκίας καὶ ἤδη
ὅτι ἀμφίθυρος εἴη) ἐδόκει μοι ταύτῃ πειρᾶσθαι σωθῆναι,
ἐνθυμουμένῳ ὅτι, ἐὰν μὲν λάθω, σωθήσομαι, ἐὰν δὲ ληφθῶ,
ἡγούμην μέν, εἰ Θέογνις εἴη πεπεισμένος ὑπὸ τοῦ Δαμνίπ-

— ἐν τοιούτῳ: 'in such a straight.'
Cf. xxx. 3, εἰς τοῦτο κατέστημεν, and
Xen. *Anab.* i. 7. 5, διὰ τὸ ἐν τοιούτῳ
εἶναι τοῦ κινδύνου προσιόντος.— τοῦ γε
ἀποθανεῖν ὑπάρχοντος: 'as there was
death to start with, at any rate.' On
the inf., see G. 1547; H. 959.

14. ἥκω κτλ.: note the short sentences, spoken with bated breath. —
ἀδικῶ: translate as pf. (GMT. 27; H.
827). — ἀπόλλυμαι: translate as fut.
(GMT. 32); see on ἐλάμβανον, § 27. —
πρόθυμον: properly used only of persons, here transferred to δύναμιν. So
with ὁρμή, Plut. *Philop.* 9. The phrase
= πρόθυμον παράσχου σεαυτὸν κατὰ τὴν
σεαυτοῦ δύναμιν. — εἰς: of purpose or
end, rare in the orators. Cf. § 18, and
Isocr. viii. 59, εἰς τὰς ἐκκλησίας ἀργύριον ἂν παρέχοιμεν. G. 1207 d; H. 796 c.
— διδοίη: indir. disc.; the tense of the
apod. shows the form of condition.

15. ἀμφίθυρος: *i.e.* it ran back to
the next street and hence had a back
as well as a front entrance. — ταύτῃ:
this way, dat. of manner. G. 1181;
H. 779 a. See App. — ἡγούμην: here
the construction introduced by ἐνθυμουμένῳ ὅτι is varied. The natural
apod. to ἐὰν ληφθῶ would have been
ἢ οὐδὲν ἧττον ἀφεθήσομαι ἢ ὁμοίως ἀπο-
θανοῦμαι. But the further supposition
about Theognis came into Lysias's
mind, and he inserted ἡγούμην to prevent one cond. clause from following directly upon another (ἐὰν ληφθῶ,
εἰ Θέογνις εἴη); hence the apod. of
ληφθῶ becomes indir. discourse. —
μέν: belongs properly to εἰ εἴη, not
with ἡγούμην, but μέν is sometimes
thus attached to the main verb upon
which two contrasted clauses depend;
cf. Plat. *Rep.* 334 C, εἰκὸς μὲν, οὓς ἄν
τις ἡγῆται χρηστούς, φιλεῖν, οὓς δ' ἂν

που χρήματα λαβεῖν, οὐδὲν ἧττον ἀφεθήσεσθαι, εἰ δὲ μή,
16 ὁμοίως ἀποθανεῖσθαι. ταῦτα διανοηθεὶς ἔφευγον, ἐκείνων
ἐπὶ τῇ αὐλείῳ θύρᾳ τὴν φυλακὴν ποιουμένων· τριῶν δὲ
θυρῶν οὐσῶν, ἃς ἔδει με διελθεῖν, ἅπασαι ἀνεῳγμέναι
ἔτυχον. ἀφικόμενος δὲ εἰς Ἀρχένεω τοῦ ναυκλήρου ἐκεῖνον πέμπω εἰς ἄστυ, πευσόμενον περὶ τοῦ ἀδελφοῦ· ἥκων
90 δὲ ἔλεγεν ὅτι Ἐρατοσθένης αὐτὸν ἐν τῇ ὁδῷ λαβὼν εἰς τὸ
17 δεσμωτήριον ἀπαγάγοι. καὶ ἐγὼ μὲν τοιαῦτα πεπυσμένος
τῆς ἐπιούσης νυκτὸς διέπλευσα Μέγαράδε. Πολεμάρχῳ
δὲ παρήγγειλαν οἱ τριάκοντα τὸ ἐπ' ἐκείνων εἰθισμένον
παράγγελμα, πίνειν κώνειον, πρὶν τὴν αἰτίαν εἰπεῖν δι'
95 ἥντινα ἔμελλεν ἀποθανεῖσθαι· οὕτω πολλοῦ ἐδέησε κριθῆ-
18 ναι καὶ ἀπολογήσασθαι. καὶ ἐπειδὴ ἀπεφέρετο ἐκ τοῦ

πονηρούς, μισεῖν. — ὁμοίως : all the
same.

16. αὐλείῳ θύρᾳ : the front door,
by which one would pass from the
αὐλή into the street. — τριῶν θυρῶν :
on their position, see App. — ἀνεῳγμέναι ἔτυχον : 'happened to be standing open,' lit. to have been opened.
Thus the pf. partic. retains its ordinary force. GMT. 147; see on § 27.
— ἄστυ : Athens, where Polemarchus
lived; the shipcaptain, like Lysias,
lived in the Piraeus. — ἥκων : came
back; see on xvi. 4.

17. ἐπί : of time. G. 1210, 1 b;
H. 799, 1 c. — κώνειον : not the tree
which we erroneously call hemlock
(the hemlock-spruce), but the wild
plant conium maculatum, 'poi-
son hemlock,' of the umbelliferae
order, like carrots, parsnips, etc.
From the leaves is distilled the poi-
son, called coniine or conia. — πρὶν
εἰπεῖν : here = without telling. On

this use of πρίν, cf. Aesch. iii. 235,
πλείους ἢ χιλίους καὶ πεντακοσίους
τῶν πολιτῶν ἀκρίτους ἀπέκτειναν (sc. οἱ
τριάκοντα) πρὶν καὶ τὰς αἰτίας ἀκοῦσαι
ἐφ' αἷς ἔμελλον ἀποθνήσκειν. — ἀποθανεῖσθαι : on the tense, see on κινδυνεύειν, xvi. 13. — πολλοῦ ἐδέησε : on
this personal use of the act. of δέω,
cf. xxiii. 13; xxiv. 1; and see H. 743 b.
For the dependent inf., see G. 1521.
— κριθῆναι κτλ. : this neglect of the
legal forms is dwelt upon in §§ 81
and 82. It was an Athenian view
that ἀοικήτους (uninhabitable) εἶναι
ταύτας τῶν πόλεων ἐν αἷς ἄκριτοί τινες
ἀπόλλυνται τῶν πολιτῶν, Isocr. xv. 22;
yet even under the democracy men
were sometimes executed untried.
Cf. xix. 7, xxv. 26, and the proposal
in xxii. 2. For the Thirty's practice,
see Aeschines quoted above. The
same number is given by Isocr. vii.
67; Arist. Resp. Ath. 35.

δεσμωτηρίου τεθνεώς, τριῶν ἡμῖν οἰκιῶν οὐσῶν ἐξ οὐδεμιᾶς
εἴασαν ἐξενεχθῆναι, ἀλλὰ κλεισίον μισθωσάμενοι προύθεντο αὐτόν· καὶ πολλῶν ὄντων ἱματίων αἰτοῦσιν οὐδὲν
100 ἔδοσαν εἰς τὴν ταφήν, ἀλλὰ τῶν φίλων ὃ μὲν ἱμάτιον ὃ δὲ
προσκεφάλαιον ὃ δὲ ὅ τι ἕκαστος ἔτυχεν ἔδωκεν εἰς τὴν
19 ἐκείνου ταφήν. καὶ ἔχοντες μὲν ἑπτακοσίας ἀσπίδας τῶν
ἡμετέρων, ἔχοντες δὲ ἀργύριον καὶ χρυσίον τοσοῦτον,
χαλκὸν δὲ καὶ κόσμον καὶ ἔπιπλα καὶ ἱμάτια γυναικεῖα
105 ὅσα οὐδεπώποτε ᾤοντο κτήσεσθαι, καὶ ἀνδράποδα εἴκοσι
καὶ ἑκατόν, ὧν τὰ μὲν βέλτιστα ἔλαβον, τὰ δὲ λοιπὰ εἰς
τὸ δημόσιον ἀπέδοσαν, εἰς τοσαύτην ἀπληστίαν καὶ
αἰσχροκέρδειαν ἀφίκοντο καὶ τοῦ τρόπου τοῦ αὐτῶν ἀπό-
δειξιν ἐποιήσαντο· τῆς γὰρ Πολεμάρχου γυναικὸς χρυ-
110 σοῦς ἑλικτῆρας, οὓς ἔχουσα ἐτύγχανεν, ὅτε τὸ πρῶτον
ἦλθεν εἰς τὴν οἰκίαν Μηλόβιος, ἐκ τῶν ὤτων ἐξείλετο.

18. οὐσῶν: concessive, like ὄντων
and ἔχοντες below. G. 1563, 6; H.
969 e. — ἐξενεχθῆναι: this, like
effero, was the regular word used
of funerals. The corpse, washed and
anointed, was dressed in white,
crowned with flowers and laid out
(cf. προύθεντο) in the front part of the
house on a couch (κλίνη) about which
were set the flasks called λήκυθοι.
Friends and relatives attended (but
see on § 87) this lying in state (the
πρόθεσις), and the funeral (ἐκφορά,
§ 87) followed early the next morning. See Hermann, *Privatalt.* p. 362
ff., or Becker's *Charicles,* English
edition, p. 385 ff., and on § 21 below.
— κλεισίον: hut, hovel. See App. —
ἔτυχεν: on the omission of the partic.
δούς, see G. 1586 ; H. 984 a ; cf.
XXIV. 20.

19. τοσοῦτον: with reference to
§ 11. — χαλκόν: raw material for
shields. — κόσμον: *ornaments,* 'ob-
jects of *vertu,*' cf. Hdt. iii. 123, τὸν
κόσμον τὸν ἐκ τοῦ ἀνδρεῶνος τοῦ Πολυ-
κράτεος. This included also men's
and women's ornaments (Aesch.
Theb. 397, Hdt. v. 92. 7), services of
plate (Ath. p. 231 B), *etc.* — καὶ τοῦ
τρόπου: after εἰς τοσαύτην a clause
with ὥστε might follow, cf. XXXII. 19;
but instead another statement is
added in a co-ordinate clause. This
statement is then justified by τῆς γὰρ
κτλ. So XIII. 80, οὗτος δὲ οὕτω τολ-
μηρὸς καὶ ἐκεῖ ἐγένετο · συνηκολούθει
γὰρ κτλ. But see App. — ἑλικτῆρας:
called also ἐνώτια, ἐλλόβια. Cf. in au-
res. — ὅτε τὸ πρῶτον: as soon as,
although generally τὸ πρῶτον means
the first time. See App.

20 καὶ οὐδὲ κατὰ τὸ ἐλάχιστον μέρος τῆς οὐσίας ἐλέου παρ'
αὐτῶν ἐτυγχάνομεν, ἀλλ' οὕτως εἰς ἡμᾶς διὰ τὰ χρήματα
ἐξημάρτανον, ὥσπερ οὐδ' ἂν ἕτεροι μεγάλων ἀδικημάτων
115 ὀργὴν ἔχοντες, οὐ τούτων ἀξίους γ' ὄντας τῇ πόλει, ἀλλὰ
πάσας μὲν τὰς χορηγίας χορηγήσαντας, πολλὰς δ' εἰσφορὰς εἰσενεγκόντας, κοσμίους δ' ἡμᾶς αὐτοὺς παρέχοντας
καὶ πᾶν τὸ προσταττόμενον ποιοῦντας, ἐχθρὸν δ' οὐδένα
κεκτημένους, πολλοὺς δ' Ἀθηναίων ἐκ τῶν πολεμίων λυσα-
120 μένους τοιούτων ἠξίωσαν, οὐχ ὁμοίως μετοικοῦντας ὥσπερ
21 αὐτοὶ ἐπολιτεύοντο.   οὗτοι γὰρ πολλοὺς μὲν τῶν πολιτῶν
εἰς τοὺς πολεμίους ἐξήλασαν, πολλοὺς δ' ἀδίκως ἀποκτεί-
ναντες ἀτάφους ἐποίησαν, πολλοὺς δ' ἐπιτίμους ὄντας
ἀτίμους κατέστησαν, πολλῶν δὲ θυγατέρας μελλούσας

20. οὐδ' ἂν ἕτεροι, *sc.* ἐξήμαρτον
(G. 1313; H. 863), of which ἔχοντες
is protasis. G. 1413; H. 902. On
the ethics, *cf.* §§ 2 and 60. — πόλει :
dat. of interest or relation. G. 1172;
H. 771; *cf.* Antiphon, VI. 10, χάριτος
ἄξιον εἶναι τῇ πόλει. — χορηγίας : on
the duty of the Chorēgus, see Gow,
§ 211; Gilbert, *Antiq.* p. 359; Smith,
Dict. Antiq. s.v. To gain good-will
speakers would often recount the
performance of this and other public duties; see on § 38, and *cf.* VII.
31; XXXII. 24.   This scheme often
worked well.   But it is amusing
to note how Lysias, having used
it himself here, warns the judges
against its employment by his adversary in § 38. — εἰσφοράς: special war-
taxes, levied according to property;
see Gow, p. 132; Gilbert, *Antiq.* p.
364.   *Cf.* VII. 31; XXII. 13. — κοσμίους: for the meaning, see on VII. 41.
— λυσαμένους: the λύσις αἰχμαλώτων

was one of those acts of humanity of
which speakers had good reason to
be proud; *cf.* Dem. VIII. 70; ἔχων
καὶ τριηραρχίας εἰπεῖν καὶ χορηγίας καὶ
χρημάτων εἰσφορὰς καὶ λύσεις αἰχμαλώτων καὶ τοιαύτας ἄλλας φιλανθρωπίας.
— ἠξίωσαν: a new construction (anacoluthon, H. 1063), for all the par-
ticiples might depend on the first
ἡμᾶς, but now ἠξίωσαν τοιούτων picks
up the threads and sums up the
whole. — οὐχ ὁμοίως: litotes. 'We
as metics were *better* than they as
citizens.'

21. εἰς τοὺς πολεμίους : in the
orators, εἰς is rarely used when *persons* are the end of motion.   See
App. On the thought, *cf.* § 95 end.
— ἀτάφους : because they had not
the usual rites; see on § 18 and *cf.* 96,
also Cic. *Quinct.* 50, si funus id
habendum est quo non amici
conveniunt ad exsequias co-
honestendas. — ἀτίμους : on ἀτι-

22 ἐκδίδοσθαι ἐκώλυσαν. καὶ εἰς τοσοῦτόν εἰσι τόλμης
ἀφιγμένοι ὥσθ᾽ ἥκουσιν ἀπολογησόμενοι, καὶ λέγουσιν
ὡς οὐδὲν κακὸν οὐδ᾽ αἰσχρὸν εἰργασμένοι εἰσίν. ἐγὼ δ᾽
ἐβουλόμην ἂν αὐτοὺς ἀληθῆ λέγειν· μετῆν γὰρ ἂν καὶ
23 ἐμοὶ τούτου τἀγαθοῦ οὐκ ἐλάχιστον μέρος. νῦν δὲ οὔτε
130 πρὸς τὴν πόλιν αὐτοῖς τοιαῦτα ὑπάρχει οὔτε πρὸς ἐμέ·
τὸν ἀδελφὸν γάρ μου, ὥσπερ καὶ πρότερον εἶπον, Ἐρατοσθένης ἀπέκτεινεν, οὔτε αὐτὸς ἰδίᾳ ἀδικούμενος οὔτε εἰς
τὴν πόλιν ὁρῶν ἐξαμαρτάνοντα, ἀλλὰ τῇ ἑαυτοῦ παρανο-
24 μίᾳ προθύμως ἐξυπηρετῶν. ἀναβιβασάμενος δ᾽ αὐτὸν
135 βούλομαι ἐρέσθαι, ὦ ἄνδρες δικασταί. τοιαύτην γὰρ
γνώμην ἔχω· ἐπὶ μὲν τῇ τούτου ὠφελείᾳ καὶ πρὸς ἕτερον
περὶ τούτου διαλέγεσθαι ἀσεβὲς εἶναι νομίζω, ἐπὶ δὲ τῇ
τούτου βλάβῃ καὶ πρὸς αὐτὸν τοῦτον ὅσιον καὶ εὐσεβές.
ἀνάβηθι οὖν μοι καὶ ἀπόκριναι, ὅ τι ἄν σε ἐρωτῶ.

μία, see Introd. § 51. — ἐκώλυσαν:
by confiscating the property of their
fathers or brothers (cf. XVI. 10) so that
there was no money for the dowry,
all-important in Greek marriages.

22. ἐβουλόμην ἄν: potential, referring to present time, = vellem.
G. 1339; cf. VII. 12. — οὐχ ἐλάχιστον:
litotes, cf. οὐχ ὁμοίως, § 20.

23. νῦν δέ: but as it is, as things
are. — πρός: of personal relations
(G. 1216, 3 b; H. 805, 3 b), cf. § 53
and XVIII. 6, τοιαῦτα ἐνομίζετο τὰ
ὑπάρχοντα αὐτῷ πρὸς τὸ ὑμέτερον πλῆθος εἶναι, and XVI. 10, with βεβίωκα
and ἐνειμάμην. — τοιαῦτα: i.e. οἷα
λέγουσιν ὡς οὐδὲν κακὸν κτλ., § 22. —
ἀπέκτεινεν: not, of course, with his
own hand; cf. § 67. — οὔτε ἀδικούμενος: a personal wrong would have
excused him, for popular ethics were

not yet beyond the 'eye for an eye'
stage; cf. Plat. Rep. 332 B, ὀφείλεται
δέ γε, οἶμαι, παρά γε τοῦ ἐχθροῦ τῷ
ἐχθρῷ, ὅπερ καὶ προσήκει (appropriate),
κακόν τι (where Plato is giving the
popular doctrine, not his own). See
on §§ 2 and 60. Plato himself defends
the Christian view.

24. ἀναβιβασάμενος: ἀνα-, because
of the platform, βῆμα, Introd. § 44.
— ἐρέσθαι: a speaker might cross-
question his opponent; cf. XXII. 5,
and see Introd. § 48. — ἀσεβές: to
speak to or have dealings with the
murderer of one's kinsman was, according to the popular view, ἀσεβές,
as such a one was ἐναγής or μιαρός.
But Lysias says that, to secure revenge (Greek ethics again), it is even
ὅσιον and εὐσεβές to speak to Eratosthenes.

25 Ἀπήγαγες Πολέμαρχον ἢ οὔ; Τὰ ὑπὸ τῶν ἀρχόντων
προσταχθέντα δεδιὼς ἐποίουν. Ἦσθα δ' ἐν τῷ βουλευ-
τηρίῳ, ὅτε οἱ λόγοι ἐγίγνοντο περὶ ἡμῶν; Ἦ. Πότερον
συνηγόρευες τοῖς κελεύουσιν ἀποκτεῖναι ἢ ἀντέλεγες;
Ἀντέλεγον. Ἵνα ἀποθάνωμεν ἢ ἵνα μὴ ἀποθάνωμεν;
145 Ἵνα μὴ ἀποθάνητε. Ἡγούμενος ἡμᾶς ἄδικα πάσχειν ἢ
δίκαια; Ἄδικα.

26 Εἶτ', ὦ σχετλιώτατε πάντων, ἀντέλεγες μὲν ἵνα σώσειας,
συνελάμβανες δὲ ἵνα ἀποκτείνειας; καὶ ὅτε μὲν τὸ πλῆθος
ἦν ὑμῶν κύριον τῆς σωτηρίας τῆς ἡμετέρας, ἀντιλέγειν
150 φῂς τοῖς βουλομένοις ἡμᾶς ἀπολέσαι, ἐπειδὴ δὲ ἐπὶ σοὶ
μόνῳ ἐγένετο καὶ σῶσαι Πολέμαρχον καὶ μή, εἰς τὸ δεσμωτήριον ἀπήγαγες; εἶθ' ὅτι μέν, ὡς φῄς, ἀντειπὼν οὐδὲν
ὠφέλησας, ἀξιοῖς χρηστὸς νομίζεσθαι, ὅτι δὲ συλλαβὼν
ἀπέκτεινας, οὐκ ἐμοὶ καὶ τουτοισὶ δοῦναι δίκην;

27 Καὶ μὴν οὐδὲ τοῦτο εἰκὸς αὐτῷ πιστεύειν, εἴπερ ἀληθῆ
λέγει φάσκων ἀντειπεῖν, ὡς αὐτῷ προσετάχθη. οὐ γὰρ
δή που ἐν τοῖς μετοίκοις πίστιν παρ' αὐτοῦ ἐλάμβανον.

---

25. τὰ ... ἐποίουν: instead of a
direct answer Eratosthenes excuses
himself by giving his reason for obe-
dience. But his other answers are
straight to the point. — οἱ λόγοι:
refers to § 6. — συνηγόρευες: *did you
concur?*

26. εἶτα: *and so*, used in indig-
nant or ironical inquiry.— τὸ πλῆθος
ὑμῶν: *the majority of you;* but *cf.* § 42.
— ἀντιλέγειν: represents the impf.,
see on xvi. 6, ἱππεύειν, and *cf.* ἀντέλεγον above. It shows the *attitude* of
Eratosthenes, which was one of opposition. The arrest, however, was a
single act, hence the aor. ἀπήγαγες.
— ἐπί: *in the power of.* — ἀξιοῖς:

claim. — τουτοισί: the -ί adds emphasis, and a gesture often accompanied a word so emphasised; *cf.*
h i c e and *celui-ci*. — δοῦναι: depends,
like νομίζεσθαι, on ἀξιοῖς which is
understood after the strong οὐκ. Cf.
XIV. 23, εἴ τις ὑμῶν τὸν Ἀλκιβιάδην
ἀξιώσει διὰ μὲν τοὺς βοηθοῦντας σῴζε-
σθαι, διὰ δὲ τὴν αὐτοῦ πονηρίαν μὴ ἀπολέσθαι. See App.

27. τοῦτο: here refers forward. —
δή που: adds an ironical or sarcastic
tone; *cf.* XXXI. 28. — ἐν τοῖς μετοίκοις: *in the case of mere metics; cf.*
Xen. *Anab.* v. 8. 15, ἐν ἐμαυτῷ πεῖραν
(*experiment*) λαβών. — πίστιν: here
not *oath*, as in § 9, but *guarantee*,

ἔπειτα τῷ ἧττον εἰκὸς ἦν προσταχθῆναι ἢ ὅστις ἀντειπών
γε ἐτύγχανε καὶ γνώμην ἀποδεδειγμένος; τίνα γὰρ εἰκὸς
160 ἦν ἧττον ταῦτα ὑπηρετῆσαι ἢ τὸν ἀντειπόντα οἷς ἐκεῖνοι
28 ἐβούλοντο πραχθῆναι; ἔτι δὲ τοῖς μὲν ἄλλοις Ἀθηναίοις
ἱκανή μοι δοκεῖ πρόφασις εἶναι τῶν γεγενημένων εἰς τοὺς
τριάκοντα ἀναφέρειν τὴν αἰτίαν, αὐτοὺς δὲ τοὺς τριάκοντα,
ἐὰν εἰς σφᾶς αὐτοὺς ἀναφέρωσι, πῶς ὑμᾶς εἰκὸς ἀποδέ-
29 χεσθαι; εἰ μὲν γάρ τις ἦν ἐν τῇ πόλει ἀρχὴ ἰσχυροτέρα
ὑφ᾽ ἧς αὐτῷ προσετάττετο παρὰ τὸ δίκαιον ἀνθρώπους
ἀπολλύναι, ἴσως ἂν εἰκότως αὐτῷ συγγνώμην εἴχετε· νῦν
δὲ παρὰ τοῦ ποτε καὶ λήψεσθε δίκην, εἴπερ ἐξέσται τοῖς
τριάκοντα λέγειν ὅτι τὰ ὑπὸ τῶν τριάκοντα προσταχθέντα
30 ἐποίουν; καὶ μὲν δὴ οὐκ ἐν τῇ οἰκίᾳ ἀλλ᾽ ἐν τῇ ὁδῷ,
σῴζειν τ᾽ αὐτὸν καὶ τὰ τούτοις ἐψηφισμένα παρόν, συλλα-

---

assurance, as in § 77. Metics were
not important enough persons to
make their cases the test of a man's
loyalty to the Thirty. Had Eratosthenes objected, the Thirty would
not have made a test case of it. —
ἐλάμβανον: the impf. here expresses
likelihood; see on ἐκέρδαινον, VII. 32;
so the pres. above, § 14. — ἔπειτα: *besides*. — ἐτύγχανε: with the *impf*. of
this verb the aor. partic. retains its
own past time. GMT. 146, and *cf.*
§ 64. The pf. partic. following keeps
its own time as usual; see on § 16. —
γνώμην: the article is often omitted
with this word. — ταῦτα: cogn. acc.
G. 1051; H. 715.

28. ἔτι δέ: *and another point.* —
πρόφασις: here not *pretext*, but
ground for excuse. In XXIV. 1, it
means *occasion.* — εἰς σφᾶς αὐτούς:
there is a fallacy here, for Erato-

sthenes would set himself apart from
the others because of his protest.

29. προσετάττετο: the rel. clause
is assimilated to conform to the
protasis, and must be translated
accordingly; *cf.* XXXI. 26. G. 1440;
H. 919 b; *cf.* ἦσαν, § 98. — νῦν δέ:
see on § 23. — παρὰ τοῦ ποτε καί:
the ποτέ makes τοῦ more general, as
we say 'whom in the world,' and the
καί strengthens λήψεσθαι, 'will you
ever punish?' *Cf.* XXIV. 12, καὶ ἔλεγεν,
and Xen. *Hellen.* ii. 3. 47, τοῦτον τί
ποτε καὶ καλέσαι χρή;

30. καὶ μὲν δή: *furthermore.* —
σῴζειν: with αὐτόν it has the lit.
meaning *save*, but with τὰ ἐψηφισμένα
it means *keep to.* The whole thought
is made clear in § 31; he might have
pretended not to see Polemarchus. —
τέ: might properly follow αὐτόν, but
the idea is σῴζειν τ᾽ αὐτὸν καὶ σῴζειν

βῶν ἀπήγαγεν. ὑμεῖς δὲ πᾶσιν ὀργίζεσθε, ὅσοι εἰς τὰς
οἰκίας ἦλθον τὰς ὑμετέρας ζήτησιν ποιούμενοι ἢ ὑμῶν ἢ
31 τῶν ὑμετέρων τινός· καίτοι εἰ χρὴ τοῖς διὰ τὴν ἑαυτῶν
175 σωτηρίαν ἑτέρους ἀπολέσασι συγγνώμην ἔχειν, ἐκείνοις
ἂν δικαιότερον ἔχοιτε· κίνδυνος γὰρ ἦν πεμφθεῖσι μὴ
ἐλθεῖν καὶ καταλαβοῦσιν ἐξάρνοις γενέσθαι. τῷ δὲ
Ἐρατοσθένει ἐξῆν εἰπεῖν ὅτι οὐκ ἀπήντησεν, ἔπειτα ὅτι
οὐκ εἶδεν· ταῦτα γὰρ οὔτ' ἔλεγχον οὔτε βάσανον εἶχεν,
180 ὥστε μηδ' ὑπὸ τῶν ἐχθρῶν βουλομένων οἷόν τ' εἶναι
32 ἐξελεγχθῆναι. χρῆν δέ σε, ὦ Ἐρατόσθενες, εἴπερ ἦσθα
χρηστός, πολὺ μᾶλλον τοῖς μέλλουσιν ἀδίκως ἀποθανεῖσθαι μηνυτὴν γενέσθαι ἢ τοὺς ἀδίκως ἀπολουμένους συλ-
33 λαμβάνειν. νῦν δέ σου τὰ ἔργα φανερὰ γεγένηται οὐχ

τὰ κτλ. *Cf.* § 62, 66, and Dein. i. 6,
δικάσαι τε περὶ τοῦ σώματος καὶ τῆς
ψυχῆς. — **παρόν**: 'though he might
have'; the partic. in the acc. absol.
representing impf. time (G. 1289;
H. 856 a) in a potential expression
without ἄν. *Cf.* μέλλοντα, § 99, and see
on χρῆν, § 32. — **ὀργίζεσθε**: the Thirty
obliged good citizens to share their
illegal work (βουλόμενοι ὡς πλείστους
ἀναπλῆσαι αἰτιῶν, Plat. *Apol.* 32 C),
such as searching houses. The
thought is, 'you scorn such people,
but you can pardon them, for they
did it in fear for their lives; but this
defence will not hold for Eratosthenes.'

31. ἐκείνοις: refers to ὅσοι κτλ.,
§ 30. — **δικαιότερον**: *sc.* than Eratosthenes. — **κίνδυνος** κτλ.: Socrates
refused to obey such an order, but
he said, ἴσως ἂν διὰ ταῦτ' ἀπέθανον, εἰ
μὴ ἡ ἀρχὴ (the Thirty's) διὰ ταχέων

κατελύθη, Plat. *Apol.* 32 D. — **ἐξῆν
εἰπεῖν**: *might have said* (but he
didn't); see on χρῆν, § 32. — **ἔπειτα**:
i.e. if it was proved that he did meet
him. — **ταῦτα**: refers merely to ὅτι
οὐκ εἶδεν. — **εἶχεν**: 'carried with it,'
'involved'; *cf.* Cic. *de Or.* i. 125,
stultitia excusationem non
habet. — **βουλομένων**: may be concessive or conditional.

32. χρῆν δέ σε μηνυτὴν γενέσθαι:
you ought to have become an informer
(implying that he did not become
one). On the omission of ἄν in such
an expression, see G. 1400; H. 897;
GMT. 416 ff.; and *cf.* ἐξῆν, § 31, vii.
26; κάλλιον ἦν, § 52; ἄξιον ἦν, § 64;
οἷόν τ' ἦν, vii. 26; κρεῖττον ἦν, vii. 27;
ἀσφαλέστερον ἦν, vii. 24; εἰκὸς ἦν,
xxiii. 15; συνέφερε, xxii. 13. But
in § 48, ἄν is used. — **μηνυτήν**: here
in a good sense, an unusual usage;
cf. § 48.

185 ὡς ἀνιωμένου ἀλλ' ὡς ἡδομένου τοῖς γιγνομένοις, ὥστε
τούσδε ἐκ τῶν ἔργων χρὴ μᾶλλον ἢ ἐκ τῶν λόγων τὴν
ψῆφον φέρειν, ἃ ἴσασι γεγενημένα τῶν τότε λεγομένων
τεκμήρια λαμβάνοντας, ἐπειδὴ μάρτυρας περὶ αὐτῶν οὐχ
οἷόν τε παρασχέσθαι. οὐ γὰρ μόνον ἡμῖν παρεῖναι οὐκ
190 ἐξῆν, ἀλλ' οὐδὲ παρ' αὐτοῖς εἶναι, ὥστ' ἐπὶ τούτοις ἐστὶ
πάντα τὰ κακὰ εἰργασμένοις τὴν πόλιν πάντα τἀγαθὰ
34 περὶ αὐτῶν λέγειν. τοῦτο μέντοι οὐ φεύγω, ἀλλ' ὁμολογῶ
σοι, εἰ βούλει, ἀντειπεῖν. θαυμάζω δὲ τί ἄν ποτ' ἐποίησας
συνειπών, ὁπότε ἀντειπεῖν φάσκων ἀπέκτεινας Πολέμαρχον.
195 Φέρε δή, τί ἄν, εἰ καὶ ἀδελφοὶ ὄντες ἐτυγχάνετε αὐτοῦ
ἢ καὶ ὑεῖς; ἀπεψηφίζεσθε; δεῖ γάρ, ὦ ἄνδρες δικασταί,
Ἐρατοσθένη δυοῖν θάτερον ἀποδεῖξαι, ἢ ὡς οὐκ ἀπήγαγεν
αὐτόν, ἢ ὡς δικαίως τοῦτ' ἔπραξεν. οὗτος δὲ ὡμολόγηκεν
ἀδίκως συλλαβεῖν, ὥστε ῥᾳδίαν ὑμῖν τὴν διαψήφισιν περὶ
35 αὐτοῦ πεποίηκε. καὶ μὲν δὴ πολλοὶ καὶ τῶν ἀστῶν καὶ
τῶν ξένων ἥκουσιν εἰσόμενοι τίνα γνώμην περὶ τούτων

---

33. ἀνιωμένου: impf. in time, like
ἡδομένου. — τούσδε: used of persons
actually present. — τότε: refers to the
session mentioned in §§ 6 and 26. —
ψῆφον: see Introd. § 49. — παρεῖναι:
the sessions of the Thirty's senate
were private, unlike the practice of
the democracy. — παρ' αὐτοῖς: in our
own homes or country; cf. chez nous.
The word-play in παρεῖναι and παρ'
αὐτοῖς εἶναι cannot be expressed in
English. — αὐτοῖς: the refl. pron. of
the third person here refers to the
first person, ἡμῖν. G. 995; H. 686.

34. φεύγω: evade, contest. Lysias
cannot prove that Eratosthenes did
not protest, but he grants the point
only to turn to the judges and make

it an argument against him. — ποτέ:
see on § 29. — φάσκων: though you
assert. — τί ἄν: on the ellipsis of the
verb, cf. § 20; XXXI. 28. The force
of ἄν is carried over to ἀπεψηφίζεσθε.
See on XVI. 8. — καὶ ἀδελφοὶ κτλ.:
the idea is 'you would not acquit a
man who had made such an admission even were he your nearest
kinsman.' — ὑεῖς: the forms with ι
(υἱεῖς etc.) do not belong to the prose
of the fifth and fourth century. See
App. — ὡμολόγηκεν: in fact he had
admitted (§ 25) only that the vote of
the Thirty was unjust.

35. τίνα γνώμην ἔξετε: this is to be
a test case and the vote is to be a political precedent. — μαθόντες: with the

ἕξετε. ὧν οἱ μὲν ὑμέτεροι ὄντες πολῖται μαθόντες ἀπίασιν
ὅτι ἢ δίκην δώσουσιν ὧν ἂν ἐξαμάρτωσιν, ἢ, πράξαντες
μὲν ὧν ἐφίενται, τύραννοι τῆς πόλεως ἔσονται, δυστυχή-
205 σαντες δὲ τὸ ἴσον ὑμῖν ἕξουσιν· ὅσοι δὲ ξένοι ἐπιδημοῦσιν,
εἴσονται πότερον ἀδίκως τοὺς τριάκοντα ἐκκηρύττουσιν ἐκ
τῶν πόλεων ἢ δικαίως. εἰ γὰρ δὴ αὐτοὶ οἱ κακῶς πεπονθότες λαβόντες ἀφήσουσιν, ἦ που σφᾶς γ' αὐτοὺς ἡγή-
36 σονται περιέργους ὑπὲρ ὑμῶν τιμωρουμένους.   οὐκ οὖν
210 δεινὸν εἰ τοὺς μὲν στρατηγούς, οἳ ἐνίκων ναυμαχοῦντες
ὅτε διὰ χειμῶνα οὐχ οἷοί τ' ἔφασαν εἶναι τοὺς ἐκ τῆς
θαλάττης ἀνελέσθαι, θανάτῳ ἐζημιώσατε, ἡγούμενοι
χρῆναι τῇ τῶν τεθνεώτων ἀρετῇ παρ' ἐκείνων δίκην λαβεῖν,
τούτους δέ, οἳ ἰδιῶται μὲν ὄντες καθ' ὅσον ἐδύναντο ἐποίη-

knowledge. — ὧν ἂν ἐξαμάρτωσιν :
whatever offence they shall have committed. The time of the aor. subjv.
here precedes that of δώσουσιν. GMT.
90. — ἢ πράξαντες κτλ.: the second
alternative, that of escape from
punishment, is subdivided, showing
what, in case Eratosthenes is acquitted, will be the results of success
(πράξαντες μέν) or failure (δυστυχήσαντες δέ) in future attempts at
tyranny. πράξαντες here = διαπρά-
ξαντες. On δυστυχήσαντες, cf. § 98. —
τὸ ἴσον: 'equal rights' with good
citizens ; cf. § 92. — ἐκκηρύττουσιν :
the regular word used of formal ban-
ishment, cf. §§ 95, 97. Some of the
Thirty may not have accompanied
the majority to Eleusis. See p. 26.
— ἦ που : of course ; an emphatic
way of beginning an apodosis, cf.
VII. 8. On the form of condition,
cf. § 11. — περιέργους : over-careful,
taking needless trouble.

36. εἰ : that. G. 1424 ; H. 926 ; cf.
§ 88. — εἰ, μέν, δέ : on the sequence,
cf. VII. 35. — στρατηγούς : the com-
manders at Arginusae, B.C. 406. —
ἐνίκων : were victorious. GMT. 37 ;
H. 827 a. — ὅτε : since. Logically,
ὅτε would introduce οἷοί τ' ἦσαν, but
ἔφασαν is introduced to put the excuse
into the mouths of the generals themselves. — τῇ ἀρετῇ : 'in honour of the
valour'; dat. of interest. — τούτους :
might be governed by a verb like οὐ
κολάσεσθε, in contrast to ἐζημιώσατε,
but after the complicated clauses
which follow there is an anacoluthon
(see on § 20), and οὐ χρὴ αὐτούς takes
up the threads and asks a new question. — ἰδιῶται κτλ. : as members of
the political clubs whose leaders be-
trayed, so it is supposed, the fleet at
Aegos Potami, the battle here referred to. — ἐποίησαν ἡττηθῆναι : is
contrasted with ἐνίκων, as is ὁμολογοῦσιν ἑκόντες κτλ. with διὰ χειμῶνα

215 σαν ἡττηθῆναι ναυμαχοῦντες, ἐπειδὴ δὲ εἰς τὴν ἀρχὴν
κατέστησαν, ὁμολογοῦσιν ἑκόντες πολλοὺς τῶν πολιτῶν
ἀκρίτους ἀποκτιννύναι, οὐκ ἄρα χρὴ αὐτοὺς καὶ τοὺς
παῖδας ὑφ' ὑμῶν ταῖς ἐσχάταις ζημίαις κολάζεσθαι;

37 Ἐγὼ τοίνυν, ὦ ἄνδρες δικασταί, ἠξίουν ἱκανὰ εἶναι τὰ
220 κατηγορημένα· μέχρι γὰρ τούτου νομίζω χρῆναι κατηγορεῖν, ἕως ἂν θανάτου δόξῃ τῷ φεύγοντι ἄξια εἰργάσθαι·
ταύτην γὰρ ἐσχάτην δίκην δυνάμεθα παρ' αὐτῶν λαβεῖν.
ὥστ' οὐκ οἶδ' ὅ τι δεῖ πολλὰ κατηγορεῖν τοιούτων ἀνδρῶν,
οἳ οὐδ' ἂν ὑπὲρ ἑνὸς ἑκάστου τῶν πεπραγμένων δὶς ἀπο-
38 θανόντες δίκην δοῦναι δύναιντ' ἀξίαν. οὐ γὰρ δὴ οὐδὲ
τοῦτο αὐτῷ προσήκει ποιῆσαι, ὅπερ ἐν τῇδε τῇ πόλει
εἰθισμένον ἐστί, πρὸς μὲν τὰ κατηγορούμενα μηδὲν ἀπολογεῖσθαι, περὶ δὲ σφῶν αὐτῶν ἕτερα λέγοντες ἐνίοτε
ἐξαπατῶσιν ὑμᾶς, ἀποδεικνύντες ὡς στρατιῶται ἀγαθοί
230 εἰσιν, ἢ ὡς πολλὰς τῶν πολεμίων ναῦς ἔλαβον τριηραρχήσαντες, ἢ ὡς πόλεις πολεμίας οὔσας φίλας ἐποίησαν·

... ἀνελέσθαι. — τοὺς παῖδας : the
visiting of the sins of the fathers upon
the children, is a commonplace in
Greek.

37. Here begins the argument ἔξω
τοῦ πράγματος. See p. 29. — ἕως ἂν
δόξῃ : until it shall appear. G. 1465 ;
H. 921. — τῷ φεύγοντι : dat. of
agent. — ταύτην : assimilated to the
gender of δίκην, this as the extreme
penalty. H.632 a ; cf. VII. 23, XXIV. 10.
— αὐτῶν : does not mean the Thirty
but refers, in the constructio ad
sensum, to the collective idea of
defendants in φεύγοντι. H. 633 ; cf.
§ 58, XXII. 2, and XXXI. 3, 9. — ὅ τι :
why. G. 1061 ; H. 719 c. — οὐδ' ἂν :
on the position of ἂν, which belongs

to δύναιντο, cf. § 82. The verb of the
prot. is ἀποθανόντες.

38. πρὸς τὰ κατηγορούμενα κτλ. :
on the custom, cf. § 20, and XXVI. 3,
αὐτὸν ἀκούω μὲν ὑπὲρ τῶν αὐτοῦ κατη-
γορουμένων διὰ βραχέων ἀπολογήσεσθαι,
λέξειν δὲ ὡς πολλὰ εἰς τὴν πόλιν ἀνηλώκασι. — λέγοντες ἐξαπατῶσιν : instead
of ἐξαπατᾶν in antithesis to ἀπολογεῖσθαι, the construction shifts to the
indic. which gives an actual narrative ; cf. XXII. 19. — τριηραρχήσαντες :
the trierarchy, like the choregy (see
on § 20) was one of the public duties
performed by rich citizens ; see Gow,
p. 133 ; Gilbert, Antiq. p. 370 ; and
Smith, Dict. Antiq. s.v. On Eratosthenes as trierarch, cf. § 42. — φίλας

39 ἐπεὶ κελεύετε αὐτὸν ἀποδεῖξαι ὅπου τοσούτους τῶν πολεμίων ἀπέκτειναν ὅσους τῶν πολιτῶν, ἢ ναῦς ὅπου τοσαύτας
ἔλαβον ὅσας αὐτοὶ παρέδοσαν, ἢ πόλιν ἥντινα τοιαύτην
40 προσεκτήσαντο οἵαν τὴν ὑμετέραν κατεδουλώσαντο. ἀλλὰ
γὰρ ὅπλα τῶν πολεμίων τοσαῦτα ἐσκύλευσαν ὅσαπερ
ὑμῶν ἀφείλοντο; ἀλλὰ τείχη τοιαῦτα εἷλον οἷα τὰ τῆς
ἑαυτῶν πατρίδος κατέσκαψαν; οἵτινες καὶ τὰ περὶ τὴν
Ἀττικὴν φρούρια καθεῖλον, καὶ ὑμῖν ἐδήλωσαν ὅτι οὐδὲ
240 τὸν Πειραιᾶ Λακεδαιμονίων προσταττόντων περιεῖλον, ἀλλ'
ὅτι ἑαυτοῖς τὴν ἀρχὴν οὕτω βεβαιοτέραν ἐνόμιζον εἶναι.
41 Πολλάκις οὖν ἐθαύμασα τῆς τόλμης τῶν λεγόντων ὑπὲρ
αὐτοῦ, πλὴν ὅταν ἐνθυμηθῶ ὅτι τῶν αὐτῶν ἐστιν αὐτούς τε
πάντα τὰ κακὰ ἐργάζεσθαι καὶ τοὺς τοιούτους ἐπαινεῖν.
42 οὐ γὰρ νῦν πρῶτον τῷ ὑμετέρῳ πλήθει τἀναντία ἔπραξεν,

ἐποίησαν: cf. Isocr. XVI. 21, πόλεις
... λόγῳ πείσας φίλας ὑμῖν ἐποίησε.

39. ἐπεί: states the reason for οὐ
προσήκει above. — κελεύετε: on the
imv. thus used, cf. Dem. XXXIX. 32,
ἐπεὶ σὺ δεῖξον ὅστις Ἀθηναίων κτλ. —
ὅσους τῶν πολιτῶν: for the number
slain, see on § 17. — παρέδοσαν: sc. at
the surrender of Athens to Sparta.

40. ἀλλὰ γάρ: often used in an
abrupt question, cf. § 83; the γάρ,
of course, is not translatable. ἀλλὰ
is used also without γάρ, XXIV. 24.
— ἀφείλοντο: cf. § 95. The Thirty
disarmed εἴ who were not in the
catalogue of the Three Thousand;
cf. Arist. Resp. Ath. 37. 2, ἀναιρεθέν-
τος δὲ Θηραμένους τὰ ὅπλα παρείλοντο
πάντων πλὴν τῶν τρισχιλίων. Cf. Xen.
Hellen. ii. 3. 20 ff., who sets the disarming before the death of Theramenes. On the gen. ὑμῶν, cf. XXIV.

13, and see G. 1118; H. 748 a. —
οἵτινες: used scornfully, 'why they,'
cf. ὅς, § 65, and XXXII. 13, 20. —
φρούρια: the facts are not known.
The object of the Thirty was to make
Attica an unfortified country. — τὸν
Πειραιᾶ: see on § 70. — περιεῖλον:
dismantled.

41. πολλάκις ἐθαύμασα: see on § 3;
hence the subjv. ἐνθυμηθῶ, not the opt.
G. 1268. — τῶν λεγόντων: does not
refer to their defenders in court
(συνήγοροι, cf. § 86, and p. 29), but
to their supporters in general. — τῶν
αὐτῶν: pred. gen. denoting nature.
H. 732 c. — τοὺς τοιούτους: i.e. those
who are, like them, κακοί.

42. οὐ γάρ: 'and he is κακός, for
this is not the first time,' etc. — τῷ
ὑμετέρῳ πλήθει: a common phrase for
the democracy, cf. § 43, and XXIV.
25, XXXI. 15. — τἀναντία ἔπραξεν:

ἀλλὰ καὶ ἐπὶ τῶν τετρακοσίων ἐν τῷ στρατοπέδῳ ὀλιγαρχίαν καθιστὰς ἔφευγεν ἐξ Ἑλλησπόντου τριήραρχος καταλιπὼν τὴν ναῦν, μετὰ Ἰατροκλέους καὶ ἑτέρων, ὧν τὰ ὀνόματα οὐδὲν δέομαι λέγειν. ἀφικόμενος δὲ δεῦρο τἀναντία
τοῖς βουλομένοις δημοκρατίαν εἶναι ἔπραττε. καὶ τούτων
μάρτυρας ὑμῖν παρέξομαι.

ΜΑΡΤΥΡΕΣ.

43   Τὸν μὲν τοίνυν μεταξὺ βίον αὐτοῦ παρήσω· ἐπειδὴ δὲ
ἡ ναυμαχία καὶ ἡ συμφορὰ τῇ πόλει ἐγένετο, δημοκρατίας
ἔτι οὔσης, ὅθεν τῆς στάσεως ἦρξαν, πέντε ἄνδρες ἔφοροι
255 κατέστησαν ὑπὸ τῶν καλουμένων ἑταίρων, συναγωγεῖς μὲν
τῶν πολιτῶν, ἄρχοντες δὲ τῶν συνωμοτῶν, ἐναντία δὲ τῷ

'worked against,' cf. § 64. — **ἐπὶ τῶν τετρακοσίων**: not to be taken lite-rally, but as applying to a time just before the Four Hundred were actu-ally established. While the oligarchi-cal intrigues were going on in the army and fleet at Samos (Thuc. viii. 47 ff.), the like work was being done in other places dependent on Athens (Thuc. viii. 64); and Eratosthenes probably engaged in it on the Helles-pont. Unsuccessful there, he de-serted his ship and joined the oli-garchs in Athens itself. — **καθιστάς**: impf. partic., cf. § 49, xxiv. 7; here of attempted action. G. 1255; H. 832. —**Ἰατροκλέους**: otherwise unknown.

43. μεταξύ: i.e. between the time of the Four Hundred (B.C. 412–11) and Aegos Potami (405).—**παρήσω**: had Lysias known of anything to Era-tosthenes's discredit, we should prob-ably learn of it here; see p. 24, and on xxxi. 20. — **ἡ ναυμαχία**

κτλ.: the accepted phrase for these events. The orators were care-ful how they reminded the people of their misfortunes; cf. xxxi. 8. — **ὅθεν ... ἦρξαν**: the antecedent of this clause is the next clause which in English would precede; cf. Isaeus vi. 8, ὡς δ' ἐξὸν αὐτῷ ταῦτ' ἔπραξεν, ὅθεν δικαιότατα ἡγοῦμαι τὰ τοιαῦτ' εἶναι μαν-θάνειν, τούτον ὑμῖν αὐτὸν παρέξομαι τὸν νόμον. — **ἔφοροι**: these men, chosen after the battle but before the sur-render of Athens (cf. § 44 f.; Curtius, Hist. of Greece, III, p. 563), were not constitutional officers, but were se-lected merely by the oligarchical clubs (ἑταιρεῖαι, cf. ἑταίρων) to be the direc-tors of their revolutionary move-ment. Their title, after that of the Spartan ephors, is significant. — **κατέστησαν**: in effect a passive, hence ὑπό. — **συνωμοτῶν**: cf. coniu-rati, and on their oaths of secrecy, cf. §§ 47 and 77.

ὑμετέρῳ πλήθει πράττοντες· ὧν Ἐρατοσθένης καὶ Κριτίας
44 ἦσαν. οὗτοι δὲ φυλάρχους τε ἐπὶ τὰς φυλὰς κατέστησαν,
καὶ ὅ τι δέοι χειροτονεῖσθαι καὶ οὕστινας χρείη ἄρχειν
260 παρήγγελλον, καὶ εἴ τι ἄλλο πράττειν βούλοιντο κύριοι
ἦσαν· οὕτως οὐχ ὑπὸ τῶν πολεμίων μόνον ἀλλὰ καὶ ὑπὸ
τούτων πολιτῶν ὄντων ἐπεβουλεύεσθε, ὅπως μήτ' ἀγαθὸν
45 μηδὲν ψηφιεῖσθε πολλῶν τε ἐνδεεῖς ἔσεσθε. τοῦτο γὰρ
καλῶς ἠπίσταντο, ὅτι ἄλλως μὲν οὐχ οἷοί τε ἔσονται περι-
265 γενέσθαι, κακῶς δὲ πραττόντων δυνήσονται· καὶ ὑμᾶς
ἡγοῦντο τῶν παρόντων κακῶν ἐπιθυμοῦντας ἀπαλλαγῆναι
46 περὶ τῶν μελλόντων οὐκ ἐνθυμήσεσθαι. ὡς τοίνυν τῶν
ἐφόρων ἐγένετο, μάρτυρας ὑμῖν παρέξομαι, οὐ τοὺς τότε
συμπράττοντας (οὐ γὰρ ἂν δυναίμην), ἀλλὰ τοὺς αὐτοῦ
47 Ἐρατοσθένους ἀκούσαντας. καίτοι κἀκεῖνοι εἰ ἐσωφρόνουν, κατεμαρτύρουν ἂν αὐτῶν καὶ τοὺς διδασκάλους τῶν
σφετέρων ἁμαρτημάτων σφόδρ' ἂν ἐκόλαζον, καὶ τοὺς
ὅρκους, εἰ ἐσωφρόνουν, οὐκ ἂν ἐπὶ μὲν τοῖς τῶν πολιτῶν
κακοῖς πιστοὺς ἐνόμιζον, ἐπὶ δὲ τοῖς τῆς πόλεως ἀγαθοῖς

---

44. φυλάρχους: not the cavalry
officers of xvi. 6, but men selected,
one in each φυλή, to 'work' under
the ephors, who managed the political 'machine.' See App. — ἐπί:
on this use, cf. xxviii. 14, οἱ μὲν γὰρ
ἐπὶ τοῦτ' ἐχειροτονήθησαν, ἵνα κτλ. —
ἄρχειν: to hold the offices. — παρήγγελλον: they passed the word; really
a military term, but here used as in
§ 76, where the working of this
'machine' is illustrated. — ὅπως . . .
ψηφιεῖσθε: object clause. G. 1372;
H. 885. See App. — πολλῶν: sc.
ἀγαθῶν. The chief reference is to the
necessaries of life, lacking during
the siege.

45. πραττόντων: sc. ὑμῶν. Cf.
§ 64, and on the omission, see G. 1568;
H. 972 a.

46. οὐ γὰρ κτλ.: their oaths (§ 47)
would prevent them from testifying.

47. κἀκεῖνοι: refers to τοὺς συμπράττοντας. — αὐτῶν: i.e. their leaders. — τοὺς ὅρκους: as the following
οὐκ refers to both the μέν and the δέ
clause succeding, a different oath is
meant in each case; in the first, the
oath sworn as a member of a ἑται-
ρεία (cf. on § 43); in the second the
oath of allegiance taken when a
young man came of age. — ἐπί: in
the case of, 'where it is a question
of.' Cf. Isocr. xviii. 24, καίτοι δεινὸν

275 ῥᾳδίως παρέβαινον. πρὸς μὲν οὖν τούτους τοσαῦτα λέγω,
τοὺς δὲ μάρτυράς μοι κάλει. καὶ ὑμεῖς ἀνάβητε.

ΜΑΡΤΥΡΕΣ.

48 Τῶν μὲν μαρτύρων ἀκηκόατε. τὸ δὲ τελευταῖον εἰς τὴν
ἀρχὴν καταστὰς ἀγαθοῦ μὲν οὐδενὸς μετέσχεν, ἄλλων δὲ
πολλῶν. καίτοι εἴπερ ἦν ἀνὴρ ἀγαθός, ἐχρῆν ἂν πρῶτον
280 μὲν μὴ παρανόμως ἄρχειν, ἔπειτα τῇ βουλῇ μηνυτὴν
γίγνεσθαι περὶ τῶν εἰσαγγελιῶν ἁπασῶν, ὅτι ψευδεῖς εἶεν,
καὶ Βάτραχος καὶ Αἰσχυλίδης οὐ τἀληθῆ μηνύουσιν, ἀλλὰ
τὰ ὑπὸ τῶν τριάκοντα πλασθέντα εἰσαγγέλλουσι, συγκεί-
49 μενα ἐπὶ τῇ τῶν πολιτῶν βλάβῃ. καὶ μὲν δή, ὦ ἄνδρες
285 δικασταί, ὅσοι κακόνοι ἦσαν τῷ ὑμετέρῳ πλήθει, οὐδὲν
ἔλαττον εἶχον σιωπῶντες· ἕτεροι γὰρ ἦσαν οἱ λέγοντες
καὶ πράττοντες ὧν οὐχ οἷόν τ᾽ ἦν μείζω κακὰ γενέσθαι τῇ
πόλει. ὁπόσοι δ᾽ εὐνοί φασιν εἶναι, πῶς οὐκ ἐνταῦθα
ἔδειξαν, αὐτοί τε τὰ βέλτιστα λέγοντες καὶ τοὺς ἐξαμαρτά-

εἰ ἐπὶ μὲν τοῖς ὑμετέροις αὐτῶν πράγμασιν
ἐμμένετε τοῖς ὅρκοις, ἐπὶ δὲ τῇ τούτου
συκοφαντίᾳ παραβαίνειν ἐπιχειρήσετε.—
παρέβαινον: the force of ἄν continues;
see on XVI. 8. — **κάλει** : addressed to
the κῆρυξ, 'crier'; cf. XXXI. 16.

48. ἀρχήν : sc. τὴν τῶν τριάκοντα,
for the ephors were not magistrates.
— **ἄλλων** : ironical for κακῶν. — **ἐχρῆν
ἄν**: 'he would have had.' See on § 32,
and for the use of ἄν here, cf. VII. 22,
and see G. 1401 ; H. 897 a. See
App. — **τῇ βουλῇ** : under the Thirty
the oligarchical senate took the place
of the democratic Heliastic courts.
— **μηνυτήν** : see on § 32. — **εἶεν** and
μηνύουσιν : on the change of mood
(GMT. 670), cf. Xen. Anab. ii. 1. 3,
οὗτοι ἔλεγον ὅτι Κῦρος μὲν τέθνηκεν,

Ἀριαῖος δὲ πεφευγὼς εἴη. — **Βάτραχος**:
he is called in [Lys.] VI. 45, ὁ πάντων
πονηρότατος, γενόμενος ἐπὶ τῶν τριάκοντα μηνυτής, where μηνυτής has its
usual infamous sense. Among the
lost orations of Lysias was one ὑπὲρ
τοῦ Βατράχου φόνου (Harp. s.v. φηγού-
σιον), possibly written on the death
of this same man. Nothing further
is known of Aeschylides. — **συγκεί-
μενα**: concocted; cf. III. 26, πάντα αὐτῷ
ταῦτα σύγκειται καὶ μεμηχάνηται.

49. καὶ μὲν δή : see on § 30. —
οὐδὲν ἔλαττον εἶχον : were none the
worse off, 'lost nothing.' See on
XXXII. 1. — **ὦν** : the antecedent is
the omitted obj. of πράττοντες, the
gen. depends on the comparative. —
πῶς : 'how was it that?' — **ἐξαμαρ-**

50 νοντας ἀποτρέποντες; ἴσως δ᾽ ἂν ἔχοι εἰπεῖν ὅτι ἐδεδοίκει,
καὶ ὑμῶν τοῦτο ἐνίοις ἱκανὸν ἔσται. ὅπως τοίνυν μὴ
φανήσεται ἔν τῳ λόγῳ τοῖς τριάκοντα ἐναντιούμενος· εἰ
δὲ μή, ἐνταυθοῖ δῆλος ἔσται ὅτι ἐκεῖνά τ᾽ αὐτῷ ἤρεσκε καὶ
τοσοῦτον ἐδύνατο ὥστε ἐναντιούμενος μηδὲν κακὸν παθεῖν
295 ὑπ᾽ αὐτῶν. χρῆν δ᾽ αὐτὸν ὑπὲρ τῆς ὑμετέρας σωτηρίας
ταύτην τὴν προθυμίαν ἔχειν, ἀλλὰ μὴ ὑπὲρ Θηραμένους,
51 ὃς εἰς ὑμᾶς πολλὰ ἐξήμαρτεν. ἀλλ᾽ οὗτος τὴν μὲν πόλιν
ἐχθρὰν ἐνόμιζεν εἶναι, τοὺς δ᾽ ὑμετέρους ἐχθροὺς φίλους,
ὡς ἀμφότερα ταῦτα ἐγὼ πολλοῖς τεκμηρίοις παραστήσω,
300 καὶ τὰς πρὸς ἀλλήλους διαφορὰς οὐχ ὑπὲρ ὑμῶν ἀλλ᾽
ὑπὲρ ἑαυτῶν γιγνομένας, ὁπότεροι μόνοι ταῦτα πράξουσι
52 καὶ τῆς πόλεως ἄρξουσι. εἰ γὰρ ὑπὲρ τῶν ἀδικουμένων
ἐστασίαζον, ποῦ κάλλιον ἦν ἀνδρὶ ἄρχοντι ἢ Θρασυ-

τάνοντας: for its time, see on καθιστάς, § 42, πυνθανεσθαι, §ι

50. ἐδεδοίκει: *was afraid*, and so
was silent on occasions when he
should have spoken ; *cf.* §§ 48 and
49. — **ὅπως φανήσεται** : on this Attic
colloquial use of the fut. indic. (G.
1352 ; H. 886 ; GMT. 271 ff.), *cf.* i.
21, quoted below. The thought is :
' He will say that he was afraid. But
then he must be careful not to let it
appear that he ever opposed (ἐναντιούμενος is impf., see on ἔχοντες, xvi. 5)
the Thirty ; otherwise (that is, if he
ever *did* oppose them) it will be clear
that he was not in fear of them, and
that he opposed them whenever he
wished, and was silent only when
he agreed with them.' — **ἔν τῳ λόγῳ** :
' anywhere in discussion.' — **εἰ δὲ μή**:
otherwise. The phrase is used in
Greek even when the clause would
not be negative if completed. G. 1417;

H. 906 b ; *cf.* i. 21, ὅπως τοίνυν ταῦτα
μηδεὶς ἀνθρώπων πεύσεται· εἰ δὲ μή (*i.e.*
if anybody does hear of it), οὐδέν σοι
κύριον ἔσται. — **δῆλος ἔσται ὅτι** : for
the personal use, see on xxxi. 6. —
ἐναντιούμενος : concessive.

51. ἀμφότερα: *i.e.* that the state was
his enemy and that your foes were
his friends. The orator proposes to
establish (παραστήσω) these facts καὶ
τὰς διαφορὰς ... γιγνομένας, ' and that
their dissensions were arising.' The
change here from the dir. obj. to the
partic. in indir. disc. is so harsh that
it is probable that after καί some
word like ἀποδείξω has fallen out.
See App. — **ὁπότεροι** : *i.e.* the advanced oligarchs under Critias or
the moderates under Theramenes. —
ταῦτα : used of something well understood, here the plans of the oligarchs ;
cf. ταῦτ᾽ ἔπραττεν, § 65.

52. κάλλιον ἦν : see on χρῆν, § 32.

βούλου Φυλὴν κατειληφότος, τότε ἐπιδείξασθαι τὴν αὑτοῦ
305 εὔνοιαν; ὃ δ᾽ ἀντὶ τοῦ ἐπαγγείλασθαί τι ἢ πρᾶξαι ἀγαθὸν
πρὸς τοὺς ἐπὶ Φυλῇ, ἐλθὼν μετὰ τῶν συναρχόντων εἰς
Σαλαμῖνα καὶ Ἐλευσῖνάδε τριακοσίους τῶν πολιτῶν ἀπήγαγεν εἰς τὸ δεσμωτήριον καὶ μιᾷ ψήφῳ αὐτῶν ἁπάντων
53 θάνατον κατεψηφίσατο. ἐπειδὴ δὲ εἰς τὸν Πειραιᾶ ἤλθομεν
310 καὶ αἱ ταραχαὶ γεγενημέναι ἦσαν καὶ περὶ τῶν διαλλαγῶν
οἱ λόγοι ἐγίγνοντο, πολλὰς ἑκάτεροι ἐλπίδας εἴχομεν πρὸς
ἀλλήλους ἔσεσθαι ὡς ἀμφότεροι ἐδείξαμεν. οἱ μὲν γὰρ
54 ἐκ Πειραιῶς κρείττους ὄντες εἴασαν αὐτοὺς ἀπελθεῖν· οἱ
δὲ εἰς τὸ ἄστυ ἐλθόντες τοὺς μὲν τριάκοντα ἐξέβαλον πλὴν

—τοὺς ἐπὶ Φυλῇ : ἐπί is used, not ἐν,
because the fort of Phyle lay high up
in the pass on Mount Parnes. See
App.—Σαλαμῖνα καὶ Ἐλευσῖνάδε : by
the wholesale slaughter of the citizens
of Salamis (cf. XIII. 44 ; Diod. xiv. 32)
and Eleusis (Xen. Hellen. ii. 4. 8 ff.)
the Thirty cleared these places in
order to use them as refuges in case
of need.— μιᾷ ψήφῳ: illegal, as being
contrary to the common procedure
which provided that, when several
parties were accused, a separate vote
should be taken on each ; cf. Xen.
Hellen. i. 7. 34 ; Plat. Apol. 32 B.
On the trial, see Curtius, Hist. of
Greece, III, p. 540 ff.

53. ἤλθομεν : observe how Lysias
here and in other speeches (e.g. XXIV.
25) constantly takes it for granted
that all his hearers belonged to the
patriotic party. Yet among them
and even among the present judges
may have been members of the Three
Thousand. So in the preceding section he speaks as if the Three Thousand had had nothing to do with

the condemnation of the Eleusinians ;
but see Xen. Hellen. ii. 4. 9 ff. —
—ταραχαί : disturbances, a purposely
mild word used of the battle between
Athenian citizens. — διαλλαγῶν : the
standing word for the reconciliation
brought about by Pausanias.— λόγοι:
negotiations. — πρὸς ἀλλήλους ἔσεσθαι ὡς : the expression is unusually
condensed : 'that we should be in
our relations to each other (πρός as
in § 23) as we both showed ourselves.'
It is clear that some idea like 'for-
getting and forgiving' is understood.
— αὐτούς : the party of the city is
meant, but this is a strange use of
αὐτός.   See App.

54. ἐλθόντες: when they had returned;
see on XVI. 4. — τοὺς τριάκοντα ἐξέβαλον : an exaggerated statement, the
truth being that the Thirty were merely deposed. Cf. Xen. Hellen. ii. 4. 23,
ἐψηφίσαντο (sc. οἱ τρισχίλιοι) ἐκείνους
μὲν (the Thirty) καταπαῦσαι, ἄλλους
δὲ ἑλέσθαι, and Arist. Resp. Ath. 38,
τοὺς μὲν τριάκοντα κατέλυσαν, αἱροῦνται
δὲ δέκα τῶν πολιτῶν αὐτοκράτορας ἐπὶ

315 Φείδωνος καὶ Ἐρατοσθένους, ἄρχοντας δὲ τοὺς ἐκείνοις
ἐχθίστους εἵλοντο, ἡγούμενοι δικαίως ἂν ὑπὸ τῶν αὐτῶν
τούς τε τριάκοντα μισεῖσθαι καὶ τοὺς ἐν Πειραιεῖ φιλεῖσθαι.
55 τούτων τοίνυν Φείδων γενόμενος καὶ Ἱπποκλῆς καὶ Ἐπι-
χάρης ὁ Λαμπτρεὺς καὶ ἕτεροι οἱ δοκοῦντες εἶναι ἐναντιώ-
320 τατοι Χαρικλεῖ καὶ Κριτίᾳ καὶ τῇ ἐκείνων ἑταιρείᾳ, ἐπειδὴ
αὐτοὶ εἰς τὴν ἀρχὴν κατέστησαν, πολὺ μείζω στάσιν καὶ
πόλεμον ἐπὶ τοὺς ἐν Πειραιεῖ τοῖς ἐξ ἄστεως ἐποίησαν.
56 ᾧ καὶ φανερῶς ἐπεδείξαντο ὅτι οὐχ ὑπὲρ τῶν ἐν Πειραιεῖ
οὐδ' ὑπὲρ τῶν ἀδίκως ἀπολλυμένων ἐστασίαζον, οὐδ' οἱ
325 τεθνεῶτες αὐτοὺς ἐλύπουν οὐδ' οἱ μέλλοντες ἀποθανεῖσθαι,
57 ἀλλ' οἱ μεῖζον δυνάμενοι καὶ θᾶττον πλουτοῦντες. λαβόντες γὰρ τὰς ἀρχὰς καὶ τὴν πόλιν ἀμφοτέροις ἐπολέμουν,
τοῖς τε τριάκοντα πάντα κακὰ εἰργασμένοις καὶ ὑμῖν

τὴν τοῦ πολέμου κατάλυσιν. The majority of the Thirty then withdrew
to Eleusis. — ἄρχοντας : the Ten
just mentioned in the quotation
from Aristotle ; so Xen. *ibid.* 24,
καὶ εἵλοντο δέκα, ἕνα ἀπὸ φυλῆς. —
ἐκείνοις : *i.e.* to the Thirty as a government. Eratosthenes and Phidon
clearly belonged to a more moderate
set than Critias and Charicles. Having coupled them together, Lysias
goes on to show that Phidon (and
by inference Eratosthenes) was not a
true patriot, else he would have been
true to the purpose for which he was
elected, namely to reconcile the
parties (*cf.* § 58).

55. τούτων : *i.e.* the Ten. — γενόμενος : on the number, see on § 12.
— Ἱπποκλῆς : unknown, unless he
be the naval officer of Thuc. viii. 13.
— Λαμπτρεύς : Lamptrae was a deme
of the tribe Erechtheïs. — ἐναντιώτα-

τοι : Epichares, however, was a
senator under the Thirty ; so Andoc.
I. 95, who in § 99 calls him their tool
and a sycophant. — Χαρικλεῖ : he with
Critias was chief of the advanced
oligarchs ; *cf.* Arist. *Pol.* 1305 B, 25,
ἐν τοῖς τριάκοντα οἱ περὶ Χαρικλέα ἴσχυ-
σαν τοὺς τριάκοντα δημαγωγοῦντες. —
ἑταιρείᾳ : see on § 43. — αὐτοί : emphatic : ' they in their turn.' —
πολὺ . . . ἐποίησαν : on the facts, *cf.*
Xen. *Hellen.* ii. 4. 24 ff. ; Arist. *Resp.*
Ath. 38.

57. λαβόντες : *taking possession of;*
the usual word of legal succession to
an office would be παραλαβόντες,
which indeed is used of these very
Ten by Arist. *Resp. Ath.* 38. — τοῖς
τε τριάκοντα : there is nothing in Xen.
to suggest actual hostilities between
the Ten and the Thirty. Both sent
to Sparta for help against Thrasybulus, *Hellen.* ii. 4. 28. But it is

πάντα κακὰ πεπονθόσι. καίτοι τοῦτο πᾶσι δῆλον ἦν, ὅτι
330 εἰ μὲν ἐκεῖνοι δικαίως ἔφευγον, ὑμεῖς ἀδίκως, εἰ δ' ὑμεῖς
δικαίως, οἱ τριάκοντα ἀδίκως· οὐ γὰρ δὴ ἑτέρων ἔργων
αἰτίαν λαβόντες ἐκ τῆς πόλεως ἐξέπεσον, ἀλλὰ τούτων.
58 ὥστε σφόδρα χρὴ ὀργίζεσθαι, ὅτι Φείδων αἱρεθεὶς ὑμᾶς
διαλλάξαι καὶ καταγαγεῖν τῶν αὐτῶν ἔργων Ἐρατοσθένει
335 μετεῖχε καὶ τῇ αὐτῇ γνώμῃ τοὺς μὲν κρείττους αὐτῶν δι'
ὑμᾶς κακῶς ποιεῖν ἕτοιμος ἦν, ὑμῖν δὲ ἀδίκως φεύγουσιν
οὐκ ἠθέλησεν ἀποδοῦναι τὴν πόλιν, ἀλλ' ἐλθὼν εἰς Λακε-
δαίμονα ἔπειθεν αὐτοὺς στρατεύεσθαι, διαβάλλων ὅτι
Βοιωτῶν ἡ πόλις ἔσται, καὶ ἄλλα λέγων οἷς ᾤετο πείσειν
59 μάλιστα. οὐ δυνάμενος δὲ τούτων τυχεῖν, εἴτε καὶ τῶν
ἱερῶν ἐμποδὼν ὄντων εἴτε καὶ αὐτῶν οὐ βουλομένων,
ἑκατὸν τάλαντα ἐδανείσατο, ἵνα ἔχοι ἐπικούρους μισθού-

clear that the Ten held a middle
ground. — **ἔφευγον**: *were in exile*,
the pres. approaching the sense of
the perf. in this sense. GMT. 27
and 37. — **αἰτίαν λαβόντες**: instead of
the usual αἰτίαν ἔχοντες, *cf.* XXII. 18.
— **ἐξέπεσον**: used as pass. of ἐξέβαλον.
G. 1241; H. 820.

58. αἱρεθεὶς ὑμᾶς διαλλάξαι κτλ.:
cf. § 55 and Arist. *Resp. Ath.* 38
(quoted on § 54), who adds οἱ δὲ παραλαβόντες τὴν ἀρχὴν ἐφ' οἷς μὲν ᾑρέθησαν
οὐκ ἔπραττον, ἐπρέσβευσαν δ' εἰς Λακε-
δαίμονα βοήθειαν μεταπεμπόμενοι καὶ
χρήματα δανειζόμενοι. — **τῇ αὐτῇ γνώμῃ**:
sc. Ἐρατοσθένει. Lysias's object in
thus bringing forward Phidon is
twofold; to show that Phidon and
Eratosthenes were hand and glove,
both equally opposed to the patriots,
and also to prevent Phidon from
pointing to any merits of his own

when appearing as συνήγορος (see
Introd. § 36) for Eratosthenes. —
τοὺς κρείττους αὐτῶν: the main body
of the Thirty, then in Eleusis. — **δι'
ὑμᾶς**: *through your means; cf.* § 60
and VII. 5. — **οὐκ ἠθέλησεν**: 'he
could not bring himself,' *cf.* XXXI. 1;
but below in § 69 it means as usual
he refused. *Cf.* VII. 35; XXXII. 12. —
ἔπειθεν: of attempted action. G. 1255;
H. 832. — **αὐτούς**: for the number, see
on αὐτῶν, § 37. — **Βοιωτῶν κτλ.**: this
would excite Spartan jealousy, and it
was a credible story, for Thrasybulus
had set out from Thebes to seize
Phyle, with the collusion of the Thebans (Diod. xiv. 32). See on § 95.

59. ἱερῶν ἐμποδὼν ὄντων: this re-
calls the well-known reason for the
Spartans' refusal to aid the Athenians promptly at Marathon. *Cf.*
Hdt. vi. 106.

σθαι, καὶ Λύσανδρον ἄρχοντα ᾐτήσατο, εὐνούστατον μὲν
ὄντα τῇ ὀλιγαρχίᾳ, κακονούστατον δὲ τῇ πόλει, μισοῦντα
60 δὲ μάλιστα τοὺς ἐν Πειραιεῖ. μισθωσάμενοι δὲ πάντας
ἀνθρώπους ἐπ' ὀλέθρῳ τῆς πόλεως καὶ ὅλας πόλεις ἐπάγοντες καὶ τελευτῶντες Λακεδαιμονίους καὶ τῶν συμμάχων
ὁπόσους ἐδύναντο πεῖσαι, οὐ διαλλάξαι ἀλλ' ἀπολέσαι
παρεσκευάζοντο τὴν πόλιν, εἰ μὴ δι' ἄνδρας ἀγαθούς, οἷς
350 ὑμεῖς δηλώσατε παρὰ τῶν ἐχθρῶν δίκην λαβόντες, ὅτι καὶ
61 ἐκείνοις χάριν ἀποδώσετε. ταῦτα δὲ ἐπίστασθε μὲν καὶ
αὐτοί, καὶ οἶδ' ὅτι οὐ δεῖ μάρτυρας παρασχέσθαι· ὅμως
δέ· ἐγώ τε γὰρ δέομαι ἀναπαύσασθαι, ὑμῶν τ' ἐνίοις ἥδιον
ὡς πλείστων τοὺς αὐτοὺς λόγους ἀκούειν.

ΜΑΡΤΥΡΕΣ.

62 Φέρε δὴ καὶ περὶ Θηραμένους ὡς ἂν δύνωμαι διὰ

60. πάντας ἀνθρώπους : on the
meaning, without the article, see on
XVI. 15, and *cf.* Dem. VIII. 5, Φίλιπ-
πος συσκευάζεται πάντας ἀνθρώπους ἐφ'
ἡμᾶς. — ὅλας πόλεις : an effective exaggeration, hardly supported by the
facts. See App. — τελευτῶντες : the
partic. as adv.; *cf.* XXXII. 11, 12.
G. 1564; H. 968 a. — εἰ μὴ διά: means
'had it not been for.' G. 1414; H.
905 a, 2; GMT. 476, 3. *Cf.* Isocr.
V. 92, φαίνονται γὰρ κἀκεῖνοι κρατήσαν-
τες ἂν τῶν βασιλέως πραγμάτων, εἰ μὴ
διὰ Κῦρον. Gildersleeve, *A. J. P.*
XVI, p. 396, explains the ellipsis as
that of the negative involved in the
leading clause. Thus, εἰ μὴ διά = εἰ
μὴ οὐκ ἀπώλεσαν, *unless they had failed
to destroy.* For the apod. without
ἄν, see on ἐγίγνετο, VII. 13; ἔμελλε, VII.
24. — ἄνδρας ἀγαθούς : both avowed

and secret friends of Athens are
meant, as in Argos, Thebes, Corinth,
and elsewhere, including all who
were jealous of Lysander. The patriotic party is of course included, and
perhaps that of the second Ten. — οἷς
δηλώσατε : on this idiomatic use of
the rel. with imv., *cf.* § 99. Translate
by *must.*

61. ὅμως δέ : *sc.* παρέξομαι. — πλείστων : on the gen. of the person, see
G. 1103; H. 742 c.

62. φέρε δή : *come now*, a phrase
frequently prefixed to the subjv. of
exhortation. G. 1345. — Θηραμένους :
Eratosthenes, himself a moderate
oligarch, would naturally class himself with Theramenes, the victim of
Critias and a martyr, in popular
esteem, to the good cause. Lysias
must therefore paint Theramenes in

βραχυτάτων διδάξω. δέομαι δ' ὑμῶν ἀκοῦσαι ὑπέρ τ'
ἐμαυτοῦ καὶ τῆς πόλεως. καὶ μηδενὶ τοῦτο παραστῇ
ὡς Ἐρατοσθένους κινδυνεύοντος Θηραμένους κατηγορῶ·
πυνθάνομαι γὰρ ταῦτα ἀπολογήσεσθαι αὐτὸν ὅτι ἐκείνῳ
63 φίλος ἦν καὶ τῶν αὐτῶν ἔργων μετεῖχε. καίτοι σφόδρ' ἂν
αὐτὸν οἶμαι μετὰ Θεμιστοκλέους πολιτευόμενον προσ-
ποιεῖσθαι πράττειν ὅπως οἰκοδομηθήσεται τὰ τείχη, ὁπότε
καὶ μετὰ Θηραμένους ὅπως καθαιρεθήσεται. οὐ γάρ μοι
δοκοῦσιν ἴσου ἄξιοι γεγενῆσθαι· ὃ μὲν γὰρ Λακεδαιμο-
365 νίων ἀκόντων ᾠκοδόμησεν αὐτά, οὗτος δὲ τοὺς πολίτας
64 ἐξαπατήσας καθεῖλε. περιέστηκεν οὖν τῇ πόλει τοὐναντίον ἢ ὡς εἰκὸς ἦν. ἄξιον μὲν γὰρ ἦν καὶ τοὺς φίλους
τοὺς Θηραμένους προσαπολωλέναι, πλὴν εἴ τις ἐτύγχανεν

the darkest colours, to show the
people that they did not know their
idol ; hence what follows must be
taken with a good deal of salt. See
App. — τέ: on its position, *cf.* § 30.
— παραστῇ ... κατηγορῶ: 'let nobody fancy that my speech is directed
against Theramenes, although Eratosthenes is the man who is on trial.'
Cf. Dem. XVIII. 15, εἶτα κατηγορεῖ μὲν
ἐμοῦ, κρίνει (*he brings to trial*) δὲ τοῦ-
τονί. Lysias anticipates that he will
be charged by the other side with
leaving the real question which is at
issue. See App. For παραστῇ in this
sense, *cf.* VII. 17. — κινδυνεύοντος:
this verb is often used of defendants.

63. καίτοι σφόδρα ... γεγενῆσθαι:
spoken with sneering irony, and made
more bitter by σφόδρα, to which emphatic word ἄν is attached. 'He
says he acted with Theramenes. Of
course, then, if he had been in the
government along with Themistocles

he would pretend, I suppose, that he
joined him in building the walls,
since he joined even (observe the καί
after ὁπότε, *cf.* XXII. 16) a person like
Theramenes in pulling them down.
Of course he would, for Themistocles
and Theramenes were men of very
different metal' (the inference being
that, as Themistocles was the better,
Eratosthenes would have urged that
he did even more to help him than
to help Theramenes). The litotes in
οὐκ ἴσου ἄξιοι and the scoffing tone in
μοι δοκοῦσιν should be noted. — ἐξαπατήσας: for the facts, *cf.* § 68 ff.

64. περιέστηκεν: *has come about.*
Cf. Thuc. vi. 24. 2, τοὐναντίον περιέστη
αὐτῷ. — εἰκὸς ἦν: 'might have been
expected'; on the omission of ἄν here
and with ἄξιον ἦν, see on § 32. — πλὴν
εἰ: *unless*, where πλήν represents the
apodosis. GMT. 477; *cf.* Plat. *Apol.*
18 C, οὐδὲ τὰ ὀνόματα οἷόν τε αὐτῶν
εἰδέναι, πλὴν εἴ τις κωμῳδιοποιὸς τυγχά-

ἐκείνῳ τἀναντία πράττων· νῦν δὲ ὁρῶ τάς τε ἀπολογίας
370 εἰς ἐκεῖνον ἀναφερομένας τούς τ' ἐκείνῳ συνόντας τιμᾶσθαι
πειρωμένους, ὥσπερ πολλῶν ἀγαθῶν αἰτίου ἀλλ' οὐ
65 μεγάλων κακῶν γεγενημένου. ὃς πρῶτον μὲν τῆς προτέρας
ὀλιγαρχίας αἰτιώτατος ἐγένετο, πείσας ὑμᾶς τὴν ἐπὶ τῶν
τετρακοσίων πολιτείαν ἑλέσθαι. καὶ ὁ μὲν πατὴρ αὐτοῦ
375 τῶν προβούλων ὢν ταῦτ' ἔπραττεν, αὐτὸς δὲ δοκῶν εὐνού-
στατος εἶναι τοῖς πράγμασι στρατηγὸς ὑπ' αὐτῶν ᾑρέθη.
66 καὶ ἕως μὲν ἐτιμᾶτο, πιστὸν ἑαυτὸν παρεῖχεν· ἐπειδὴ δὲ
Πείσανδρον μὲν καὶ Κάλλαισχρον καὶ ἑτέρους ἑώρα
προτέρους αὑτοῦ γιγνομένους, τὸ δὲ ὑμέτερον πλῆθος οὐκέτι
380 βουλόμενον τούτων ἀκροᾶσθαι, τότ' ἤδη διά τε τὸν πρὸς

νει ὤν. — **τἀναντία πράττων** : cf. § 42.
The aor. partic. could not have been
used ; see on § 27. — **γεγενημένου** : sc.
αὐτοῦ. See on § 45.

65. ὅς : for the meaning, see on
οἵτινες, § 40. — **αἰτιώτατος** : an exaggeration. The orator Antiphon (see
Introd. § 14) was the real author of
the scheme according to Thucydides
(viii. 68), who, however, mentions
with him Pisander and Theramenes
as the chief leaders in the establish-
ment of the Four Hundred ; so Arist.
Resp. Ath. 32. In xxv. 9 Lysias mentions Phrynichus and Pisander (and in
XIII. 73 only Phrynichus), as the found-
ers of the Four Hundred. In Xen.
Hellen. ii. 3. 30, Critias says : οὗτος
(Theramenes) κατὰ τὸν πατέρα Ἅγνωνα
(*taking pattern by his father Hagnon*)
προπετέστατος (*most headlong*) ἐγένετο
τὴν δημοκρατίαν μεταστῆσαι εἰς τοὺς
τετρακοσίους. — **προβούλων** : ' com-
missioners.' They were at first ten.
Afterwards, with the twenty συγγρα-
φεῖς (Thuc. viii. 1. 3 ; 67. 1 ; Arist.

Resp. Ath. 29), they matured the
measures which led to the election
of the Four Hundred. — **ταῦτα** : for
the meaning, see on § 51. — **τοῖς**
πράγμασι : *i.e.* the government of the
Four Hundred. — **ὑπ' αὐτῶν** : for the
facts, see App.

66. πιστόν : *loyal, sc.* to the Four
Hundred. — **ἐπειδὴ** κτλ. : fear and
jealousy, according to Lysias, were
the only motives influencing Theramenes, and this is also the view of
Thucydides (viii. 89). But he adds
that the pretext for assailing the
Four Hundred was that the Five
Thousand were a name, not a reality. This ' pretext ' is made the sole
reason for Theramenes's action in
Arist. *Resp. Ath.* 33, αἰτιώτατοι δ' ἐγένοντο τῆς καταλύσεως (*sc.* of the Four
Hundred) Ἀριστοκράτης καὶ Θηραμένης, οὐ συναρεσκόμενοι τοῖς ὑπὸ τῶν
τετρακοσίων γιγνομένοις· ἅπαντα γὰρ
δι' αὐτῶν ἔπραττον, οὐδὲν ἐπαναφέροντες
τοῖς πεντακισχιλίοις. — **τότ' ἤδη** : tum
demum, *then, and not till then.*

ἐκείνους φθόνον καὶ τὸ παρ' ὑμῶν δέος μετέσχε τῶν
67 Ἀριστοκράτους ἔργων. βουλόμενος δὲ τῷ ὑμετέρῳ πλήθει
δοκεῖν πιστὸς εἶναι, Ἀντιφῶντα καὶ Ἀρχεπτόλεμον φιλτά-
τους ὄντας αὐτῷ κατηγορῶν ἀπέκτεινεν, εἰς τοσοῦτον δὲ
385 κακίας ἦλθεν, ὥστε ἅμα μὲν διὰ τὴν πρὸς ἐκείνους πίστιν
ὑμᾶς κατεδουλώσατο, διὰ δὲ τὴν πρὸς ὑμᾶς τοὺς φίλους
68 ἀπώλεσε. τιμώμενος δὲ καὶ τῶν μεγίστων ἀξιούμενος,
αὐτὸς ἐπαγγειλάμενος σώσειν τὴν πόλιν αὐτὸς ἀπώλεσε,
φάσκων πρᾶγμα ηὑρηκέναι μέγα καὶ πολλοῦ ἄξιον. ὑπέ-
390 σχετο δὲ εἰρήνην ποιήσειν μήτε ὅμηρα δοὺς μήτε τὰ τείχη
καθελὼν μήτε τὰς ναῦς παραδούς· ταῦτα δὲ εἰπεῖν μὲν
69 οὐδενὶ ἠθέλησεν, ἐκέλευσε δὲ αὐτῷ πιστεύειν. ὑμεῖς δέ, ὦ
ἄνδρες Ἀθηναῖοι, πραττούσης μὲν τῆς ἐν Ἀρείῳ πάγῳ
βουλῆς σωτήρια, ἀντιλεγόντων δὲ πολλῶν Θηραμένει,

—Ἀριστοκράτους: son of Scellius,
was a taxiarch under the Four Hundred (Thuc. viii. 92. 4), and was a
noted ' aristocrat.' Aristophanes
puns on his name, *Aves*, 125, ΕΠ.
ἀριστοκρατεῖσθαι δῆλος εἶ ζητῶν. ΕΥ.
ἐγώ; ἥκιστα· καὶ τὸν Σκελλίου βδελύτ-
τομαι. He was one of the generals
put to death after Arginusae.

67. Ἀντιφῶντα: see on § 65. —
Ἀρχεπτόλεμον: son of Hippodamus
(Ar. *Eq*. 327), and a favourer of peace
with Sparta.—κατηγορῶν: the decree,
moved by Andron, by which they
were accused of high treason, is given
in Ps.-Plut. *Vitae X Oratt*., 834 A.
The charge was of intrigue with
Sparta. — ἀπέκτεινεν: not, of course,
with his own hand; *cf*. § 23.

68. τιμώμενος κτλ.: Lysias skips
to 405 b.c., for there was nothing in
the record of Theramenes as general

from 411 to 408 with which to find
fault. Of his behaviour in the accusation of the generals (*cf*. § 36), Lysias
could say nothing without accusing
the people of a judicial murder.—
αὐτός: *of his own accord* (*cf*. § 70,
xxxi. 15), repeated with ἀπώλεσε to
emphasize the attack ; *cf*. Xen. *Anab*.
iii. 2. 4, αὐτὸς ὀμόσας ἡμῖν, αὐτὸς δεξιὰς
δούς, αὐτὸς ἐξαπατήσας.—ὑπέσχετο δέ:
there is nothing adversative in δέ
here to the English mind ; *cf*. § 9.
One might expect γάρ.

69. πραττούσης ... σωτήρια: the
Areopagus had at this period legally
no political power, but appears, in
the case of this crisis and of some
others, to have used its influence in
an informal way. Probably it was
trying here to reconcile the parties.
— πολλῶν: among them was Cleo-
phon, as we know from xiii. 7 ff.—

395 εἰδότες δὲ ὅτι οἱ μὲν ἄλλοι ἄνθρωποι τῶν πολεμίων ἕνεκα
τἀπόρρητα ποιοῦνται, ἐκεῖνος δ' ἐν τοῖς αὑτοῦ πολίταις
οὐκ ἠθέλησεν εἰπεῖν ταῦτα ἃ πρὸς τοὺς πολεμίους ἔμελλεν
ἐρεῖν, ὅμως ἐπετρέψατε αὐτῷ πατρίδα καὶ παῖδας καὶ
70 γυναῖκας καὶ ὑμᾶς αὐτούς. ὃ δὲ ὧν μὲν ὑπέσχετο οὐδὲν
400 ἔπραξεν, οὕτως δὲ ἐνετεθύμητο ὡς χρὴ μικρὰν καὶ ἀσθενῆ
γενέσθαι τὴν πόλιν, ὥστε περὶ ὧν οὐδεὶς πώποτε οὔτε τῶν
πολεμίων ἐμνήσθη οὔτε τῶν πολιτῶν ἤλπισε, ταῦθ' ὑμᾶς
ἔπεισε πρᾶξαι, οὐχ ὑπὸ Λακεδαιμονίων ἀναγκαζόμενος,

ἐν τοῖς κτλ.: see on § 6. — ἐπετρέψατε:
this was the occasion when Theramenes was sent alone, πρεσβευτὴν αὐτο-
κράτορα, xiii. 10. Lysias says nothing
here of the facts that ambassadors
had already been sent to the Spartans
to sue for peace on favourable terms
(cf. xiii. 8, Xen. Hellen. ii. 2. 11 ff.),
and that Theramenes, after his return (from Lysander, not from Sparta), was sent to Sparta with nine
others (Xen. Hellen. ii. 2. 17), who
finally brought the Spartan terms to
Athens.

70. ἐνετεθύμητο: 'was so firmly
convinced.' — οὔτε τῶν πολεμίων
ἐμνήσθη κτλ.: in answer to the first
embassy mentioned above, the Spartans had required that the long walls
should be taken down for ten stadia
(xiii. 8, Xen. Hellen. ii. 2. 15). The
final terms, doubtless previously
agreed upon between the oligarchs
and Lysander, required the entire
demolition of those walls, the dis-
mantling of the Piraeus, the surrender of all but twelve ships, the return
of the exiles, and that Athens should
join the Spartan alliance; Xen. ibid.

20, cf. Plut. Lys. 14. These were the
terms on which peace was made at
an assembly held probably in April,
404 B.C. Aristotle says that it was
stipulated that Athens should assume
its ancient form of government, and
this is the only condition mentioned
in Resp. Ath. 34. 3, τῆς εἰρήνης γενομένης αὐτοῖς ἐφ' ᾧ τε πολιτεύσονται τὴν
πάτριον πολιτείαν. Cf. Diod. xiv. 3. It
does not seem likely that this provision was among the actual con-
ditions of peace; at any rate, the
question of changing the form of
government (τὴν ὑπάρχουσαν πολιτείαν
καταλῦσαι) was not considered until a
second assembly, the one mentioned
in the next section, which was held
in the summer or early in September.
In this speech, therefore, Lysias apparently confuses the two meetings;
but the knowledge possessed by his
hearers might acquit him of intentional deceit. He states the terms
more exactly in xiii. 14. — ἔπεισε: sc.
in his speech announcing the terms,
Xen. Hellen. ii. 2. 22, λέγων ὡς χρὴ πείθεσθαι τοῖς Λακεδαιμονίοις καὶ τὰ τείχη
περιαιρεῖν. — οὐχ κτλ.: see on § 71.

ἀλλ' αὐτὸς ἐκείνοις ἐπαγγελλόμενος, τοῦ τε Πειραιῶς τὰ
405 τείχη περιελεῖν καὶ τὴν ὑπάρχουσαν πολιτείαν καταλῦσαι,
εὖ εἰδὼς ὅτι, εἰ μὴ πασῶν τῶν ἐλπίδων ἀποστερήσεσθε,
71 ταχεῖαν παρ' αὐτοῦ τὴν τιμωρίαν κομιεῖσθε. ‖ καὶ τὸ
τελευταῖον, ὦ ἄνδρες δικασταί, οὐ πρότερον εἴασε τὴν
ἐκκλησίαν γενέσθαι, ἕως ὁ ὡμολογημένος ὑπ' ἐκείνων
410 καιρὸς ἐπιμελῶς ὑπ' αὐτοῦ ἐτηρήθη καὶ μετεπέμψατο μὲν
τὰς μετὰ Λυσάνδρου ναῦς ἐκ Σάμου, ἐπεδήμησε δὲ τὸ τῶν
72 πολεμίων στρατόπεδον. τότε δὲ τούτων ὑπαρχόντων καὶ
παρόντος Λυσάνδρου καὶ Φιλοχάρους καὶ Μιλτιάδου περὶ
τῆς πολιτείας τὴν ἐκκλησίαν ἐποίουν, ἵνα μήτε ῥήτωρ
415 αὐτοῖς μηδεὶς ἐναντιοῖτο μηδὲ διαπειλοῖτο ὑμεῖς τε μὴ τὰ
τῇ πόλει συμφέροντα ἕλοισθε, ἀλλὰ τἀκείνοις δοκοῦντα

71. Here Aristotle (*Resp. Ath.* 34. 3) differs from Lysias. According to the former, Theramenes, who with other moderates had wished for a return to the old government (the constitution of Solon?), opposed the institution of the Thirty : Λυσάνδρου δὲ προσθεμένου (*joining*) τοῖς ὀλιγαρχικοῖς, καταπλαγεὶς ὁ δῆμος ἠναγκάσθη χειροτονεῖν τὴν ὀλιγαρχίαν. So Diod. xiv. 3, with the addition that Lysander threatened to kill Theramenes unless he ceased his opposition. Xenophon gives no details of this second assembly, *Hellen.* ii. 3. 2. — οὐ πρότερον... ἕως : instead of the usual οὐ πρότερον πρίν. — ἐκείνων : *i.e.* the Spartans. — καιρός : *the right moment*. Probably this was the surrender of Samos. — ἐκ Σάμου : Lysander had therefore sailed thither after the capitulation of Athens to reduce this island ; so Diod. xiv. 3. According to Xen. *Hellen.* ii. 3. 3, he did not go until

after the institution of the Thirty. See App. — ἐπεδήμησε : 'had entered the city.' The impf. would denote a state of being in the city. G. 1260 ; H. 841 ; *cf.* vii. 36, xxiii. 15. On the augment, see on ἐξεκλησίαζετε, § 73. — στρατόπεδον : *i.e.* the army of King Agis ; *cf.* Xen. *Hellen.* ii. 3. 3.

72. τούτων ὑπαρχόντων : it was all a previously arranged affair. — παρόντος : for the sing., see on ἐξιοῦσι, § 12. — Φιλοχάρους : an Athenian, like Miltiades, as the names indicate. They may have been leaders among the oligarchs, sent to fetch Lysander when the time was ripe. — ῥήτωρ : a term for any one who addressed the assembly, whether or not a practised speaker ; see on xxxi. 27. — ἐναντιοῖτο : on the tense of this verb and of διαπειλοῖτο as contrasted with the aorists following, see App. to xvi. 6.

73 ψηφίσαισθε. ἀναστὰς δὲ Θηραμένης ἐκέλευσεν ὑμᾶς
τριάκοντα ἀνδράσιν ἐπιτρέψαι τὴν πόλιν καὶ τῇ πολιτείᾳ
χρῆσθαι ἣν Δρακοντίδης ἀπέφαινεν. ὑμεῖς δ' ὅμως καὶ
420 οὕτω διακείμενοι ἐθορυβεῖτε ὡς οὐ ποιήσοντες ταῦτα·
ἐγιγνώσκετε γὰρ ὅτι περὶ δουλείας καὶ ἐλευθερίας ἐν
74 ἐκείνῃ τῇ ἡμέρᾳ ἐξεκλησιάζετε. Θηραμένης δέ, ὦ ἄνδρες
δικασταί (καὶ τούτων ὑμᾶς αὐτοὺς μάρτυρας παρέχομαι),
εἶπεν ὅτι οὐδὲν αὐτῷ μέλοι τοῦ ὑμετέρου θορύβου, ἐπειδὴ
425 πολλοὺς μὲν Ἀθηναίων εἰδείη τοὺς τὰ ὅμοια πράττοντας
αὐτῷ, δοκοῦντα δὲ Λυσάνδρῳ καὶ Λακεδαιμονίοις λέγοι.
μετ' ἐκεῖνον δὲ Λύσανδρος ἀναστὰς ἄλλα τε πολλὰ εἶπε
καὶ ὅτι παρασπόνδους ὑμᾶς ἔχοι, καὶ ὅτι οὐ περὶ πολιτείας
ὑμῖν ἔσται ἀλλὰ περὶ σωτηρίας, εἰ μὴ ποιήσαιθ' ἃ Θηρα-

73. **Δρακοντίδης:** cf. Arist. *Resp. Ath.* 34. 3, ἔγραψε (*moved*) δὲ τὸ ψήφισμα (*i.e.* the decree establishing the Thirty) Δρακοντίδης Ἀφιδναῖος. He was a low fellow, often cast in suits, and the butt of comic poets; cf. Schol. Ar.*Vesp.* 157. He was one of the Thirty. — ἀπέφαινεν: 'proceeded to declare'; the proper word would be ἔγραφε (see Arist. just quoted), but Lysias selects a word which shows that their plan was all arranged beforehand. — ὅμως ... διακείμενοι: 'in spite of being in such a plight.' — ἐθορυβεῖτε: the regular word used of large bodies of people, signifying sometimes approval, sometimes disapproval; here the latter, as in Plat. *Apol.* 21 A, καὶ ὅπερ λέγω μὴ θορυβεῖτε, ὦ ἄνδρες. — ὡς οὐ ποιήσοντες: a construction closely resembling indir. disc. Cf. xxxii. 23, and see GMT. 919. — ἐξεκλησιάζετε: on the augment, see G. 543; H. 362 a; and

App. On the tense in indir. disc., cf. vii. 12. G. 1489; H. 936.

74. **παρέχομαι:** an appeal to the judges as witnesses was not unusual. Cf. vii. 25, xxii. 12, and Plat. *Apol.* 19 D, μάρτυρας δὲ αὐτοὺς ὑμῶν τοὺς πολλοὺς παρέχομαι. — δοκοῦντα κτλ.: a shameless admission. On the fact, cf. Critias's words, Xen. *Hellen.* ii. 3. 25, σὺν τῇ Λακεδαιμονίων γνώμῃ τήνδε τὴν πολιτείαν καθίσταμεν. — παρασπόνδους: because the walls had not been wholly demolished to conform to the treaty. Cf. Plut. *Lys.* 15, ἔφη τὴν πόλιν εἰληφέναι παρασπονδοῦσαν· ἑστάναι γὰρ τὰ τείχη τῶν ἡμερῶν, ἐν αἷς ἔδει καθῃρῆσθαι, παρῳχηκμένων.—οὐ περὶ...ἔσται: 'it would not be a question of forms of government.' Cf. Ar. *Eq.* 87, περὶ πότου (*drinking*) γοῦν ἐστί σοι;—ἔσται, ποιήσαισθε, κελεύοι: on the change of mood, see G. 1498. — ἀλλὰ περὶ σωτηρίας: 'but a matter of life or death.'

75 μένης κελεύοι. τῶν δ᾽ ἐν τῇ ἐκκλησίᾳ ὅσοι ἄνδρες ἀγαθοὶ
ἦσαν, γνόντες τὴν παρασκευὴν καὶ τὴν ἀνάγκην, οἳ μὲν
αὐτοῦ μένοντες ἡσυχίαν ἦγον, οἳ δ᾽ ᾤχοντο ἀπιόντες, τοῦτο
γοῦν σφίσιν αὐτοῖς συνειδότες ὅτι οὐδὲν κακὸν τῇ πόλει
ἐψηφίσαντο· ὀλίγοι δέ τινες καὶ πονηροὶ καὶ κακῶς βου-
76 λευόμενοι τὰ προσταχθέντα ἐχειροτόνησαν· παρήγγελτο
γὰρ αὐτοῖς δέκα μὲν οὓς Θηραμένης ἀπέδειξε χειροτονῆ-
σαι, δέκα δὲ οὓς οἱ καθεστηκότες ἔφοροι κελεύοιεν, δέκα δ᾽
ἐκ τῶν παρόντων· οὕτω γὰρ τὴν ὑμετέραν ἀσθένειαν ἑώρων
καὶ τὴν αὐτῶν δύναμιν ἠπίσταντο, ὥστε πρότερον ᾔδεσαν
77 τὰ μέλλοντα ἐν τῇ ἐκκλησίᾳ πραχθήσεσθαι. ταῦτα δὲ οὐκ
ἐμοὶ δεῖ πιστεῦσαι, ἀλλὰ ἐκείνῳ· πάντα γὰρ τὰ ὑπ᾽ ἐμοῦ
εἰρημένα ἐν τῇ βουλῇ ἀπολογούμενος ἔλεγεν, ὀνειδίζων
μὲν τοῖς φεύγουσιν, ὅτι δι᾽ αὐτὸν κατέλθοιεν, οὐδὲν φροντιζόντων Λακεδαιμονίων, ὀνειδίζων δὲ τοῖς τῆς πολιτείας
445 μετέχουσιν, ὅτι πάντων τῶν πεπραγμένων τοῖς εἰρημένοις

---

75. παρασκευήν: 'the plot.' It
was a 'put-up job'; see on VII. 18.—
ᾤχοντο ἀπιόντες: *were off and away;*
see on § 13.—**γοῦν:** *at least, at any
rate.*

76. Lysias is our only authority
for the details given in this section.—
παρήγγελτο: for the meaning, see
on § 44.—**ἀπέδειξε:** *nominated*, indir.
disc., but not changed to the opt.,
since it is a dependent aorist indicative. G. 1499; H. 935 c. Of the
ten nominated by Theramenes one
was perhaps Eratosthenes; all probably shared Theramenes's moderate
views. — **καθεστηκότες:** sc. ὑπὸ τῶν
ἑταίρων, cf. § 43.—**κελεύοιεν:** indir.
disc. like ἀπέδειξε, but here changed
since it represents the pres. indicative. — **ἐκ τῶν παρόντων:** a hollow

concession, for the assembly was
intimidated. — **πρότερον:** *beforehand,*
i.e. in their clubs.

77. ἐν τῇ βουλῇ: on the occasion
when Theramenes's name was struck
from the list. *Cf.* Xen. Ḥellen. ii.
3. 24 ff. But his speech, as given by
Xenophon, contains nothing of what
now follows in Lysias. See App. —
δι᾽ αὐτόν: on this use of διά, see
on § 58. — **οὐδὲν φροντιζόντων:** 'car-
ing nothing about it.' The exiles
returned after the surrender (see on
§ 70). The Spartans personally cared
only to make Athens weak, and it
was only after the intrigues of Lysander and the Athenian oligarchs that
the terms of peace were fixed in
detail as stated on § 70. — **τοῖς εἰρημένοις τρόποις ὑπ᾽ ἐμοῦ:** called by

τρόποις ὑπ' ἐμοῦ αὐτοῖς αἴτιος γεγενημένος τοιούτων
τυγχάνοι, πολλὰς πίστεις αὐτοῖς ἔργῳ δεδωκὼς καὶ παρ'
78 ἐκείνων ὅρκους εἰληφώς. καὶ τοσούτων καὶ ἑτέρων κακῶν
καὶ αἰσχρῶν καὶ πάλαι καὶ νεωστὶ καὶ μικρῶν καὶ μεγά-
450 λων αἰτίῳ γεγενημένῳ τολμήσουσιν αὐτοὺς φίλους ὄντας
ἀποφαίνειν, οὐχ ὑπὲρ ὑμῶν ἀποθανόντος Θηραμένους ἀλλ'
ὑπὲρ τῆς αὑτοῦ πονηρίας, καὶ δικαίως μὲν ἐν ὀλιγαρχίᾳ
δίκην δόντος — ἤδη γὰρ αὐτὴν κατέλυσε — δικαίως δ' ἂν
ἐν δημοκρατίᾳ· δὶς γὰρ ὑμᾶς κατεδουλώσατο, τῶν μὲν
455 παρόντων καταφρονῶν, τῶν δὲ ἀπόντων ἐπιθυμῶν, καὶ τῷ
καλλίστῳ ὀνόματι χρώμενος δεινοτάτων ἔργων διδάσκαλος
καταστάς.

79　Περὶ μὲν τοίνυν Θηραμένους ἱκανά μοί ἐστι τὰ κατη-
γορημένα· ἥκει δ' ὑμῖν ἐκεῖνος ὁ καιρός, ἐν ᾧ δεῖ συγγνώ-

Frohberger a unique instance in
Lysias of the separation of a pre-
positional phrase from the partic. to
which it belongs. For the normal
order, see three lines above. G. 969;
H. 667 a. See App. — τοιούτων :
'such a return.' — πίστεις : for the
meaning, see on § 27.

78. καί: its frequent repetition
here (ἀθροισμός) adds great weight.
— τολμήσουσιν : on the pl., see p. 28,
note 25. — ὑπέρ : repeated for the
sake of parallelism ; before πονηρίας
it has the meaning of ἕνεκα, cf. § 37.
— οὐχ ὑπὲρ ... Θηραμένους : though
it was not for you that Theramenes died. — ἤδη ... κατέλυσε : the
government of the Four Hundred is
meant; cf. § 66. See App. — ἄν : belongs to δόντος, understood from
above. See on § 20 ; and for the
apod. thus expressed by a partic.,

G. 1418. The idea is that, had he
lived, he would have been justly
punished by the restored democracy
after the fall of the Thirty. — τῶν
μὲν παρόντων ... ἐπιθυμῶν : the
'paronomasia' and 'homoeoteleuton'
(see the lexicon) lend the air of a
proverb to this passage; cf. Theopom-
pus ap. Athen. 261 A, τῶν μὲν ὑπαρχόντων ἡμέλουν, τῶν δ' ἀπόντων ἐπεθύμουν.
This 'belittling what you have and
wanting what you have not' is the
opposite of the characteristic of the
ἀνὴρ σώφρων (see on μετρίως, XVI. 3).
Cf. [Isocr.] I. 29, στέργε τὰ παρόντα,
ζήτει δὲ τὰ βέλτιστα. Nicias bids the
Athenians before the Sicilian expedition μὴ δυσέρωτας εἶναι τῶν ἀπόντων,
Thuc. vi. 13. — τῷ καλλίστῳ ὀνόματι :
Theramenes had come forward as
σωτήρ, cf. § 68.

79. ἐκεῖνος ὁ καιρός : 'that long-

460 μην καὶ ἔλεον μὴ εἶναι ἐν ταῖς ὑμετέραις γνώμαις, ἀλλὰ
παρὰ Ἐρατοσθένους καὶ τῶν τούτου συναρχόντων δίκην
λαβεῖν, μηδὲ μαχομένους μὲν κρείττους εἶναι τῶν πολε-
80 μίων, ψηφιζομένους δὲ ἥττους τῶν ἐχθρῶν. μηδ' ὧν φασι
μέλλειν πράξειν πλείω χάριν αὐτοῖς ἴστε, ἢ ὧν ἐποίησαν
465 ὀργίζεσθε· μηδ' ἀποῦσι μὲν τοῖς τριάκοντα ἐπιβουλεύετε,
παρόντας δ' ἀφῆτε· μηδὲ τῆς τύχης, ἢ τούτους παρέδωκε
τῇ πόλει, κάκιον ὑμεῖς ὑμῖν αὐτοῖς βοηθήσητε.

81 Κατηγόρηται μὲν Ἐρατοσθένους καὶ τῶν τούτου φίλων,
οἷς τὰς ἀπολογίας ἀνοίσει καὶ μεθ' ὧν αὐτῷ ταῦτα πέ-
470 πρακται. ὁ μέντοι ἀγὼν οὐκ ἐξ ἴσου τῇ πόλει καὶ Ἐρατο-
σθένει· οὗτος μὲν γὰρ κατήγορος καὶ δικαστὴς αὐτὸς ἦν
τῶν κρινομένων, ἡμεῖς δὲ νυνὶ εἰς κατηγορίαν καὶ ἀπολο-
82 γίαν καθέσταμεν. καὶ οὗτοι μὲν τοὺς οὐδὲν ἀδικοῦντας

expected hour.'—**πολεμίων**: this, like
ἐχθρῶν, refers to the Thirty, in the
civil war and in the political or legal
arena.—**ψηφιζομένους**: 'at the ballot
box.'

80. **ὧν**: assimilated like the following ὧν to the case of the omitted
antec., which would be a causal gen.
—**ὀργίζεσθε**: imv., like ἴστε and ἐπιβουλεύετε. Note the change in tense:
ἐπιβουλεύετε, 'keep plotting'; ἀφῆτε
(subjv.), 'let them off' (once for all).
G. 1346; H. 874 a. On the gen. with
ὀργίζεσθαι, see on xxxi. 11.—**ἀποῦσι**:
the main body of the Tyrants was still
in Eleusis.—**τῆς τύχης** κτλ.: cf. Isocr.
v. 152, αἰσχρόν ἐστι καλῶς τῆς τύχης
ἡγουμένης ἀπολειφθῆναι, καὶ μὴ παρασχεῖν σαυτὸν εἰς ὃ βούλεταί σε προαγα-
γεῖν.

81. 'My accusation is finished.
But Eratosthenes and his country do

not stand on equal terms. He is
granted a fair trial; the patriots
were condemned unheard.'—**κατηγόρηται μέν**: see App.—**οἷς ἀνοίσει**:
a rare construction (cf. vii. 17), instead of the usual εἰς and acc., §§ 28,
64.—**οὐκ ἐξ ἴσου**: not on an equality.
Cf. Ar. Ran. 867, οὐκ ἐξ ἴσου γάρ ἐστιν
ἀγὼν νῷν.—**αὐτός**: 'in one and the
same person,' like idem. Under the
Thirty the functions of the civil
courts seem to have been entirely
suspended. The Thirty had power
to kill anybody whose name was
not in the catalogue (see on § 17,
Arist. Resp. Ath. 37; Xen. Hellen.
ii. 3. 51), and their senate anybody
whose name was in the catalogue
(Xen. ibid.). In general it was a
time of lawlessness; see on vii. 27. —
ἡμεῖς...καθέσταμεν: 'we have settled
down to the regular forms of law.'

ἀκρίτους ἀπέκτειναν, ὑμεῖς δὲ τοὺς ἀπολέσαντας τὴν πόλιν
475 κατὰ τὸν νόμον ἀξιοῦτε κρίνειν, παρ' ὧν οὐδ' ἂν παρανόμως βουλόμενοι δίκην λαμβάνειν ἀξίαν τῶν ἀδικημάτων
ὧν τὴν πόλιν ἠδικήκασι λάβοιτε.   τί γὰρ ἂν παθόντες
83 δίκην τὴν ἀξίαν εἴησαν τῶν ἔργων δεδωκότες; πότερον εἰ
αὐτοὺς ἀποκτείναιτε καὶ τοὺς παῖδας αὐτῶν, ἱκανὴν ἂν τοῦ
480 φόνου δίκην λάβοιμεν, ὧν οὗτοι πατέρας καὶ υἷς καὶ
ἀδελφοὺς ἀκρίτους ἀπέκτειναν; ἀλλὰ γὰρ εἰ τὰ χρήματα
τὰ φανερὰ δημεύσαιτε, καλῶς ἂν ἔχοι ἢ τῇ πόλει, ἧς οὗτοι
πολλὰ εἰλήφασιν, ἢ τοῖς ἰδιώταις, ὧν τὰς οἰκίας ἐξεπόρ-
84 θησαν; ἐπειδὴ τοίνυν πάντα ποιοῦντες δίκην παρ' αὐτῶν
485 ἱκανὴν οὐκ ἂν δύναισθε λαβεῖν, πῶς οὐκ αἰσχρὸν ὑμῖν καὶ
ἡντινοῦν ἀπολιπεῖν, ἥντινά τις βούλοιτο παρὰ τούτων
λαμβάνειν; πᾶν δ' ἄν μοι δοκεῖ τολμῆσαι, ὅστις νυνί,
οὐχ ἑτέρων ὄντων τῶν δικαστῶν ἀλλ' αὐτῶν τῶν κακῶς
πεπονθότων, ἥκει ἀπολογησόμενος πρὸς αὐτοὺς τοὺς
490 μάρτυρας τῆς τούτου πονηρίας· τοσοῦτον ἢ ὑμῶν κατα-

---

82. Further reasons why the issue
between Eratosthenes and the city is
not a fair one. — οὐδ' ἄν: on the
position of ἄν (which belongs to
λάβοιτε), cf. § 37. So in the following
τί γὰρ ἄν. — ἀδικημάτων: depends on
ἀξίαν.

83. ὧν: its antecedent is the subj.
of λάβοιμεν. — υἷς: on the form, see
on § 34. — ἀλλὰ γάρ: see on § 40.
— φανερά: a word used, speaking
roughly, of 'real' in distinction from
'personal' property; see on xxxii. 4.
— καλῶς ἂν ἔχοι: would it be enough?
Cf. Eur. Hel. 1579, ἔτ', ὦ ξέν', εἰς τὸ
πρόσθεν, ἢ καλῶς ἔχει, πλεύσωμεν; ...
ὁ δ' εἶφ'· ἅλις μοι. — ἧς: for the case,
see on § 40.

84. ἡντινοῦν: any whatsoever. H.
1002 a; cf. xxii. 15. — βούλοιτο: an
opt. without ἄν in a rel. clause de-
pending on an expression of propriety (here impropriety) in a primary
tense (GMT. 555). Cf. Plat. Rep. 332 A,
ἀποδοτέον οὐδ' ὁπωστιοῦν τότε, ὁπότε τις
μὴ σωφρόνως ἀπαιτοῖ, a deposit should
not be returned on any account when
the person who asks it back is not in
his right mind. — πᾶν: 'anything and
everything.' — ὅστις: for the meaning,
see on xxiii. 12. — ἥκει ἀπολογησόμενος: cf. § 22, and see p. 27, note 20.
— τοσοῦτον: sums up the foregoing
and draws the inference; hence without γάρ. See on τοιαῦτα, § 1, and cf.
οὕτως, xxxii. 21.

85 πεφρόνηκεν ἢ ἑτέροις πεπίστευκεν. ὧν ἀμφοτέρων ἄξιον
ἐπιμεληθῆναι, ἐνθυμουμένους ὅτι οὔτ' ἂν ἐκεῖνα ἐδύναντο
ποιεῖν μὴ ἑτέρων συμπραττόντων, οὔτ' ἂν νῦν ἐπεχείρησαν
ἐλθεῖν μὴ ὑπὸ τῶν αὐτῶν οἰόμενοι σωθήσεσθαι, οἳ οὐ τού-
495 τοις ἤκουσι βοηθήσοντες, ἀλλὰ ἡγούμενοι πολλὴν ἄδειαν
σφίσιν ἔσεσθαι καὶ τοῦ λοιποῦ ποιεῖν ὅ τι ἂν βούλωνται,
εἰ τοὺς μεγίστων κακῶν αἰτίους λαβόντες ἀφήσετε.

86 Ἀλλὰ καὶ τῶν συνερούντων αὐτοῖς ἄξιον θαυμάζειν,
πότερον ὡς καλοὶ κἀγαθοὶ αἰτήσονται, τὴν αὐτῶν ἀρετὴν
500 πλείονος ἀξίαν ἀποφαίνοντες τῆς τούτων πονηρίας—ἐβουλόμην μέντ' ἂν αὐτοὺς οὕτω προθύμους εἶναι σώζειν τὴν
πόλιν, ὥσπερ οὗτοι ἀπολλύναι—ἢ ὡς δεινοὶ λέγειν ἀπολο-
γήσονται καὶ τὰ τούτων ἔργα πολλοῦ ἄξια ἀποφανοῦσιν·
ἀλλ' οὐχ ὑπὲρ ὑμῶν οὐδεὶς αὐτῶν οὐδὲ τὰ δίκαια πώποτε
505 ἐπεχείρησεν εἰπεῖν.

87 Ἀλλὰ τοὺς μάρτυρας ἄξιον ἰδεῖν, οἳ τούτοις μαρτυροῦν-
τες αὐτῶν κατηγοροῦσι, σφόδρα ἐπιλήσμονας καὶ εὐήθεις
νομίζοντες ὑμᾶς εἶναι, εἰ διὰ μὲν τοῦ ὑμετέρου πλήθους

---

85. **ἐκεῖνα**: 'those crimes.' — **ἐδύναντο**: impf., used of repeated actions
in *past* time in a supposition contrary to fact. G. 1397 ; H. 895 a. *Cf.*
XIII. 36, *εἰ μὲν οὖν ἐν τῷ δικαστηρίῳ
ἐκρίνοντο* (*if their several trials had
been held in court*), *ῥᾳδίως ἂν ἐσῴζοντο*.
— **ἐλθεῖν**: sc. before the court. — **οἱ ...
βοηθήσοντες**: former members of the
oligarchical party are meant, present,
acc. to Lysias, not to speak for Eratosthenes, but to see how this test case
was going to be decided. — **ἄδειαν**:
immunity. — **καί**: *also.* — **ποιεῖν**: depends on ἄδειαν as in XXII. 19, but in
XXX. 34 we have τοῦ ποιεῖν. See App.

86. **ἀλλὰ καί**: transition to a brief

attack on the συνήγοροι (*cf.* XXXI. 32,
and see Introd. § 36), some of whom
may be included under οἱ ... βοηθήσοντες, § 85. — **καλοὶ κἀγαθοί**: Lysias
employs sneeringly one of the terms
regularly applied by oligarchs to
themselves. Other terms were βέλ-
τιστοι, χρηστοί. — **αἰτήσονται**: the
simple verb is used of συνήγοροι also
in XXX. 33, but more commonly ἐξαιτεῖσθαι, as in XXX. 31. — **ἐβουλόμην
ἄν**: *I could wish;* see on § 22. — **οὐδὲ
τὰ δίκαια**: *not even what was just.*

87. **εὐήθεις**: a common ironical
term signifying ἄφρονας, as in XVI. 6.—
διά: observe the use of gen. and acc.
here. The δέ clause is best subordi-

ἀδεῶς ἡγοῦνται τοὺς τριάκοντα σώσειν, διὰ δὲ Ἐρατοσθένη
510 καὶ τοὺς συνάρχοντας αὐτοῦ δεινὸν ἦν καὶ τῶν τεθνεώτων
88 ἐπ' ἐκφορὰν ἐλθεῖν. καίτοι οὗτοι μὲν σωθέντες πάλιν ἂν
δύναιντο τὴν πόλιν ἀπολέσαι· ἐκεῖνοι δέ, οὓς οὗτοι ἀπώλεσαν, τελευτήσαντες τὸν βίον πέρας ἔχουσι τῆς τῶν
ἐχθρῶν τιμωρίας. οὐκ οὖν δεινὸν εἰ τῶν μὲν ἀδίκως
515 τεθνεώτων οἱ φίλοι συναπώλλυντο, αὐτοῖς δὲ τοῖς τὴν
πόλιν ἀπολέσασιν ἐπ' ἐκφορὰν πολλοὶ ἥξουσιν, ὁπότε
89 βοηθεῖν τοσοῦτοι παρασκευάζονται; καὶ μὲν δὴ πολλῷ
ῥᾷον ἡγοῦμαι εἶναι ὑπὲρ ὧν ὑμεῖς ἐπάσχετε ἀντειπεῖν ἢ
ὑπὲρ ὧν οὗτοι πεποιήκασιν ἀπολογήσασθαι. καίτοι λέ-
520 γουσιν ὡς Ἐρατοσθένει ἐλάχιστα τῶν τριάκοντα κακὰ
εἴργασται, καὶ διὰ τοῦτο αὐτὸν ἀξιοῦσι σωθῆναι· ὅτι δὲ
τῶν ἄλλων Ἑλλήνων πλεῖστα εἰς ὑμᾶς ἐξημάρτηκεν, οὐκ
οἴονται χρῆναι αὐτὸν ἀπολέσθαι;

nated by using *while* and *yet* in translation. — **ἐπί**: of the object sought.
G. 1210, 3 c ; H. 799, 3 c. — **ἐκφοράν**:
see on §§ 18, 21, 96, *cf.* Aeschines III.
235, (οἱ τριάκοντα) οὐδ' ἐπὶ τὰς ταφὰς
καὶ ἐκφορὰς τῶν τελευτησάντων εἴων τοὺς
προσήκοντας παραγίγνεσθαι.

88. καίτοι: *and yet.* — **πέρας ἔχουσι**
... **τιμωρίας:** *have no opportunity left
for taking vengeance on their foes.*
The gen. ἐχθρῶν is objective. The
phrase πέρας ἔχειν means 'be at an
end,' *cf.* Lycurg. *Leocr.* 60, περὶ τὰς
πόλεις (*in the case of cities*) συμβαίνει
πέρας ἔχειν τὴν ἀτυχίαν ὅταν ἀνάστατοι
(*utterly overthrown*) γένωνται. The
Thirty, if spared, might return and
revenge themselves by setting up
another oligarchy (πάλιν ... ἀπολέσαι); the patriot dead were helpless.
— **δεινὸν εἰ**: see on § 36. — **συναπώλ**-

λυντο: for the tense, see on ἐλάμβανον,
§ 27. — **ἐπ' ἐκφορὰν κτλ.**: bitterly sarcastic. Lysias takes a favourable
verdict for granted.

89. καὶ μὲν δή: *and yet certainly.*
— **ῥᾷον εἶναι**: the inf. is impf. in
time here and the clause represents
ῥᾷον ἦν, *it were easier* (without ἄν,
see on § 32), but as understood after
ἤ it is present, representing ἐστί. —
— **ἀντειπεῖν**: sc. in answer to what
the Thirty were doing. — **τῶν τριάκοντα**: part. genitive. *Cf.* XXI. 6,
ἡ ναῦς ἄριστά μοι ἔπλει παντὸς τοῦ στρατοπέδου. — **τῶν ἄλλων Ἑλλήνων**: *i.e.*
all except the Thirty. The genitive,
considered as partitive, is, strictly
speaking, illogical, since Eratosthenes
was one of the Thirty. But this use
of τῶν ἄλλων after a superlative is
common enough from Homer down.

future west n-d

90 Ὑμεῖς δὲ δείξετε ἥντινα γνώμην ἔχετε περὶ τῶν πραγ-
525 μάτων. εἰ μὲν γὰρ τούτου καταψηφιεῖσθε, δῆλοι ἔσεσθε
ὡς ὀργιζόμενοι τοῖς πεπραγμένοις· εἰ δὲ ἀποψηφιεῖσθε,
ὀφθήσεσθε τῶν αὐτῶν ἔργων ἐπιθυμηταὶ τούτοις ὄντες, καὶ
οὐχ ἕξετε λέγειν ὅτι τὰ ὑπὸ τῶν τριάκοντα προσταχθέντα
91 ἐποιεῖτε· νυνὶ μὲν γὰρ οὐδεὶς ὑμᾶς ἀναγκάζει παρὰ τὴν
530 ὑμετέραν γνώμην ἀποψηφίζεσθαι. ὥστε συμβουλεύω μὴ
τούτων ἀποψηφισαμένους ὑμῶν αὐτῶν καταψηφίσασθαι.
μηδ᾽ οἴεσθε κρύβδην εἶναι τὴν ψῆφον· φανερὰν γὰρ τῇ
πόλει τὴν ὑμετέραν γνώμην ποιήσετε.

92 Βούλομαι δὲ ὀλίγα ἑκατέρους ἀναμνήσας καταβαίνειν,
535 τούς τε ἐξ ἄστεως καὶ τοὺς ἐκ Πειραιῶς, ἵνα τὰς ὑμῖν διὰ
τούτον γεγενημένας συμφορὰς παραδείγματα ἔχοντες τὴν

Cf. *Il.* ii. 673, Νιρεύς, ὃς κάλλιστος ἀνὴρ
ὑπὸ Ἴλιον ἦλθεν τῶν ἄλλων Δαναῶν,
Plat. *Rep.* 603 E, ἀνὴρ ἐπιεικὴς ... υἱὸν
ἀπολέσας ... ῥᾷστα οἴσει τῶν ἄλλων.
Cf. expressions like Thuc. i. 50. 2,
ναυμαχία ... μεγίστη δὴ τῶν πρὸ αὑτῆς.
Tacitus imitates the Greek usage; *cf.*
Agr. 34, hi ceterorum Britan-
norum fugacissimi. *Cf.* Milton's
"Adam, the goodliest of men since
born | His sons, the fairest of her
daughters Eve." In Greek, the genitive is thought to be ablatival, or
is sometimes called the genitive of
separation, expressing the point from
which the comparison is made. See
App.

90. δείξετε: in this and the following section Lysias is really addressing
τοὺς ἐξ ἄστεως, hence the menacing
fut. tense here and in the following
protases, for which see on § 11. —
δῆλοι ἔσεσθε ὡς ὀργιζόμενοι: a case
of ὡς with the partic. in indir. dis-

course. *Cf.* Xen. *Anab.* i. 5. 9, δῆλος
ἦν Κῦρος ὡς σπεύδων, *Cyrus showed
that he was hastening.* G. 1593;
GMT. 916. On the personal use of
δῆλος here, see G. 1589; H. 981. —
τὰ ὑπὸ ... ἐποιεῖτε: with reference to
Eratosthenes's defence in §§ 25, 29.

91. νυνί: more emphatic than νῦν.
—κρύβδην: of course the actual balloting was, as usual, to be secret.
The meaning is that the result of the
vote will be recognized as a test of
the feelings of the City party. On
adverbs in the predicate as here, *cf.*
Dem. xix. 239, οὐ γὰρ εἰ κρύβδην ἐστὶν
ἡ ψῆφος, λήσει τοὺς θεούς, and Isocr.
iv. 5, ὥστ᾽ ἤδη μάτην εἶναι τὸ μεμνῆσθαι
περὶ τούτων. See App.

92. The orator abandons his threat-
ening tone, and in the following sections appeals to the sense of honour
and of shame in the City party; then
he arouses the spirit of vengeance in
the party of the Piraeus. — καταβαί-

ψῆφον φέρητε. καὶ πρῶτον μὲν ὅσοι ἐξ ἄστεώς ἐστε,
σκέψασθε ὅτι ὑπὸ τούτων οὕτω σφόδρα ἤρχεσθε, ὥστε
ἀδελφοῖς καὶ ὑέσι καὶ πολίταις ἠναγκάζεσθε πολεμεῖν
540 τοιοῦτον πόλεμον, ἐν ᾧ ἡττηθέντες μὲν τοῖς νικήσασι τὸ
93 ἴσον ἔχετε, νικήσαντες δ' ἂν τούτοις ἐδουλεύετε. καὶ τοὺς
ἰδίους οἴκους οὗτοι μὲν ἐκ τῶν πραγμάτων μεγάλους ἐκτή-
σαντο, ὑμεῖς δὲ διὰ τὸν πρὸς ἀλλήλους πόλεμον ἐλάττους
ἔχετε· συνωφελεῖσθαι μὲν γὰρ ὑμᾶς οὐκ ἠξίουν, συνδια-
545 βάλλεσθαι δ' ἠνάγκαζον, εἰς τοσοῦτον ὑπεροψίας ἐλθόντες
ὥστε οὐ τῶν ἀγαθῶν κοινούμενοι πιστοὺς ὑμᾶς ἐκτῶντο,
94 ἀλλὰ τῶν ὀνειδῶν μεταδιδόντες εὔνους ᾤοντο εἶναι. ἀνθ'
ὧν ὑμεῖς νῦν ἐν τῷ θαρραλέῳ ὄντες καθ' ὅσον δύνασθε
καὶ ὑπὲρ ὑμῶν αὐτῶν καὶ ὑπὲρ τῶν ἐκ Πειραιῶς τιμωρή-
550 σασθε, ἐνθυμηθέντες μὲν ὅτι ὑπὸ τούτων πονηροτάτων
ὄντων ἤρχεσθε, ἐνθυμηθέντες δὲ ὅτι μετ' ἀνδρῶν νῦν
ἀρίστων πολιτεύεσθε καὶ τοῖς πολεμίοις μάχεσθε καὶ

νειν : sc. ἀπὸ τοῦ βήματος. — παραδείγματα : 'warnings.' — οὕτω σφόδρα
ἤρχεσθε : 'their government was so
severe.' Cf. Ar. Av. 508, ἦρχον δ'
οὕτω σφόδρα τὴν ἀρχήν. — τοιοῦτον
ἐν ᾧ : 'of such a sort that.' — ἡττηθέντες : concessive. — τὸ ἴσον : for the
meaning, see on § 35. Isocrates says
that it resulted ὥστε μηδὲν ἔλαττον
ἔχειν τοὺς ἐκβαλόντας τῶν κατελθόντων,
VII. 67. — νικήσαντες : prot. of ἂν ἐδουλεύετε, which is pres. in time.

93. οἴκους : for the meaning, cf.
XXXII. 23, and Xen. Oec. vi. 4, οἶκος
δ' ἡμῖν ἐφαίνετο ὅπερ (the same as)
κτῆσις ἡ σύμπασα. — μεγάλους ἐκτή-
σαντο : how they did this may be
seen from §§ 6, 8, 11, 19, 99; cf.
Arist. Resp. Ath. 35. 4, ἀπέκτεινον

τοὺς καὶ ταῖς οὐσίαις καὶ τῷ γένει καὶ
τοῖς ἀξιώμασιν προέχοντας. — συνωφελεῖσθαι ... ἠνάγκαζον : 'they did not
suffer you to share their advantages
(cf. XVI. 5), but obliged you to share
their dishonour.' See on § 30. —
ὑμᾶς : obj. with ἐκτῶντο, but subj.
with εὔνους εἶναι. — ἐκτῶντο : of attempted action. See on καθιστάς, § 42.
— εἶναι : pres. after a 'verb of expecting'; see on ποιήσειν, § 9.

94. ἀνθ' ὧν : 'to pay for this.' —
ἐν τῷ θαρραλέῳ : because the democracy was restored. — νῦν ἀρίστων :
by the hyperbaton (H. 1062) of νῦν,
which belongs to πολιτεύεσθε, a strong
emphasis is given to ἀρίστων, a term
applied to the patriots for their en-
durance and courage (cf. § 97). —

περὶ τῆς πόλεως βουλεύεσθε, ἀναμνησθέντες δὲ τῶν ἐπικούρων, οὓς οὗτοι φύλακας τῆς σφετέρας ἀρχῆς καὶ τῆς
95 ὑμετέρας δουλείας εἰς τὴν ἀκρόπολιν κατέστησαν. καὶ
πρὸς ὑμᾶς μὲν ἔτι πολλῶν ὄντων εἰπεῖν τοσαῦτα λέγω.
ὅσοι δ᾽ ἐκ Πειραιῶς ἐστε, πρῶτον μὲν τῶν ὅπλων ἀναμνήσθητε, ὅτι πολλὰς μάχας ἐν τῇ ἀλλοτρίᾳ μαχεσάμενοι
οὐχ ὑπὸ τῶν πολεμίων ἀλλ᾽ ὑπὸ τούτων εἰρήνης οὔσης
560 ἀφῃρέθητε τὰ ὅπλα, ἔπειθ᾽ ὅτι ἐξεκηρύχθητε μὲν ἐκ τῆς
πόλεως, ἣν ὑμῖν οἱ πατέρες παρέδοσαν, φεύγοντας δὲ ὑμᾶς
96 ἐκ τῶν πόλεων ἐξῃτοῦντο. ἀνθ᾽ ὧν ὀργίσθητε μὲν ὥσπερ
ὅτ᾽ ἐφεύγετε, ἀναμνήσθητε δὲ καὶ τῶν ἄλλων κακῶν ἃ
πεπόνθατε ὑπ᾽ αὐτῶν, οἳ τοὺς μὲν ἐκ τῆς ἀγορᾶς τοὺς δ᾽
565 ἐκ τῶν ἱερῶν συναρπάζοντες βιαίως ἀπέκτειναν, τοὺς δὲ
ἀπὸ τέκνων καὶ γονέων καὶ γυναικῶν ἀφέλκοντες φονέας
αὐτῶν ἠνάγκασαν γενέσθαι καὶ οὐδὲ ταφῆς τῆς νομιζομένης εἴασαν τυχεῖν, ἡγούμενοι τὴν αὑτῶν ἀρχὴν βεβαιο-

ἐπικούρων: Callibius and his seven
hundred mercenaries; see on § 6 and
App. to § 60.

95. τοσαῦτα: see on οὐχ ὅσον, § 11.
— ἀφῃρέθητε τὰ ὅπλα: for the facts,
see on § 40. — ἐξεκηρύχθητε ἐκ τῆς
πόλεως: more exact would have been
ἐκ τοῦ ἄστεως (see on § 16), for after
the execution of Theramenes the
Thirty προεῖπον τοῖς ἔξω τοῦ καταλόγου
μὴ εἰσιέναι εἰς τὸ ἄστυ, Xen. Hellen. ii.
4. 1; so Lys. xxv. 22, xxxi. 8. The
Piraeus was not forbidden them.
On the verb ἐκκηρύττω, see on § 35.
— ἐκ τῶν πόλεων: i.e. the cities belonging to the Spartan alliance, which
now included nearly all Greece (hence
πανταχόθεν, § 97); cf. Diod. xiv. 6,
Λακεδαιμόνιοι ... ἐψηφίσαντο τοὺς Ἀθη-

ναίων φυγάδας ἐξ ἁπάσης τῆς Ἑλλάδος
ἀγωγίμους (subject to arrest) τοῖς τριάκοντα εἶναι. But Thebes (see on § 58),
Argos, Megara, and Chalcis (cf. xxiv.
25) harboured them.

96. ὅτ᾽ ἐφεύγετε: when you were
in exile. — ἐκ τῆς ἀγορᾶς: cf. Xen.
Hellen. ii. 4. 14 quoted on § 8, and
Dem. xxii. 52, τοῦτο κατηγοροῦσι
τῶν τριάκοντα, ὅτι τοὺς ἐκ τῆς ἀγορᾶς
ἀπῆγον. The agora was under the
protection of the θεοὶ ἀγοραῖοι. — ἐκ
τῶν ἱερῶν: cf. § 98. Theramenes was
dragged from the altar, Xen. Hellen.
ii. 3. 55. — φονέας αὐτῶν: by forcing
them to drink hemlock; cf. § 17. —
ταφῆς τῆς νομιζομένης: cf. §§ 18, 21;
xxxi. 21; xxxii. 8. — βεβαιοτέραν:
surer than or too secure for.

97 τέραν εἶναι τῆς παρὰ τῶν θεῶν τιμωρίας. ὅσοι δὲ τὸν
570 θάνατον διέφυγον, πολλαχοῦ κινδυνεύσαντες καὶ εἰς πολλὰς πόλεις πλανηθέντες καὶ πανταχόθεν ἐκκηρυττόμενοι,
ἐνδεεῖς ὄντες τῶν ἐπιτηδείων, οἱ μὲν ἐν πολεμίᾳ τῇ πατρίδι
τοὺς παῖδας καταλιπόντες, οἱ δ' ἐν ξένῃ γῇ, πολλῶν ἐναν-
τιουμένων ἤλθετε εἰς τὸν Πειραιᾶ. πολλῶν δὲ καὶ μεγά-
575 λων κινδύνων ὑπαρξάντων ἄνδρες ἀγαθοὶ γενόμενοι τοὺς
μὲν ἠλευθερώσατε, τοὺς δ' εἰς τὴν πατρίδα κατηγάγετε.
98 εἰ δὲ ἐδυστυχήσατε καὶ τούτων ἡμάρτετε, αὐτοὶ μὲν ἂν
δείσαντες ἐφεύγετε μὴ πάθητε τοιαῦτα οἷα καὶ πρότερον,
καὶ οὔτ' ἂν ἱερὰ οὔτε βωμοὶ ὑμᾶς ἀδικουμένους διὰ τοὺς
580 τούτων τρόπους ὠφέλησεν, ἃ καὶ τοῖς ἀδικοῦσι σωτήρια
γίγνεται. οἱ δὲ παῖδες ὑμῶν, ὅσοι μὲν ἐνθάδε ἦσαν, ὑπὸ
τούτων ἂν ὑβρίζοντο, οἱ δ' ἐπὶ ξένης μικρῶν ἂν ἕνεκα
συμβολαίων ἐδούλευον ἐρημίᾳ τῶν ἐπικουρησόντων.
99 Ἀλλὰ γὰρ οὐ τὰ μέλλοντα ἔσεσθαι βούλομαι λέγειν,

97. **πλανηθέντες** κτλ.: for the facts,
see on § 95. — **πολεμίᾳ**: pred. position, 'which had now become a hostile country.' — **τοὺς μέν, τοὺς δέ**:
the two sets of children mentioned
above. — **εἰς τὴν πατρίδα**: with κατά-
γειν, κατιέναι, κατέρχεσθαι, technical
expressions used of a return from
exile, the *terminus ad quem* is usually
omitted; *cf.* §§ 58, 77; xvi. 6.

98. **ἐδυστυχήσατε**: for the meaning, see on § 35. — **τούτων**: refers
back to ἠλευθερώσατε and κατηγάγετε.
— **δείσαντες**: 'in utter fear,' emphatic in position, preceding instead
of following ἐφεύγετε. *Cf.* μαθόντες,
§ 35. — **πάθητε**: subjv., as ἐφεύγετ' ἄν
is primary. GMT. 172. — **ἦσαν**: for
the tense, see on § 29. — **ἐπὶ ξένης**:

'in foreign lands,' a common expression in the orators. — **συμβολαίων**: *loans*. — **ἐδούλευον**: not actual
slavery, but enforced work done for
the lender until the debt was paid;
cf. Isocr. xiv. 48, τοὺς παῖδας ... πολλοὺς μὲν μικρῶν ἕνεκα συμβολαίων δου-
λεύοντας, ἄλλους δ' ἐπὶ θητείαν ἰόντας.
— **ἐρημίᾳ τῶν ἐπικουρησόντων**: 'for
lack of any to succour them.' *Cf.*
διαδεξόμενον, xxiv. 6, and Isocr. xix.
29, δι' ἔνδειαν τοῦ θεραπεύσοντος. GMT.
826.

99. **ἀλλὰ γάρ**: *but enough! for* ——.
A phrase used in changing the subject; *cf.* vii. 9, xxii. 11, xxiv. 14. —
μέλλοντα: 'would be going.' *Cf.*
vii. 24, and see on παρόν, § 30. G.
1402, 3; GMT. 428. For a different

585 τὰ πραχθέντα ὑπὸ τούτων οὐ δυνάμενος εἰπεῖν· οὐδὲ γὰρ
ἑνὸς κατηγόρου οὐδὲ δυοῖν ἔργον ἐστίν, ἀλλὰ πολλῶν.
ὅμως δὲ τῆς ἐμῆς προθυμίας οὐδὲν ἐλλέλειπται, ὑπέρ τε
τῶν ἱερῶν, ἃ οὗτοι τὰ μὲν ἀπέδοντο τὰ δ' εἰσιόντες ἐμίαι-
νον, ὑπέρ τε τῆς πόλεως, ἣν μικρὰν ἐποίουν, ὑπέρ τε τῶν
590 νεωρίων, ἃ καθεῖλον, καὶ ὑπὲρ τῶν τεθνεώτων, οἷς ὑμεῖς,
ἐπειδὴ ζῶσιν ἐπαμῦναι οὐκ ἠδύνασθε, ἀποθανοῦσι βοηθή-
100 σατε. οἶμαι δ' αὐτοὺς ἡμῶν τε ἀκροᾶσθαι καὶ ὑμᾶς
εἴσεσθαι τὴν ψῆφον φέροντας, ἡγουμένους, ὅσοι μὲν ἂν
τούτων ἀποψηφίσησθε, αὐτῶν θάνατον κατεψηφισμένους
595 ἔσεσθαι, ὅσοι δ' ἂν παρὰ τούτων δίκην λάβωσιν, ὑπὲρ
αὐτῶν τὰς τιμωρίας πεποιημένους.

sense, cf. XXII. 20. — οὐ δύναμενος:
a return to the thought of § 1. —
ἱερῶν: ἱερά is a general term, including not only the buildings themselves but also their sacred implements
and treasures as well as the holy pre-
cincts (τεμένη) about them, and it
doubtless is not meant that the
Thirty sold actual temples. — τὰ μέν,
τὰ δέ: partitive apposition. H. 624 d.
— μικράν: cf. XIII. 46, ὥστε μηδὲν
διαφέρειν τῆς ἐλαχίστης πόλεως τὴν
πόλιν. — νεωρίων: the νεώρια consisted of νεώσοικοι, ναυπήγια, and
σκευοθήκη (arsenal). — καθεῖλον: in
order to ensure the downfall of
democratic Athens, whose power lay
in her ships, the νεώσοικοι, which had
cost three thousand talents, were sold
for three by the Thirty ἐπὶ καθαιρέσει,
to be torn down; Isocr. VII. 66. — οἷς
βοηθήσατε: for the rel. with imv.,
see on § 60. — ἠδύνασθε: see App.

100. This passage appeals to the
popular belief that the dead were

conscious of what went on in the
world in matters of peculiar interest
to them. See App. — ἡμῶν: i.e.
Lysias and others who were accusing
Eratosthenes. Lysias never uses the
pl. ἡμεῖς of himself alone (Frohberger). — εἴσεσθαι ... φέροντας: not
know that you are casting (indir.
disc.), but be aware of your casting
your votes (G. 1582; GMT. 884; cf.
XVI. 20); for εἰδέναι when used in
connexion with a verb of hearing
approaches closely in meaning to
ἰδεῖν. Cf. Isocr. XII. 168, τίς γὰρ οὐκ
οἶδεν ἢ τίς οὐκ ἀκήκοε; Dem. IV. 3, καὶ
παρ' ἄλλων ἀκούουσι καὶ τοῖς εἰδόσιν αὐτοῖς ἀναμιμνῃσκομένοις. — ἀποψηφίσησθε: shall have acquitted; GMT. 90.
— κατεψηφισμένους ἔσεσθαι: fut.
perf. G. 706; H. 467 a; GMT. 80 and
114. Cf. XXII. 19. — κατηγορῶν: see
on λέγοντι, § 1. — ἀκηκόατε κτλ.: a
strong climax. Aristotle seems to
have had this passage in mind in
Rhet. III. 19, τελευτὴ δὲ τῆς λέξεως

Παύσομαι κατηγορῶν. ἀκηκόατε, ἑωράκατε, πεπόνθατε,
ἔχετε· δικάζετε.

ἁρμόττει ἡ ἀσύνδετος ὅπως ἐπίλογος
ἀλλὰ μὴ λόγος ᾖ· Εἴρηκα, ἀκηκόατε,
ἔχετε, κρίνατε. — ἔχετε: sc. in your

power. Cf. Lycurg. Leocr. 27, τοῦτον
ἔχοντες ἐν τῇ ὑμετέρᾳ ψήφῳ οὐκ ἀπο-
κτενεῖτε;

FOR MANTITHEUS.

INTRODUCTION.

THE Greek title of this speech shows that Mantitheus, having been elected to an office, had come up before the Senate to pass his δοκιμασία.[1] We do not know positively what the office was, but it is most probable that it was that of Senator. The outgoing Senate conducted the δοκιμασία of its successor.[2] The principal charge against Mantitheus was that he had served in the cavalry under the Thirty Tyrants (§ 3), and this service, as we know from another oration of Lysias,[3] was enough to keep a man out of the Senate. Finally, the language of § 8 strengthens the theory that the office in question was that of Senator.

While any connexion whatever with the Tyrants was remembered against a man for years (cf. VII. 27, XXIV. 25), it was natural that service in their cavalry should be the cause of particular hatred. For the cavalry had been prominent from the first with the Thirty and the Spartan troops against the patriots,[4] in the slaughter at Eleusis,[5] with the first board of Ten,[6] and in the last stage of the struggle after the Thirty had withdrawn from the city.[7] Pausanias, also, had employed them in his half-hearted contest against Thrasybulus.[8] The hatred felt for the cavalry was shown four years later, in 399 B.C., when the Spartan Thibron applied to Athens for a cavalry contingent to serve against Tissaphernes. The Athenians sent three hundred men who had been in the Thirty's cavalry, νομίζοντες κέρδος τῷ δήμῳ, εἰ ἀποδημοῖεν καὶ ἐναπόλοιντο.[9]

[1] See Introd. § 8.
[2] M. and S. p. 238; Gilbert, *Antiq.* p. 266; Arist. *Resp. Ath.* 45. 3.
[3] XXVI. 10; *cf.* And. I. 75.
[4] Xen. *Hellen.* ii. 4. 2 and 10.
[5] *Ibid.* 8 and 9.
[6] Arist. *Resp. Ath.* 38. 2.
[7] Xen. *Hellen.* ii. 4. 26.
[8] *Ibid.* 31.
[9] *Ibid.* iii. 1. 4.

In view of all this, it was vital that Mantitheus should refute the charge. He does this by documentary evidence. On entrance into service, each cavalryman received a certain sum (called the κατάστασις[10]) from the State to help pay for his outfit. The restored democracy determined to recover for the treasury the money which had been thus paid out to the Thirty's cavalry. A decree was passed (§ 6) that the phylarchs[11] should make out a list of these men and hand it over to the syndics,[12] to whom was entrusted the business of recovering the money. This list was the document on which Mantitheus relied, and he points out that his name was not on it. He contends also that fear of punishment would prevent the phylarchs from falsifying it (§ 7). His enemies, also, relied upon a document, — the Thirty's own list of cavalry, called the σανίδιον[13] in § 6. But Mantitheus asserts that this was full of falsifications, and that it deserved no credit. In fact, this list probably contained the names of all whom the Thirty *expected* to serve in the cavalry, though some of them escaped service by absence from Athens or in other ways. It should be observed, however, that his own argument, based on the absence of his name from the phylarchs' list, is somewhat fallacious; for he might have served without having received a κατάστασις, since he arrived so late in the Thirty's term (§ 4). Believing, however, that he has

[10] Sauppe, *Philologus*, XV, 69; Gilbert, *Antiq.* p. 322; Boeckh, *Staatshaush.* I, p. 319. Martin (*Les Cavaliers Athéniens*, p. 335 ff.) holds (*cf.* Harp. *s.v.*) that the κατάστασις was regularly refunded to the State at the end of the cavalryman's service; so Gilbert, *Antiq.* p. 322.

[11] The phylarch was the officer who commanded the cavalry contingent of a tribe; the two hipparchs commanded the whole body from the ten tribes.

[12] The σύνδικοι (§ 7) were a board originating in the many lawsuits that followed the illegal acts of the Thirty. Their existence may be traced from 398 to 387 B.C. (M. and S. p. 124; *cf.* XIX. 32). They had jurisdiction, ἡγεμονία (that is, they prepared the business and presided over the court), in all cases in which property held by a citizen was claimed by the State, or in which a citizen claimed property which had been confiscated by the State.

[13] Called σανίδες in XXVI. 10 (quoted in the note on § 6); and explained in Hesych. *s.v.* σανίς by λεύκωμα, a word which occurs in [Lys.] IX. 6. These words were applied to all sorts of bulletin boards, which were either painted white or covered with gypsum.

proved his point, and hence that there is no legal hindrance to his becoming a Senator, he devotes the rest of his speech to a statement of the reasons why he deserves the honour.

He gives an account of his entire life, showing that he has been a good brother (§ 10), and a good citizen, especially in war (§§ 11–17). Towards the end we find reason to think that, in support of the main charge, it had been alleged that he was aristocratic (§§ 18, 19) as well as forth-putting (§§ 20, 21). He had evidently given some ground for the former suspicion by his outward appearance and bearing, but he calls upon the court to judge him by what he has done, not by what he has seemed to be. As for the latter, he admits that he may have exceeded the golden mean, but urges that it was with an honorable ambition.

Of Mantitheus himself we know only what he tells us. We should not have even his name except for the Greek title of the speech. He must have been at least thirty years old, since no younger man could enter the Senate,[14] and he was probably not much older (§§ 11 and 20). Of his family we have only the same source of information.[15] It had been prominent in the state (§ 20), but we are not told in what measures. Probably, however, it was of the oligarchical party. This might account for the father's connexion with a foreign prince (§ 4), and for the secondary charge against Mantitheus himself of aristocratic leanings. Blass thinks[16] that the disaster to his father (§ 10) means his fall at Aegos Potami. But had he fallen there, the son would not be silent about such a proof of the loyalty of the family. It is certainly suspicious that we hear not a word more of this father, and perhaps the coupling of his συμφορά with the state's is an artful concealment of some punishment inflicted on him by the people,[17] as a result of which

14 Schömann, *Gr. Alt.*³, I, p. 380; Gilbert, *Antiq.* p. 265.

15 It has been supposed, with probability, that the Mantitheus, son of Mantias, of the deme Thoricus, mentioned by Dem. xxxix. 27 ff., was grandson of our speaker. The grandfather of the Demosthenic Mantitheus bore the same name. Thoricus belonged to the tribe Acamantis, and to this tribe belonged also the deme Cerameis, probably that of the phylarch Orthobulus in § 13 (Köhler, *Hermes*, V, 10 f.; *CIA*. II, 19).

16 *Att. Bereds.* I, p. 517.

17 So Frohberger, p. 4, note 33.

Mantitheus was obliged to address the Assembly in his own behalf at an early age (§ 20).

In this oration Lysias has given us a striking proof of his power of suiting the speech to the speaker, and this has always been reckoned among his finest works. We can almost see the bright, ambitious young Athenian, eager to distinguish himself, and ready to defend his good name against all comers.

The speech could not have been delivered before 394 B.C., because in it (§ 15) the events of that year are mentioned, nor after 389, because in the spring of that year Thrasybulus died.[18] The sportive tone and lack of bitterness in the reference to him (*ibid.*) show that he was still alive. Perhaps he was present, and Frohberger suggests that there may have been some sparring between him and Mantitheus at a recent meeting of the Assembly.

---

[18] Clinton, *F. H.;* Frohberger, *Philologus*, XVII, 437 ff. On the exact date of the speech, see Blass, *Att. Bereds.* I, p. 518 (who sets it at 392), Fuhr p. 118, Frohberger p. 6 (who set it in the preceding year).

ΕΝ ΒΟΥΛΗΙ

ΜΑΝΤΙΘΕΩΙ ΔΟΚΙΜΑΖΟΜΕΝΩΙ ΑΠΟΛΟΓΙΑ.

1 Εἰ μὴ συνῄδη, ὦ βουλή, τοῖς κατηγόροις βουλομένοις
ἐκ παντὸς τρόπου κακῶς ἐμὲ ποιεῖν, πολλὴν ἂν αὐτοῖς
χάριν εἶχον ταύτης τῆς κατηγορίας· ἡγοῦμαι γὰρ τοῖς
ἀδίκως διαβεβλημένοις τούτους εἶναι μεγίστων ἀγαθῶν
5 αἰτίους, οἵτινες ἂν αὐτοὺς ἀναγκάζωσιν εἰς ἔλεγχον τῶν
2 αὐτοῖς βεβιωμένων καταστῆναι. ἐγὼ γὰρ οὕτω σφόδρα
ἐμαυτῷ πιστεύω, ὥστ᾽ ἐλπίζω καὶ εἴ τις πρός με τυγχάνει
ἀηδῶς διακείμενος, ἐπειδὰν ἐμοῦ λέγοντος ἀκούσῃ περὶ
τῶν πεπραγμένων, μεταμελήσειν αὐτῷ καὶ πολὺ βελτίω
3 με εἰς τὸν λοιπὸν χρόνον ἡγήσεσθαι. ἀξιῶ δέ, ὦ βουλή,
ἐὰν μὲν τοῦτο μόνον ὑμῖν ἐπιδείξω, ὡς εὔνους εἰμὶ τοῖς
καθεστηκόσι πράγμασι καὶ ὡς ἠνάγκασμαι τῶν αὐτῶν

1. **χάριν εἶχον**: gratiam habe-
rem; for a similar paradoxical opening, cf. XXIV. 1, and the advice of
Dionysius (below, p. 161), and of
Cicero, Inv. I. 25, sin res dabit,
non inutile est ab aliqua re
nova aut ridicula (cf. Lys. VII. 1)
incipere. — **τούτους οἵτινες**: the
antecedent is not really definite (H.
699 a), such persons as. Hence ἂν
ἀναγκάζωσιν. G. 1431, 1; H. 914, B.
— **εἰς ἔλεγχον... καταστῆναι**: to submit to an investigation of their behaviour in the past. Cf. XXXII. 12. —
βεβιωμένων: a somewhat rare use of

the partic. as subst.; see Kr. Spr. 52,
3, 5, and cf. Dem. XVIII. 265, ἐξέτασον
τοίνυν παρ᾽ ἄλληλα τὰ σοὶ κἀμοὶ βεβιω-
μένα.

2. **ἐμαυτῷ**: naïvely said and characteristic of Mantitheus. Generally
and more modestly the cause, not the
man, is mentioned. — **μεταμελήσειν**:
indir. disc., after a verb of expecting.
See on ποιήσειν, XII. 9. G. 1286;
H. 948 a.

3. **ἀξιῶ**: think fit, require. — **τοῖς
καθεστηκόσι πράγμασι**: the existing
order of things, i.e. the present constitution, referring to the restored

κινδύνων μετέχειν ὑμῖν, μηδέν πώ μοι πλέον εἶναι· ἐὰν δὲ
φαίνωμαι καὶ περὶ τὰ ἄλλα μετρίως βεβιωκὼς καὶ πολὺ
15 παρὰ τὴν δόξαν καὶ παρὰ τοὺς λόγους τοὺς τῶν ἐχθρῶν,
δέομαι ὑμῶν ἐμὲ μὲν δοκιμάζειν, τούτους δὲ ἡγεῖσθαι
χείρους εἶναι. πρῶτον δὲ ἀποδείξω ὡς οὐχ ἵππευον ἐπὶ
τῶν τριάκοντα οὐδὲ μετέσχον τῆς τότε πολιτείας.

4 Ἡμᾶς γὰρ ὁ πατὴρ πρὸ τῆς ἐν Ἑλλησπόντῳ συμφορᾶς
20 ὡς Σάτυρον τὸν ἐν τῷ Πόντῳ διαιτησομένους ἐξέπεμψε,
καὶ οὔτε τῶν τειχῶν καθαιρουμένων ἐπεδημοῦμεν οὔτε
μεθισταμένης τῆς πολιτείας, ἀλλ᾽ ἤλθομεν πρὶν τοὺς ἀπὸ
Φυλῆς εἰς τὸν Πειραιᾶ κατελθεῖν πρότερον πένθ᾽ ἡμέραις.

democracy, a common use of πράγματα. — μηδέν πώ μοι κτλ. : that I
shall gain nothing whatever by it.
Here πλέον is elliptical, no more
(than I should without this). See
Kr. Spr. 48, 3, 7; cf. Antiphon v. 95,
τί ἔσται πλέον τῷ γε ἀποθανόντι; what
good will it do the dead man? —
εἶναι: the object phrase with ἀξιῶ con-
veys also the idea of futurity and hence
is the apodosis of ἐὰν ἐπιδείξω. GMT.
445. — καὶ περὶ τὰ ἄλλα : in everything else too, i.e. in all the duties of
civic and private life. — μετρίως βεβι-
ωκώς : 'a well regulated life,' far higher
praise to the Greek mind, however,
than the English words express. It
means the avoidance of all extremes
and the possession of the virtue of
σωφροσύνη. Cf. the Delphic μηδὲν
ἄγαν. — δόξαν : 'what people think.'
The slander of his enemies had done
its work. — ἐμὲ δοκιμάζειν : to pass me
on this examination, cf. XXXI. 34. —
χείρους : knaves, the Greek, with his
finer feeling for contrasts, using a
comparative where we do not; cf.

XXXII. 1. So below, βελτίων, § 17;
see Kühn. Gr. § 542, note 7.

4. Σάτυρον: he reigned from about
407 B.C. over the kingdom of the Cim-
merian Bosporus, called also Pontus,
which included the Tauric Chersonese
(Crimea), and the neighbouring cities
on the coast; see Gilbert, Gr. Staatsalt. II, p. 188. The capital, Pantica-
peum, was one of the chief corn-
marts of Athens. — τῶν τειχῶν καθαιρουμένων : for the facts, see XII. 70.
— μεθισταμένης κτλ. : when the constitution was in course of alteration,
sc. to the government of the Thirty.
Cf. XII. 74 ff. — ἤλθομεν : came back.
Cf. XII. 54, and for ἥκω in this sense,
XII. 16. Note the difference in the
tenses of ἤλθομεν and ἐπεδημοῦμεν (for
the augment, see on XII. 71). — τοὺς
ἀπὸ Φυλῆς : cf. XII. 52. The title
'men of Phyle' was regularly applied
to the patriots after their success, as
in Dem. XXIV. 134, τῶν ἐκ Πειραιῶς
καὶ ἀπὸ Φυλῆς οὗτος ἦν. Cf. 'he was at
Lexington and Bunker Hill.' — πρότερον πένθ᾽ ἡμέραις : πρότερον modifies

5 καίτοι οὔτε ἡμᾶς εἰκὸς ἦν εἰς τοιοῦτον καιρὸν ἀφιγμένους
25 ἐπιθυμεῖν μετέχειν τῶν ἀλλοτρίων κινδύνων, οὔτ᾽ ἐκεῖνοι
φαίνονται τοιαύτην γνώμην ἔχοντες ὥστε καὶ τοῖς ἀποδη-
μοῦσι καὶ μηδὲν ἐξαμαρτάνουσι μεταδιδόναι τῆς πολιτείας, ἀλλὰ μᾶλλον ἠτίμαζον καὶ τοὺς συγκαταλύσαντας
6 τὸν δῆμον.　ἔπειτα δὲ ἐκ μὲν τοῦ σανιδίου τοὺς ἱππεύ-
30 σαντας σκοπεῖν εὔηθές ἐστιν· ἐν τούτῳ γὰρ πολλοὶ μὲν
τῶν ὁμολογούντων ἱππεύειν οὐκ ἔνεισιν, ἔνιοι δὲ τῶν ἀποδημούντων ἐγγεγραμμένοι εἰσίν.　ἐκεῖνος δ᾽ ἐστὶν ἔλεγ-
χος μέγιστος· ἐπειδὴ γὰρ κατήλθετε, ἐψηφίσασθε τοὺς
φυλάρχους ἀπενεγκεῖν τοὺς ἱππεύσαντας, ἵνα τὰς κατα-
7 στάσεις ἀναπράττητε παρ᾽ αὐτῶν.　ἐμὲ τοίνυν οὐδεὶς ἂν
ἀποδείξειεν οὔτ᾽ ἀπενεχθέντα ὑπὸ τῶν φυλάρχων οὔτε

ἦλθομεν on which the clause with πρίν
depends. GMT. 658. For emphasis
the date is given last, *and only five
days before it*, otherwise πρότερον
would as usual precede πρίν. On
the dat., see G. 1184 ; H. 781.

5. **καιρόν**: *crisis.*—**ἔχοντες**: partic.
in indir. disc. (G. 1588; H. 981),
representing the impf. (G. 1289; H.
856 a), *cf.* xxiv. 8, λαμβάνων, and
below, § 6, ἀποδημούντων. — **ἀλλὰ** . . .
τὸν δῆμον: ' No! their habit was
to disenfranchise even their accom-
plices.' Said with reference to the
fate of Theramenes (*cf.* xii. 64 and
78) and others.

6. **σανιδίου**: ' muster roll,' see p.
75, note 13. — **εὔηθες**: see on xii. 87.
— **ἱππεύειν**: impf. in time. G. 1285;
H. 853 a. *Cf.* xii. 26. — **ἀποδημούντων**: not like ὁμολογούντων in time;
see on ἔχοντες, § 5. — **ἐγγεγραμμένοι
εἰσίν**: a technical term. *Cf.* xxvi. 10,
ὡς ἱππευκότος αὐτοῦ ἐπὶ τῶν τριάκοντα

τοὔνομα ἐν ταῖς σανίσιν ἐνεγέγραπτο
and Ar. *Eq.* 1369, ὁπλίτης ἐντεθεὶς
ἐν καταλόγῳ ἐγγεγράψεται. — **ἐκεῖνος** :
' and now comes,' the dem. calling
attention to something new. H. 695 a.
On the gender assimilated to that of
the predicate, see H. 632 a, and *cf.*
xii. 37.　This is rare with ἐκεῖνος. —
κατήλθετε : a technical word signifying a return from exile ; see on
xii. 97.　We should use the plpf.
G. 1261. — **τοὺς φυλάρχους ἀπενεγκεῖν** :
the phylarchs (see p. 75, note 11)
were to make a return, either directly
to the people or through the σύνδικοι,
of all who had served.—**καταστάσεις** :
see p. 75, note 10. — **ἀναπράττητε** :
exact, ' get back.' On the mood after
a secondary tense, see G. 1369 ;
H. 881 a.　*Cf.* xii. 7 and 12, xxxi.
30.　In such cases the practice of
Lysias is about equally divided between the subjv. and opt.　GMT.
320[1].　See App.

παραδοθέντα τοῖς συνδίκοις. καίτοι πᾶσι ῥάδιον τοῦτο
γνῶναι, ὅτι ἀναγκαῖον ἦν τοῖς φυλάρχοις, εἰ μὴ ἀποδείξειαν τοὺς ἔχοντας τὰς καταστάσεις, αὐτοῖς ζημιοῦσθαι.
40 ὥστε πολὺ ἂν δικαιότερον ἐκείνοις τοῖς γράμμασιν ἢ τούτοις πιστεύοιτε· ἐκ μὲν γὰρ τούτων ῥάδιον ἦν ἐξαλειφθῆ-
ναι τῷ βουλομένῳ, ἐν ἐκείνοις δὲ τοὺς ἱππεύσαντας ἀναγ-
8 καῖον ἦν ὑπὸ τῶν φυλάρχων ἀπενεχθῆναι. ἔτι δέ, ὦ
βουλή, εἴπερ ἵππευσα, οὐκ ἂν ἦ ἔξαρνος ὡς δεινόν τι
45 πεποιηκώς, ἀλλ᾽ ἠξίουν, ἀποδείξας ὡς οὐδεὶς ὑπ᾽ ἐμοῦ τῶν
πολιτῶν κακῶς πέπονθε, δοκιμάζεσθαι. ὁρῶ δὲ καὶ ὑμᾶς
ταύτῃ τῇ γνώμῃ χρωμένους καὶ πολλοὺς μὲν τῶν τότε
ἱππευσάντων βουλεύοντας, πολλοὺς δ᾽ αὐτῶν στρατηγοὺς
καὶ ἱππάρχους κεχειροτονημένους. ὥστε μηδὲν δι᾽ ἄλλο
50 με ἡγεῖσθε ταύτην ποιεῖσθαι τὴν ἀπολογίαν ἢ ὅτι περι-
φανῶς ἐτόλμησάν μου καταψεύσασθαι. ἀνάβηθι δέ μοι
καὶ μαρτύρησον.

ΜΑΡΤΥΡΙΑ.

9 Περὶ μὲν τοίνυν ταύτης τῆς αἰτίας οὐκ οἶδ᾽ ὅ τι δεῖ
πλείω λέγειν· δοκεῖ δέ μοι, ὦ βουλή, ἐν μὲν τοῖς ἄλλοις

---

7. συνδίκοις: see p. 75, note 12. —
τοῦτο: here refers forward. G. 1005 ;
H. 696 a. — ἐκείνοις: the phylarchs'
lists, not yet produced in evidence
and therefore more remote, while
τούτοις means the σανίδιον, which had
already been presented by the accusers. G. 1004 ; H. 695. — ῥάδιον
ἦν: the list was perhaps posted or kept
in a public place. Thus the κατάλογος
(in which the Thirty kept making
changes, Arist. Resp. Ath. 36. 2) was
in the Senate house when Critias
wiped out first Theramenes's name
and then the man himself. See Xen.

Hellen. ii. 3. 51, ἐγὼ οὖν, ἔφη, Θηραμένην
τουτονὶ ἐξαλείφω ἐκ τοῦ καταλόγου. —
ἀναγκαῖον ἦν: with acc. and inf. here,
but with dat. and inf. above. See App.
8. ἠξίουν: ἄν is understood from
above. G. 1314, cf. XII. 47, XXIV. 11.
— βουλεύοντας: = βουλευτὰς ὄντας.
On the law here violated, see p. 74,
note 3. — ἱππάρχους: see p. 75, note
11. — κεχειροτονημένους: military
officers were chosen by a show of
hands, not by the lot. — μαρτύρησον: sc. to the facts in §§ 4-8.
9. This section serves as a transition and introduction to the main

55 ἀγῶσι περὶ αὐτῶν μόνων τῶν κατηγορημένων προσήκειν
ἀπολογεῖσθαι, ἐν δὲ ταῖς δοκιμασίαις δίκαιον εἶναι παντὸς
τοῦ βίου λόγον διδόναι. δέομαι οὖν ὑμῶν μετ᾽ εὐνοίας
ἀκροάσασθαί μου. ποιήσομαι δὲ τὴν ἀπολογίαν ὡς ἂν
δύνωμαι διὰ βραχυτάτων.

10 Ἐγὼ γὰρ πρῶτον μὲν οὐσίας μοι οὐ πολλῆς καταλει-
φθείσης διὰ τὰς συμφορὰς καὶ τὰς τοῦ πατρὸς καὶ τὰς
τῆς πόλεως, δύο μὲν ἀδελφὰς ἐξέδωκα, ἐπιδοὺς τριάκοντα
μνᾶς ἑκατέρᾳ, πρὸς τὸν ἀδελφὸν δ᾽ οὕτως ἐνειμάμην ὥστ᾽
ἐκεῖνον πλέον ὁμολογεῖν ἔχειν ἐμοῦ τῶν πατρῴων, καὶ
65 πρὸς τοὺς ἄλλους ἅπαντας οὕτως βεβίωκα ὥστε μηδεπώ-
11 ποτέ μοι μηδὲ πρὸς ἕνα μηδὲν ἔγκλημα γενέσθαι. καὶ
τὰ μὲν ἴδια οὕτως διῴκηκα· περὶ δὲ τῶν κοινῶν μοι μέγιστον ἡγοῦμαι τεκμήριον εἶναι τῆς ἐμῆς ἐπιεικείας, ὅτι
τῶν νεωτέρων ὅσοι περὶ κύβους ἢ πότους ἢ τὰς τοιαύτας

part of the speech in which, having
already disproved the charge, the
speaker proceeds to show that he is
a deserving person. Hence the re-
quest δέομαι οὖν κτλ., often found at
the beginning of an oration, esp. in
Demosthenes. — ὡς ἂν δύνωμαι : on
the mood, see G. 1434; H. 916. —
On the general nature of the δοκιμασία, see Introd. § 8.

10. πρῶτον μέν : first the speaker
shows his unselfish behaviour towards his relations and others, sum-
ming up with τὰ μὲν ... διῴκηκα.—
τὰς τοῦ πατρός: see p. 76. — ἐξέδωκα, ἐπιδούς : technical words, cf.
XXXII. 8. Of the bride herself, ἐπι-
φέρεσθαι was used, cf. XIX. 14, τὴν
ἐμὴν μητέρα ἔλαβεν (he married) οὐδὲν
ἐπιφερομένην (without a dowry). When
a girl's father died, her brother be-

came her κύριος, and was obliged by
law to maintain her and to provide
a dowry on her marriage. Here,
therefore, the speaker is making a
virtue of necessity. — τριάκοντα μνᾶς:
about $540 (but see p. 206), an average
dowry for one in moderate circumstances; cf. XXXII. 8, and Boeckh,
Staatsh. I, p. 598. — ἐνειμάμην : cf.
XXXII. 4. Daughters had no right
of inheritance if a man left sons. —
πρὸς τοὺς κτλ. : in my relations with.
See on XII. 23.— μηδεπώποτε... γενέσθαι: there has never been any ground
of complaint at all against me on the
part of a single solitary man. Cf.
XXXII. 2, and see App.— μηδὲ πρὸς ἕνα:
ne unum quidem, more emphatic
than πρὸς μηδένα. See on XXXI. 30.

11. ἐπιεικείας : see on μετρίως, § 3.
— κύβους : these, like the Roman

70 ἀκολασίας τυγχάνουσι τὰς διατριβὰς ποιούμενοι, πάντας
αὑτοὺς ὄψεσθέ μοι διαφόρους ὄντας, καὶ πλεῖστα τούτους
περὶ ἐμοῦ λογοποιοῦντας καὶ ψευδομένους. καίτοι δῆλον
ὅτι, εἰ τῶν αὐτῶν ἐπεθυμοῦμεν, οὐκ ἂν τοιαύτην γνώμην
12 εἶχον περὶ ἐμοῦ. ἔτι δ᾽, ὦ βουλή, οὐδεὶς ἂν ἀποδεῖξαι
75 περὶ ἐμοῦ δύναιτο οὔτε δίκην αἰσχρὰν οὔτε γραφὴν οὔτε
εἰσαγγελίαν γεγενημένην· καίτοι ἑτέρους ὁρᾶτε πολλάκις
εἰς τοιούτους ἀγῶνας καθεστηκότας. πρὸς τοίνυν τὰς
στρατείας καὶ τοὺς κινδύνους τοὺς πρὸς τοὺς πολεμίους
13 σκέψασθε οἷον ἐμαυτὸν παρέχω τῇ πόλει. πρῶτον μὲν
80 γάρ, ὅτε τὴν συμμαχίαν ἐποιήσασθε πρὸς Βοιωτοὺς καὶ
εἰς Ἁλίαρτον ἔδει βοηθεῖν, ὑπὸ Ὀρθοβούλου κατειλεγ-
μένος ἱππεύειν, ἐπειδὴ πάντας ἑώρων τοῖς μὲν ἱππεύουσιν

tesserae and our dice, had six
sides, numbered from one to six,
and three or two dice were used in
the game.—τὰς διατριβὰς ποιούμενοι:
with περί and acc., the only occurrence in Lysias of this common expression (Lutz, Präpositionen, p.139).
Cf. διατρίβειν, XXIV. 20. — λογοποιοῦντας : ‘cooking up stories,’ see on
XXII. 14 and cf. Theophr. Char. 8,
ἡ δὲ λογοποιία ἐστὶ σύνθεσις ψευδῶν λόγων καὶ πράξεων ὧν βούλεται ὁ λογο-
ποιῶν. — εἰ ... ἐπεθυμοῦμεν: if we had
the same tastes. For the augment,
see on ἐξεκλησιάζετε, XII. 73.

12. δίκην : in its special meaning
of private suit, Introd. § 36. — αἰσ-
χράν : e.g. if he had been accused
of not portioning his sisters. — εἰσαγγελίαν : impeachment, see Introd.
n. 167.—πολλάκις : emphatic, as is
shown by its separation from καθεστηκότας. — τοίνυν : besides, cf. VII.
18.

13. πρῶτον μέν : followed up by
μετὰ ταῦτα τοίνυν in § 15. — τὴν συμμαχίαν : the alliance, still existing
(hence the article), was effected in
the autumn of 395 B.C., by Thrasybulus of Stiria and his namesake of
Collytus. For a fragment of the
treaty, still extant, see Hicks, Greek
Hist. Inscr. p. 122 = CIA. II, 6. —
Ἁλίαρτον : in Boeotia on Lake Co-
païs. During the Corinthian war, in
395 B.C., an expedition was sent
thither from Athens to help the
Thebans against the Spartans. The
latter were beaten and Lysander was
killed before the Athenians arrived.
Xen. Hellen. iii. 5. 17 ff. — Ὀρθοβούλου : phylarch of the speaker's
tribe. The κατάλογος (cf. XXXII. 5),
prepared by officers called καταλογεῖς
(Arist. Resp. Ath. 49, 2), was brought
before the Senate by the phylarchs
and hipparchs for the δοκιμασία.
— δεῖν : depends on νομίζοντας. —

ἀσφάλειαν εἶναι δεῖν νομίζοντας, τοῖς δ᾽ ὁπλίταις κίνδυνον
ἡγουμένους, ἑτέρων ἀναβάντων ἐπὶ τοὺς ἵππους ἀδοκιμά-
85στων παρὰ τὸν νόμον, ἐγὼ προσελθὼν ἔφην τῷ Ὀρθο-
βούλῳ ἐξαλεῖψαί με ἐκ τοῦ καταλόγου, ἡγούμενος αἰσχρὸν
εἶναι τοῦ πλήθους μέλλοντος κινδυνεύειν ἄδειαν ἐμαυτῷ
παρασκευάσαντα στρατεύεσθαι. καί μοι ἀνάβηθι, Ὀρθό-
βουλε.

ΜΑΡΤΥΡΙΑ.

14   Συλλεγέντων τοίνυν τῶν δημοτῶν πρὸ τῆς ἐξόδου, εἰδὼς
αὐτῶν ἐνίους πολίτας μὲν χρηστοὺς ὄντας καὶ προθύμους,
ἐφοδίων δὲ ἀπορούντας, εἶπον ὅτι χρὴ τοὺς ἔχοντας παρέχειν τὰ ἐπιτήδεια τοῖς ἀπόρως διακειμένοις. καὶ οὐ μόνον
τοῦτο συνεβούλευον τοῖς ἄλλοις, ἀλλὰ καὶ αὐτὸς ἔδωκα
95δυοῖν ἀνδροῖν τριάκοντα δραχμὰς ἑκατέρῳ, οὐχ ὡς πολλὰ
κεκτημένος, ἀλλ᾽ ἵνα παράδειγμα τοῦτο τοῖς ἄλλοις γένηται. καί μοι ἀνάβητε.

ΜΑΡΤΥΡΕΣ.

15   Μετὰ ταῦτα τοίνυν, ὦ βουλή, εἰς Κόρινθον ἐξόδου γενο-

τοῖς ὁπλίταις κίνδυνον: sc. probably
because Sparta's strength lay in her
heavy infantry.— ἡγουμένους : nearly
equivalent to νομίζοντας. Lysias was
fond of synonymous words or phrases
at the ends of contrasted clauses ; cf.
VII. 26; XII. 7, 48; XXIV. 18; XXXI. 17.
— ἔφην : = ἐκέλευον (cf. § 16) used
thus in prose only here and in Xen.
Cyr. iv. 6. 11, ἃ οἱ μάγοι ἔφασαν τοῖς
θεοῖς ἐξελεῖν. See App.— κινδυνεύειν :
on the tense, see G. 1254 ; H. 846.
   14. συλλεγέντων: the Athenian was
a citizen soldier enlisted and serving
by tribe and deme. Cf. Isaeus, II. 42,

ἐστράτευμαι ἐν τῇ φυλῇ τῇ ἐκείνου καὶ
ἐν τῷ δήμῳ. — ἐφοδίων : travelling expenses, funds, viaticum. The hop-
lites generally received two obols a
day for pay (μισθός) and two for ration
money (σιτηρέσιον), Boeckh, Staatsh.
I, 340; but the rich often helped poor
members of their demes with money
for equipments. See on XXXI. 15. —
τοὺς ἔχοντας : the rich, cf. XXXII. 9.
   — γένηται : on the mood, cf. ἀναπράττητε, § 6, and on the tense, see G.
1272 ; H. 851.
   15. εἰς Κόρινθον: i.e. the Corinthian
war, 394 B.C., in which 6000 Athe-

μένης καὶ πάντων προειδότων ὅτι δεήσει κινδυνεύειν,
100 ἑτέρων ἀναδυομένων ἐγὼ διεπραξάμην ὥστε τῆς πρώτης
τεταγμένος μάχεσθαι τοῖς πολεμίοις· καὶ μάλιστα τῆς
ἡμετέρας φυλῆς δυστυχησάσης καὶ πλείστων ἐναποθανόντων, ὕστερος ἀνεχώρησα τοῦ σεμνοῦ Στειριῶς τοῦ
16 πᾶσιν ἀνθρώποις δειλίαν ὠνειδικότος.   καὶ οὐ πολλαῖς
105 ἡμέραις ὕστερον μετὰ ταῦτα ἐν Κορίνθῳ χωρίων ἰσχυρῶν
κατειλημμένων, ὥστε τοὺς πολεμίους μὴ δύνασθαι παριέναι, Ἀγησιλάου δ᾽ εἰς τὴν Βοιωτίαν ἐμβαλόντος ψηφισα-
μένων τῶν ἀρχόντων ἀποκληρῶσαι τάξεις αἵτινες βοηθήσουσι, — φοβουμένων ἁπάντων (εἰκότως, ὦ βουλή· δεινὸν
110 γὰρ ἦν ἀγαπητῶς ὀλίγῳ πρότερον σεσωμένους ἐφ᾽ ἕτερον

nians took part under Thrasybulus.
Sparta won a victory at Nemea where
the Athenian loss was heavy. Cf.
Xen. Hellen. iv. 2. 9–23. — ὥστε μάχεσθαι : on the mood, see G. 1450 ;
H. 953. The same verb takes the
obj. inf. in XIII. 72, τὰ μέντοι ὀνόματα
διαπράττονται ... προσγραφῆναι εἰς τὴν
στήλην. — τῆς πρώτης : sc. τάξεως,
which here means rank, but cf. § 16.
On the gen., see G. 1095, 1096 ; H.
732 a.— δυστυχησάσης : his tribe was
therefore one of the six posted opposite to the Spartans, cf. Xen. Hellen.
iv. 2. 19–22.— ἐναποθανόντων: the ἐν-
refers to δυστυχησάσης, and means ἐν
τῇ δυστυχίᾳ. Cf. Thuc. ii. 52. 3, τά τε
ἱερὰ ἐν οἷς ἐσκήνηντο νεκρῶν πλέα ἦν,
αὐτοῦ ἐναποθνῃσκόντων (sc. ἐν τοῖς ἱεροῖς),
and Xen. Hellen. iii. 1. 4, quoted on
p. 74. — τοῦ σεμνοῦ Στειριῶς : (See
App.) Thrasybulus of the deme
Stiria, the leader of the men of
Phyle, is meant. On σεμνός, properly reverend, majestic, augustus,

but here used sarcastically, cf. Ar.
Ran. 178, ὡς σεμνὸς ὁ κατάρατος, how
airy the knave is ! Thrasybulus's
overbearing manner won him the
epithets αὐθάδης and ὑπερόπτης τοῦ
δήμου, schol. Ar. Eccl. 203. — πᾶσιν
ἀνθρώποις: without the article, the
whole world, everybody. Cf. VII. 13 ;
XII. 60 ; XXIV. 20 ; XXXI. 11 ; XXXII.
19. Mantitheus himself was evidently
smarting.

16. κατειλημμένων: sc. by the Athenians and allies, to prevent the Spartans from joining Agesilaus who was
returning from Asia by way of Phocis.
— ὥστε ... παριέναι: denotes purpose.
G. 1452; H. 953 a.— ἐμβαλόντος: gives
the reason for the action of the generals. G. 1563, 2 ; H. 953 a. — τάξεις :
the body of infantry furnished by
each tribe was called a τάξις. — αἵτινες βοηθήσουσι : denoting purpose,
cf. XXIV. 6. G. 1442; H. 911.—ἀγαπητῶς: lit. gladly, as in Dem. XIX.
219, τὴν εἰρήνην ἐποιήσασθ᾽ ἀγαπητῶς.

κίνδυνον ἰέναι) προσελθὼν ἐγὼ τὸν ταξίαρχον ἐκέλευον
17 ἀκληρωτὶ τὴν ἡμετέραν τάξιν πέμπειν. ὥστ᾽ εἴ τινες
ὑμῶν ὀργίζονται τοῖς τὰ μὲν τῆς πόλεως ἀξιοῦσι πράττειν, ἐκ δὲ τῶν κινδύνων ἀποδιδράσκουσιν, οὐκ ἂν δικαίως
115 περὶ ἐμοῦ τὴν γνώμην ταύτην ἔχοιεν· οὐ γὰρ μόνον τὰ
προσταττόμενα ἐποίουν προθύμως, ἀλλὰ καὶ κινδυνεύειν
ἐτόλμων. καὶ ταῦτ᾽ ἐποίουν οὐχ ὡς οὐ δεινὸν ἡγούμενος
εἶναι Λακεδαιμονίοις μάχεσθαι, ἀλλ᾽ ἵνα, εἴ ποτε ἀδίκως
εἰς κίνδυνον καθισταίμην, διὰ ταῦτα βελτίων ὑφ᾽ ὑμῶν
120 νομιζόμενος ἁπάντων τῶν δικαίων τυγχάνοιμι. καί μοι
ἀνάβητε τούτων μάρτυρες.

ΜΑΡΤΥΡΕΣ.

18 Τῶν τοίνυν ἄλλων στρατειῶν καὶ φρουρῶν οὐδεμιᾶς
ἀπελείφθην πώποτε, ἀλλὰ πάντα τὸν χρόνον διατετέλεκα
μετὰ τῶν πρώτων μὲν τὰς ἐξόδους ποιούμενος, μετὰ τῶν
125 τελευταίων δὲ ἀναχωρῶν. καίτοι χρὴ τοὺς φιλοτίμως καὶ
κοσμίως πολιτευομένους ἐκ τῶν τοιούτων σκοπεῖν, ἀλλ᾽
οὐκ εἴ τις κομᾷ, διὰ τοῦτο μισεῖν· τὰ μὲν γὰρ τοιαῦτα

Hence, with the implication *too
glad*, = μόλις, *barely, hardly*. See on
ἀγαπήσειν, XII. II.

17. ἀποδιδράσκουσι : this word,
regularly implying something dis-
graceful, is applied to deserters, runaway slaves, *etc.*; *cf.* Plat. *Crit.* 53 D,
ὡς γελοίως ἐκ τοῦ δεσμωτηρίου ἀπεδί-
δρασκες (*what a funny time you had
when you cleared out of the prison*)
... διφθέραν (*goatskin*) λαβὼν ἢ ἄλλα
οἷα δὴ εἰώθασιν ἐνσκευάζεσθαι οἱ ἀπο-
διδράσκοντες ('runaways').—**ἂν ἔχοιεν** :
on the potential opt. after an indic.
in prot. (G. 1421, 1 ; H. 901 b), *cf.*
XXII. 18.—**ἵνα ... τυγχάνοιμι** : a naïve

confession of the speaker's practical
reason for patriotism.

18. ἀπελείφθην : *missed*. The preceding gen. is of separation. G. 1117;
H. 748. — **πώποτε, πάντα τὸν χρόνον** : these words with the two verbs
to which they belong are strongly
contrasted by the chiastic order. —
ποιούμενος : supplementary partic.
with διατετέλεκα. G. 1580 ; H. 981.
—**κοσμίως** : for the meaning, see on
VII. 41. — **σκοπεῖν** : this verb, in the
sense of 'form a judgment about,' is
frequently used with ἐκ and the gen.;
cf. § 19 ; VII. 13, 34. — **κομᾷ** : *wears
his hair long*, as Mantitheus appar-

ἐπιτηδεύματα οὔτε τοὺς ἰδιώτας οὔτε τὸ κοινὸν τῆς πόλεως
βλάπτει, ἐκ δὲ τῶν κινδυνεύειν ἐθελόντων πρὸς τοὺς πολε-
19 μίους ἅπαντες ὑμεῖς ὠφελεῖσθε. ὥστε οὐκ ἄξιον ἀπ'
ὄψεως, ὦ βουλή, οὔτε φιλεῖν οὔτε μισεῖν οὐδένα, ἀλλ' ἐκ
τῶν ἔργων σκοπεῖν· πολλοὶ μὲν γὰρ μικρὸν διαλεγόμενοι
καὶ κοσμίως ἀμπεχόμενοι μεγάλων κακῶν αἴτιοι γεγόνα-
σιν, ἕτεροι δὲ τῶν τοιούτων ἀμελοῦντες πολλὰ κἀγαθὰ
135 ὑμᾶς εἰσιν εἰργασμένοι.
20 Ἤδη δέ τινων ἠσθόμην, ὦ βουλή, καὶ διὰ ταῦτα ἀχθομένων μοι, ὅτι νεώτερος ὢν ἐπεχείρησα λέγειν ἐν τῷ
δήμῳ. ἐγὼ δὲ τὸ μὲν πρῶτον ἠναγκάσθην ὑπὲρ τῶν ἐμαυτοῦ πραγμάτων δημηγορῆσαι, ἔπειτα μέντοι καὶ ἐμαυτῷ
140 δοκῶ φιλοτιμότερον διατεθῆναι τοῦ δέοντος, ἅμα μὲν τῶν
προγόνων ἐνθυμούμενος ὅτι οὐδὲν πέπαυνται τὰ τῆς

ently did. After the Persian wars it was the fashion for Athenian boys on reaching the age of eighteen to cut off their hair and dedicate it to their patron divinities, afterwards wearing it short. But the knights and ultra-fashionable young men of Mantitheus's time wore it long, a Spartan fashion; hence those who followed it were suspected of being aristocrats and 'Laconizers.' — ἐκ τῶν ἐθελόντων: the agent viewed as the *source*, hence not with ὑπό. G. 1209 c; H. 798 c. See App.

19. ἀπ' ὄψεως: *for his looks*, said with reference to κομᾷ. Causal, see G. 1205 c; H. 794 c. — μικρὸν διαλέγομενοι: *though their tones are low*. The principle of moderation (see on § 3) was observed by Athenian gentlemen in voice, gait (πρᾳότης πορείας, Plut. *Pericl.* 5) and general bearing. According to Theophrastus, *Char.* 4,

μεγάλῃ τῇ φωνῇ λαλεῖν was a mark of ἀγροικία. Cf. Dem. xxxvii. 52, Νικόβουλος δ' ἐπίφθονός ἐστι καὶ ταχέως βαδίζει καὶ μέγα φθέγγεται. — κοσμίως ἀμπεχόμενοι: *their mantles set decently*, a point on which much stress was laid. It looks as though Mantitheus had adopted a somewhat *dégagé* style.

20. ἤδη: *before now.* — καί: *besides* the above reasons. — τινῶν: for the gen., see G. 1102; H. 742. — ἀχθομένων: supplementary partic. G. 1582; H. 982. — νεώτερος: at the age of eighteen every Athenian had full civic rights and could therefore speak in the assembly, but modesty should still restrain him; see the incident of Glaucon in Xen. *Mem.* iii. 6. — πραγμάτων: possibly in connexion with the συμφοραὶ τοῦ πατρός, § 10. — καί: emphasizes ἐμαυτῷ. — διατεθῆναι: of the inward disposition.

21 πόλεως πράττοντες, ἅμα δὲ ὑμᾶς ὁρῶν (τὰ γὰρ ἀληθῆ
χρὴ λέγειν) τοὺς τοιούτους μόνους ἀξίους τινὸς νομίζοντας
εἶναι· ὥστε ὁρῶν ὑμᾶς ταύτην τὴν γνώμην ἔχοντας τίς
145 οὐκ ἂν ἐπαρθείη πράττειν καὶ λέγειν ὑπὲρ τῆς πόλεως; ἔτι
δὲ τί ἂν τοῖς τοιούτοις ἄχθοισθε; οὐ γὰρ ἕτεροι περὶ αὐτῶν κριταί εἰσιν, ἀλλ᾽ ὑμεῖς.

21. τοὺς τοιούτους: *i.e.* those who take part in public affairs. The Athenians little esteemed persons who neglected public duties. *Cf.* the words of Pericles, Thuc. ii. 40. 2, τόν τε μηδὲν τῶνδε (*politics*) μετέχοντα οὐκ ἀπράγμονα ἀλλ᾽ ἀχρεῖον νομίζομεν, and Introd. § 6, end. — **ἀξίους τινός**: *deserving of any esteem at all.* For this pregnant sense of τὶς see App. and H. 703 a, Kr. *Spr.* 51. 16. 13. — **κριταί**: the general term for persons with whom any decision rests; δικασταί could apply only to a legal issue. — **ἀλλ᾽ ὑμεῖς**: this abrupt close is a good example of Lysias's power of suiting the speech to the speaker.

AGAINST THE GRAIN–DEALERS.

INTRODUCTION.

THE Athenian corn-laws were not the result of any theory of political economy, and had nothing to do with the question of free trade or protection.[1] They sprang from the need of assuring a sufficient supply of food to a State which was unable to provide that food from its own soil. Attica was not a good agricultural country.[2] The olive[3] and fig alone yielded profitable returns. Barley[4] was the only really flourishing cereal; but the wheat crop was altogether inadequate to supply the demand. The population,[5] numbering about half a million souls, was beyond all due proportion to the area of but little over 700 square miles (about half the area of Rhode Island, less than one-tenth of that of Massachusetts). Naturally, therefore, recourse was had abroad[6] for food-stuffs, and Egypt, Sicily, Rhodes, Cyprus, and above all the fertile districts on the Pontus[7] supplied the wants of Attica. Cargoes were constantly coming from these quarters; and besides the supplies provided by the ordinary course of commerce, it was a favourite practice with foreign rulers to win the good-will of the Athenian commons by presents of grain.[8]

The Athenians had a whole series of laws intended to prevent a scarcity of grain. Solon is said to have forbidden the export of any agricultural product except olive oil.[9] While the export of grain

---

[1] On this general topic, see Büchsenschütz, *Besitz und Erwerb*, p. 541; Boeckh, *Staatsh.* I, p. 65 ff.

In this introduction I have closely followed Frohberger.

[2] Thuc. i. 2. 5 calls Attica λεπτόγεως, and Plutarch, *Solon*, 22, says τὰ πλεῖστα τῆς χώρας ἀγεννῆ καὶ φαῦλα.

[3] See Introd. to VII.

[4] Theophr. *H. P.* viii. 8. 2.

[5] Boeckh, *ibid.* p. 42.

[6] Dem. XVIII. 87.

[7] Dem. XX. 31 f.

[8] Dem. XX. 33.

[9] Plut. *Solon*, 24; *cf.* Boeckh, *ibid.* p. 67.

grown in Attica was absolutely prohibited,[10] its importation was
encouraged, and even enforced so far as the power of the law
could avail.   Athenian citizens and metics were forbidden, under
the severest penalties, to ship grain elsewhere than to Attica,[11] or
to lend money on bottomry[12] to grain-merchants unless the cargo
thus mortgaged was actually to be brought thither.[13]   The Piraeus
was the central warehouse (ἐμπόριον) for the eastern part of the
Mediterranean, and a law required that two-thirds of the cargo
of every grain-ship which put in there must be carried to the
city.[14]   One of the chief duties of the Athenian navy in time of
war was to keep open the communications with the Pontus so
as to ensure the safe delivery of grain.[15]   The Assembly, also,
at one of its regular meetings in each prytany, considered the
state of the grain supply.[16]   But the laws went even further into
particulars.   In order to prevent speculation and the artificial raising of the price of corn, retail dealers (σιτοπῶλαι) were forbidden,
on penalty of death, to buy more than fifty baskets (φορμοί[17]) at
a time.[18]

---

[10] Ulpian on Dem. *Tim.* p. 822 (§ 136).

[11] [Dem.] XXXIV. 37; XXXV. 50.
Lycurg. 27.

[12] See on XXXII. 6.

[13] [Dem.] XXXV. 50 f.

[14] Arist. *Resp. Ath.* 51. 4; Boeckh,
ibid. p. 104; M. and S. p. 99; Gilbert,
Antiq. p. 260. But for schemes of corn
merchants to avoid this port, if grain
was low here, *cf.* [Dem.] LVI. 8.

[15] Dem. XVIII. 87, 241, 301; L. 17;
Xen. *Hellen.* v. 4. 61.

[16] Arist. *Resp. Ath.* 43. 4; *cf.* Xen.
Mem. iii. 6. 13.

[17] A sort of wicker basket, perhaps
holding about a medimnus (= 52.5
liters or a bushel and a half). See
Boeckh, *ibid.* p. 104.

[18] § 5 f. It was formerly believed,
on the basis of § 8 where the Ms. has

δεῖν γὰρ αὐτοὺς ὀβολῷ μόνον πωλεῖν τιμιώτερον, that there was also a law forbidding dealers to sell at a profit of
more than one obol on the medimnus.
But such a law would have been next to
impossible to enforce, and § 12 (τῆς αὐτῆς
ἡμέρας ἐπώλουν δραχμῇ τιμιώτερον) shows
that no such law *was* enforced; nay,
the speaker there does not even hint
that the dealers were doing anything
really *unlawful* in making a profit of
a drachma.   Hence Graux's insertion
of κἄν in § 8 has been generally
accepted (see App. and Boeckh, *ibid.*
p. 104).   Yet, as Blass (*Att. Bereds.* I,
p. 471) remarks, δεῖν is hardly consis-
tent with the emendation.   It seems
probable to me that with Kocks we
should reject the whole clause δεῖν . . .
τιμιώτερον as a marginal gloss.   Wila-

The enforcement of these regulations was in the hands of a special board of magistrates, elected by lot, and called σιτοφύλακες.[19] Of these officials Aristotle (*Resp. Ath.* 51. 3) says :

ἦσαν δὲ καὶ σιτοφύλακες κληρωτοί, πέντε μὲν εἰς Πειραιέα, πέντε δ᾽ εἰς ἄστυ, νῦν δ᾽ εἴκοσι[20] μὲν εἰς ἄστυ, πεντεκαίδεκα δ᾽ εἰς Πειραιέα. οὗτοι δ᾽ ἐπιμελοῦνται, πρῶτον μὲν ὅπως ὁ ἐν ἀγορᾷ σῖτος ἀργὸς ὤνιος ἔσται δικαίως, ἔπειθ᾽ ὅπως οἵ τε μυλωθροὶ πρὸς τὰς τιμὰς τῶν κριθῶν τὰ ἄλφιτα πωλή- σουσιν καὶ οἱ ἀρτοπῶλαι πρὸς τὰς τιμὰς τῶν πυρῶν τοὺς ἄρτους, καὶ τὸν σταθ- μὸν ἄγοντας ὅσον ἂν οὗτοι τάξωσιν· ὁ γὰρ νόμος τούτους κελεύει τάττειν.

From this passage and from our speech[21] it would seem that there were ten of these officials in the time of Lysias. It was their duty to see that the unground (ἀργός) grain was offered at a fair price, that the millers sold barley meal at a price proportionate to that of barley, and that the bakers sold bread at a price proportionate to that of wheat and made loaves of a weight fixed by the σιτο- φύλακες. They had also to keep a record of all importations of grain.[22] Their duties, then, were of a prohibitory and restrictive sort, while the σιτῶναι, a committee appointed only on special occa- sions by a decree of the people, had the task of purchasing grain on an order from the State in time of war or scarcity, and of see- ing that it was sold at a price fixed by law.[23]

But speculation, whether in Athens or elsewhere, has never been prevented by legislation. The grain trade was the favourite busi- ness[24] of the great wholesale merchants (ἔμποροι), while the retail dealers (σιτοπῶλαι[25]), standing between the merchants and the con-

---

mowitz, *Aristoteles und Athen*, II, p. 377, thinks that the words were part of the advice given to the dealers by Anytus, and that they contain merely a suggestion of his, not a law.

[19] § 16. See Gilbert, *Antiq.* p. 260.

[20] The reading is doubtful in the Ms., possibly ιε´ (= πεντεκαίδεκα). For the old view of the number of these officers, see Boeckh, *ibid.* p. 105.

[21] § 8. [22] Dem. xx. 32.

[23] Bake, *Schol. Hypomnem.* III, 257. The ἀγορανόμοι (§ 16, Arist. *Resp. Ath.* 51. 1) had general charge of the mar- ket and saw that the wares sold there were pure and unadulterated.

[24] Xen. *Oec.* xx. 27 f.

[25] Metics as a rule (*cf.* § 5, Dem. xxxiv. 37) like most of the κάπηλοι (in itself rather a contemptuous term, *cf.* below, § 21, and Hermann, *Privatalt.* p. 420).

sumers, were not slow to scheme against both.　For instance, by
an understanding with the merchants, they might evade the laws
against the purchase of grain in bulk; or on the other hand, by
combining with each other to prevent competition they could
depress the price fixed by the merchants, and then, having bought
in at a low figure, they would busy themselves in spreading some
piece of bad news of a political sort which gave them an excuse for
raising the price on retail sales.　Such intrigues are described in
the following speech of Lysias and in the oration against Diony-
sodorus falsely attributed to Demosthenes.[26]　The σιτοφύλακες were
often unable to control these illegalities, and were punished for
their inaction or for their connivance with grain 'rings.'[27]　As
for the dealers, the popular feeling against them (which sometimes
broke out in riots[28]) made them an easy prey to 'sycophants'; and
yet this very fact often protected them in wrong-doing, for any
person who accused a grain-dealer laid himself open to the suspicion of 'sycophancy.'[29]

Since to break the corn-laws was to commit a crime against the
State, the proper method of procedure against the criminal was by
an εἰσαγγελία or denunciation laid before the Prytanes, who brought
it before the Senate.[30]　An investigation (κρίσις, § 3) followed, to
see whether a true bill could be found, and whether the Senate
should settle the matter itself or refer it to a regular heliastic
court.[31]　If it came before a court, the Thesmothetae presided,[32]
and the suit was ἀτίμητος, the penalty being death.[33]

The following speech was delivered before such a court by a
senator who accuses a company[34] of σιτοπῶλαι of illegal speculation.
The Senate had been so exasperated when the case was first laid
before it that some suggested that the accused should be executed
without a trial; our senator by his moderation prevented such

---

[26] LVI. 7 ff.
[27] §§ 8, 16, 21; Dem. XXIV. 136.
[28] Philostratus, *Vit. Sophist.* i. 23. 1,
p. 225.　　　[29] § 1.
[30] § 2 f.; M. and S. pp. 69, 312, 319.

[31] § 2; [Dem.] XLVII. 41 ff.; M. and
S. p. 323.
[32] Poll. viii. 87; Arist. *Resp. Ath.*
59. 2.
[33] §§ 5, 13, 19.　　[34] See on § 5.

hasty action, and the case took its regular course. But the senator, having stood for the regular forms of law, now found it necessary to make a stand for his own reputation, and was obliged to attack the 'ring' lest he should be thought the tool of it.[35] The dealers confessed their action, but attempted to shift the blame upon the σιτοφύλακες.[36] The speaker shows that such a defence, if allowed, merely includes these magistrates among the guilty.[37] He next overthrows the pretext that the dealers had broken the law with a good purpose, — to supply the consumer with grain at the cheapest possible rate.[38] In conclusion, he holds that their confession makes it necessary to condemn them, and that they have no claim to mercy.[39] The short epilogue combines an appeal to justice with a personal argument likely to have influence with the judges.[40]

This is the crisp, business-like speech of an earnest man who is merely engaged in doing his duty to the country and himself without having any personal grudge against the accused. It is well arranged and logical, and confined closely to the matter in hand. It is short, because there really could be no doubt about the facts; and it is almost bare of any rhetorical figures, for these would have been entirely out of place in such an address. On the date of its delivery nothing can be said with certainty. We must set it later than the beginning of the Corinthian war (394 B.C.), unless we are to suppose that the story that Spartans had seized Athenian grain-ships[41] was a stock 'scare' good at any time. It has been thought, but it cannot be proved, that σπονδάς in the same passage refers to the peace of Antalcidas (387 B.C.).[42]

---

[35] §§ 2–4.
[36] § 5.   [37] §§ 6–10.
[38] §§ 11–16.   [39] §§ 17–21.
[40] § 22.   [41] § 14.
[42] This peace is called σπονδαί in

Xen. *Hellen.* v. 1. 33, and just before the date of it the grain-ships in the Pontus had been stopped by Antalcidas (Xen. *ibid.* 28); hence perhaps the dearness mentioned in § 8.

ΚΑΤΑ ΤΩΝ ΣΙΤΟΠΩΛΩΝ.

1 Πολλοί μοι προσεληλύθασιν, ὦ ἄνδρες δικασταί, θαυμάζοντες ὅτι ἐγὼ τῶν σιτοπωλῶν ἐν τῇ βουλῇ κατηγόρουν καὶ λέγοντες ὅτι ὑμεῖς, εἰ ὡς μάλιστα αὐτοὺς ἀδικεῖν
ἡγεῖσθε, οὐδὲν ἧττον καὶ τοὺς περὶ τούτων ποιουμένους
5 τοὺς λόγους συκοφαντεῖν νομίζετε. ὅθεν οὖν ἠνάγκασμαι
κατηγορεῖν αὐτῶν, περὶ τούτων πρῶτον εἰπεῖν βούλομαι.

2 Ἐπειδὴ γὰρ οἱ πρυτάνεις ἀπέδοσαν εἰς τὴν βουλὴν
περὶ αὐτῶν, οὕτως ὠργίσθησαν αὐτοῖς, ὥστε ἔλεγόν τινες
τῶν ῥητόρων ὡς ἀκρίτους αὐτοὺς χρὴ τοῖς ἕνδεκα παρα-
10 δοῦναι θανάτῳ ζημιῶσαι. ἡγούμενος δὲ ἐγὼ δεινὸν εἶναι
τοιαῦτα ἐθίζεσθαι ποιεῖν τὴν βουλήν, ἀναστὰς εἶπον ὅτι

1. **θαυμάζοντες**: *sc.* because he had
at first (§ 2) seemed to side with the
dealers. Hence ἐγώ, emphatic. For
ὅτι instead of the usual εἰ after θαυμάζω, see G. 1424, and on VII. 7. —
εἰ ὡς μάλιστα κτλ.: 'no matter how
guilty.' *Cf.* § 10 and Plat. *Euthyphro*,
4 D, εἰ ὅτι μάλιστα ἀπέκτεινεν, and see
H. 651. — **καὶ τούς**: *even those*, see
p. 92. — **ποιουμένους τοὺς λόγους**:
see on XII. 2. — **συκοφαντεῖν**: see on
VII. 38.

2. **οἱ πρυτάνεις**: see Gow, p. 116;
Hermann, *Staatsalt.*, p. 488; Gilbert, *Antiq.* p. 271. The εἰσαγγελία
would be laid first before them as
executive committee of the Senate.
— **ἀπέδοσαν κτλ.**: the technical

phrase, *cf.* referre ad senatum.
— **ὠργίσθησαν**: *sc.* οἱ βουλευταί from
βουλήν. See on αὐτῶν, XII. 37. — **τῶν
ῥητόρων**: not necessarily professional
orators, but often merely persons
in the habit of speaking publicly.
See on XXXI. 27, and *cf.* Plat. *Ap.*
32 B, ἑτοίμων ὄντων ἐνδεικνύναι με
καὶ ἀπάγειν τῶν ῥητόρων. — **ἀκρίτους**:
on the illegality, see on XII. 17. —
τοῖς ἕνδεκα: they had charge of the
prisons and of executions. See Gilbert, *Antiq.* p. 256. — **θανάτῳ ζημιῶσαι**: the infin. of purpose. GMT.
772 a. *Cf.* XIII. 68, καὶ καταγνόντες
αὐτοῦ θάνατον ἀποτυμπανίσαι παρέδοτε,
Dinarch. II. 20, παραδοῦναι τοῖς ἐπὶ
τοῦτο τεταγμένοις θανάτῳ ζημιῶσαι. —

μοι δοκοίη κρίνειν τοὺς σιτοπώλας κατὰ τὸν νόμον, νομίζων, εἰ μέν εἰσιν ἄξια θανάτου εἰργασμένοι, ὑμᾶς οὐδὲν
ἧττον ἡμῶν γνώσεσθαι τὰ δίκαια, εἰ δὲ μηδὲν ἀδικοῦσιν,
3 οὐ δεῖν αὐτοὺς ἀκρίτους ἀπολωλέναι. πεισθείσης δὲ τῆς
βουλῆς ταῦτα, διαβάλλειν ἐπεχείρουν με λέγοντες ὡς ἐγὼ
σωτηρίας ἕνεκα τῆς τῶν σιτοπωλῶν τοὺς λόγους τούτους
ἐποιούμην. πρὸς μὲν οὖν τὴν βουλήν, ὅτ᾽ ἦν αὐτοῖς ἡ
κρίσις, ἔργῳ ἀπελογησάμην· τῶν γὰρ ἄλλων ἡσυχίαν
20 ἀγόντων ἀναστὰς αὐτῶν κατηγόρουν, καὶ πᾶσι φανερὸν
ἐποίησα ὅτι οὐχ ὑπὲρ τούτων ἔλεγον, ἀλλὰ τοῖς νόμοις
4 τοῖς κειμένοις ἐβοήθουν. ἠρξάμην μὲν οὖν τούτων ἕνεκα,
δεδιὼς τὰς αἰτίας· αἰσχρὸν δ᾽ ἡγοῦμαι πρότερον παύσασθαι, πρὶν ἂν ὑμεῖς περὶ αὐτῶν ὅ τι ἂν βούλησθε ψηφί-
25 σησθε.

5 Καὶ πρῶτον μὲν ἀνάβητε. εἰπὲ σὺ ἐμοί, μέτοικος εἶ;
Ναί. Μετοικεῖς δὲ πότερον ὡς πεισόμενος τοῖς νόμοις
τοῖς τῆς πόλεως, ἢ ὡς ποιήσων ὅ τι ἂν βούλῃ; Ὡς πει-

κατὰ τὸν νόμον: *i.e.* before a regular
court after the κρίσις (§ 3).

3. ἐποιούμην: *had made.* This and
the following impfs. ἔλεγον and ἐβοήθουν could not be changed to the present opt. without danger of obscurity
in the sense. G. 1488 ; H. 935 b. —
πρός: not *against*, as in XII. 38, but
in a local sense, *before, to. Cf.* XIII.
49, θαυμάζω ... ὅ τι ποτὲ τολμήσει πρὸς
ὑμᾶς ἀπολογεῖσθαι. — **ἡ κρίσις:** the
hearing before the Senate (*cf.* § 11),
held to see whether that body could
settle the case itself and mete out the
appropriate penalty, or should send
it on to a court. It corresponds
therefore to the ἀνάκρισις (see Introd.
§ 47). — **ἄλλων:** *i.e.* the ῥήτορες of § 2.

— κειμένοις: for the meaning, see on
XXXII. 23.

4. ἠρξάμην: *sc.* in the Senate. —
τὰς αἰτίας: *their charges,* referring to
διαβάλλειν, § 3. — **πρὶν ἄν ... ψηφίσησθε:** the leading clause has a negative force, hence the subjv. GMT.
647. So αἰσχρόν in Plat. *Prot.* 352 D,
αἰσχρόν ἐστι καὶ ἐμοὶ σοφίαν καὶ ἐπιστή-
μην μὴ οὐχὶ (on account of the preceding negative idea) πάντων κράτιστον
φάναι εἶναι.

5. On the ἐρώτησις, see Introd.
§ 48, and *cf.* XII. 25. — **ἀνάβητε:**
plural as addressed to the whole ring.
Cf. ψεύδονται, § 7 ; οὗτοι, § 8 ; συνίστασθαι, § 17 ; τούτων, § 22. See App.
— σύ: addressed to the leader. —

σόμενος. Ἄλλο τι οὖν ἀξιοῖς ἀποθανεῖν, εἴ τι πεποίηκας
30 παρὰ τοὺς νόμους, ἐφ' οἷς θάνατος ἡ ζημία; Ἔγωγε.
Ἀπόκριναι δή μοι, εἰ ὁμολογεῖς πλείω σῖτον συμπρίασθαι
πεντήκοντα φορμῶν, ὧν ὁ νόμος ἐξεῖναι κελεύει; Ἐγὼ
τῶν ἀρχόντων κελευόντων συνεπριάμην.

6 *Ἂν μὲν τοίνυν ἀποδείξῃ, ὦ ἄνδρες δικασταί, ὡς ἔστι
35 νόμος ὃς κελεύει τοὺς σιτοπώλας συνωνεῖσθαι τὸν σῖτον,
ἂν οἱ ἄρχοντες κελεύωσιν, ἀποψηφίσασθε· εἰ δὲ μή,
δίκαιον ὑμᾶς καταψηφίσασθαι. ἡμεῖς γὰρ ὑμῖν παρεσχόμεθα τὸν νόμον, ὃς ἀπαγορεύει μηδένα τῶν ἐν τῇ πόλει
πλείω σῖτον πεντήκοντα φορμῶν συνωνεῖσθαι.

7 Χρῆν μὲν τοίνυν, ὦ ἄνδρες δικασταί, ἱκανὴν εἶναι ταύτην τὴν κατηγορίαν, ἐπειδὴ οὗτος μὲν ὁμολογεῖ συμπρίασθαι, ὁ δὲ νόμος ἀπαγορεύων φαίνεται, ὑμεῖς δὲ κατὰ
τοὺς νόμους ὀμωμόκατε ψηφιεῖσθαι· ὅμως δ' ἵνα πεισθῆτε
ὅτι καὶ κατὰ τῶν ἀρχόντων ψεύδονται, ἀνάγκη καὶ μακρό-
8 τερον εἰπεῖν περὶ αὐτῶν. ἐπειδὴ γὰρ οὗτοι τὴν αἰτίαν εἰς
ἐκείνους ἀνέφερον, παρακαλέσαντες τοὺς ἄρχοντας ἠρωτῶμεν. καὶ οἱ μὲν τέτταρες οὐδὲν ἔφασαν εἰδέναι τοῦ

ἄλλο τι: on the phrase, without ἤ,
see App. and G. 1604; H. 1015 b. —
ἐφ' οἷς: for which, the relative referring κατὰ σύνεσιν to τί, which has,
as often, a collective force (= τι
τοιούτων). Cf. III. 48, εἴ τι πάθοιμι
ὧν Σίμων βούλεται, and see H. 633,
609, 615; Kr. Spr. 58, 4, 5. But
Lutz, Präp. p. 110, refers οἷς (denoting the ground) to νόμους. — συμπρίασθαι: bought up; cf. Arist. Pol. i.
11. 11, ἐν Σικελίᾳ δέ τις ... συνεπρίατο
πάντα τὸν σίδηρον ἐκ τῶν σιδηρείων. —
ἐγὼ τῶν ἀρχόντων κτλ.: Eratosthenes
similarly dodges a direct answer in

XII. 25. The ἄρχοντες are here the
σιτοφύλακες.

6. παρεσχόμεθα: the law was put
in with the other papers accompanying the γραφή, or written indictment.

7. ὀμωμόκατε: sc. in the dicasts'
oath. Cf. Aeschin. III. 6, ὁ νομοθέτης
τοῦτο πρῶτον ἔταξεν ἐν τῷ τῶν δικαστῶν
ὅρκῳ· ψηφιοῦμαι κατὰ τοὺς νόμους. —
καὶ μακρότερον: see App.

8. εἰς ... ἀνέφερον: see on XII. 81.
— ἠρωτῶμεν: sc. at the κρίσις, § 3. — οἱ
τέτταρες: for the article, see on
XXXII. 21. — οὐδὲν εἰδέναι τοῦ πράγματος: the same phrase occurs in

πράγματος, Ἄνυτος δ᾽ ἔλεγεν ὡς τοῦ προτέρου χειμῶνος,
ἐπειδὴ τίμιος ἦν ὁ σῖτος, τούτων ὑπερβαλλόντων ἀλλή-
50 λους καὶ πρὸς σφᾶς αὐτοὺς μαχομένων, συμβουλεύσειεν
αὐτοῖς παύσασθαι φιλονεικοῦσιν, ἡγούμενος συμφέρειν
ὑμῖν τοῖς παρὰ τούτων ὠνουμένοις ὡς ἀξιώτατον τούτους
πρίασθαι· δεῖν γὰρ αὐτοὺς κἂν ὀβολῷ μόνον πωλεῖν
9 τιμιώτερον. ὡς τοίνυν οὐ συμπριαμένους καταθέσθαι
55 ἐκέλευεν αὐτούς, ἀλλὰ μὴ ἀλλήλοις ἀντωνεῖσθαι συνεβού-
λευεν, αὐτὸν ὑμῖν Ἄνυτον μάρτυρα παρέξομαι, καὶ ὡς
οὗτος μὲν ἐπὶ τῆς προτέρας βουλῆς τούτους εἶπε τοὺς
λόγους, οὗτοι δὲ τῆτες συνωνούμενοι φαίνονται.

XIII. 71, cf. I. 42.—Ἄνυτος: one of the σιτοφύλακες of the year before. There is no evidence that he was the Anytus who accused Socrates. —ὑπερβαλλόν-των: trying to outbid. Cf. And. I. 134, ἐπεὶ δ᾽ οὐκ ἀντωνεῖτο οὐδείς, παρελθὼν ἐγὼ εἰς τὴν βουλὴν ὑπερέβαλλον. — πρὸς σφᾶς αὐτούς: = πρὸς ἀλλήλους. On this use of the reflexive for the reciprocal pronoun, here perhaps employed for variety, see G. 996, H. 686 b, and cf. XIV. 42, παρανόμως καὶ πρὸς τοὺς ἄλλους πολιτευόμενοι καὶ πρὸς σφᾶς αὐτοὺς διακείμενοι. — φιλονεικοῦσιν: on the case, cf. XII. 1. — ὠνουμένοις and πρίασθαι: observe the difference in tense. — ἀξιώτατον: the Attic idiomatic use of ἄξιος in the sense of cheap. Cf. § 22 and Ar. Eq. 645, οὑπώποτ᾽ ἀφύας (sprats) εἶδον ἀξιωτέρας, Moeris, p. 56, ἀξιωτέρας, Ἀττικῶς· εὐωνοτέρας, Ἑλληνικῶς. — κἂν ὀβολῷ μόνον: if only by a single obol, i.e. they must make some profit, however little. On the use of κἂν without a verb, see GMT. 228. But the whole sentence may be an interpolation. See App.

9. καταθέσθαι : lay or hoard it away, common in this sense. Cf. Xen. Anab. i. 3. 3, οὓς (sc. μυρίους δαρεικοὺς) ἐγὼ λαβὼν οὐκ εἰς τὸ ἴδιον κατεθέμην ἐμοί, and its use with that of παρακαταθήκη in XXXII. 16. The dealers distorted the advice of Anytus, which was not that they should buy up corn and store it away to sell high at a time of scant supply, but that they should stop running up the price (ἀντωνεῖσθαι, below, ὑπερβαλλόντων, § 8) in the wholesale market and thus be able to sell cheaper at retail, though still with profit to themselves. — ἐπί : of time, a new Senate being chosen annually. — καὶ ὡς ... φαίνονται: see App. — τῆτες: cf. Harp. s.v. τῆτες· ἀντὶ τοῦ τούτῳ τῷ ἔτει Λυσίας ἐν τῇ πρὸς Πυθόδημον ἀπολογίᾳ, εἰ γνήσιος, Ἀριστοφάνης Γήρᾳ καὶ οἱ ἄλλοι. Used also in Ar. Ach. 15, Vesp. 400. On the form, from the pronominal stem τἱα (like τήμερον), see Smyth, Greek Dialects, I, § 369. — συνωνούμενοι: impf. in time; see on XVI. 5.

ΜΑΡΤΥΡΙΑ.

10 Ὅτι μὲν τοίνυν οὐχ ὑπὸ τῶν ἀρχόντων κελευσθέντες
60 συνεπρίαντο τὸν σῖτον, ἀκηκόατε· ἡγοῦμαι δ᾽, ἂν ὡς μάλιστα περὶ τούτων ἀληθῆ λέγωσιν, οὐχ ὑπὲρ αὑτῶν αὐτοὺς
ἀπολογήσεσθαι, ἀλλὰ τούτων κατηγορήσειν· περὶ γὰρ
ὧν εἰσι νόμοι διαρρήδην γεγραμμένοι, πῶς οὐ χρὴ διδόναι
δίκην καὶ τοὺς μὴ πειθομένους καὶ τοὺς κελεύοντας τού-
65 τοις τἀναντία πράττειν;

11 Ἀλλὰ γάρ, ὦ ἄνδρες δικασταί, οἴομαι αὐτοὺς ἐπὶ μὲν
τούτῳ τῷ λόγῳ οὐκ ἐλεήσεσθαι· ἴσως δ᾽ ἐροῦσιν, ὥσπερ
καὶ ἐν τῇ βουλῇ, ὡς ἐπ᾽ εὐνοίᾳ τῆς πόλεως συνεωνοῦντο
τὸν σῖτον, ἵν᾽ ὡς ἀξιώτατον ὑμῖν πωλοῖεν. μέγιστον δ᾽
70 ὑμῖν ἐρῶ καὶ περιφανέστατον τεκμήριον ὅτι ψεύδονται.

12 ἐχρῆν γὰρ αὐτούς, εἴπερ ὑμῶν ἕνεκα ἔπραττον ταῦτα, φαί-
νεσθαι τῆς αὐτῆς τιμῆς πολλὰς ἡμέρας πωλοῦντας, ἕως ὁ
συνεωνημένος αὐτοὺς ἐπέλιπε· νῦν δ᾽ ἐνίοτε τῆς αὐτῆς
ἡμέρας ἐπώλουν δραχμῇ τιμιώτερον, ὥσπερ κατὰ μέδι-
75 μνον συνωνούμενοι. καὶ τούτων ὑμᾶς μάρτυρας παρέχομαι.

10. **ἂν ὡς μάλιστα**: see on § 1. —
τούτων: sc. τῶν ἀρχόντων.
11. **ἀλλὰ γάρ**: see on XII. 99. —
ἐπὶ μὲν τούτῳ ... ἐλεήσεσθαι: cf. Dem.
LVII. 45, πολλὰ δουλικὰ πράγματα τοὺς
ἐλευθέρους ἡ πενία βιάζεται ποιεῖν, ἐφ᾽
οἷς ἐλεέοιντ᾽ ἄν, and for the fut. mid.
as pass., see on XXXI. 26. See App.
— **ἐν τῇ βουλῇ**: i.e. at the κρίσις,
§ 3.
12. **ἔπραττον**: observe the tense,
denoting repeated action, like that
of πωλοῦντας. — **ἕως αὐτοὺς ἐπέλιπε**:
until it had failed them, a secondary

tense of the indic. (GMT. 613, 2) on
account of ἐχρῆν, for which see on
XII. 32. — **ὥσπερ κατὰ μέδιμνον**: they
had bought it in bulk, and hence
could have afforded to sell it all
at one price; but instead they often
put up the price as if they had
bought in small quantities and in a
short market. On ὥσπερ with the
partic., see App. to XII. 7. This dis-
tributive use of κατά occurs here first
in the orators. Lutz, *Präp.* p. 78. —
ὑμᾶς μάρτυρας: see App. and on
XII. 74.

13 Δεινὸν δέ μοι δοκεῖ εἶναι, εἰ ὅταν μὲν εἰσφορὰν εἰσενεγκεῖν δέῃ, ἣν πάντες εἴσεσθαι μέλλουσιν, οὐκ ἐθέλουσιν,
ἀλλὰ πενίαν προφασίζονται, ἐφ᾽ οἷς δὲ θάνατός ἐστιν ἡ
80 ζημία καὶ λαθεῖν αὐτοῖς συνέφερε, ταῦτα ἐπ᾽ εὐνοίᾳ φασὶ
τῇ ὑμετέρᾳ παρανομῆσαι. καίτοι πάντες ἐπίστασθε ὅτι
τούτοις ἥκιστα προσήκει τοιούτους ποιεῖσθαι λόγους.
τἀναντία γὰρ αὐτοῖς καὶ τοῖς ἄλλοις συμφέρει· τότε γὰρ
πλεῖστα κερδαίνουσιν, ὅταν κακοῦ τινος ἀπαγγελθέντος
14 τῇ πόλει τίμιον τὸν σῖτον πωλῶσιν. οὕτω δ᾽ ἄσμενοι τὰς
συμφορὰς τὰς ὑμετέρας ὁρῶσιν, ὥστε τὰς μὲν πρότεροι
τῶν ἄλλων πυνθάνονται, τὰς δ᾽ αὐτοὶ λογοποιοῦσιν, ἢ τὰς
ναῦς διεφθάρθαι τὰς ἐν τῷ Πόντῳ ἢ ὑπὸ Λακεδαιμονίων
ἐκπλεούσας συνειλῆφθαι, ἢ τὰ ἐμπόρια κεκλῆσθαι, ἢ τὰς
15 σπονδὰς μέλλειν ἀπορρηθήσεσθαι, καὶ εἰς τοῦτ᾽ ἔχθρας
ἐληλύθασιν, ὥστ᾽ ἐν τοῖς αὐτοῖς καιροῖς ἐπιβουλεύουσιν
ἡμῖν, ἐν οἷσπερ οἱ πολέμιοι. ὅταν γὰρ μάλιστα σίτου
τυγχάνητε δεόμενοι, ἀναρπάζουσιν οὗτοι καὶ οὐκ ἐθέλουσι

13. εἰσφοράν : see on XII. 20. —
πάντες κτλ. : hence this would be an
excellent opportunity for showing
patriotism (εὔνοια). — οὐκ ἐθέλουσιν :
for the negative οὐ, not μή, see on
XXXI. 31. — λαθεῖν : from our English
idiom we should expect ἄ with this
verb, but cf. § 21, and see on XXXII.
27. — συνέφερε : without ἄν, see on
XII. 32. — τῇ ὑμετέρᾳ : instead of the
obj. gen. G. 999; H. 694. — τἀναντία
γὰρ κτλ. : hence they are bad citizens
(cf. Dem. XVIII. 198, quoted on § 15),
while conversely a good citizen's
interests are those of his country.
Cf. XXXI. 5.
   14. λογοποιοῦσιν: the regular word
used of a canard. See on XVI. 11, and

cf. And. I. 54, ἃ ἐλογοποίουν οἱ ἐχθροὶ
περὶ ἐμοῦ, βουλόμενοι διαβάλλειν με,
Dem. VI. 14, λογοποιοῦσιν περιιόντες
τινές. — τὰς ναῦς : the grain-ships are
meant. — διεφθάρθαι: cf. [Dem.] LVI.
34, σωθείσης τε τῆς νεὼς καὶ οὐ διεφθαρ-
μένης. — κεκλῆσθαι : blockaded, cf.
Dem. II. 16, κεκλειμένων τῶν ἐμπορίων
τῶν ἐν τῇ χώρᾳ διὰ τὸν πόλεμον. — τὰς
σπονδάς : see p. 93.
   15. ἐν τοῖς αὐτοῖς καιροῖς: cf. Dem.
XVIII. 198, ὅτῳ συνενηνόχασιν οἱ αὐτοὶ
καιροὶ καὶ τοῖς τῆς πόλεως ἐχθροῖς, οὐκ
ἔνι τοῦτον εὔνουν εἶναι τῇ πατρίδι. —
ἀναρπάζουσιν : snap it up, a word
often used of stealing or pillage, cf.
Hom. Od. XV. 427, ἀλλά μ᾽ ἀνήρπαξαν
(kidnapped) Τάφιοι, ληίστορες ἄνδρες,

πωλεῖν, ἵνα μὴ περὶ τῆς τιμῆς διαφερώμεθα, ἀλλ᾽ ἀγαπῶ-
95 μεν ἂν ὁποσουτινοσοῦν πριάμενοι παρ᾽ αὐτῶν ἀπέλθωμεν·
ὥστ᾽ ἐνίοτε εἰρήνης οὔσης ὑπὸ τούτων πολιορκούμεθα.

16 οὕτω δὲ πάλαι περὶ τῆς τούτων πανουργίας καὶ κακονοίας
ἡ πόλις ἔγνωκεν, ὥστ᾽ ἐπὶ μὲν τοῖς ἄλλοις ὠνίοις ἅπασι
τοὺς ἀγορανόμους φύλακας κατεστήσατε, ἐπὶ δὲ ταύτῃ
100 μόνῃ τῇ τέχνῃ χωρὶς σιτοφύλακας ἀποκληροῦτε· καὶ
πολλάκις ἤδη παρ᾽ ἐκείνων πολιτῶν ὄντων δίκην τὴν
μεγίστην ἐλάβετε, ὅτι οὐχ οἷοί τ᾽ ἦσαν τῆς τούτων πονηρίας ἐπικρατῆσαι. καίτοι τί χρὴ αὐτοὺς τοὺς ἀδικοῦντας
ὑφ᾽ ὑμῶν πάσχειν, ὁπότε καὶ τοὺς οὐ δυναμένους φυλάτ-
105 τειν ἀποκτείνετε;

17 Ἐνθυμεῖσθαι δὲ χρὴ ὅτι ἀδύνατον ὑμῖν ἐστιν ἀποψηφί-
σασθαι. εἰ γὰρ ἀπογνώσεσθε ὁμολογούντων αὐτῶν ἐπὶ
τοὺς ἐμπόρους συνίστασθαι, δόξεθ᾽ ὑμεῖς ἐπιβουλεύειν
τοῖς εἰσπλέουσιν. εἰ μὲν γὰρ ἄλλην τινὰ ἀπολογίαν

Xen. *Anab.* i. 3. 14, οἱ Κίλικες ... ὧν
πολλοὺς καὶ πολλὰ χρήματα ἔχομεν
ἀνηρπακότες. — **διαφερώμεθα** : *bicker,
haggle.* Cf. x. 7, ἐγὼ δ᾽ οἶμαι δεῖν
ὑμᾶς ... οὐ περὶ τῶν ὀνομάτων διαφέρεσθαι, ἀλλὰ τῆς τούτων διανοίας (*meaning*). — **ἀγαπῶμεν** : see on XII. 11. —
ὁποσουτινοσοῦν : see on XII. 84. —
ἀπέλθωμεν: 'get off'; on the tense as
compared with διαφερώμεθα, see App.
to XVI. 6. — **πολιορκούμεθα**: 'we are
kept in a state of siege.'

16. πάλαι ἔγνωκεν: *has long known,*
this perfect being equivalent (G.
1263; H. 849) to a present with
πάλαι. G. 1258; H. 826. — **ἀγορανόμους**: on these officers see p. 91,
note 23; on the σιτοφύλακες see p. 91.
— **τέχνη** : a general term, including

our 'business' as well as 'trade' and
'profession.' Thus Lysias uses it
also of a fuller, XXIII. 7, a perfumer,
frag. I. § 2 (quoted on XXIV. 20), a
stonemason, *frag.* 69, and of the
cripple's employment, XXIV. 4. It
is used of a physician in Hdt. iii. 131.
— **χωρίς** : *by itself.* — **πολλάκις ἐλάβετε** : for the tense, see on XII. 3. —
ἤδη : *before now, cf.* § 18. — **πολιτῶν
ὄντων** : in contrast with grain-dealers
who were generally metics. A logically unjust though characteristic
appeal to the sympathies of the
court. — **ἀποκτείνετε** : *cf.* ἀπέθνησκον,
§ 21.

17. συνίστασθαι : often used of a
political 'combine,' as in XXX. 10,
Κλεοφῶν τὴν βουλὴν ἐλοιδόρει, φάσκων

110 ἐποιοῦντο, οὐδεὶς ἂν εἶχε τοῖς ἀποψηφισαμένοις ἐπιτιμᾶν·
ἐφ᾽ ὑμῖν γὰρ ὁποτέροις βούλεσθε πιστεύειν· νῦν δὲ πῶς
οὐ δεινὰ ἂν δόξαιτε ποιεῖν, εἰ τοὺς ὁμολογοῦντας παρα-
18 νομεῖν ἀζημίους ἀφήσετε; ἀναμνήσθητε δέ, ὦ ἄνδρες
δικασταί, ὅτι πολλῶν ἤδη ἐχόντων ταύτην τὴν αἰτίαν,
115 ἀρνουμένων καὶ μάρτυρας παρεχομένων, θάνατον κατέ-
γνωτε, πιστοτέρους ἡγησάμενοι τοὺς τῶν κατηγόρων
λόγους. καίτοι πῶς ἂν οὐ θαυμαστὸν εἴη, εἰ περὶ τῶν
αὐτῶν ἁμαρτημάτων δικάζοντες μᾶλλον ἐπιθυμεῖτε παρὰ
19 τῶν ἀρνουμένων δίκην λαμβάνειν; καὶ μὲν δή, ὦ ἄνδρες
120 δικασταί, πᾶσιν ἡγοῦμαι φανερὸν εἶναι ὅτι οἱ περὶ τῶν
τοιούτων ἀγῶνες κοινότατοι τυγχάνουσιν ὄντες τοῖς ἐν τῇ
πόλει, ὥστε πεύσονται ἥντινα γνώμην περὶ αὐτῶν ἔχετε,
ἡγούμενοι, ἂν μὲν θάνατον τούτων καταγνῶτε, κοσμιωτέρους ἔσεσθαι τοὺς λοιπούς· ἂν δ᾽ ἀζημίους ἀφῆτε, πολ-

---

συνεστάναι καὶ οὐ τὰ βέλτιστα βουλεύειν
τῇ πόλει, or, as here, of a 'corner,'
cf. § 21. The retail dealers must
have stocked up and then refused to
buy, except at their own price, from
the importers. Such a 'ring' would
keep grain-ships away from Athens.
— τοῖς εἰσπλέουσιν : i.e. τοῖς ἐμπόροις,
as in § 21. — ἄλλην : i.e. other than
their admission that they bought up
grain, but only at the suggestion of
the magistrates. — ὁποτέροις : either
party, plaintiff or defendant. — ἂν
δόξαιτε, ... εἰ ἀφήσετε : on the mixed
form of condition, see G. 1421, 2 ;
H. 901.
    18. ἤδη : see on § 16. — ἐχόντων
... αἰτίαν : charged with the same
thing. Cf. XIII. 62, οὐδεμίαν αἰτίαν
αἰσχρὰν ἔσχον, Xen. Anab. vii. 6. 11,
ἐγὼ νῦν ὑφ᾽ ὑμῶν αἰτίας ἔχω. — ἐπιθυ-

μεῖτε : for the mixed form of condition, see on XVI. 17, and cf. Ant.
III. γ. 9, πῶς ἂν πρέποντα πάσχοιμεν,
εἰ ... θανάτῳ ζημιούμεθα ; Plat. Apol.
25 B, πολλὴ γὰρ ἄν τις εὐδαιμονία εἴη
περὶ τοὺς νέους, εἰ εἷς μὲν μόνος αὐτοὺς
διαφθείρει. — παρὰ τῶν ἀρνουμένων :
the antithesis ἢ παρὰ τῶν ὁμολογούντων is easily understood from the
context. See App.
    19. κοινότατοι : of the most general
interest, cf. Isocr. v. 10, νομίσας οὐ-
δέποτ᾽ ἂν εὑρεθῆναι καλλίω ταύτης ὑπόθεσιν (idea) οὐδὲ κοινοτέραν οὐδὲ μᾶλλον
ἅπασιν ἡμῖν συμφέρουσαν. — ὥστε πεύσονται κτλ. : this is to be a test case ;
see on XII. 35.— κοσμιωτέρους : for the
meaning, see on VII. 41, and with the
whole sentence, cf. XXVII. 7, ἐὰν δὲ
καταψηφισάμενοι θανάτου τιμήσητε ...
τοὺς ἄλλους κοσμιωτέρους ποιήσετε. —

125 λὴν ἄδειαν αὐτοῖς ἐψηφισμένοι ἔσεσθε ποιεῖν ὅ τι ἂν βού-
20 λωνται. χρὴ δέ, ὦ ἄνδρες δικασταί, μὴ μόνον τῶν παρε-
ληλυθότων ἕνεκα αὐτοὺς κολάζειν, ἀλλὰ καὶ παραδείγματος ἕνεκα τῶν μελλόντων ἔσεσθαι· οὕτω γὰρ ἔσονται
μόγις ἀνεκτοί. ἐνθυμεῖσθε δὲ ὅτι ἐκ ταύτης τῆς τέχνης
130 πλεῖστοι περὶ τοῦ σώματός εἰσιν ἠγωνισμένοι. καὶ οὕτω
μεγάλα ἐξ αὐτῆς ὠφελοῦνται, ὥστε μᾶλλον αἱροῦνται καθ᾽
ἑκάστην ἡμέραν περὶ τῆς ψυχῆς κινδυνεύειν ἢ παύσασθαι
21 παρ᾽ ὑμῶν ἀδίκως κερδαίνοντες. καὶ μὲν δὴ οὐδ᾽ ἂν ἀντιβολῶσιν ὑμᾶς καὶ ἱκετεύωσι, δικαίως ἂν αὐτοὺς ἐλεήσαιτε,
135 ἀλλὰ πολὺ μᾶλλον τῶν τε πολιτῶν οἳ διὰ τὴν τούτων

ἐψηφισμένοι ἔσεσθε: here the construction with ἡγούμενοι is abandoned. See on XII. 38. For the
tense, see on XII. 100. — ποιεῖν: with
ἄδειαν, cf. XII. 85.

20. παραδείγματος: *warning*. See
on XXXI. 30. — τῶν μελλόντων ἔσεσθαι: *the future*. But see on XII. 99.
— οὕτω: *in the latter case*, i.e., if you
punish them. — μόγις: *only just, barely*. Cf. Aesch. *Prom.* 131, πατρῴας
μόγις παρειποῦσα φρένας, and so μόλις
in Thuc. VI. 23, μόλις οὕτως οἷοί τε
ἐσόμεθα τῶν μὲν κρατεῖν κτλ. — ἐκ ταύτης: the preposition denotes the
cause; cf. III. 48, ἠναγκάσθην ἐκ τοιούτων τῶν πραγμάτων εἰς τοιούτους
ἀγῶνας καταστῆναι. — περὶ τοῦ σώματος: *for their life.* For this sense of
σῶμα, cf. I. 50, ἐγὼ γὰρ νῦν καὶ περὶ
τοῦ σώματος καὶ περὶ τῶν χρημάτων καὶ
περὶ τῶν ἄλλων ἁπάντων κινδυνεύω, so
in XXIX. 11; used also of civil status,
cf. V. 1, VII. 26, XXIII. 12; and in the
literal meaning *body*, XXIV. 3. Below,
περὶ ψυχῆς is a mere synonym for
περὶ σώματος in the first sense, and so

the two are combined in Dinarch. I.
16, ἡ βουλὴ ... κυρία δικάσαι τε περὶ τοῦ
σώματος καὶ τῆς ψυχῆς ἑκάστου τῶν
πολιτῶν. For ψυχή meaning 'heart'
(metaphorically), cf. XXXII. 12, and
denoting the intellectual or spiritual
part as contrasted with σῶμα, XXIV. 3.
— ἐξ αὐτῆς: denoting the source; see
App. to XVI. 18. — κινδυνεύειν and
παύσασθαι: note the difference in
tense. See App.

21. ἀντιβολῶσιν καὶ ἱκετεύωσιν:
see on XXXII. 11. He is thinking of
such scenes as those described in
XXVII. 12, καὶ νῦν ἴσως ποιήσουσιν ἅπερ
καὶ πρότερον ἦσαν εἰθισμένοι καὶ δημόται
καὶ φίλοι, κλάοντες ἐξαιτεῖσθαι αὐτοὺς
παρ᾽ ὑμῶν, and in Plat. *Apol.* 34 C,
ἀγῶνα ἀγωνιζόμενος ἐδεήθη τε καὶ ἱκέτευσε τοὺς δικαστὰς μετὰ πολλῶν δα-
κρύων, παιδία τε αὐτοῦ ἀναβιβασάμενος,
ἵνα ὅτι μάλιστα ἐλεηθείη, καὶ ἄλλους
τῶν οἰκείων καὶ φίλων πολλούς. On the
verb ἐλεέω which follows, see App.
to § 11. — τῶν πολιτῶν: on the position of the genitive (belonging to the
antecedent of οἵ), cf. XXIII. 4 and 6.

πονηρίαν ἀπέθνῃσκον, καὶ τοὺς ἐμπόρους ἐφ᾽ οὓς οὗτοι
συνέστησαν· οἷς ὑμεῖς χαριεῖσθε καὶ προθυμοτέρους ποιήσετε, δίκην παρὰ τούτων λαμβάνοντες. εἰ δὲ μή, τίν᾽
αὐτοὺς οἴεσθε γνώμην ἕξειν, ἐπειδὰν πύθωνται ὅτι τῶν
140 καπήλων, οἳ τοῖς εἰσπλέουσιν ὡμολόγησαν ἐπιβουλεύειν,
ἀπεψηφίσασθε;

22 Οὐκ οἶδ᾽ ὅ τι δεῖ πλείω λέγειν· περὶ μὲν γὰρ τῶν
ἄλλων τῶν ἀδικούντων, ὅτου δικάζονται δεῖ παρὰ τῶν
κατηγόρων πυθέσθαι, τὴν δὲ τούτων πονηρίαν ἅπαντες
145 ἐπίστασθε. ἂν οὖν τούτων καταψηφίσησθε, τά τε δίκαια
ποιήσετε καὶ ἀξιώτερον τὸν σῖτον ὠνήσεσθε· εἰ δὲ μή,
τιμιώτερον. // —   12/

These are the πολῖται mentioned in
§ 16. — οἷς : not repeated in the acc.
with ποιήσετε, see on § 13.

22. ὅτου δικάζονται : on this genitive of the crime (G. 1121; H. 745),
cf. x. 2, κακηγορίας δικάζεσθαι, Dem.

LIV. 41, παθὼν ὑπὸ Κόνωνος ταῦθ᾽ ὧν
δικάζομαι, though the verb is middle
in both examples. See App. — τιμιώτερον : clearly an ad captandum
argument. But the short epilogue
contains also an appeal to justice.

AGAINST PANCLEON.

INTRODUCTION.

THE word ἀντιγραφή, which properly signified the written answer put in by the defendant to the charges brought against him, was also used as a general term covering the point or points which defendants might choose to plead in their answers. There were, however, special terms of more limited meaning. For example, if at the ἀνάκρισις a defendant objected, on any ground whatever, to the admissibility of the suit, — as, for instance, that it was not brought in accordance with proper legal forms or before the proper magistrate, — he put in what was called a παραγραφή.[1] The παραγραφή was, therefore, a special kind of ἀντιγραφή.[2] If it convinced the accuser of an error in his opening proceedings, he withdrew the case or took it to the proper court. Otherwise the issue raised by the παραγραφή was made the subject of an ἀνάκρισις (the original suit meanwhile coming to a standstill), and was then brought before a regular court for settlement. In this court the bringer of the παραγραφή had the privilege of speaking first.[3] The loser ran the risk of *epobelia*.[4]

The speech *Against Pancleon* was written for a case of this sort.[5] The speaker, a man unknown to us, had brought a private[6] suit

---

[1] In general see M. and S. p. 833 ff., especially pp. 849–855; Gilbert, *Antiq.* p. 407 f.

[2] M. and S. p. 849. It differed from the διαμαρτυρία (see on § 13) in its form, in that it was made and defended by the accused, and was not dependent upon the evidence of witnesses. Another term for this method of procedure seems to have been ἐξωμοσία (M. and S. p. 854).

[3] M. and S. p. 850. He would probably prefer to do so; *cf.* Dem. XVIII. 7.

[4] M. and S. p. 851; see Introd. § 49.

[5] The Greek title is therefore erroneous, and it should read: πρὸς τὴν Παγκλέωνος παραγραφήν (M. and S. p. 853, note 243).   [6] *Cf.* δίκης, §§ 1, 10.

against one Pancleon, a fuller by trade, whom he had summoned before the polemarch[7] in the belief that he was a metic. But Pancleon, who seems to have had a good deal of experience in lawsuits,[8] raised in his ἀντιγραφή the point that the suit μὴ εἰσαγώγιμον εἶναι.[9] That is, he put in what we call a 'plea to the jurisdiction' (in Roman law exceptio fori), on the ground that he was not a metic at all, but a person entitled to the rights of Attic citizenship, inasmuch as he was a Plataean.[10] Hence our speaker had to overthrow this παραγραφή (for such it was in effect, though the special term is not used in the speech[11]) before the original suit could go on. It is clear from the manner of the speech itself that he spoke first, contrary to the practice in other cases of this sort as known to us.[12]

After the shortest possible preface,[13] the speaker explains that although Pancleon had said at the outset[14] that he was a Plataean-Athenian of the deme Decelea, yet inquiries made among members of that deme brought out the fact that none of them had ever heard of him; further, it appeared that suits had already been tried against him before the polemarch; hence the speaker laid his suit there.[15] These inquiries were carried on more extensively after Pancleon had repeated his claim formally before that magistrate, the only result of them being that one person said that he had a runaway slave named Pancleon.[16] Some days after, this person, whose name was Nicomedes, seized upon Pancleon as his slave; the speaker happened to be present, and afterwards attended the

[7] Who had jurisdiction in matters concerning metics; M. and S. p. 66 ff.; Gilbert, *Antiq.* p. 254; Arist. *Resp. Ath.* 58. 2; *cf.* the Roman praetor peregrinus.

[8] *Cf.* §§ 3, 4, 9, 13 f.

[9] § 5.

[10] After the siege and destruction of Plataea by Spartans and Thebans (Thuc. iii. 20–24, and 68) in 428 and 427 B.C., the remnant of the Plataeans was received by the Athenians and given rights of citizenship, the men

being distributed among the demes and tribes. For a full account of this, with the decree, *cf.* [Dem.] LIX. 94–106.

[11] Only the general term ἀντιγραφή is used, §§ 5, 10; see M. and S. p. 853.

[12] M. and S. p. 853; Blass, *Att. Bereds.* I, p. 619. Otherwise the speaker would have referred to Pancleon's arguments and would not have given so full a statement of the case.

[13] § 1. [14] § 2.

[15] §§ 2–3.

[16] §§ 5–8.

proceedings in a suit which followed ; there he, with his witnesses, saw a woman disputing with Nicomedes the claim to Pancleon ; the result was that Pancleon's friends carried him off without waiting for a verdict.[17] From this incident the inference might be drawn that Pancleon himself could not prove that he was even a freeman.[18] To complete the evidence, it appeared that Pancleon, in a suit brought against him by Aristodicus, had raised this same plea to the jurisdiction ; that he had apparently been unable to overthrow the evidence (given by a διαμαρτυρία) that he was no Plataean ; and that he had allowed Aristodicus to win the original suit as brought before the polemarch.[19] Hereupon, with a three-line epilogue,[20] the speaker rests his case.

In this speech there is used but little argument, for it consists of hardly anything but a brief statement of facts. This sufficed,[21] for the speaker needed only to show the judges that he had had good grounds for bringing the suit before the polemarch. But incidentally (and herein lies the art of the oration) he leads the hearer to believe that Pancleon, far from being a Plataean, was actually a slave, and he does this without making any direct charge to this effect. At the very moment when the judges might have expected him to do so, he draws back and, as it were, puts it into Pancleon's own mouth.[22] By this neat turn and by the whole tone of the speech he avoids showing any needless bitterness, and escapes the suspicion that he was prosecuting a poor fellow from mere ὕβρις.[23]

This oration and the Twenty-fourth illustrate a custom of the Athenians which nowadays we see existing only in our small country towns. It was the regular practice to drop in during the day at the various shops about the ἀγορά to have a chat with one's friends, to hear the news, and to exchange the latest bits of gossip. Thus in the Twenty-fourth oration, § 20, we find the perfumers',

17 §§ 9–11. 18 § 12.
19 §§ 13–15. 20 § 16.
  21 And there is no reason to believe,
with Francken (*Comm. Lys.* p. 164) that

we have only an epitome of the actual speech ; see Blass, *Att. Bereds.* I, p. 620.
  22 § 12. *Cf.* Introd. to XXXI, note 19.
  23 § 5.

the cobblers', and the barbers' shops made use of in this way; so, too, people gathered about the bankers' tables.[24] Certain sets of people seem to have had their particular haunts; for the speaker of our oration knew that Deceleans were to be found at a barber's shop near the Hermae,[25] and he was told that the Plataeans met at the green-cheese market.[26] He went therefore to these places to ask about his man. Such resorts took the place of our clubs, and he who did not frequent them was considered an unsociable and rather stuck-up person.[27] Of all these resorts, the barbers' shops were the favourite, and ancient literature contains many allusions to the chatter and gossip that abounded in them.[28] Theophrastus dubbed them 'wineless symposia.'[29] The barber himself has been in all ages a type of garrulity. Everybody knows the story of king Archelaus (a contemporary of Lysias), which is constantly turning up as a new joke in our comic papers.[30] Another barber nearly lost his life by his desire to be the first to retail the latest news. This was the man who heard in the Piraeus from one of his customers the news of the defeat in Sicily. Up he rushed to the city and began to spread the news; but, being unable to give the name of his informant, he was actually bound to the wheel to be tortured as an unpatriotic liar, when, fortunately for him, the sad news was confirmed by official messengers.[31]

In the oration against Pancleon there is nothing by which the date of its delivery can be fixed.

---

[24] [Lys.] IX. 5. On the general subject, see Hermann, *Privatalt.* p. 126; Wilamowitz, *Phil. Untersuch.* I, p. 196.

[25] § 3. [26] § 6.

[27] Dem. XXV. 52, οὐδὲ προσφοιτᾷ πρός τι τούτων τῶν ἐν τῇ πόλει κουρείων ἢ μυροπωλίων ἢ τῶν ἄλλων ἐργαστηρίων οὐδὲ πρὸς ἕν.

[28] E.g., Ar. *Plut.* 338; *Av.* 1441. See Hermann, *ibid.*

[29] Apud Plut. p. 679 A, Θεόφραστος ἄοινα συμπόσια παίζων ἐκάλει τὰ κουρεῖα, διὰ τὴν λαλιὰν τῶν προσκαθιζόντων.

[30] χαριέντως γοῦν ὁ βασιλεὺς Ἀρχέλαος, ἀδολέσχου (talkative) κουρέως περιβαλόντος αὐτῷ τὸ ὠμόλινον (towel), καὶ πυθομένου· πῶς σε κείρω, βασιλεῦ; σιωπῶν, ἔφη, Plut. p. 509 B.

[31] Plut. *ibid.* and *Nicias*, 30. The best account of Greek and Roman barbers is by F. W. Nicolson in vol. II, p. 41 ff. of the *Harvard Studies in Classical Philology.*

ΚΑΤΑ ΠΑΓΚΛΕΩΝΟΣ

ΟΤΙ ΟΤΚ ΗΝ ΠΛΑΤΑΙΕΤΣ.

1 Πολλὰ μὲν λέγειν, ὦ ἄνδρες δικασταί, περὶ τουτουὶ τοῦ
πράγματος οὔτ᾿ ἂν δυναίμην οὔτε μοι δοκεῖ δεῖν· ὡς δὲ
ὀρθῶς τὴν δίκην ἔλαχον τουτῳὶ Παγκλέωνι οὐκ ὄντι Πλαταιεῖ, τοῦτο ὑμῖν πειράσομαι ἀποδεῖξαι.

2 Ὡς γὰρ ἀδικῶν με πολὺν χρόνον οὐκ ἐπαύετο, ἐλθὼν
ἐπὶ τὸ γναφεῖον ἐν ᾧ εἰργάζετο προσεκαλεσάμην αὐτὸν
πρὸς τὸν πολέμαρχον, νομίζων μέτοικον εἶναι. εἰπόντος
δὲ τούτου ὅτι Πλαταιεὺς εἴη, ἠρόμην ὁπόθεν δημοτεύοιτο,
παραινέσαντός τινος τῶν παρόντων προσκαλέσασθαι καὶ
10 πρὸς τὴν φυλὴν ἧστινος εἶναι σκήπτοιτο. ἐπειδὴ δὲ ἀπε-
κρίνατο ὅτι Δεκελειόθεν, προσκαλεσάμενος αὐτὸν καὶ

---

1. ὀρθῶς : i.e. before the proper
court. — δίκην ἔλαχον : see Introd.
§46.— Πλαταιεῖ : see p. 105, note 10.

2. ὡς : instead of ἐπειδή or ὅτε, the
only instance in Lysias of this temporal use and very rare in the other
earlier orators (Fuhr). — ἐπί : not
into. See on XII. 8. — γναφεῖον : the
fuller, γναφεύς, scoured and cleansed
home-made cloth, and washed and
cleaned soiled clothing. See, in general, Smith, Dict. Antiq. s.v. fullo.—
προσεκαλεσάμην : see Introd. § 46. —
τῶν παρόντων : probably one of the
speaker's κλητῆρες. See Introd. § 46.
—καί: also. —ἧστινος...σκήπτοιτο :
of which he alleged that he was a

member.—τοὺς δικάζοντας : a body of
forty men, chosen by lot, four from
each tribe, acted in divisions of four
for their appropriate tribes. Such
were called οἱ κατὰ δήμους δικασταί.
Cases of αἰκία and βίαια (see on § 12),
together with nearly all those which
concerned rights to property, came
before them. If the amount at issue
was not over ten drachmae, their
decision was final; otherwise they
sent the case to the public arbitrators
and, if necessary, to the courts. See
Arist. Resp. Ath. 53; M. and S.
p. 88 ff.; Gilbert, Antiq. p. 377. —
Ἱπποθωντίδι : Decelea belonged to
that tribe.

3 πρὸς τοὺς τῇ Ἱπποθωντίδι δικάζοντας, ἐλθὼν ἐπὶ τὸ κουρεῖον τὸ παρὰ τοὺς Ἑρμᾶς, ἵνα οἱ Δεκελεῖς προσφοιτῶσιν,
ἠρώτων, οὕς τε ἐξευρίσκοιμι Δεκελέων ἐπυνθανόμην εἴ
15 τινα γιγνώσκοιεν Δεκελειόθεν δημοτευόμενον Παγκλέωνα.
ἐπειδὴ δὲ οὐδεὶς ἔφασκεν γιγνώσκειν αὐτόν, πυθόμενος
ὅτι καὶ ἑτέρας δίκας τὰς μὲν φεύγοι τὰς δ' ὠφλήκοι παρὰ
τῷ πολεμάρχῳ, ἔλαχον καὶ ἐγώ.

4   Πρῶτον μὲν οὖν ὑμῖν Δεκελέων οὓς ἠρόμην μάρτυρας
20 παρέξομαι, ἔπειτα δὲ καὶ τῶν ἄλλων τῶν λαχόντων τε
δίκας αὐτῷ πρὸς τὸν πολέμαρχον καὶ καταδικασαμένων,
ὅσοι τυγχάνουσι παρόντες.   καί μοι ἐπίλαβε τὸ ὕδωρ.

ΜΑΡΤΥΡΕΣ.

5 Ἐκ μὲν τούτων πεισθεὶς πρὸς τὸν πολέμαρχον αὐτῷ

---

3. παρὰ τοὺς Ἑρμᾶς: along by the
Hermae (i.e. as you go by them),
cf. III. 17, ἤδη δὲ αὐτοῖς οὖσι παρὰ τὴν
Λάμπωνος οἰκίαν, And. I. 38, ἐπεὶ δὲ
παρὰ τὸ προπύλαιον τὸ Διονύσου ἦν. The
speaker means a celebrated row of
Hermae (square pillars terminating in
the head of Hermes) in that part of the
market near which were shops.   See
App. — ἵνα: generally with verbs of
rest, hence οἵ might have been used
here, but cf. Dinarch. II. 10, τόπος
... ἵν' ἐξῆν ἀπάγειν τοὺς ἐκ δεσμωτηρίου
κλέπτοντας, Thuc. iv. 74, ἵναπερ ὥρ-
μητο. — ἠρώτων: I made inquiries. —
τέ: for its use without καί, see on
XXXI. 2. — φεύγοι, ὠφλήκοι: note
the difference in tense. Some suits
were still pending. — παρὰ τῷ πολεμάρχῳ: the dat. of a word denoting
a magistrate or board is very common with παρά in such contexts.

See Lutz, Präp. p. 147, and on VII.
14.

4. Δεκελέων οὕς: for the position
of the gen., cf. τῶν ἄλλων ὅσους, § 6,
and see on XXII. 21.— πρὸς τὸν πολέμαρχον: the acc. (with πρός) of a
word denoting a magistrate or board
is common with expressions denoting appearance or action before such
officers. Cf. §§ 2 and 5, and see Lutz,
Präp. p. 160. — καταδικασαμένων:
without the article, as this partic.
refers to the same persons as λαχόντων. The mere bringing suit would
be no proof that Pancleon was a
metic, but conviction would prove it.
— ἐπίλαβε: addressed to the officer
(ὁ ἐφύδωρ) in charge of the κλεψύδρα,
on which see Smith, Dict. Antiq.
s.v. horologium. The time taken up
by witnesses was not deducted from
that allowed to a speaker.

τὴν δίκην ἔλαχον· ἐπειδὴ δέ μοι αὐτὴν ἀντεγράψατο μὴ
25 εἰσαγώγιμον εἶναι, περὶ πολλοῦ ποιούμενος μηδενὶ δόξαι
ὑβρίζειν βούλεσθαι μᾶλλον ἢ δίκην λαβεῖν ὧν ἠδικήθην,
πρῶτον μὲν Εὐθύκριτον, ὃν πρεσβύτατόν τε Πλαταιῶν
ἐγίγνωσκον καὶ μάλιστα ᾠόμην εἰδέναι, ἠρόμην εἴ τινα
γιγνώσκοι Ἱππαρμοδώρου υὸν Παγκλέωνα Πλαταιᾶ·
6 ἔπειτα δέ, ἐπειδὴ ἐκεῖνος ἀπεκρίνατό μοι ὅτι τὸν Ἱππαρ-
μόδωρον μὲν γιγνώσκοι, υὸν δὲ ἐκείνῳ οὐδένα οὔτε Παγκλέωνα οὔτε ἄλλον οὐδένα εἰδείη ὄντα, ἠρώτων δὴ καὶ τῶν
ἄλλων ὅσους ἤδη Πλαταιᾶς ὄντας. πάντες οὖν ἀγνο-
οῦντες τὸ ὄνομα αὐτοῦ, ἀκριβέστατα ἂν ἔφασάν με πυθέ-
35 σθαι ἐλθόντα εἰς τὸν χλωρὸν τυρὸν τῇ ἕνῃ καὶ νέᾳ· ταύτῃ
γὰρ τῇ ἡμέρᾳ τοῦ μηνὸς ἑκάστου ἐκεῖσε συλλέγεσθαι
7 τοὺς Πλαταιᾶς. ἐλθὼν οὖν εἰς τὸν τυρὸν ταύτῃ τῇ ἡμέρᾳ
ἐπυνθανόμην αὐτῶν, εἴ τινα γιγνώσκοιεν Παγκλέωνα
πολίτην σφέτερον. καὶ οἱ μὲν ἄλλοι οὐκ ἔφασαν γιγνώ-
40 σκειν, εἷς δέ τις εἶπεν ὅτι τῶν μὲν πολιτῶν οὐδενὶ εἰδείη

---

5. **ἀντεγράψατο**: see p. 105, note 11,
for the special meaning here. — **μὴ
εἰσαγώγιμον εἶναι**: sc., to the polemarch (see p. 105, and Introd. § 46),
'that it was not in his jurisdiction.'
— **ὑβρίζειν**: be overbearing or high-
handed; i.e. he did not wish to seem
to be putting himself above the law.

6. **τὸν χλωρὸν τυρὸν**: χλωρός is
explained in Bekker Anec. p. 73,
ὁ νέος καὶ πρόσφατος. Cf. Ar. Ran.
559, τὸν τυρόν γε τὸν χλωρὸν τάλαν, ὃν
οὗτος (Heracles) αὐτοῖς τοῖς ταλάροις
(wicker baskets in which cheese and
fruit were sold) κατήσθιεν. On the
Athenian habit of naming places
from the wares sold there, cf. Poll.
IX. 47, οἱ Ἀττικοὶ ὠνόμαζον (τοὺς τό-

πους) ἀπὸ τῶν ἐν αὐτοῖς πιπρασκομέ-
νων, ὡς εἰ φαῖεν 'ἀπῆλθον ἐς τοὔψον
(cf. Aeschin. I. 65, and see on Lys.
XXXII. 26), καὶ ἐς τὸν οἶνον (cf. Ar.
frag. 299, Kock), καὶ ἐς τοὔλαιον
(Menander, inc. 339, Dind.) καὶ ἐς
τὰς χύτρας' (cf. Ar. Lys. 557). So
παρὰ τοὺς ἰχθῦς, Ar. Ran. 1068, and
ἀγαγόντα εἰς τὸν σίδηρον ἐπιδεῖξαι αὐτὸν
ἔφη πολλὰς μὲν μαχαίρας κτλ., Xen.
Hellen. iii. 3. 7. — **ἕνῃ καὶ νέᾳ**: the
common name for the last day of the
month, originating with Solon. Cf.
Plut. Solon, 25, Diog. Laert. i. 2. 57,
and Gow, p. 79 ff. It was a sort of
settling day in money matters; cf.
Ar. Nub. 1134.

7. **εἷς δέ τις**: this was Nicomedes,

τοῦτο ὂν τὸ ὄνομα, δοῦλον μέντοι ἔφη ἑαυτοῦ ἀφεστῶτα
εἶναι Παγκλέωνα, τήν τε ἡλικίαν λέγων τὴν τούτου καὶ
8 τὴν τέχνην ᾗ οὗτος χρῆται.   Ταῦτ᾿ οὖν ὡς ἀληθῆ ἐστι,
τόν τε Εὐθύκριτον, ὃν πρῶτον ἠρόμην, καὶ τῶν ἄλλων
45 Πλαταιῶν ὅσοις προσῆλθον, καὶ τὸν ὃς ἔφη δεσπότης
τούτου εἶναι, μάρτυρας παρέξομαι.   καί μοι ἐπίλαβε τὸ
ὕδωρ.

ΜΑΡΤΥΡΕΣ.

9   Ἡμέραις τοίνυν μετὰ ταῦτα οὐ πολλαῖς ὕστερον ἰδὼν
ἀγόμενον τουτονὶ Παγκλέωνα ὑπὸ τοῦ Νικομήδους, ὃς
50 ἐμαρτύρησεν αὐτοῦ δεσπότης εἶναι, προσῆλθον βουλόμενος εἰδέναι ὁποῖόν τι περὶ αὐτοῦ πραχθήσοιτο.   τότε μὲν
οὖν ἐπειδὴ ἐπαύσαντο μαχόμενοι, εἶπόν τινες τῶν τούτῳ
παρόντων ὅτι εἴη αὐτῷ ἀδελφὸς ὃς ἐξαιρήσοιτο αὐτὸν εἰς

§ 9.—ἀφεστῶτα : used here of a runaway slave (cf. Thuc. i. 139. 2, ἀνδρα-
πόδων ὑποδοχὴν τῶν ἀφισταμένων) instead of the usual ἀποφεύγω, ἀπο-
διδράσκω (see on XVI. 17), or δρα-
πέτης.   For the verb is properly
applied to freedmen who neglect
their duties to their patrons, thus
becoming liable to the δίκη ἀποστα-
σίου, M. and S. p. 619 ff., Arist. Resp.
Ath. 58. 3. — τὴν τέχνην : cf. § 2, and
see on XXII. 16.

8. καὶ τὸν ὃς κτλ. : equivalent to τὸν
εἰπόντα κτλ. This is a survival of the
demonstrative use of ὁ, ἡ, τό, before
a relative clause, found esp. in Plato.
H. 655 c ; Kühn. § 459, 1 a ; cf. Dem.
XXII. 64, μισεῖν τοὺς οἷόσπερ οὗτος,
Plat. Prot. 320 D, ἐκ γῆς καὶ πυρὸς
μίξαντες καὶ τῶν ὅσα πυρὶ καὶ γῇ κερά-
νυνται. Lysias has this usage only
here, but for τὸν καὶ τόν cf. I. 23, XIX.
59, and see H. 655 b ; πρὸ τοῦ, XII. 2.

9. ἀγόμενον: a master had the right
to seize upon and repossess himself
(ἄγειν εἰς δουλείαν or simply ἄγειν) of
a runaway slave wherever found.
The term (see App. to § 10) ἐξαιρεῖσθαι
or ἀφαιρεῖσθαι (with or without εἰς
ἐλευθερίαν) was used of a citizen who
opposed the claim on the ground
that the man was free. Such an opponent had to undertake to bring
the slave before the polemarch and
give security (three citizens required)
that, in case he lost the following
suit, he would pay the damages.
On the subject, see M. and S. p. 658
ff., and cf. the case of Verginia in
Livy iii. 44 ff. — ἐμαρτύρησεν : referring to the evidence just given, at
the end of § 8. — τῶν τούτῳ παρόντων : friends to whom Pancleon
had appealed with the legal word
μαρτύρομαι. Cf. § 12. — ἐξαιρήσοιτο :
no actual ἐξαίρεσις, therefore, took

ἐλευθερίαν· ἐπὶ τούτοις ἐγγυησάμενοι παρέξειν εἰς αὔριον
10 ᾤχοντο ἀπιόντες. τῇ δ' ὑστεραίᾳ τῆς τε ἀντιγραφῆς
ἕνεκα ταυτησὶ καὶ αὐτῆς τῆς δίκης ἔδοξέ μοι χρῆναι μάρτυρας λαβόντι παραγενέσθαι, ἵν' εἰδείην τόν τ' ἐξαιρησό-
μενον αὐτὸν καὶ ὅ τι λέγων ἀφαιρήσοιτο. ἐφ' οἷς μὲν
οὖν ἐξηγγυήθη, οὔτε ἀδελφὸς οὔτε ἄλλος οὐδεὶς ἦλθε,
60 γυνὴ δὲ φάσκουσα αὐτῆς αὐτὸν εἶναι δοῦλον, ἀμφισβη-
τοῦσα τῷ Νικομήδει, καὶ οὐκ ἔφη ἐάσειν αὐτὸν ἄγειν.
11 ὅσα μὲν οὖν αὐτόθι ἐρρήθη, πολὺς ἂν εἴη μοι λόγος διη-
γεῖσθαι· εἰς τοῦτο δὲ βιαιότητος ἦλθον οἵ τε παρόντες
τούτῳ καὶ αὐτὸς οὗτος, ὥστε ἐθέλοντος μὲν τοῦ Νικομή-
65 δους ἐθελούσης δὲ τῆς γυναικὸς ἀφιέναι, εἴ τις ἢ εἰς ἐλευθερίαν τοῦτον ἐξαιροῖτο ἢ ἄγοι φάσκων ἑαυτοῦ δοῦλον
εἶναι, τούτων οὐδὲν ποιήσαντες ἀφελόμενοι ᾤχοντο. ὡς
οὖν τῇ τε προτεραίᾳ ἐπὶ τούτοις ἐξηγγυήθη καὶ τότε βίᾳ
ᾤχοντο ἀφελόμενοι αὐτόν, μάρτυρας παρέξομαι ὑμῖν. καὶ
70 μοι ἐπίλαβε τὸ ὕδωρ.

ΜΑΡΤΥΡΕΣ.

12   Ῥᾴδιον τοίνυν εἰδέναι ὅτι οὐδ' αὐτὸς Παγκλέων νομίζει
ἑαυτὸν μὴ ὅτι Πλαταιᾶ εἶναι, ἀλλ' οὐδ' ἐλεύθερον. ὅστις

place on that day, but it appears that
the man in question was let go, on
the agreement of friends to produce
him next day before the polemarch
for the legal ἐξαίρεσις by his brother ;
see M. and S. p. 659. — **εἰς αὔριον** :
see App.

10. ἀντιγραφῆς and **δίκης** : the
speaker hoped to get, by being present at the ἐξαίρεσις, some useful points
on both his original suit (δίκης) and
the ἀντιγραφή of Pancleon. — **ἐφ' οἷς** :
= ἐπὶ τούτοις (§ 9) ἐφ' οἷς. — **ἀμφισβη-**

τοῦσα : *laying a claim against.* Cf.
XVII. 5, ἡμῖν οἱ Ἐρασιφῶντος οἰκεῖοι
τούτων τῶν χρημάτων ἠμφισβήτουν, and
XXIV. 14.

11. ἐθέλοντος, ἐθελούσης : note the
anaphora, used only here in this
speech.

12. ἑαυτόν : the subject is expressed
for emphasis. H. 940 b ; Kr. *Spr.*
55, 2, 3. — **μὴ ὅτι** : 'not to speak of,'
stronger than *not only.* G. 1504 ;
H. 1035 a. — **ὅστις ἐβουλήθη ... οὐ-**
δενὶ χαλεπόν κτλ. : see on XXXI. 22.

γὰρ ἐβουλήθη βίᾳ ἀφαιρεθεὶς ἐνόχους καταστῆσαι τοὺς
ἑαυτοῦ ἐπιτηδείους τοῖς βιαίοις μᾶλλον ἢ κατὰ τοὺς νόμους
75 εἰς τὴν ἐλευθερίαν ἐξαιρεθεὶς δίκην λαβεῖν παρὰ τῶν
ἀγόντων αὐτόν, οὐδενὶ χαλεπὸν γνῶναι ὅτι εὖ εἰδὼς ἑαυτὸν
ὄντα δοῦλον ἔδεισεν ἐγγυητὰς καταστήσας περὶ τοῦ σώματος ἀγωνίσασθαι.

13 Ὅτι μὲν οὖν Πλαταιεὺς εἶναι πολλοῦ δεῖ, οἶμαι ὑμᾶς ἐκ
80 τούτων σχεδόν τι γιγνώσκειν· ὅτι δὲ οὐδ᾽ αὐτός, ὃς
ἄριστα οἶδε τὰ αὑτοῦ, ἡγήσατο δόξαι ἂν ὑμῖν Πλαταιεὺς
εἶναι, ἐξ ὧν ἔπραξε ῥᾳδίως μαθήσεσθε. ἐν τῇ ἀντωμοσίᾳ
γὰρ τῆς δίκης ἣν αὐτῷ ἔλαχεν Ἀριστόδικος οὑτοσί,
ἀμφισβητῶν μὴ πρὸς τὸν πολέμαρχον εἶναί οἱ τὰς δίκας,

— ἐνόχους καταστῆσαι κτλ.: i.e. they
would stand guilty of forcible ab-
duction instead of lawful ἐξαίρεσις,
and were liable to the δίκη βιαίων
with a penalty of double the value of
the plaintiff's loss. M. and S. pp.
646, 660. — δίκην λαβεῖν κτλ.: if Pancleon had really been a free man, he
was morally bound to bring the
action just mentioned against the
two persons who asserted that he
was a slave. — εἰδὼς ἑαυτὸν ὄντα :
the acc. of the partic. is used when
a reflexive is the object of a verb
that takes the partic. in indir.
discourse. GMT. 905. — σώματος :
used of his civil status. See on
VII. 26.

13. εἶναι πολλοῦ δεῖ : he is far from
being. See on XII. 17. — σχεδόν τι :
'pretty well,' cf. XIII. 33, σχεδόν τι
οἶμαι ὑμᾶς ἐπίστασθαι. — ἀντωμοσίᾳ :
properly used only of the defendant's
oath at the ἀνάκρισις, but here of the
proceedings in general there. See M.

and S. p. 827 ff. — μὴ εἶναι : the negative idea of ἀμφισβητῶν repeated, and
so after διεμαρτυρήθη. See on VII. 18.—
οἱ : this indir. reflexive is rarely used
by the orators, but by Lysias in XIII.
41, six times in Andocides, twice in
Antiphon, once in Isaeus. Kr. Spr.
51, 2, 4 ; Kühn. § 455, 5, 9 ; Dyroff,
Gesch. d. Pron. Reflex. p. 361 ff. —
διεμαρτυρήθη : at the anacrisis, Pancleon had claimed that he was a
citizen (being a Plataean), and that
consequently the polemarch had no
jurisdiction in his case. Thereupon
Aristodicus brought in a διαμαρτυρία
(that is, he presented witnesses to
prove that Pancleon's objection
would not hold), and διεμαρτυρήθη,
'testimony was brought to show'
that he was not a Plataean. See M.
and S. p. 842 ff., esp. p. 848, and on
the repetition in μή of the negative
idea, cf. Isaeus VI. 4, διεμαρτύρησεν
Ἀνδροκλῆς οὑτοσὶ μὴ ἐπίδικον εἶναι τὸν
κλῆρον.

14 διεμαρτυρήθη μὴ Πλαταιεὺς εἶναι, ἐπισκηψάμενος δὲ τῷ
μάρτυρι οὐκ ἐπεξῆλθεν, ἀλλ' εἴασε καταδικάσασθαι αὐτοῦ
τὸν Ἀριστόδικον. ἐπειδὴ δὲ ὑπερήμερος ἐγένετο, ἐξέτεισε
τὴν δίκην, καθ' ὅ τι ἔπειθε. καὶ τούτων, ὡς ἀληθῆ ἐστι,
μάρτυρας ἐγὼ παρέξομαι ὑμῖν. καί μοι ἐπίλαβε τὸ ὕδωρ.

ΜΑΡΤΥΡΕΣ.

15 Πρὶν τοίνυν ταῦτα ὁμολογηθῆναι αὐτῷ, δεδιὼς τὸν
Ἀριστόδικον, μεταστὰς ἐντεῦθεν Θήβησι μετῴκει. καίτοι
οἶμαι εἰδέναι ὑμᾶς ὅτι εἴπερ ἦν Πλαταιεύς, πανταχοῦ
μᾶλλον ἢ Θήβησιν εἰκὸς ἦν αὐτὸν μετοικῆσαι. ὡς οὖν
ἐκεῖ ᾤκει πολὺν χρόνον, τούτων ὑμῖν μάρτυρας παρέξομαι.
95 καί μοι ἐπίλαβε τὸ ὕδωρ.

14. **ἐπισκηψάμενος** : concessive.
The ἐπίσκηψις was the notice of in-
tention to bring a δίκη ψευδομαρτυριῶν,
action for false witness. It had to be
given before the judges voted ; Arist.
Resp. Ath. col. 36. See M. and S.
p. 491. — **ἐπεξῆλθεν** : prosecuted. —
ὑπερήμερος : a term was fixed for
the settlement of fines or damages,
though we do not know what it was.
But of course the parties could agree
upon an extension (cf. [Dem.] XLVII.
49, μελλούσης μοι ἤδη ἐξήκειν τῆς ὑπερη-
μερίας ... ἐδεόμην δ' αὐτοῦ ἀναβαλέσθαι
τὴν ὑπερημερίαν), or, as here, could
settle it by compromise (ὁμολογία, see
below, § 15) after the term had ex-
pired ; see M. and S. p. 964. — **καθ'
ὅ τι ἔπειθε** : as ἐκτίνω generally means
to pay in full, this relative clause
modifies it by showing that there
was a compromise, and means *on the
terms he persuaded him to accept*, i.e.
'on the best terms possible.' For a

like ellipse with πείθω, cf. [Dem.] L.
42, τὸ ἐπιτριηράρχημα ἀπέδωκε τῷ
Ἀγνίᾳ τοῦ χρόνου οὗ ἐπανήλωσεν ὑπὲρ
αὐτῶν, ὅσον ἔπεισε, and an inscription
from Orchomenus, Boeotia, ap. Cauer,
Delectus Inscr. Graec. 295, 134, ἀπο-
δόμεν τὰν πόλιν Ἐρχομενίων Νικαρέτη
Θίωνος, ὃ ἐπίθωσαν οὔπὲρ τᾶν οὐπεραμε-
ριάων τᾶν ἐπὶ Ξενοκρίτω ἄρχοντος ἐν
Θεσπιῆς, ἀργουρίω δραχμὰς μουρίας κτλ.
For καθ' ὅ τι, cf. καθ' ὅσον, Lys. XXXI.
8, and the common phrase καθ' ὅσον
δύναμαι, also Lycurg. *Leocr.* 16, καθ' ὅ
τι ἂν αὐτοῖς δοκῇ.

15. **ὁμολογηθῆναι** : the regular
word in such affairs, see on § 14,
and [Dem.] XLII. 12, XLVII. 77 ff. —
μετῴκει : *he lived as a foreigner*, cf.
XII. 20, XXII. 5 ; note the difference
in meaning of the aor. μετοικῆσαι. See
on XII. 71. — **πανταχοῦ μᾶλλον** : on
account of the long hostility between
the two places ; see note 10, p. 105. —
εἰκὸς ἦν : without ἄν, see on XII. 32.

ΜΑΡΤΥΡΕΣ.

16 Ἐξαρκεῖν μοι νομίζω τὰ εἰρημένα, ὦ ἄνδρες δικασταί·
ἐὰν γὰρ διαμνημονεύητε, οἶδ᾽ ὅτι τά τε δίκαια καὶ τἀληθῆ
ψηφιεῖσθε· ἃ καὶ ἐγὼ ὑμῶν δέομαι.

FOR THE CRIPPLE.

INTRODUCTION.

THE system of public charities or state aid to the poor, which we expect to find organized in every civilized modern country, did not exist in Greek antiquity.[1] There was not so great a need for it. In the small states of ancient Greece, property was more evenly divided than it is now; Greeks, indeed, never had, even in the time of the decadence, any such great private fortunes as were common in Rome. Though there were always beggars from the time of Odysseus down, yet these were as a rule rarely natives of the country in which they begged, but were generally, as he pretended to be, exiles or unfortunates from another land. In the best days of Athens the sight of a citizen begging in public was, according to Isocrates,[2] an unknown thing, and this disgrace befell the State only after the misfortunes of the Peloponnesian war and the troubles in the time of the Thirty. But from the earliest times and during the whole history of the city there must always have been cases of indigency arising from physical inability to work, and it was the boast of Athens that she alone of all Greek states made charitable provision for them.[3] This was done not by means of a poor-house, but by allowances.

The earliest known case of the sort is that of Thersippus, a wounded soldier in whose favour Solon obtained a decree that he should be supported at the public cost.[4] Upon this precedent Pisistratus based a general law applying to all such veterans.[5] The

---

[1] On the general subject, see Boeckh, *Staatshaush.* I, 308 ff., 570 ff.; Hermann, *Privatalt.* p. 94 f.   [2] VII. 83.

[3] Aristid. I, p. 310, Dind.
[4] Plut. *Solon.* 31.
[5] *Ibid.; cf.* Boeckh, *ibid.* p. 309.

next known instance is that of the cripple in Lysias's oration. We see from this that the charity had been extended, and we learn how it was administered. It was no longer confined to old soldiers; for if Lysias's man had ever served, he would certainly have enlarged upon the fact. His allowance amounted to one obol a day,[6] it was voted originally by the Senate,[7] and had to be confirmed annually by that body.[8] The people in the Assembly seem to have voted each year on the whole list of allowances, not troubling themselves ordinarily about individuals.[9] Although the grant was made on the ground that the recipient was incapacitated for work, yet it is clear that the letter of the law was not rigidly enforced; for our cripple had a trade,[10] he could walk, though only with sticks or crutches,[11] and even ride,[12] and that too in the days before stirrups and saddles with trees were known. But in spite of this, more than one Senate had satisfied itself that he was really ἀδύνατος within the meaning of the law, for every year the incoming Senate held a δοκιμασία on such cases.[13] And at this investigation, charges might be made even against the character of the beneficiary.[14]

In the speech of Aeschines against Timarchus,[15] the orator tells how the accused, himself well off, had suffered his own uncle, a poor old blind man, to be reckoned among the cripples (ἐν τοῖς ἀδυνάτοις μισθοφοροῦντα), and how, when he failed to come up for his δοκιμασία on the appointed day,[16] but presented himself later with a petition to the Senate, the cruel Timarchus, though himself a Senator, had not a word to say in his behalf, but allowed him to lose τὸν τῆς πρυτανείας μισθόν. From this passage we learn that the allowance, called μισθός, was paid by the prytany, and from

[6] §§ 13, 26. For the evidence that this was a *day's* allowance, see Aristotle, quoted on p. 118.

[7] §§ 7, 22. [8] § 26. [9] § 22.

[10] § 4. What was it? It required him to go about, § 10; he calls himself δημιουργός, § 19. For the meaning of τέχνη, see on XXII. 16.

[11] § 12.

[12] § 10 ff.

[13] § 26.

[14] §§ 15, 19. On the general nature of all δοκιμασίαι, see Introd. § 8.

[15] §§ 103, 104.

[16] § 104, ἀπολειφθέντος τοῦ πρεσβύτου τῆς γιγνομένης τοῖς ἀδυνάτοις δοκιμασίας, ἱκετηρίαν θέντος εἰς τὴν βουλὴν ὑπὲρ τοῦ μισθοῦ, and the scholium thereon.

the scholium that 'cripples' were τοὺς ὁπωσδηποτοῦν ἠχρειωμένους πρὸς ἐπικουρίαν αὐτῶν.[17]

This brings us down to the more exact statement of the law by Aristotle (*Resp. Ath.* 49. 4), as follows : δοκιμάζει δὲ καὶ τοὺς ἀδυνάτους ἡ βουλή· νόμος γάρ ἐστιν ὃς κελεύει τοὺς ἐντὸς τριῶν μνῶν κεκτημένους, καὶ τὸ σῶμα πεπηρωμένους ὥστε μὴ δύνασθαι μηδὲν ἔργον ἐργάζεσθαι, δοκιμάζειν μὲν τὴν βουλήν, διδόναι δὲ δημοσίᾳ τροφὴν δύο ὀβολοὺς ἑκάστῳ τῆς ἡμέρας. Two new facts come out here,—first, that the allowance had been increased to two obols; and, second, that it was given to all whose property amounted to less than three minae. The time when this change and this limitation were made remains at present unknown.[18]

Lysias wrote the Twenty-fourth oration for a pensioner of this sort.[19] His cripple seems to have been a celebrity, — perhaps a somewhat impudent fellow, but one who had a lively wit and humour of his own. He attracted the idlers of the market[20] to his little shop, where they would doubtless lounge to exchange a joke, — often rather a biting one, for the man was probably a privileged character. He made friends, however, even among the rich ; witness the loan of horses to him. Such a man would of course make enemies, too, by his ever-ready tongue, and it was

[17] The statement in the scholium that the allowance was three obols seems due to a confusion with the heliast's pay ; see Boeckh, *ibid.* p. 310.

[18] According to Harp., *s.v.* ἀδύνατοι, Philochorus (died in 261 B.C.) said that the allowance was nine drachmae a prytany (= about one and a half obols a day). Harpocration also quotes Aristotle and Lysias on the amount. The sum of five obols a day named in Bekker, *Anec.* p. 345, 15, is a clear error. Hesychius and Suidas add nothing new, the former following Aristotle, the latter Harpocration. It has been thought that the amount may have varied with the degree of poverty ; see Boeckh,

ibid. p. 310 ; also Hartmann, *Quaest. Gr.* II, p. 1 ff.

[19] Others who received public support (τροφή) of a different sort (elsewhere as well as in Athens) were the children of men who had fallen in war, Arist. *Polit.* 1268 a, 6 ff. Among private charities may be mentioned the fitting out of poor men for campaigns by their richer comrades (see on XVI. 14), and the λύσις αἰχμαλώτων (see on XII. 20). Then there were the ἔρανοι and the θίασοι, see Boeckh, *ibid.* p. 312.

[20] On the life in the agora, see p. 106. On the character of the Cripple, see Devries's excellent analysis, in his *Ethopoiia,* p. 34 ff.

perhaps one of them — maybe a man of higher station with whom he had gone too far in a joke — that raised objections to his allowance at the annual δοκιμασία.[21] But the accuser got more than he had bargained for. Lysias doubtless knew the man, saw the humour of the situation, marked it for his own, and wrote a speech (probably free of charge) which must have confounded the plaintiff. It was an excellent opportunity for the exhibition of that ἠθοποιία in which Lysias excelled, and he made the most of it. The speech is a very lucky hit, a mixture of serious pleading and of witty retort[22]; now in earnest, now employing intentional absurdity,[23] now jesting,[24] now a comical parody of the solemn and sententious[25]; passing "from grave to gay, from lively to severe." But the soberness and gravity are really all ironical and used for comic effect, and the speech contains no real pathos unless it be in the concluding appeal that after all it's only an obol that he needs, poor wretch, to make him happy.[26]

Both ancient and modern critics[27] have doubted whether this oration was really the work of Lysias. It has been thought most unlikely that Lysias should have written a speech for such a man, or that the Senate would have listened to so elaborate, and withal so impudent an address, on such a trifling matter. But, as Blass well remarks, neither modern nor ancient critics can tell on what

---

[21] The word εἰσαγγελία in the Ms. Greek title is a manifest error; see M. and S. p. 312. A different title is given by Suidas, who has s.v. ἀνάπηρον: Λυσίας ἐν τῷ περὶ τοῦ διδομένου τοῖς ἀδυνάτοις ὀβολοῦ.

[22] Cf. ὁμοίως τούτῳ, § 21.

[23] As, e.g., the notion that he might be choregus or archon, §§ 9, 13, — that he could have been ἐν δυνάμει in the time of the Thirty, § 25, — that his two sticks proved that he was stronger than those who used one, § 12, — that his infirmity was as desirable as an heiress, § 14.

[24] Cf. συκοφαντεῖ, § 2; his reductio ad absurdum of the charge so as to apply it to all Athens, § 20; jokes παρὰ προσδοκίαν, as οὐδέν, § 6; φθόνου, § 1.

[25] Gnomic thoughts, §§ 3, 10, 16 ff.; affected and grandiose words, too high for his real station, ἰᾶσθαι, § 3; ἐλεημονέστατοι, § 7; φιλοσοφεῖν, § 10; πρᾳόνως, § 15; κωμῳδεῖν, § 18; δειλαιότατος, § 23; his allusions to δαίμων and τύχη, § 22; antitheses, §§ 7, 16, 17, 18.

[26] § 26.

[27] Harp. s.v. ἀδύνατοι. Boeckh, ibid. p. 309.

subjects Lysias would choose to write, or the Athenians to lend an ear.[28] And it is now generally agreed that we have in it one of the most typical of the works of Lysias.[29]

On the date, nothing can be said further than that the speech was delivered some time after the fall of the Thirty.[30]

---

[28] *Att. Bereds.* I, 637. Blass himself, p. 633, classes it among 'bagatelle' speeches with the lost orations *On the Cruet-stand, On the Golden Tripod, Defence of the Dog,* etc.

[29] Wilamowitz, *Phil. Untersuch.* I, p. 196, calls it Lysias's best speech.

[30] § 25.

ΠΡΟΣ ΤΗΝ ΕΙΣΑΓΓΕΛΙΑΝ ΠΕΡΙ ΤΟΥ ΜΗ
ΔΙΔΟΣΘΑΙ ΤΩΙ ΑΔΥΝΑΤΩΙ ΑΡΓΥΡΙΟΝ.

1 Οὐ πολλοῦ δέω χάριν ἔχειν, ὦ βουλή, τῷ κατηγόρῳ, ὅτι μοι παρεσκεύασε τὸν ἀγῶνα τουτονί. πρότερον γὰρ οὐκ ἔχων πρόφασιν ἐφ᾽ ἧς τοῦ βίου λόγον δοίην, νυνὶ διὰ τοῦτον εἴληφα. καὶ πειράσομαι τῷ λόγῳ τοῦτον μὲν 5 ἐπιδεῖξαι ψευδόμενον, ἐμαυτὸν δὲ βεβιωκότα μέχρι τῆσδε τῆς ἡμέρας ἐπαίνου μᾶλλον ἄξιον ἢ φθόνου· διὰ γὰρ οὐδὲν ἄλλο μοι δοκεῖ παρασκευάσαι τόνδε μοι τὸν κίνδυ-2 νον οὗτος ἢ διὰ φθόνον. καίτοι ὅστις τούτοις φθονεῖ οὓς οἱ ἄλλοι ἐλεοῦσι, τίνος ἂν ὑμῖν ὁ τοιοῦτος ἀποσχέσθαι 10 δοκεῖ πονηρίας; εἰ μὲν γὰρ ἕνεκα χρημάτων με συκοφαν-

---

1. On the opening, see on XVI. I. — οὐ πολλοῦ δέω: see on XII. 17, and for the neg. with this phrase, cf. Xen. *Anab.* v. 4. 32, παῖδας ... οὐ πολλοῦ δέοντας ἴσους τὸ μῆκος καὶ τὸ πλάτος εἶναι. — παρεσκεύασε: for the meaning, see on VII. 18. — πρόφασιν: for the meaning, see on XII. 28. — ἐφ᾽ ἧς: for the unusual gen., see App. — ἔχων: a secondary tense, being impf. in time; cf. δοκοῦντες, § 7. — ἐφ᾽ ἧς δοίην: an extension of the dependent deliberative construction (see on XXXII. 20) to a purely rel. clause. Cf. [Dem.] XXXV. 25, οὐκ εἴχομεν ὅτου ἐπιλαβοίμεθα οὐδ᾽ ὅτου κρατοῖμεν, and for examples of the subjv. after a

primary tense Isocr. XXI. I, οὐ προφάσεως ἀπορῶ δι᾽ ἥντινα λέγω ὑπὲρ Νικίου τουτονί, and Xen. *Anab.* i. 7. 7, οὐκ ἔχω ἱκανοὺς οἷς δῶ. See GMT. 572, and App. — ἄξιον: see App. — φθόνου: not a real antithesis to ἐπαίνου (as ψόγου would be), but purposely used παρὰ προσδοκίαν. It might excite surprise and amusement at the moment, but it prepares the way for the cripple's attack on the heartlessness of his adversary.

2. εἰ ... συκοφαντεῖ: the apod. is supplied by a significant gesture (we might turn out a pocket) or a derisive laugh. G. 1416. The apod. is often omitted with the first of two

τεῖ—, εἰ δ' ὡς ἐχθρὸν ἑαυτοῦ με τιμωρεῖται, ψεύδεται·
διὰ γὰρ τὴν πονηρίαν αὐτοῦ οὔτε φίλῳ οὔτε ἐχθρῷ πώ-
3 ποτε ἐχρησάμην αὐτῷ. ἤδη τοίνυν, ὦ βουλή, δῆλός ἐστι
φθονῶν, ὅτι τοιαύτῃ κεχρημένος συμφορᾷ τούτου βελτίων
15 εἰμὶ πολίτης. καὶ γὰρ οἶμαι δεῖν, ὦ βουλή, τὰ τοῦ σώματος δυστυχήματα τοῖς τῆς ψυχῆς ἐπιτηδεύμασιν ἰᾶσθαι.
εἰ γὰρ ἐξ ἴσου τῇ συμφορᾷ καὶ τὴν διάνοιαν ἕξω καὶ τὸν
ἄλλον βίον διάξω, τί τούτου διοίσω;

4   Περὶ μὲν οὖν τούτων τοσαῦτά μοι εἰρήσθω· ὑπὲρ ὧν
20 δέ μοι προσήκει λέγειν, ὡς ἂν οἷός τ' ὦ διὰ βραχυτάτων
ἐρῶ. φησὶ γὰρ ὁ κατήγορος οὐ δικαίως με λαμβάνειν
τὸ παρὰ τῆς πόλεως ἀργύριον· καὶ γὰρ τῷ σώματι δύνασθαι καὶ οὐκ εἶναι τῶν ἀδυνάτων, καὶ τέχνην ἐπίστασθαι
5 τοιαύτην ὥστε καὶ ἄνευ τοῦ διδομένου τούτου ζῆν. καὶ
25 τεκμηρίοις χρῆται τῆς μὲν τοῦ σώματος ῥώμης, ὅτι ἐπὶ
τοὺς ἵππους ἀναβαίνω, τῆς δ' ἐν τῇ τέχνῃ εὐπορίας, ὅτι
δύναμαι συνεῖναι δυναμένοις ἀνθρώποις ἀναλίσκειν. τὴν
μὲν οὖν ἐκ τῆς τέχνης εὐπορίαν καὶ τὸν ἄλλον τὸν ἐμὸν

---

clauses introduced by εἰ μέν and εἰ δέ.
Kühn. 577, 3 c. — ὡς ἐχθρόν με τιμω-
ρεῖται: this would be right enough.
See on XII. 2.

3. ἤδη τοίνυν: now therefore. —
συμφορᾷ: of a physical misfortune,
cf. XXXI. 10. — ψυχῆς: in its proper
contrast to σῶμα. See on XXII. 20.
— ἐπιτηδεύμασιν: pursuits, studia.
— ἰᾶσθαι: with allusion to the proverbial μὴ κακοῖς ἰῶ κακά, Aesch. frag.
349 Nauck²; cf. Hdt. iii. 53, Thuc.
v. 65, Soph. frag. 74, Ajax, 362,
Plat. Prot. 340 E. — ἐξ ἴσου: to correspond to. See below, § 9. — τὸν ἄλλον
βίον: used of his moral behaviour,

while διάνοιαν means his intelligence,
and the two are contrasted with his
physical disability, συμφορᾷ.

4. περί, ὑπέρ: synonyms, as in
§ 21. This use of ὑπέρ, somewhat
rare in the three earlier orators, becomes common later; see Lutz, Präp.
p. 93. — τέχνην: see p. 117, note 10.

5. ἐν τῇ τέχνῃ: denoting the
means. Cf. XIII. 12, ἀπέκτειναν (sc. αὐτὸν) ἐν τῇ προφάσει τούτῃ, and see on
VII. 20. Below, in ἐκ τῆς τέχνης, the
point of view is rather that of cause.
See Lutz, Präp. pp. 36, 38, 53. —
βίον: livelihood, living. Cf. Thuc.
i. 5, ἥρπαζον καὶ τὸν πλεῖστον τοῦ βίου

βίον, οἷος τυγχάνει, πάντας ὑμᾶς οἴομαι γιγνώσκειν·
6 ὅμως δὲ κἀγὼ διὰ βραχέων ἐρῶ. ἐμοὶ γὰρ ὁ μὲν πατὴρ
κατέλιπεν οὐδέν, τὴν δὲ μητέρα τελευτήσασαν πέπαυμαι
τρέφων τρίτον ἔτος τουτί, παῖδες δέ μοι οὔπω εἰσὶν οἵ με
θεραπεύσουσι· τέχνην δὲ κέκτημαι βραχέα δυναμένην
ὠφελεῖν, ἣν αὐτὸς μὲν ἤδη χαλεπῶς ἐργάζομαι, τὸν δια-
35 δεξόμενον δ᾽ αὐτὴν οὔπω δύναμαι κτήσασθαι· πρόσοδος δέ
μοι οὐκ ἔστιν ἄλλη πλὴν ταύτης, ἣν ἂν ἀφέλησθέ με, κιν-
7 δυνεύσαιμ᾽ ἂν ὑπὸ τῇ δυσχερεστάτῃ γενέσθαι τύχῃ. μὴ
τοίνυν, ἐπειδή γε ἔστιν, ὦ βουλή, σῶσαί με δικαίως, ἀπο-
λέσητε ἀδίκως· μηδὲ ἃ νεωτέρῳ καὶ μᾶλλον ἐρρωμένῳ
40 ὄντι ἔδοτε, πρεσβύτερον καὶ ἀσθενέστερον γιγνόμενον
ἀφέλησθε· μηδὲ πρότερον καὶ περὶ τοὺς οὐδὲν ἔχοντας
κακὸν ἐλεημονέστατοι δοκοῦντες εἶναι νυνὶ διὰ τοῦτον

ἐντεῦθεν ἐποιοῦντο, Ar. Pax. 1212, ἀπώ-
λεσάς μου τὴν τέχνην καὶ τὸν βίον. —
τυγχάνει : sc. ὤν, rarely (and only
here in Lysias) omitted. GMT. 902.

6. τρίτον ἔτος τουτί : abhinc tres
annos, 'going on three years,' i.e.
two years ago. On the case, see G.
1063; H. 721, and cf. Dem. LIV. 3,
ἐξῆλθον, ἔτος τουτὶ τρίτον, εἰς Πάνακτον.
The phrase belongs both to τελευτήσασαν and to πέπαυμαι. — οὔπω : a
jest, for (though his mother has
lately died) he seems to be well on in
years. Cf. §§ 7, 8, 16. — θεραπεύ-
σουσι : on the tense, cf. XVI. 16. —
τὸν διαδεξόμενον : for the tense, see
on XII. 98. A technical term. He
means a slave who is to 'relieve'
him of the actual work of his business; see Hermann, Privatalt. pp. 91,
399. — κτήσασθαι : acquire, i.e. buy,
cf. § 11. Note the difference in tense

from that of κέκτημαι. — ὑπὸ τῇ τύχῃ :
a half-personification of τύχη, on the
analogy of ὑπὸ τοῖς τυράννοις ἐγένοντο,
XXVI. 22, ὑπὸ τῷ βαρβάρῳ, XXXIII. 3 ;
see on ὑπό with gen. below, in § 17,
and for a like use with ἐπί, cf.
Antiphon v. 6, ἅπαντα γὰρ τὰ ἐν ἀδήλῳ
ἔτ᾽ ὄντα ἐπὶ τῇ τύχῃ μᾶλλον ἀνάκειται ἢ
τῇ προνοίᾳ. With both prepositions the
use of substantives really impersonal
is rare in the sense of ' in the power
of'; see Lutz, Präp. pp. 115, 179.

7. σῶσαι ... ἀδίκως : cf. XIX. 54,
βούλεσθε ἡμᾶς δικαίως σῶσαι μᾶλλον ἢ
ἀδίκως ἀπολέσαι. — ἐρρωμένῳ : as adj.
GMT. 830. — τοὺς ... κακόν : people
who had nothing the matter with
them. — ἐλεημονέστατοι : a rare adj.;
cf. Isocr. xv. 20, who says that
the Athenians ἐλεημονεστάτους ὁμολο-
γεῖσθαι καὶ πρᾳοτάτους ἁπάντων εἶναι
τῶν Ἑλλήνων. — δοκοῦντες : impf. in

τοὺς καὶ τοῖς ἐχθροῖς ἐλεεινοὺς ὄντας ἀγρίως ἀποδέξησθε·
μηδ᾽ ἐμὲ τολμήσαντες ἀδικῆσαι καὶ τοὺς ἄλλους τοὺς
8 ὁμοίως ἐμοὶ διακειμένους ἀθυμῆσαι ποιήσητε. καὶ γὰρ
ἂν ἄτοπον εἴη, ὦ βουλή, εἰ ὅτε μὲν ἁπλῆ μοι ἦν ἡ συμφορά, τότε μὲν φαινοίμην λαμβάνων τὸ ἀργύριον τοῦτο,
νῦν δ᾽ ἐπειδὴ καὶ γῆρας καὶ νόσοι καὶ τὰ τούτοις ἑπό-
9 μενα κακὰ προσγίγνεταί μοι, τότε ἀφαιρεθείην. δοκεῖ δέ
50 μοι τῆς πενίας τῆς ἐμῆς τὸ μέγεθος ὁ κατήγορος ἂν ἐπιδεῖξαι σαφέστατα μόνος ἀνθρώπων. εἰ γὰρ ἐγὼ κατασταθεὶς χορηγὸς τραγῳδοῖς προκαλεσαίμην αὐτὸν εἰς
ἀντίδοσιν, δεκάκις ἂν ἕλοιτο χορηγῆσαι μᾶλλον ἢ ἀντι-

time. — **ἀγρίως ἀποδέξησθε**: this verb
is generally used of kindly or willing
receptions (*cf.* XII. 28 and XIX. 6, τοὺς
ἐλέγχους ἤδη ἐθέλοντες ἀποδέχεσθε),
but as here in Ant. III. β. 2, δυσχερῶς
ἀποδεξαμένους μου τὴν ἀπολογίαν. —
τολμήσαντες: for the meaning, see
on XII. 5.

8. φαινοίμην λαμβάνων: not ἐφαι-
νόμην, for the impf. idea is in the
participle. See on XVI. 5. — **τότε
ἀφαιρεθείην**: on this emphatic use of
τότε after νῦν, *cf.* Dinarch. I. 93, νῦν
ἐπειδὴ ... τηνικαῦτα, Anth. Pal. ix.
138, νῦν δ᾽ ὁπότε χρῆσθαι μὴ δύναμαι,
τότ᾽ ἔχω. See App.

9. σαφέστατα μόνος ἀνθρώπων:
an exaggerated combination of the
common phrase μόνος ἀνθρώπων with
σαφέστατα ἀνθρώπων (for the latter
cf. XXIX. 2, οἷς ἐκεῖνος οἰκειότατ᾽ ἀνθρώπων ἐχρῆτο); *cf.* III. 31, ἐμίσει πάντων
ἀνθρώπων μάλιστα. So un us and the
superlative in Latin with or without
omnium, as in Cic. *Prov. Consul.*
12, un us omnium nequissimus,
Planc. 97, urbem unam mihi

amicissimam. — **κατασταθείς**: the
pass. instead of the commoner intrans. second aor. act. (used in XXI. 1,
καταστὰς δὲ χορηγός, XXVII. 3, φύλακες
ὑφ᾽ ὑμῶν καταστάντες, *cf.* XII. 48). So
Antiphon VI. 11, ἐπειδὴ χορηγὸς κατε-
στάθην, Hyperides, *Athenog.* 15. 9,
ὑπ᾽ ἐκείνου κατασταθεὶς ἄρχων. Lysias
has the aor. pass. also in XIII. 35,
ἐπειδὴ οἱ τριάκοντα κατεστάθησαν, but
the second aor. act. in the same
phrase in XII. 5; *cf.* XII. 36, 43, 55;
XIII. 34; XXI. 4; XXV. 14. See App.
— **χορηγός**: see on XII. 20. The great
expense of the Choregia is in amusing
contrast to the speaker's poverty. —
ἀντίδοσιν: 'an exchange of property.'
When a man was assigned a liturgy
but considered that it should have
been assigned to some other person,
he might challenge that person to
assume the liturgy or to exchange
properties with him. A lawsuit followed a refusal of the challenge. On
the subject, see Smith, *Dict. Antiq.*
s.v.; M. and S. p. 740 f; Gilbert,
Antiq. p. 361 ff. — **ἐξ ἴσου**: 'on an

δοῦναι ἅπαξ. καὶ πῶς οὐ δεινόν ἐστι νῦν μὲν κατηγορεῖν
55 ὡς διὰ πολλὴν εὐπορίαν ἐξ ἴσου δύναμαι συνεῖναι τοῖς
πλουσιωτάτοις, εἰ δὲ ὧν ἐγὼ λέγω τύχοι τι γενόμενον,
ὁμολογεῖν ἂν ἐμὲ τοιοῦτον εἶναι καὶ ἔτι πονηρότερον;
10 Περὶ δὲ τῆς ἐμῆς ἱππικῆς, ἧς οὗτος ἐτόλμησε μνησθῆναι πρὸς ὑμᾶς, οὔτε τὴν τύχην δείσας οὔτε ὑμᾶς αἰσχυν-
60 θείς, οὐ πολὺς ὁ λόγος. ἐγὼ γὰρ οἶμαι, ὦ βουλή, πάντας
τοὺς ἔχοντάς τι δυστύχημα τοῦτο ζητεῖν καὶ τοῦτο φιλοσοφεῖν, ὅπως ὡς ἀλυπότατα μεταχειριοῦνται τὸ συμβε-
βηκὸς πάθος. ὧν εἷς ἐγώ, καὶ περιπεπτωκὼς τοιαύτῃ
συμφορᾷ ταύτην ἐμαυτῷ ῥᾳστώνην ἐξηῦρον εἰς τὰς ὁδοὺς
11 τὰς μακροτέρας τῶν ἀναγκαίων. ὃ δὲ μέγιστον, ὦ βουλή,
τεκμήριον ὅτι διὰ τὴν συμφορὰν ἀλλ᾽ οὐ διὰ τὴν ὕβριν,
ὡς οὗτός φησιν, ἐπὶ τοὺς ἵππους ἀναβαίνω· εἰ γὰρ
ἐκεκτήμην οὐσίαν, ἐπ᾽ ἀστράβης ἂν ὠχούμην, ἀλλ᾽

equality with'; cf. § 3. — **εἰ δὲ ...
πονηρότερον**: the thought is, 'should
an ἀντίδοσις be proposed, he would
admit that I am as poor (τοιοῦτον) as I profess to be, or even
wretcheder still.' For πονηρός in this
sense, cf. Isaeus, I. 12, τελευτήσαντος
γὰρ Δεινίου καὶ τῶν πραγμάτων ἡμῖν
πονηρῶς ἐχόντων, and And. I. 118.

10. ἱππικῆς: (sc. τέχνης), horse-
manship, purposely used with a
satirical turn, meaning a little more
than mere 'riding.' Xenophon wrote
a book Περὶ Ἱππικῆς. — **τύχην**: for-
tunam, cf. [Isocr.] I. 29, κοινὴ γὰρ ἡ
τύχη καὶ τὸ μέλλον ἀόρατον, and see
on § 22. — **δείσας, αἰσχυνθείς**: cf.
XXXII. 13. — **φιλοσοφεῖν**: this word,
though purposely affected in the
mouth of the cripple, did not yet
signify speculative thought, but

meant to *make a thing one's study*;
cf. Isocr. xv. 121, τοῦτ᾽ ἐφιλοσόφει καὶ
τοῦτ᾽ ἔπραττεν, ὅπως μηδεμία τῶν πόλεων
αὐτὸν φοβήσεται, IV. 6, σκοπεῖν καὶ
φιλοσοφεῖν τοῦτον τὸν λόγον (theme).
See Jebb, *Attic Orators*, II, p. 37. —
ὧν εἷς ἐγώ: the emphasis on ἐγώ is
such that εἰμί is omitted; cf. Plat.
Euthyd. 304 C, φιλήκοος μὲν ἔγωγε καὶ
ἡδέως ἄν τι μανθάνοιμι, though the
emphasis there is secondary. On
such omissions, see Kr. *Spr.* 62, 1, 5.
— **ταύτην**: for the gender, see on
XII. 37. — **τῶν ἀναγκαίων**: partitive
genitive. See App.

11. ὃ δὲ μέγιστον κτλ.: introductory
rel. phrase, cf. XXXII. 24. — **ἀστράβης**:
a padded saddle with a back, almost
a chair, used by invalids, women, or,
as in Dem. XXI. 133, effeminate men.
It was placed on mules, whence Har-

οὐκ ἐπὶ τοὺς ἀλλοτρίους ἵππους ἀνέβαινον· νυνὶ δ'
70 ἐπειδὴ τοιοῦτον οὐ δύναμαι κτήσασθαι, τοῖς ἀλλοτρίοις
12 ἵπποις ἀναγκάζομαι χρῆσθαι πολλάκις. καίτοι πῶς
οὐκ ἄτοπόν ἐστιν, ὦ βουλή, τοῦτον ἂν αὐτόν, εἰ μὲν ἐπ'
ἀστράβης ὀχούμενον ἑώρα με, σιωπᾶν — τί γὰρ ἂν καὶ
ἔλεγεν; — ὅτι δ' ἐπὶ τοὺς ᾐτημένους ἵππους ἀναβαίνω, πει-
75 ρᾶσθαι πείθειν ὑμᾶς ὡς δυνατός εἰμι; καὶ ὅτι μὲν δυοῖν
βακτηρίαιν χρῶμαι, τῶν ἄλλων μιᾷ χρωμένων, μὴ κατηγορεῖν ὡς καὶ τοῦτο τῶν δυναμένων ἐστίν, ὅτι δ' ἐπὶ τοὺς
ἵππους ἀναβαίνω, τεκμηρίῳ χρῆσθαι πρὸς ὑμᾶς ὡς εἰμὶ
τῶν δυναμένων; οἷς ἐγὼ διὰ τὴν αὐτὴν αἰτίαν ἀμφοτέροις
80 χρῶμαι.

13 Τοσοῦτον δὲ διενήνοχεν ἀναισχυντίᾳ τῶν ἁπάντων
ἀνθρώπων, ὥστε ὑμᾶς πειρᾶται πείθειν, τοσούτους ὄντας
εἷς ὤν, ὡς οὐκ εἰμὶ τῶν ἀδυνάτων ἐγώ. καίτοι εἰ τοῦτο
πείσει τινὰς ὑμῶν, ὦ βουλή, τί με κωλύει κληροῦσθαι τῶν

pocration and others say that the
word came to mean mule. See Göll's
edition of Becker's *Charicles*, II, p. 14.
and Hermann, *Privatalt.* p. 481. —
ἵππους: the speaker could not have
been very badly disabled, for the
horse was ridden without saddle or
stirrups. — ἀνέβαινον: ἄν is understood; see on XVI. 8.

12. τί γὰρ ἂν καί: for the force of
καί, see on XII. 29, and *cf.* § 23, below.
— ᾐτημένους: *borrowed. Cf.* XIX. 27,
χαλκώματα ... αἰτησάμενος ἐχρήσατο,
Xen. *Anab.* v. I. 11, αἰτησάμενοι παρὰ
Τραπεζουντίων μακρὰ πλοῖα. — τῶν δυναμένων: for the meaning, see on
XXXII. 23. The gen. is possessive.
G. 1094, 1; see on XII. 41. — ἀμφοτέροις: *i.e.* horses and sticks.

13. τοσούτους ... ὤν: for the
phrase, see on XXXI. 31. — εἰ τοῦτο
πείσει: *if he is going to persuade*,
not a future condition. See G. 1391;
H. 893 c; GMT. 407; and *cf.* Xen.
Anab. i. 3. 16, εἰ δὲ καὶ τῷ ἡγεμόνι
πιστεύσομεν ... τί κωλύει καὶ τὰ ἄκρα
ἡμῖν κελεύειν Κῦρον προκαταλαβεῖν; —
κληροῦσθαι τῶν ἐννέα ἀρχόντων: although, by the letter of the law, members of the fourth Solonian class of
citizens (the Thetes) were not eligible
to the archonship, yet in practice at
this period the law was evaded. *Cf.*
Arist. *Resp. Ath.* 7. 3; 26. 2; and see
Gilbert, *Antiq.* pp. 153, 157. Hence
the cripple was debarred only by his
physical condition. One who was not
ὁλόκληρος (physically *perfect*) could

85 ἐννέα ἀρχόντων, καὶ ὑμᾶς ἐμοῦ μὲν ἀφελέσθαι τὸν ὀβολὸν
ὡς ὑγιαίνοντος, τούτῳ δὲ ψηφίσασθαι πάντας ὡς ἀνα-
πήρῳ; οὐ γὰρ δήπου τὸν αὐτὸν ὑμεῖς μὲν ὡς δυνάμενον
ἀφαιρήσεσθε τὸ διδόμενον, οἱ δὲ θεσμοθέται ὡς ἀδύνατον
14 ὄντα κληροῦσθαι κωλύσουσιν. ἀλλὰ γὰρ οὔτε ὑμεῖς
90 τούτῳ τὴν αὐτὴν ἔχετε γνώμην, οὔθ' οὗτος . . . εὖ ποιῶν.
ὁ μὲν γὰρ ὥσπερ ἐπικλήρου τῆς συμφορᾶς οὔσης ἀμφισ-
βητήσων ἥκει καὶ πειρᾶται πείθειν ὑμᾶς ὡς οὐκ εἰμὶ τοιοῦτος οἷον ὑμεῖς ὁρᾶτε πάντες· ὑμεῖς δὲ (ὃ τῶν εὖ φρο-
νούντων ἔργον ἐστί) μᾶλλον πιστεύετε τοῖς ὑμετέροις αὐ-
95 τῶν ὀφθαλμοῖς ἢ τοῖς τούτου λόγοις.
15 Λέγει δ' ὡς ὑβριστής εἰμι καὶ βίαιος καὶ λίαν ἀσελ-
γῶς διακείμενος, ὥσπερ, εἰ φοβερῶς ὀνομάσειε, μέλλων
ἀληθῆ λέγειν, ἀλλ' οὐκ, ἂν πάνυ πραόνως, ταῦτα ποιήσων.
ἐγὼ δ' ὑμᾶς, ὦ βουλή, σαφῶς οἶμαι δεῖν διαγιγνώσκειν
100 οἷς τ' ἐγχωρεῖ τῶν ἀνθρώπων ὑβρισταῖς εἶναι καὶ οἷς οὐ

not perform the religious functions
of the office. See M. and S. p. 240;
Boeckh, *Staatsh.* I, p. 593. For the
use of κληροῦσθαι, see on XXXI. 33;
and for the gen., see on XXXII. 5.
— ἀφελέσθαι and ἀφαιρήσεσθε: for
the different constructions following
them, see on XXXI. 19. — θεσμοθέται:
these had charge of the drawing of
the lots for the choice of magistrates;
cf. Aeschin. III. 13.

14. ἀλλὰ γάρ: see on XII. 99. —
εὖ ποιῶν: on the lacuna, see App.
— ὥσπερ ἐπικλήρου: when there were
no sons, a man's daughter was called
ἐπίκληρος and went with the inheritance. To keep this in the family
(see on XXXII. 4), the nearest relative
was entitled to marry her, and, to

make this possible, even marriages
made before she became an ἐπίκληρος
might be annulled. Many lawsuits
arose from such cases. On the subject, see M. and S. p. 614 ff.; Smith,
Dict. Antiq. s.v. Epiclerus. Hence
the cripple jestingly speaks of his
συμφορά as an ἐπίκληρος, dowered as it
is with his allowance. — ἀμφισβητή-
σων: the regular word used of claims
to property or to an heiress.

15. λίαν: a rather rare adv., but
occurring four times in this speech
(§§ 16, 21, 25). — φοβερῶς ὀνομάσειε:
'call me dreadful names,' *i.e.* ὑβριστής, βίαιος κτλ. — πραόνως: (as if
from a πραόνους), used also in Ar.
Ran. 856, for the usual πράως. —
ταῦτα ποιήσων: *i.e.* ἀληθῆ λέξων.

16 προσήκει. οὐ γὰρ τοὺς πενομένους καὶ λίαν ἀπόρως διακειμένους ὑβρίζειν εἰκός, ἀλλὰ τοὺς πολλῷ πλείω τῶν
ἀναγκαίων κεκτημένους· οὐδὲ τοὺς ἀδυνάτους τοῖς σώμα-
σιν ὄντας, ἀλλὰ τοὺς μάλιστα πιστεύοντας ταῖς αὑτῶν
105 ῥώμαις· οὐδὲ τοὺς ἤδη προβεβηκότας τῇ ἡλικίᾳ, ἀλλὰ
17 τοὺς ἔτι νέους καὶ νέαις ταῖς διανοίαις χρωμένους. οἱ μὲν
γὰρ πλούσιοι τοῖς χρήμασιν ἐξωνοῦνται τοὺς κινδύνους,
οἱ δὲ πένητες ὑπὸ τῆς παρούσης ἀπορίας σωφρονεῖν
ἀναγκάζονται· καὶ οἱ μὲν νέοι συγγνώμης ἀξιοῦνται τυγ-
110 χάνειν παρὰ τῶν πρεσβυτέρων, τοῖς δὲ πρεσβυτέροις
18 ἐξαμαρτάνουσιν ὁμοίως ἐπιτιμῶσιν ἀμφότεροι· καὶ τοῖς
μὲν ἰσχυροῖς ἐγχωρεῖ μηδὲν αὐτοῖς πάσχουσιν οὓς ἂν
βουληθῶσιν ὑβρίζειν, τοῖς δὲ ἀσθενέσιν οὐκ ἔστιν οὔτε
ὑβριζομένοις ἀμύνεσθαι τοὺς ὑπάρξαντας οὔτε ὑβρίζειν
115 βουλομένοις περιγίγνεσθαι τῶν ἀδικουμένων. ὥστε μοι
δοκεῖ ὁ κατήγορος εἰπεῖν περὶ τῆς ἐμῆς ὕβρεως οὐ σπου-
δάζων, ἀλλὰ παίζων, οὐδ᾽ ὑμᾶς πεῖσαι βουλόμενος ὡς
εἰμὶ τοιοῦτος, ἀλλ᾽ ἐμὲ κωμῳδεῖν βουλόμενος, ὥσπερ τι
καλὸν ποιῶν.

16. For the commonplaces of this
section, *cf.* Arist. *Rhet.* II. p. 1378 b,
28, οἱ νέοι καὶ οἱ πλούσιοι ὑβρισταί·
ὑπερέχειν γὰρ οἴονται ὑβρίζοντες, and
Ar. *Plut.* 564, where Πενία says :
κοσμιότης οἰκεῖ μετ᾽ ἐμοῦ, τοῦ πλούτου
δ᾽ ἐστὶν ὑβρίζειν. — Note the unusual
(for Lysias) number of antitheses.

17. ἐξωνοῦνται τοὺς κινδύνους : *sc.*
by compromising with or bribing persons whom they have wronged ; *cf.*
XXVII. 6, μέρει τῶν ἀδικημάτων ('of
their ill-gotten gains') τὸν κίνδυνον
ἐξεπρίαντο. — ὑπὸ τῆς ἀπορίας: see on
§ 6, and XII. 3.—ἀμφότεροι: *i.e.* young
and old.

18. τοὺς ὑπάρξαντας : frequently
used absolutely of the person who
gives the provocation, as in Isocr.
XVI. 44, οὐδ᾽ ἀμυνόμενος ἀλλ᾽ ὑπάρχων
(ultro) ἠδίκεις αὐτούς, [Dem.] LIX. 15,
τιμωρεῖσθαι τὸν ὑπάρξαντα, Menander,
frag. 358 Kock, ὡς οὐχ ὑπάρχων, ἀλλὰ
τιμωρούμενος, but also with a genitive
as [Dem.] LIX. 1, τῆς ἔχθρας πρότερος
οὗτος ὑπῆρξεν. So the simple verb ;
cf. Lys. IV. 11, εἰ οὗτος ἦρχε χειρῶν
ἀδίκων ἢ ἐγὼ πρότερος τοῦτον ἐπάταξα
and τὸν ἄρξαντα τῆς πληγῆς with οἱ
ἄρχοντες in Ant. IV. β. 2. — τῶν ἀδικουμένων : 'their victims.' — βουλόμενος : for its repetition, see on XVI.

19 Ἔτι δὲ καὶ συλλέγεσθαί φησιν ἀνθρώπους ὡς ἐμὲ
πονηροὺς καὶ πολλούς, οἳ τὰ μὲν ἑαυτῶν ἀνηλώκασι, τοῖς
δὲ τὰ σφέτερα σῴζειν βουλομένοις ἐπιβουλεύουσιν. ὑμεῖς
δὲ ἐνθυμήθητε πάντες ὅτι ταῦτα λέγων οὐδὲν ἐμοῦ κατηγορεῖ μᾶλλον ἢ τῶν ἄλλων ὅσοι τέχνας ἔχουσιν, οὐδὲ τῶν
125 ὡς ἐμὲ εἰσιόντων μᾶλλον ἢ τῶν ὡς τοὺς ἄλλους δημιουρ-
20 γούς. ἕκαστος γὰρ ὑμῶν εἴθισται προσφοιτᾶν ὃ μὲν
πρὸς μυροπώλιον, ὃ δὲ πρὸς κουρεῖον, ὃ δὲ πρὸς σκυτο-
τομεῖον, ὃ δ᾽ ὅποι ἂν τύχῃ, καὶ πλεῖστοι μὲν ὡς τοὺς
ἐγγυτάτω τῆς ἀγορᾶς κατεσκευασμένους, ἐλάχιστοι δὲ ὡς
130 τοὺς πλεῖστον ἀπέχοντας αὐτῆς· ὥστ᾽ εἴ τις ὑμῶν πονηρίαν καταγνώσεται τῶν ὡς ἐμὲ εἰσιόντων, δῆλον ὅτι καὶ
τῶν παρὰ τοῖς ἄλλοις διατριβόντων· εἰ δὲ κἀκείνων,
ἁπάντων Ἀθηναίων· ἅπαντες γὰρ εἴθισθε προσφοιτᾶν
καὶ διατρίβειν ἀμουγέπου.

13. — ὥσπερ ... ποιῶν : doing a fine
thing, as it were.   See App. to xii. 7.
In connexion with κωμῳδεῖν, however,
ποιῶν possibly means composing.

19. συλλέγεσθαι : of course, as
Rauchenstein remarks, the accuser
had not objected to the men, but to
their character, and the stress would
be on πονηρούς, not on συλλέγεσθαι or
πολλούς. The defence, however, very
neatly pretends to misunderstand the
charge and reverses the emphasis by
putting συλλέγεσθαι first and πολλούς
after instead of, as usual, before the
other adjective.   Thus the accuser
is made to blame the habits of all
Athens.   On these habits and on the
shops mentioned in the next section,
see p. 107.

20. ὅποι ἂν τύχῃ : sc. προσφοιτᾶν.
See on xii. 18. — κατεσκευασμένους :

properly the verb means fit up, as
πρῶτον μὲν διδασκαλεῖον (for a chorus)
ᾗ ἦν ἐπιτηδειότατον τῆς ἐμῆς οἰκίας
κατεσκεύασα, Antiphon vi. 11 ; in the
middle, set up shop, open a business,
κατασκευάζομαι τέχνην μυρεψικήν· ἀφορ-
μῆς (see on § 24) δὲ δέομαι, Lys. frag.
i. 2, also with τὴν τράπεζαν, Isaeus,
frag. 15. 3, and κατεσκευασμένος λαμ-
πρότατον ἰατρεῖον, Antiphanes, frag.
208 Kock ; used absolutely as here
(though not of shopkeeping), Thuc.
ii. 17. 3, κατεσκευάσαντο δὲ καὶ ἐν
τοῖς πύργοις τῶν τειχῶν πολλοί (sc.
of the Athenians crowded into the
city during the Peloponnesian war).
— καταγνώσεται : for the acc. and
the gen., see G. 1123; H. 752 a.
— πάντων Ἀθηναίων : without the
article, see on xvi. 15. — ἀμουγέπου : i.e. ἀμοῦ γέ που, somewhere or

21 Ἀλλὰ γὰρ οὐκ οἶδ' ὅ τι δεῖ λίαν με ἀκριβῶς ἀπολογού-
μενον πρὸς ἓν ἕκαστον ὑμῖν τῶν εἰρημένων ἐνοχλεῖν
πλείω χρόνον. εἰ γὰρ ὑπὲρ τῶν μεγίστων εἴρηκα, τί δεῖ
περὶ τῶν ὁμοίως τούτῳ φαύλων σπουδάζειν; ἐγὼ δ' ὑμῶν,
ὦ βουλή, δέομαι πάντων τὴν αὐτὴν ἔχειν περὶ ἐμοῦ διά-
22 νοιαν, ἥνπερ καὶ πρότερον. μηδ' οὗ μόνου μεταλαβεῖν
ἔδωκεν ἡ τύχη μοι τῶν ἐν τῇ πατρίδι, τούτου διὰ τουτονὶ
ἀποστερήσητέ με· μηδ' ἃ πάλαι κοινῇ πάντες ἔδοτέ μοι,
νῦν οὗτος εἷς ὢν πείσῃ πάλιν ὑμᾶς ἀφελέσθαι. ἐπειδὴ
γάρ, ὦ βουλή, τῶν μεγίστων ἀρχῶν ὁ δαίμων ἀπεστέρη-
145σεν ἡμᾶς, ἡ πόλις ἡμῖν ἐψηφίσατο τοῦτο τὸ ἀργύριον,
ἡγουμένη κοινὰς εἶναι τὰς τύχας τοῖς ἅπασι καὶ τῶν
23 κακῶν καὶ τῶν ἀγαθῶν. πῶς οὖν οὐκ ἂν δειλαιότατος
εἴην, εἰ τῶν μὲν καλλίστων καὶ μεγίστων διὰ τὴν συμφορὰν ἀπεστερημένος εἴην, ἃ δ' ἡ πόλις ἔδωκε προνοηθεῖσα
150τῶν οὕτως διακειμένων διὰ τὸν κατήγορον ἀφαιρεθείην;

other. The nom. ἁμός is cited by ancient grammarians as Doric for τὶς, and the stem appears in οὐδαμοῖ, οὐδαμοῦ. Though ἁμουγέπου occurs elsewhere only in Schol. Plat. *Soph.* 259 D, we find ἁμωσγέπως, Lys. XIII. 7, ἁμηγέπῃ, Plat. *Rep.* 474 C, Ar. *Ach.* 608, ἁμόθεν γέ ποθεν, Plat. *Gorg.* 492 D. See Bl.-Kühn. *Gr.* I, p. 614.

21. ἀλλὰ γάρ: see on XII. 99. — **ὑμῖν:** belongs to ἐνοχλεῖν, a hyperbaton as in § 27. See on XII. 94. — **ὑπέρ** and **περί:** see on § 4. — **μεγίστων:** i.e. his infirmity and poverty. — **τῶν ὁμοίως τούτῳ φαύλων:** the point of the gibe lies in the double sense of φαῦλος, as in our *common, mean, slight;* cf. Shakespeare's 'Away, slight man!'

22. οὗ μόνου: partitive gen. with μεταλαβεῖν. The relative clause here precedes the antecedent; see on XII. 43. — **πάντες . . . εἷς ὤν:** see on XXXI. 31. — **ὁ δαίμων:** for the relation between δαίμων and τύχη, cf. Dem. XVIII. 208, τῇ τύχῃ δ', ἣν ὁ δαίμων ἔνειμεν ἑκάστοις, ταύτῃ κέχρηνται, and Eur. *Med.* 671, ἄπαιδές ἐσμεν δαίμονός τινος τύχῃ. Thus Lysias here employs the words; cf. also XIII. 63, ἡ δὲ τύχη καὶ ὁ δαίμων περιεποίησε, and [Lys.] II. 78, ὁ δαίμων ὁ τὴν ἡμετέραν μοῖραν εἰληχὼς ἀπαραίτητος. — **ἡμᾶς:** not equiv. to ἐμέ, for he now speaks of the whole class of ἀδύνατοι. **κοινὰς κτλ.:** see on § 10.

23. δειλαιότατος: the use of this generally poetic word increases the

μηδαμῶς, ὦ βουλή, ταύτῃ θῆσθε τὴν ψῆφον. διὰ τί γὰρ
24 ἂν καὶ τύχοιμι τοιούτων ὑμῶν; πότερον ὅτι δι' ἐμέ τις εἰς
ἀγῶνα πώποτε καταστὰς ἀπώλεσε τὴν οὐσίαν; ἀλλ' οὐδ'
ἂν εἰς ἀποδείξειεν. ἀλλ' ὅτι πολυπράγμων εἰμὶ καὶ θρα-
155 σὺς καὶ φιλαπεχθήμων; ἀλλ' οὐ τοιαύταις ἀφορμαῖς
25 τοῦ βίου τυγχάνω χρώμενος. ἀλλ' ὅτι λίαν ὑβριστὴς
καὶ βίαιος; ἀλλ' οὐδ' ἂν αὐτὸς φήσειεν, εἰ μὴ βούλοιτο
καὶ τοῦτο ψεύδεσθαι τοῖς ἄλλοις ὁμοίως. ἀλλ' ὅτι ἐπὶ
τῶν τριάκοντα γενόμενος ἐν δυνάμει κακῶς ἐποίησα πολ-
160 λοὺς τῶν πολιτῶν; ἀλλὰ μετὰ τοῦ ὑμετέρου πλήθους
ἔφυγον εἰς Χαλκίδα, καὶ ἐξόν μοι μετ' ἐκείνων ἀδεῶς
26 πολιτεύεσθαι μεθ' ὑμῶν εἱλόμην κινδυνεύειν ἁπάντων. μὴ
τοίνυν, ὦ βουλή, μηδὲν ἡμαρτηκὼς ὁμοίων ὑμῶν τύχοιμι

parody of pathos. *Cf.* Aeschin. i. 172, ἐκκοπεὶς ὁ δείλαιος ἀμφοτέρους τοὺς ὀφθαλμοὺς καὶ τὴν γλῶτταν ἀποτμηθείς. — ταύτῃ κτλ.: *cf.* Isaeus, viii. 46, ᾗ δίκαιόν ἐστι, ταύτῃ τὴν ψῆφον τίθεσθε. τύχοιμι ... ὑμῶν: *cf.* xviii. 23, οἵων ὑμῶν ἐν τοῖς κινδύνοις τεύξονται, and And. iii. 21, ποίων τινῶν Λακεδαιμονίων τυγχάνοντας;

24. πότερον, ἀλλά, ἀλλά: a favourite formula in abrupt questions, *cf.* xxxi. 24; for ἀλλά, see on xii. 40. — **οὐδ' ἂν εἷς**: see on xxxi. 30. — **πολυπράγμων**: the regular word applied to a *busybody*. — **ἀφορμαῖς τοῦ βίου**: 'condition in life,' referring to his description in § 16. ἀφορμή, *starting point*, as a military term means 'base of operations,' Thuc. i. 90. 2, τήν τε Πελοπόννησον πᾶσιν ἔφασαν ἱκανὴν εἶναι ... ἀφορμήν, and in business 'capital,' *cf.* Lys. *frag.* 1. 2 (quoted on § 20), Dem. xlv. 5, τὰ χρήματα ... ἃ τῆς

τραπέζης εἶχεν ἀφορμήν, but it is also used in a more general sense, as here, in Dem. xxi. 137, τὴν βίαν καὶ τὴν φιλοπραγμοσύνην ὁρῶντας τὴν τούτου καὶ τὴν ἀφορμήν, ἥπερ ἰσχυρόν ποιεῖ καὶ φοβερὸν τὸν κατάπτυστον τουτονί.

25. γενόμενος ἐν δυνάμει: see on vii. 27. — **πλήθους**: see on xii. 42. — **εἰς Χαλκίδα**: in Euboea. For the facts, see on xii. 95. — **ἁπάντων**: an exaggeration of the facts like that in xii. 53; *cf.* xiii. 47, συλλήβδην ἅπαντες ὑπὸ τῶν τριάκοντα ἐκ τῆς πατρίδος ἐξηλάθητε. See App.

26. ὁμοίων τοῖς πολλὰ ἠδικηκόσιν: = οἵων ὑμῶν τυγχάνουσιν οἱ πόλλ' ἠδικηκότες. For a similar brachylogy (H. 1058), *cf.* Xen. *Oec.* xiii. 11, ἀθυμία (*sc.* δοκεῖ) ἐγγίγνεσθαι τοῖς ἀγαθοῖς, ὅταν ὁρῶσι ... τῶν ὁμοίων τυγχάνοντας ἑαυτοῖς τοὺς μήτε πονεῖν μήτε κινδυνεύειν ἐθέλοντας, and so with ἴσος, *ibid.* 12, οὐδ' ὁπωστιοῦν τῶν ἴσων ἀξιῶ τοὺς ἀμείνους τοῖς κακίοσι τυγχάνειν. See Kühn.

τοῖς πολλὰ ἠδικηκόσιν, ἀλλὰ τὴν αὐτὴν ψῆφον θέσθε περὶ
165 ἐμοῦ ταῖς ἄλλαις βουλαῖς, ἀναμνησθέντες ὅτι οὔτε χρήματα διαχειρίσας τῆς πόλεως δίδωμι λόγον αὐτῶν, οὔτε
ἀρχὴν ἄρξας οὐδεμίαν εὐθύνας ὑπέχω νῦν αὐτῆς, ἀλλὰ
27 περὶ ὀβολοῦ μόνον ποιοῦμαι τοὺς λόγους. καὶ οὕτως
ὑμεῖς μὲν τὰ δίκαια γνώσεσθε πάντες, ἐγὼ δὲ τούτων ὑμῖν
170 τυχὼν ἕξω τὴν χάριν, οὗτος δὲ τοῦ λοιποῦ μαθήσεται μὴ
τοῖς ἀσθενεστέροις ἐπιβουλεύειν ἀλλὰ τῶν ὁμοίων αὑτῷ
περιγίγνεσθαι.

§ 543, 3, Anm., Kr. *Spr.* 48, 13, 9. —
ταῖς ἄλλαις βουλαῖς : on the facts see
p. 117. — εὐθύνας : see Introd. § 7. —
περὶ ὀβολοῦ μόνον : a really pathetic
note is struck here, in strong contrast
to the general tone of this speech. —
ποιοῦμαι τοὺς λόγους : see on XII. 2.

27. τούτων : refers to δίκαια. —
ὑμῖν : for the hyperbaton, see on
§ 21.

AGAINST PHILON.

INTRODUCTION.

THE speeches *For Mantitheus* and *Against Philon* are counterparts. Each was delivered at the δοκιμασία [1] of a senator, but in the former a candidate defends himself, in the latter a candidate is attacked. Philon, a citizen of the deme Acharnae,[2] a man unknown to us except from what we learn of him here, had played a contemptible part during the time of the Thirty. He was forced, like others, to leave the city, but, far from joining or assisting the patriots under Thrasybulus, he went across the boundary into Boeotia, and, setting his private interests above his country's good,[3] lived the life of a freebooter, preying upon his weaker countrymen. After the fall of the Tyrants he returned to Athens and was chosen by lot to the Senate.[4] At his δοκιμασία, a member of the outgoing Senate[5] accused him in the present oration.

After an introduction [6] designed to show that no private grudge, but simply his respect for the senatorial oath, brings him forward against Philon, the speaker gives his definition of what a good senator ought to be,[7] and then shows, by way of strong contrast, what the accused really is. During the year of anarchy, he says, Philon sided with neither party,[8] but got together all his property

---

[1] On this subject in general, see Introd. § 8.

[2] § 16.   [3] § 17.

[4] § 33.   [5] See p. 74.

[6] §§ 1–4.   [7] §§ 5–7.

[8] No allusion whatever is made in this speech (*cf.* § 27 f.) to the traditional 'law' of Solon, which is said to have required every citizen to adopt the one side or the other in a civil disturbance. If this was ever a real *law*, and not merely a doctrine or ideal principle, evidently it was obsolete in the time of Lysias, else reference to it would have been made in this speech. The 'law' appears first in Arist. *Resp. Ath.* 8.5; *cf.* also Plut. *Solon,* 20, *Moral.* p. 550 B, 823 F; Cic. *Att.* x. 1. 2; Gell. II. 12. On the subject, see Lüders, in *Jahrbb.* XCVII, p. 54.

and went to live in Oropus.[9] Without the excuse, which others had, of physical disability or of poverty, he held himself aloof, showed no interest in the contest, and contributed neither arms nor money to the patriots, as so many others had done.[10] Far from such thoughts, his mind was set only on his own personal profit, and he seems to have behaved like a perfect pirate, organizing raids against those helpless citizens whose age prevented them from leaving their country homes or from defending themselves.[11] Worse than all the rest, his character was so notorious in his own family that his very mother did not dare to trust him with the money for her burial.[12] There is no ground whatever for giving him the senatorship, — on the contrary, he deserves punishment, not reward.[13] As for his claim that there was no law forbidding citizens to leave the scene of action at a crisis, this very fact is one of the heaviest counts against him.   There was no law because nobody had ever imagined that an Athenian could be guilty of such vile desertion.   The very metics lent a hand in the hour of peril, and they were rewarded for their devotion.   Shall not this wretch suffer — if nothing worse — the disgrace of exclusion from the Senate?[14] His whole record shows him unfit for the post, and those who are now his advocates never thought of asking his aid when the State was really in need.[15] He himself can never complain of his rejection by a body whose corporate existence he never lifted a finger to save.[16] This rejection, concludes the speaker, is assured in advance by the essential difference between the unheard-of baseness of Philon and the high character of the men who are his judges.[17]

This speech is not lacking in fire and force, and it gives us a lifelike picture of a man of despicable character.[18] Yet it

---

[9] § 8–9.

[10] §§ 10–16.

[11] §§ 17–19.

[12] §§ 20–23.

[13] §§ 24–26.

[14] §§ 27–30.

[15] §§ 31–32.

[16] § 33.

[17] § 34. In the foregoing summary I have followed chiefly Blass, *Att. Bereds.* I, p. 481 ff.

[18] Dante would have put him among the 'accidious,' with those caitiff angels

Che non furon ribelli
Nè fur fedeli a Dio, *ma per sè foro.*

L'Inferno, III, 38.

is somewhat more rhetorical in parts than is usual with the works of Lysias.[19] This may be because it deals so much with a question of high principle, affecting the national life, rather than with the individuality of one man, whether the speaker or the accused. But there is no overcolouring, and the orator never allows himself to go too far. All his statements are carefully supported by witnesses. And at the very climax of his passion (§§ 27–29), where there was danger that his audience would feel that he was proving too much, the ideal of moderation prevails and the accuser, instead of allowing himself to call for exile or capital punishment of this traitor, returns to the actual case in hand and asks merely that Philon be rejected.[20] In this oration, therefore, Lysias again shows himself a master of the principle of suiting the speech to the speaker. The accuser, actuated by no personal enmity against the accused, should not exhibit bitterness; still, aside from his senatorial rank, the very fact that he came forward voluntarily would lead his hearers, in spite of his protestation of inexperience,[21] to expect from him a speech that was, in its artistic construction, something beyond the common.

We have nothing upon which to base an exact date for the delivery of the speech. Blass sets it at about 398 B.C., Weidner a little earlier.

[19] *E.g.*, Paronomasia, §§ 9, 11, 17, 24, 26, 32. Gnomic thoughts, §§ 6, 11. Antithesis, §§ 2, 28. Hypophora, § 24 f. Parallelism, § 17. It is noticeable also that the articular infinitive is used eleven times in this speech, out of but thirty-six occurrences in the whole of Lysias; see Birklein, *Entwickel. der subst. Infin.* p. 60.

[20] See Rauchenstein's introduction.

[21] § 2 ; see Blass, *ibid.* p. 484.

ΚΑΤΑ ΦΙΛΩΝΟΣ ΔΟΚΙΜΑΣΙΑΣ.

1 Ὤιμην μέν, ὦ βουλή, οὐκ ἄν ποτ᾽ εἰς τοῦτο τόλμης
Φίλωνα ἀφικέσθαι, ὥστε ἐθελῆσαι εἰς ὑμᾶς ἐλθεῖν δοκι-
μασθησόμενον· ἐπειδὴ δὲ οὐχ ἕν τι μόνον ἀλλὰ πολλὰ
τολμηρός ἐστιν, ἐγὼ δὲ ὀμόσας εἰσῆλθον εἰς τὸ βουλευ-
2 τήριον τὰ βέλτιστα βουλεύσειν τῇ πόλει, ἔνεστί τε ἐν τῷ
ὅρκῳ ἀποφανεῖν εἴ τίς τινα οἶδε τῶν λαχόντων ἀνεπιτήδειον ὄντα βουλεύειν, ἐγὼ τὴν κατὰ τουτουὶ Φίλωνος ποιήσομαι κατηγορίαν, οὐ μέντοι γε ἰδίαν ἔχθραν οὐδεμίαν
μεταπορευόμενος, οὐδὲ τῷ δύνασθαι καὶ εἰωθέναι λέγειν
10 ἐν ὑμῖν ἐπαρθείς, ἀλλὰ τῷ πλήθει τῶν ἁμαρτημάτων
αὐτοῦ πιστεύων καὶ τοῖς ὅρκοις οἷς ὤμοσα ἐμμένειν ἀξιῶν.

1. **ᾤμην μέν** : 'until now I believed'; so begins Isaeus VII. I. *Cf.*
Lys. VII. I. — **ἐθελῆσαι** : 'bring himself,' see on XII. 58. — **εἰς ὑμᾶς** :
cf. XXXII. I. — **ὀμόσας** : the oath of
office of a senator is meant ; *cf.*
[Dem.] LIX. 4, *ὀμωμοκὼς δὲ τὰ βέλτιστα βουλεύσειν τῷ δήμῳ τῷ Ἀθηναίων,*
Xen. *Mem.* i. I. 17, *τὸν βουλευτικὸν
ὅρκον ὀμόσας, ἐν ᾧ ἦν κατὰ τοὺς νόμους
βουλεύσειν.* — **τὰ βέλτιστα βουλεύσειν** :
cf. § 31 and XXX. 10, *Κλεοφῶν τὴν βουλὴν ἐλοιδόρει, φάσκων συνεστάναι καὶ οὐ
τὰ βέλτιστα βουλεύειν τῇ πόλει.*

2. **ἔνεστί τε** : for the simple *τε* used
to connect clauses, *cf.* XXIII. 3, XXXII.

1, 22. — **ἀποφανεῖν** : preserving the
tense of the oath, *cf.* Xen. quoted
above. — **τῶν λαχόντων**: *sc. τῷ κυάμῳ,*
and see on § 33. — **ἀνεπιτήδειον** : part
of the inquiry at the *δοκιμασία* of
magistrates was *εἴτ᾽ ἐπιτήδειοί εἰσιν
ἄρχειν εἴτε καὶ μή,* Poll. VIII. 44. —
ἰδίαν ἔχθραν : personal enmity (a
proper ground in cases like XII. 2)
would be out of place when one
spoke for the State. — **μεταπορευόμενος** : in this sense unique in Attic
where the usual word is *μέτειμι* or
μετέρχομαι. — **τῷ δύνασθαι** : causal.
G. 1547 ; H. 959. See App. and p.
135, note 19.

3 γνώσεσθε μὲν οὖν ὅτι οὐκ ἀπὸ ἴσης παρασκευῆς ἐγώ τε
τοῦτον ἐλέγξω οἷός ἐστι καὶ οὗτος ἐπεχείρησε πονηρὸς
εἶναι. ὅμως δ᾽ εἴ τι ἐγὼ ἐλλείποιμι τῷ λόγῳ τῆς κατηγο-
15 ρίας, οὐκ ἂν δίκαιος εἴη οὗτος διὰ τοῦτο ὠφεληθῆναι,
ἀλλὰ μᾶλλον, ὅ τι ἱκανῶς διδάξαιμι, ἐκ τούτων ἀποδοκι-
4 μασθῆναι. ἐνδεῶς μὲν γὰρ διὰ τὴν ἀπειρίαν πάντων τῶν
τούτῳ πεπραγμένων, ἱκανῶς δὲ διὰ τὴν περὶ αὐτὸν κακίαν
εἰρηκὼς ἂν εἴην. ἀξιῶ δὲ καὶ ὑμῶν, οἵτινες δυνατώτεροι
20 ἐμοῦ εἰσι λέγειν, ἀποφῆναι μείζω ὄντα αὐτοῦ τὰ ἁμαρτήματα, καὶ ἐξ ὧν ἂν ἐγὼ ὑπολίπω, πάλιν αὐτοὺς περὶ ὧν
ἴσασι κατηγορῆσαι Φίλωνος· οὐ γὰρ ἐκ τῶν ὑπ᾽ ἐμοῦ
μόνου λεγομένων δεῖ ὑμᾶς περὶ αὐτοῦ ὁποῖός ἐστι σκέ-
ψασθαι.

5 Ἐγὼ γὰρ οὐκ ἄλλους τινάς φημι δίκαιον εἶναι βουλεύειν περὶ ἡμῶν ἢ τοὺς πρὸς τῷ εἶναι πολίτας καὶ ἐπιθυμοῦντας τούτου. τούτοις μὲν γὰρ μεγάλα τὰ διαφέροντά

---

3. οὐκ ἀπὸ ἴσης παρασκευῆς κτλ.:
'I am not so well prepared.' For
the use of ἀπό, cf. XXI. 10, καὶ ταῦτα
οὐκ ἀπὸ τύχης ἐγίγνετο, ἀλλ᾽ ἀπὸ παρασκευῆς τῆς ἐμῆς. — **καὶ οὗτος κτλ.:** 'as
he was when he entered upon his
course of wickedness.' Note τε ... καί.
— **δίκαιος:** 'entitled.' On the personal usage, cf. § 20, and see G. 1527;
H. 944 a. But a different sense must
be given it with ἀποδοκιμασθῆναι.
— **ὅ τι:** singular, though τούτων is
plural; see on XII. 37.

4. τὴν ἀπειρίαν: my lack of acquaintance. — **περὶ αὐτόν:** 'attaching
to him'; cf. Isocr. XII. 76, τῆς περὶ
αὐτὸν δόξης, his own fame. See App.
— **εἰρηκὼς ἂν εἴην:** the rare perf. opt.
GMT. 103, 104. He is anticipating

the end of his speech. — **ἐξ ὧν κτλ.:**
the other senators are to continue
the accusation through the material
which the speaker leaves unused. —
πάλιν αὐτούς: themselves in their
turn, contrasted with ἐγώ.

5. Here the speaker gives his conception of a good senator. — **περί:**
approaches closely the meaning of
ὑπέρ with gen. Cf. XXXIV. 10, ἄνδρας
ἀγαθοὺς περὶ τῆς πατρίδος καὶ ἡμῶν αὐτῶν γίγνεσθαι. — **πρὸς τῷ εἶναι:** besides being. See App. — **ἐπιθυμοῦντας τούτου:** (sc. τοῦ εἶναι πολίτας)
'are really in love with their condition.' — **τὰ διαφέροντα:** the difference, the odds, in another sense in
XXXII. 1. On the phrase, cf. Thuc. ii.
43. 5, μεγάλα τὰ διαφέροντα, ἤν τι πταί-

ἔστιν εὖ τε πράττειν τὴν πόλιν τήνδε καὶ ἀνεπιτηδείως,
διὰ τὸ ἀναγκαῖον σφίσιν αὐτοῖς ἡγεῖσθαι εἶναι μετέχειν
30 τὸ μέρος τῶν δεινῶν, ὥσπερ καὶ τῶν ἀγαθῶν μετέχουσι·
6 ὅσοι δὲ φύσει μὲν πολῖταί εἰσι, γνώμῃ δὲ χρῶνται ὡς
πᾶσα γῆ πατρὶς αὐτοῖς ἐστιν ἐν ᾗ ἂν τὰ ἐπιτήδεια ἔχωσιν,
οὗτοι δῆλοί εἰσιν ὅτι κἂν παρέντες τὸ τῆς πόλεως κοινὸν
ἀγαθὸν ἐπὶ τὸ ἑαυτῶν ἴδιον κέρδος ἔλθοιεν διὰ τὸ μὴ τὴν
7 πόλιν ἀλλὰ τὴν οὐσίαν πατρίδα ἑαυτοῖς ἡγεῖσθαι. ἐγὼ
τοίνυν ἀποφανῶ Φίλωνα τουτονὶ περὶ πλείονος ποιησά-
μενον τὴν ἰδίαν ἀσφάλειαν ἢ τὸν κοινὸν τῆς πόλεως κίνδυνον, καὶ ἡγησάμενον κρεῖττον εἶναι αὐτὸν ἀκινδύνως
τὸν βίον διάγειν ἢ τὴν πόλιν σῴζειν ὁμοίως τοῖς ἄλλοις
40 πολίταις κινδυνεύοντα.
8 Οὗτος γάρ, ὦ βουλή, ὅτε ἡ συμφορὰ τῇ πόλει ἦν (ἧς
ἐγώ, καθ' ὅσον ἀναγκάζομαι, κατὰ τοσοῦτον μέμνημαι),
ἐκκεκηρυγμένος ἐκ τοῦ ἄστεως ὑπὸ τῶν τριάκοντα μετὰ

σωσιν. — ἀνεπιτηδείως : unbecoming-
ly, used euphemistically, cf. XIII. 51,
πονηρὰ καὶ οὐκ ἐπιτήδεια τῷ δήμῳ. —
διὰ τό κτλ.: join διὰ τὸ ἡγεῖσθαι. The
order shows that ἀναγκαῖον and μετέχειν are emphatic, and the following words are strengthened by the
chiasm. — τὸ μέρος: the gen. could
not stand here after μετέχειν. Cf. τί,
§ 9. — ὥσπερ καί: even as.

6. πᾶσα γῆ πατρὶς κτλ.: the Greek
of the good old sort, to whom his
native land was μήτηρ and τροφός
(cf. Plat. Menex. 237 B, Isocr. IV. 25),
had a low opinion of what we call a
'citizen of the world.' This latter
notion appears in Eurip. Frag. Phaë-
thon, 777 Nauck², ὡς πανταχοῦ γε πατρὶς ἡ βόσκουσα γῆ, and Ar. Plut. 1151,
πατρὶς γάρ ἐστι πᾶσ' ἵν' ἂν πράττῃ τις

εὖ. Andocides on the other hand says
ἄλλοθί τε γὰρ ὢν πάντα τὰ ἀγαθὰ ἔχειν
στερόμενος τῆς πατρίδος οὐκ ἂν δεξαίμην,
I. 5. — δῆλοι ... ὅτι: instead of the
usual participial constr. (GMT. 907,
912) because of παρέντες. For another
instance, also caused by the structure
of the sentence, cf. XII. 50. — κἂν :
see App.

8. ἡ συμφορά : i.e. Aegos Potami
and what followed ; cf. XII. 43. —
ἧς ἐγώ ... μέμνημαι : a common
apology, cf. XIII. 43, ἀνιῶμαι μὲν οὖν
ὑπομιμνήσκων τὰς γεγενημένας συμφορὰς
τῇ πόλει, ἀνάγκη δ' ἐστίν, and see on
XII. 43 ; so Cic. Vatin. 21, ac ne
diutius loquar de auguratu
tuo, quod inuitus facio ut
recorder ruinas rei publicae.
— ἐκκεκηρυγμένος: see on XII. 95. —

τοῦ ἄλλου πλήθους τῶν πολιτῶν, τέως μὲν ᾤκει ἐν ἀγρῷ,
45 ἐπειδὴ δὲ οἱ ἀπὸ Φυλῆς κατῆλθον εἰς τὸν Πειραιᾶ, καὶ οὐ
μόνον οἱ ἐκ τῶν ἀγρῶν ἀλλὰ καὶ οἱ ἐκ τῆς ὑπερορίας οἱ
μὲν εἰς τὸ ἄστυ οἱ δ᾽ εἰς τὸν Πειραιᾶ συνελέγοντο καὶ
καθ᾽ ὅσον ἕκαστος οἷός τ᾽ ἦν, κατὰ τοσοῦτον ἐβοήθει τῇ
πατρίδι, τἀναντία ἅπασι τοῖς ἄλλοις πολίταις ἐποίησε·
9 συσκευασάμενος γὰρ τὰ ἑαυτοῦ ἐνθένδε εἰς τὴν ὑπερορίαν
ἐξῴκησε, καὶ ἐν Ὠρωπῷ μετοίκιον κατατιθεὶς ἐπὶ προστάτου ᾤκει, βουληθεὶς παρ᾽ ἐκείνοις μετοικεῖν μᾶλλον ἢ μεθ᾽
ἡμῶν πολίτης εἶναι. οὐ τοίνυν οὐδ᾽ ὥσπερ ἔνιοί τινες
τῶν πολιτῶν μετεβάλλοντο, ἐπειδὴ ἑώρων τοὺς ἀπὸ Φυλῆς
55 ἐν οἷς ἔπραττον εὐτυχοῦντας, οὐδὲ τούτων τι τῶν εὐτυχη-
μάτων ἠξίωσε μετασχεῖν, ἐπὶ κατειργασμένοις μᾶλλον
ἐλθεῖν βουλόμενος ἢ συγκατελθεῖν κατεργασάμενός τι
τῶν τῇ κοινῇ πολιτείᾳ συμφερόντων· οὐ γὰρ ἦλθεν εἰς

οἱ ἀπὸ Φυλῆς: see on XVI. 4. — οἱ ἐκ
τῆς ὑπερορίας : including the exiles,
like the invalid (XXIV. 25), as well
as persons absent on business or for
other reasons, like Mantitheus, XVI. 4.
Such persons on returning joined
each the party he preferred, as the
invalid joined the patriots, and Cal-
limachus (Isocr. XVIII. 48) the Thirty.
9. ἐξῴκησε : *emigrated*, see on
XXXII. 14. — Ὠρωπῷ : this city, near
the border of Attica and Boeotia,
belonged to the Athenian alliance
until 411, when it was lost by
treachery. It then became an in-
dependent oligarchy under Thebes.
In 402 it was annexed to Boeotia.
— μετοίκιον : the tax paid by a resi-
dent foreigner ; see Introd. § 15. — ἐπὶ
προστάτου ᾤκει : an expression found
(acc. to Lutz, *Präp.* p. 101) else-

where in the orators only in Lycurg.
Leocr. 145, οἰκήσας ἐν Μεγάροις ἐπὶ προστάτου.　In it the local sense merges
into manner.　Cf. Thuc. ii. 63. 3, εἴ
που ἐπὶ σφῶν αὐτῶν αὐτόνομοι οἰκήσειαν,
and see H. 799, 1 d.　On the προστάτης, see Introd. § 15. — ἐκείνοις : refers
to Ὠρωπῷ. See on αὐτῶν, XII. 37. —
μετεβάλλοντο : the regular word of
changes from one political party to
another ; cf. XVIII. 5, XXV. 9. — τὶ :
see on μέρος, § 5. — ἐπὶ κατειργασμένοις : ' after it was all over.'　On
this sense of ἐπί, cf. Hdt. viii. 94,
ἐπ᾽ ἐξεργασμένοισι ἐλθεῖν ἐς τὸ στρατόπεδον (so ix. 77, cf. Aesch. *Pers.*
525), and Xen. *Hellen.* iii. 4. 6,
ἐπὶ τούτοις ῥηθεῖσι, Hdt. i. 170, ἐπὶ
διεφθαρμένοισι Ἴωσι.　Note the double
paronomasia in κατειργασμένοις with
κατεργασάμενος and in ἐλθεῖν with

τὸν Πειραιᾶ, οὐδ᾽ ἔστιν ὅπου ἑαυτὸν ὑμῖν τάξαι παρέσχεν.
10 καίτοιγε ὅστις εὐτυχοῦντας ὁρῶν ἡμᾶς ἐτόλμα προδιδόναι,
τί ποτε ὡς μὴ ἐβουλόμεθά γε πράττοντας ἐποίησεν ἄν;
ὅσοι μὲν τοίνυν διὰ συμφορὰς ἰδίας οὐ μετέσχον τῶν τότε
γενομένων τῇ πόλει κινδύνων, συγγνώμης τινὸς ἄξιοί εἰσι
τυχεῖν· οὐδενὶ γὰρ οὐδὲν ἑκούσιον δυστύχημα γίγνεται·
11 ὅσοι δὲ γνώμῃ τοῦτο ἔπραξαν, οὐδεμιᾶς συγγνώμης ἄξιοί
εἰσιν· οὐ γὰρ διὰ δυστυχίαν ἀλλὰ δι᾽ ἐπιβουλὴν ἐποίησαν αὐτό. καθέστηκε δέ τι ἔθος δίκαιον πᾶσιν ἀνθρώποις τῶν αὐτῶν ἀδικημάτων μάλιστα ὀργίζεσθαι τοῖς
μάλιστα δυναμένοις μὴ ἀδικεῖν, τοῖς δὲ πένησιν ἢ ἀδυνά-
70 τοις τῷ σώματι συγγνώμην ἔχειν διὰ τὸ ἡγεῖσθαι ἄκοντας

συγκατελθεῖν, and see on § 11.—τάξαι:
the regular word of an appointment
to military duty. Cf. Plat. Apol. 28 D,
ὅτε μέν με οἱ ἄρχοντες ἔταττον. On
the mood, denoting purpose, see
GMT. 772.

10. ὡς μὴ ἐβουλόμεθα: a euphemism
for κακῶς, like aliter atque vel-
lemus. Cf. Dem. XXII. 62, πολλὰ
γὰρ ἡμῶν ἕκαστος οὐχ ὡς βούλεται
πράττει, Isocr. XIX. 39, τῆς ἀναχωρήσεως οὐχ οἵας ἠβουλόμεθα γενομένης.
The clause has μή because it is connected with πράττοντας, an impf.
partic. serving as protasis of ἐποίησεν
ἄν. — συμφορὰς ἰδίας: such as physical disability (cf. XXIV. 3) or poverty.
— ἑκούσιον: of his own wish or will.
An involuntary failure of duty was
of course excusable; cf. Dem. XXIV.
49, τοῖς γὰρ ἄκουσιν ἁμαρτοῦσι μέτεστι
συγγνώμης, οὐ τοῖς ἐπιβουλεύσασιν, and
Arist. N. E. iii. 1. 1, ἐπὶ μὲν τοῖς ἑκου-
σίοις ἐπαίνων καὶ ψόγων γινομένων, ἐπὶ
δὲ τοῖς ἀκουσίοις συγγνώμης.

11. γνώμη (on purpose), συγγνώμης: paronomasia. See on § 9, and
cf. Thuc. ii. 62. 3, μὴ φρονήματι μόνον, ἀλλὰ καὶ καταφρονήματι. — καθέστηκε: it is settled or agreed, stronger
than ἔστι. Cf. Thuc. i. 76. 2, ἀεὶ
καθεστῶτος (it being an established
rule) τὸν ἥσσω ὑπὸ τοῦ δυνατωτέρου
κατείργεσθαι. So the perf. of δοκεῖ,
as δεδογμένον γέ ἐστι τὸ Σωκράτη διαφέρειν τινὶ τῶν πολλῶν ἀνθρώπων, Plat.
Apol. 34 E. — πᾶσιν ἀνθρώποις: see
on XVI. 15. — ἀδικημάτων: the gen.
of the cause with ὀργίζεσθαι, because
the gen. belongs also to συγγνώμην
ἔχειν. In XII. 80 it is used for con-
cinnity with the following clause, so
in XXVII. 11. Elsewhere in Lysias
this verb is construed with ὑπέρ (XII.
2), ἀντί (XII. 96), διά (XXI. 9), ἐπί
(XXXII. 21): Frohberger. — ἀδυνάτοις
τῷ σώματι: cf. XXIV. 4.

12. Application of the foregoing
general principle to the case of
Philon. Note the chiastic order in

12 αὐτοὺς ἁμαρτάνειν. οὗτος τοίνυν οὐδεμιᾶς συγγνώμης
ἄξιός ἐστι τυχεῖν· οὔτε γὰρ τῷ σώματι ἀδύνατος ἦν
ταλαιπωρεῖν, ὡς καὶ ὑμεῖς ὁρᾶτε, οὔτε τῇ οὐσίᾳ ἄπορος
λῃτουργεῖν, ὡς ἐγὼ ἀποδείξω. ὅστις οὖν ὅσον δυνατὸς
75 ἦν ὠφελεῖν, τοσοῦτον κακὸς ἦν, πῶς οὐκ ἂν εἰκότως ὑπὸ
13 πάντων ὑμῶν μισοῖτο; ἀλλὰ μὴν οὐδ' ἀπεχθήσεσθέ γε
τῶν πολιτῶν οὐδενὶ τοῦτον ἀποδοκιμάσαντες· ὃς οὔ τι
τοὺς ἑτέρους ἀλλ' ἀμφοτέρους φανερός ἐστι προδοὺς, ὥστε
μήτε τοῖς ἐν τῷ ἄστει γενομένοις φίλον προσήκειν εἶναι
80 τοῦτον, — οὐ γὰρ ἠξίωσεν ὡς αὐτοὺς ἐλθεῖν κινδυνεύον-
τας, — μήτε τοῖς τὸν Πειραιᾶ καταλαβοῦσιν, — οὐδὲ γὰρ
14 τούτοις ἠθέλησε συγκατελθεῖν. εἰ μέντοι τι μέρος περίεστι τῶν πολιτῶν ὅ τι τῶν αὐτῶν μετέσχε τούτῳ πραγμάτων, μετ' ἐκείνων, ἐάν ποτε (ὃ μὴ γένοιτο) λάβωσι τὴν
85 πόλιν, βουλεύειν ἀξιούτω.

Ὡς οὖν ᾤκει τε ἐν Ὠρωπῷ ἐπὶ προστάτου καὶ ἐκέκτητο
ἱκανὴν οὐσίαν καὶ οὔτ' ἐν τῷ Πειραιεῖ οὔτ' ἐν τῷ ἄστει
ἔθετο τὰ ὅπλα, ἵνα εἰδῆτε ὅτι ταῦτα πρῶτον ἀληθῆ λέγω,
ἀκούσατε τῶν μαρτύρων.

which the two points are taken up :
τοῖς πένησιν : ἀδυνάτοις τῷ σώματι : :
τῷ σώματι ἀδύνατος : τῇ οὐσίᾳ ἄπορος.
—λῃτουργεῖν: in a wide sense, including such public contributions as are
mentioned in § 15.

13. τοὺς ἑτέρους : one party.

14. περίεστι : remains, is left over.
The whole sentence is of course
sarcastic:— τῶν αὐτῶν πραγμάτων :
cf. XII. 62. — ὃ μὴ γένοιτο : a regular
formula of deprecation, like our
' Heaven forbid.' Cf. Dem. XXI. 209,
ἐνθυμεῖσθ', ὦ ἄνδρες δικασταί, εἰ γένοιτο, ὃ μὴ γένοιτο οὐδ' ἔσται, οὗτοι

κύριοι τῆς πολιτείας. — ἐάν... πόλιν : a
secondary prot., really part of the
apodosis. GMT. 510. The main prot.
is εἰ ... πραγμάτων. — λάβωσι τὴν
πόλιν : cf. XII. 57. — ἔθετο τὰ ὅπλα :
equiv. to οὐδ' ἔστιν ... τάξαι παρέσχεν,
§ 9, 'took his post,' &c. for battle or
service in general. Cf. Dem. XXI. 145,
αὐτὸς ὑπὲρ τοῦ δήμου θέμενος τὰ ὅπλα, δὶς
μὲν ἐν Σάμῳ, τρίτον δ' ἐν αὐτῇ τῇ πόλει,
τῷ σώματι τὴν εὔνοιαν, οὐ χρήμασι οὐδὲ
λόγοις ἐνεδείξατο τῇ πατρίδι. —πρῶτον:
to begin with. Cf. Dem. XXXVII. 8,
ὡς οὖν ταῦτα πρῶτον ἀληθῆ λέγω, τούτων τοὺς μάρτυρας ὑμῖν παρέξομαι.

ΜΑΡΤΥΡΕΣ.

15 Ὑπολείπεται τοίνυν αὐτῷ λέγειν ὡς τῷ μὲν σώματι δι'
ἀσθένειάν τιν' ἐπιγενομένην ἀδύνατος κατέστη βοηθῆσαι
εἰς τὸν Πειραιᾶ, ἀπὸ δὲ τῶν ὑπαρχόντων ἐπαγγειλάμενος
αὐτὸς ἢ χρήματ' εἰσενεγκεῖν εἰς τὸ πλῆθος τὸ ὑμέτερον ἢ
ὁπλίσαι τινὰς τῶν ἑαυτοῦ δημοτῶν, ὥσπερ καὶ ἄλλοι πολ-
95 λοὶ τῶν πολιτῶν αὐτοὶ οὐ δυνάμενοι λῃτουργεῖν τοῖς σώ-
16 μασιν. ἵνα οὖν μὴ ἐγγένηται αὐτῷ ψευσαμένῳ ἐξαπατῆσαι, καὶ περὶ τούτων ἤδη σαφῶς ὑμῖν ἀποδείξω, ἐπειδὴ
ὕστερον οὐκ ἐξέσται μοι παρελθόντι ἐνθάδ' ἐλέγχειν αὐτόν. καί μοι κάλει Διότιμον τὸν Ἀχαρνέα καὶ τοὺς αἱρε-
100 θέντας μετ' αὐτοῦ τοὺς δημότας ὁπλίσαι ἀπὸ τῶν εἰσενεχ-
θέντων χρημάτων.

15. τῷ σώματι: it was the duty of a good citizen to serve the state τῷ σώματι καὶ τοῖς χρήμασι, Lys. xxv. 4; cf. And. II. 18, ἐκεῖνος ἂν εἴη πολὺ πλείστου ἄξιος ἀνήρ, ὅστις τοῖς ἑαυτοῦ παρακινδυνεύων χρήμασί τε καὶ σώματι τολμῴη ἀγαθόν τι ποιεῖν τοὺς ἑαυτοῦ πολίτας. To give money only was less glorious (cf. Dem. xxi. 145 quoted on § 14), but becoming, if physical or other disability forbade the other. — ἐπιγενομένην: having fallen upon; cf. Dem. xxxvi. 7, ἐπιγενομένης δ' ἀρρωστίας τῷ Πασίωνι. This disability was at least a thing of the past; cf. § 12. — τῶν ὑπαρχόντων: his belongings, possessions, somewhat differently in xxxii. 28. — ἐπαγγειλάμενος αὐτός: see on xii. 68. — εἰσενεγκεῖν: a sudden change from the construction with ὡς after λέγειν to the infinitive. A like change occurs in xiii. 78, and the reverse in xiii. 9; even after εἶπον the former

occurs in Thuc. i. 87. 4. — τὸ πλῆθος κτλ. : see on xii. 26. — ὥσπερ καὶ ἄλλοι: others besides the infirm helped out their poorer comrades; cf. xvi. 14, and the case of Lysias himself, Introd. § 20.

16. ἐξαπατῆσαι: sc. by the method of defence described in xii. 38. — καὶ περὶ τούτων: sc. as well as on the first points, on which evidence has already been given. — οὐκ ἐξέσται: the passage shows that in the δοκιμασία, at least of senators, an accuser could speak but once. — παρελθόντι ἐνθάδε: sc. to the speaker's platform; the verb is technical in this sense. — κάλει: see on xii. 47. — Διότιμον: not otherwise known unless he is identical with Διότιμος Διομνήστου Ἀχαρνεύς, CIA. II, 1917. The deme Acharnae was north of Athens. — ὁπλίσαι: on the mood, cf. τάξαι, § 9.

ΜΑΡΤΥΡΙΑ ΤΩΝ ΑΙΡΕΘΕΝΤΩΝ ΜΕΤΑ ΔΙΟΤΙΜΟΥ.

17　Οὗτος τοίνυν οὐχ ὅπως ὠφελήσει τὴν πόλιν ἐν τοιούτῳ
καιρῷ καὶ τοιαύτῃ καταστάσει διενοήθη, ἀλλ᾽ ὅπως τι
κερδανεῖ ἀπὸ τῶν ὑμετέρων συμφορῶν παρεσκευάσατο·
105 ὁρμώμενος γὰρ ἐξ Ὠρωποῦ, τοτὲ μὲν αὐτὸς μόνος, τοτὲ
δ᾽ ἑτέροις ἡγούμενος οἷς τὰ ὑμέτερα δυστυχήματα εὐτυ-
18 χήματα ἐγεγόνει, περιιὼν κατὰ τοὺς ἀγροὺς καὶ ἐντυγχά-
νων τῶν πολιτῶν τοῖς πρεσβυτέροις, οἳ κατέμειναν ἐν τοῖς
δήμοις ὀλίγα μὲν τῶν ἐπιτηδείων ἔχοντες, τἀναγκαῖα δέ,
110 εὖνοι μὲν ὄντες τῷ πλήθει, ἀδύνατοι δὲ ὑπὸ τῆς ἡλικίας
βοηθεῖν, τούτους ἀφῃρεῖτο τὰ ὑπάρχοντα, περὶ πλείονος
ποιούμενος αὐτὸς μικρὰ κερδαίνειν ἢ ἐκείνους μηδὲν ἀδι-
κεῖν· οἳ νῦν αὐτὸν δι᾽ αὐτὸ τοῦτο οὐχ οἷοί τέ εἰσιν ἐπεξελθεῖν ἅπαντες, δι᾽ ὅπερ καὶ τότε ἀδύνατοι τῇ πόλει βοηθεῖν
19 ἦσαν.　οὐ μέντοι τοῦτόν γε χρὴ διὰ τὴν ἐκείνων ἀδυνα-
μίαν δὶς ὠφεληθῆναι, τότε τ᾽ ἀφελόμενον ἃ εἶχον, νῦν τε

---

17. καταστάσει : here used in a rather general sense, *political condition*, as in Plat. *Rep.* 492 E, ἐν τοιαύτῃ καταστάσει πολιτειῶν, but more often the sense is narrower, meaning *constitution*, as frequently in Arist. *Resp. Ath.*, *e.g.* 41, 42. — **διενοήθη, παρεσκευάσατο**: on these synonymous endings of the clauses, see on XVI. 13. —**ὁρμώμενος**: often used, in a military sense, of one's base of operations, as in Xen. *Anab.* i. 1. 9, ἐπολέμει ἐκ Χερρονήσου ὁρμώμενος τοῖς Θρᾳξί. See on ἀφορμαῖς, XXIV. 24. Oropus was Philon's headquarters. — **αὐτὸς μόνος, ἑτέροις** : for a like contrast, *cf.* XXXII. 27; sometimes the former member is strengthened into μόνος

αὐτὸς καθ᾽ αὑτόν, XXVI. 11. — **οἷς ...
ἐγεγόνει** : the typical good citizen suffered with his country, but not so the bad ; *cf.* XXII. 13, 14.

18. δήμοις : of course the country demes are meant. — **τἀναγκαῖα** : ' necessaries of life,' which would be included among ἐπιτήδεια, *provisions*, in general. — **ὑπό** : causal; see on VII. 21. — **τὰ ὑπάρχοντα** : see on § 15. — **αὐτόν** : with ἐπεξελθεῖν the dat. would be commoner; see App.—**ἅπαντες**: as the words κἂν ὁστισοῦν κτλ. in § 19 show, the speaker had but few witnesses or fellow-accusers ; hence this explanation of the fact that so few appeared against a man like Philon. — **δι᾽ αὐτὸ τοῦτο** : *i.e.* their age and poverty.

δοκιμασθέντα ὑφ' ὑμῶν· ἀλλὰ κἂν ὁστισοῦν παραγένηται
τῶν ἀδικηθέντων, μέγα αὐτὸ ἡγήσασθε εἶναι καὶ τοῦτον
ὑπερμισήσατε, ὅστις ἐτόλμησεν, οἷς ἕτεροι διδόναι παρ'
120 ἑαυτῶν τι προῃροῦντο διὰ τὴν ἀπορίαν οἰκτίραντες αὐτούς,
τούτων ἀφαιρεῖσθαι τὰ ὑπάρχοντα. κάλει μοι τοὺς μάρτυρας.

ΜΑΡΤΥΡΕΣ.

20　Οὐ τοίνυν ἔγωγε οἶδα ὅ τι ὑμᾶς διαφερόντως δεῖ γιγνώσκειν περὶ αὐτοῦ ἢ οἱ οἰκεῖοι γιγνώσκουσι· τοιαῦτα γάρ
125 ἐστιν, ὥστ' εἰ καὶ μηδὲν αὐτῷ ἄλλο ἡμάρτητο, διὰ μόνα
ταῦτα δίκαιον εἶναι ἀποδοκιμασθῆναι. οἷα μὲν οὖν ζῶσα
ἡ μήτηρ αὐτοῦ κατηγόρει παρήσω· ἐξ ὧν δὲ τελευτῶσα
τὸν βίον διεπράξατο τεκμαιρομένοις ῥᾴδιόν ἐστιν ὑμῖν
21 γνῶναι ὁποῖός τις ἦν περὶ αὐτήν. ἐκείνη γὰρ τούτῳ μὲν
130 ἠπίστησεν ἀποθανοῦσαν ἑαυτὴν ἐπιτρέψαι, Ἀντιφάνει δὲ
οὐδὲν προσήκουσα πιστεύσασα ἔδωκεν εἰς τὴν ἑαυτῆς

19. ὁστισοῦν : *anybody at all.* H.
1002 a. — **μέγα :** 'a great point,' 'of
great weight.' *Cf.* Eur. *Phoen.* 549 f.,
τί τὴν τυραννίδ', ἀδικίαν εὐδαίμονα,
τιμᾷς ὑπέρφευ καὶ μέγ' ἥγησαι τόδε ;
and Xen. *Cyr.* v. 3. 19, μέγα ποιοῦμαι
φίλιον τοῦτο τὸ χωρίον τοῖς ἐνθάδε συμ-
μάχοις καταλείπων. — **παρ' ἑαυτῶν :**
from their own means, a common use
of παρά with reflexives (Lutz, *Präp.*
p. 143), *cf.* xxvi. 24, οὐ φάσκων αὐτοὺς
λύσεσθαι, εἰ μὴ τοῦτο (*i.e.* a sum of
thirty mìnae) αὐτῷ παρὰ σφῶν αὐτῶν
παράσχοιεν. — **τούτων ἀφαιρεῖσθαι τὰ
ὑπάρχοντα :** the same verb in § 18
takes two accs., and the like variety
occurs in xxiv. 13. G. 1069, 1071 ;
H. 724, 748 a.

20. γιγνώσκειν : *feel.* — **τοιαῦτα :**
referring to the state of mind of Phi-

lon's relatives. See App.—**δίκαιον :** see
on § 3. — **κατηγόρει :** *reproached.* —
παρήσω : a favourite rhetorical de-
vice, rousing suspicion in the jury's
mind against the accused, often
groundlessly. See on xii. 43, and *cf.*
Auct. *ad Herenn.* iv. 37, ut utilius
sit occulte fecisse suspitio-
nem, quam eius modi intendisse
orationem, quae redarguatur.

21. οὐδὲν προσήκουσα : concessive
and subordinate to πιστεύσασα. To
pass over (παραλιποῦσα) one's own
son and enjoin the charge of the
ταφῇ νομιζομένη (see on xii. 96) to a
comparative stranger was to cast on
the former the worst of stigmas. The
thought of burial by one's children
was a comforting hope ; *cf.* xiii. 45,
where it is said of the aged, ἤλπιζον

ταφὴν τρεῖς μνᾶς ἀργυρίου, παραλιποῦσα τοῦτον υἱὸν ὄντα
ἑαυτῆς. ἆρα δῆλον ὅτι εὖ ᾔδει αὐτὸν οὐδὲ διὰ τὸ προσή-
22 κειν αὐτῇ τὰ δέοντα ἂν ποιήσαντα; καίτοι εἰ μήτηρ, ἣ
135 πέφυκε καὶ ἀδικουμένη ὑπὸ τῶν ἑαυτῆς παίδων μάλιστα
ἀνέχεσθαι καὶ μίκρ᾽ ὠφελουμένη μεγάλα ἔχειν ἡγεῖσθαι
διὰ τὸ εὐνοίᾳ μᾶλλον ἢ ἐλέγχῳ τὰ γιγνόμενα δοκιμάζειν,
ἐνόμιζε τοῦτον κἂν ἀπὸ τεθνεώσης φέρειν ἑαυτῆς, τί χρὴ
23 ὑμᾶς περὶ αὐτοῦ διανοηθῆναι; ὅστις γὰρ περὶ τοὺς
140 ἑαυτοῦ ἀναγκαίους τοιαῦτα ἁμαρτάνει ἁμαρτήματα, τί
ἂν περὶ γε τοὺς ἀλλοτρίους ποιήσειεν; ὡς οὖν καὶ
ταῦτ᾽ ἀληθῆ ἐστιν, ἀκούσατε αὐτοῦ τοῦ λαβόντος τὸ
ἀργύριον καὶ θάψαντος αὐτήν.

ΜΑΡΤΥΡΙΑ.

24　Τί ἂν οὖν βουληθέντες ὑμεῖς τοῦτον δοκιμάσαιτε;

ὑπὸ τῶν σφετέρων αὐτῶν παίδων γηρο-
τροφέντες, ἐπειδὴ τελευτήσειαν τὸν βίον
ταφήσεσθαι. Of the son's duty to his
father the law of Solon enjoined,
ἀποθανόντα δὲ αὐτὸν θαπτέτω καὶ τἆλλα
ποιείτω τὰ νομιζόμενα, Aeschin. I. 13.
Neglect of this duty meant rejection
at the δοκιμασία, see Introd. § 8. —
τρεῖς μνᾶς : not a large sum for the
purpose, in fact the smallest mentioned in the authors ; cf. Boeckh,
Staatsh. I, p. 146, and Lys. xxxii. 21.
— ἆρα δῆλον : the addition of δῆλον
shows that ἆρα here = nonne. Kr.
Spr. 69, 9.
22. εἰ μήτηρ : if a mother. The
speaker begins with a general
thought, but at ἐνόμιζε τοῦτον passes
to the particular case, as in xii. 84,
xxiii. 12. — μικρὰ ... δοκιμάζειν :

tried by the test of a mother's love
(εὐνοίᾳ), not by any legal scrutiny
(ἐλέγχῳ), even small services from
her children seem great. Cf. Soph.
El. 770, δεινὸν τὸ τίκτειν (motherhood)
ἐστίν· οὐδὲ γὰρ κακῶς πάσχοντι (even
though wronged) μῖσος ὧν τέκῃ προσ-
γίγνεται. — φέρειν : plunder, rob. The
expression was proverbial, Arist.
Rhet. II. 6. 5, τὸ κερδαίνειν ἀπ᾽ ἀδυνάτων, οἷον πενήτων ἢ τεθνεώτων· ὅθεν καὶ
ἡ παροιμία, τὸ κἂν ἀπὸ νεκροῦ φέρειν.
24. τί βουληθέντες : used (though
generally the partic. is pres.) in an im-
patient sort of question to which the
speaker believes that no well ground-
ed answer can be given. Cf. I. 45,
τί ἂν οὖν βουλόμενος ἐκινδύνευον ; Plat.
Phaed. 63 A, τί γὰρ ἂν βουλόμενοι
ἄνδρες σοφοὶ ὡς ἀληθῶς δεσπότας

145 πότερον ὡς οὐχ ἡμαρτηκότα; ἀλλὰ τὰ μέγιστα περὶ τὴν
πατρίδα ἠδίκηκεν· ἀλλ' ὡς ἔσται βελτίων; τοιγάρτοι
πρότερον βελτίων γενόμενος περὶ τὴν πόλιν ὕστερον βουλεύειν ἀξιούτω, φανερόν τι ἀγαθὸν ὥσπερ τότε κακὸν
ποιήσας. σωφρονέστερον γάρ ἐστιν ὕστερον πᾶσι τῶν
150 ἔργων τὰς χάριτας ἀποδιδόναι· δεινὸν γὰρ ἔμοιγε δοκεῖ
εἶναι, εἰ ἐξ ὧν μὲν ἤδη ἡμάρτηκε μηδέποτε τιμωρηθήσεται,
25 ἐξ ὧν δὲ μέλλει εὖ ποιήσειν ἤδη τετιμήσεται. ἀλλ' ἄρα
ἵνα βελτίους ὦσιν οἱ πολῖται ὁρῶντες ἅπαντας ὁμοίως
τιμωμένους, διὰ τοῦτο δοκιμαστέος ἐστίν; ἀλλὰ κίνδυνος
155 καὶ τοὺς χρηστούς, ἐὰν αἰσθάνωνται ὁμοίως τοὺς πονηροὺς τιμωμένους, παύσεσθαι τῶν χρηστῶν ἐπιτηδευμάτων,
τῶν αὐτῶν ἡγουμένους εἶναι τούς τε κακοὺς τιμᾶν καὶ τῶν

ἀμείνους αὐτῶν φεύγοιεν ; — **πότερον,
ἀλλὰ, ἀλλὰ** (§ 25): see on XXIV. 24.
— **ὡς οὐχ ἡμαρτηκότα** : on the ground
that he has not offended.   See on
XII. 2. — **περὶ ... ἠδίκηκεν** : elsewhere
Lys. uses the simple acc. with ἀδικέω;
here he may have been influenced by
his use of περί with acc. twice in § 23
as well as with πόλιν below. In Dem.
περί and acc. is freq. with ἀδικέω, and
Fuhr adds CIA. II, 811 c, 154, ἐάν
τις ἀδικῇ περὶ τὰ ἐν τοῖς νεωρίοις. —
ὡς ἔσται : on the ground that he will
be a better man, the somewhat rare
use of ὡς in a causal sentence with
indic., seeming to have the 'subjective' force (i.e. it expresses the
ground on which the subject of δοκιμάσαιτε is supposed to act), as with
the partic. ἡμαρτηκότα above. See Kr.
Spr. 65, 8, and App. — **τοιγάρτοι** :
accordingly, then, said with reference
to Philon's promised improvement
implied in ὡς ἔσται βελτίων. — **πᾶσι** :

see App. — **ἤδη, ἤδη** : Rauchenstein
notes this poignant repetition (observe also the jingle in τιμωρηθήσεται
and τετιμήσεται, cf. § 26), in which the
first ἤδη refers to the past, already,
and the second means at once, immediately. For the latter sense (which
is often also the feeling of the fut.
perf., see G. 1266; GMT. 79), cf.
Dem. VIII. 2, κἂν ἤδη δοκῇ κἂν ἐπι-
σχοῦσιν (after waiting a while), Xen.
Anab. i. 4. 16, ἐγὼ μὲν ἤδη ὑμᾶς ἐπαι-
νῶ· ὅπως δὲ καὶ ὑμεῖς ἐμὲ ἐπαινέσετε
ἐμοὶ μελήσει.

25. ἄρα : gives an ironical tone to
the clause; cf. § 28, Plat. Apol. 37 D,
ἄλλοι δὲ ἄρα αὐτὰς οἴσουσι ῥᾳδίως;—
ὁμοίως: = ἐξ ἴσου, sc. ἑαυτοῖς. — **παύσεσθαι** : an inf. after κίνδυνός ἐστι is
ordinarily pres. or aor., cf. XII. 31
(G. 1521).   But the fut. (G. 1277)
may also be used, as with κινδυνεύει
in Plat. Rep. 459 C. — **τῶν αὐτῶν** :
for the case, see on XII. 41.

26 ἀγαθῶν ἀμνημονεῖν. ἄξιον δὲ καὶ τόδε ἐνθυμηθῆναι, ὅτι
εἰ μέν τις φρούριόν τι προὔδωκεν ἢ ναῦς ἢ στρατόπεδόν
160 τι, ἐν ᾧ μέρος τι ἐτύγχανε τῶν πολιτῶν ὄν, ταῖς ἐσχάταις
ἂν ζημίαις ἐζημιοῦτο, οὗτος δὲ προδοὺς ὅλην τὴν πόλιν
οὐχ ὅπως μὴ τιμωρηθήσεται ἀλλ᾽ ὅπως τιμήσεται παρασκευάζεται. καίτοι δικαίως γ᾽ ἂν ὅστις φανερῶς ὥσπερ
οὗτος προὔδωκε τὴν ἐλευθερίαν, οὐ περὶ τοῦ βουλεύειν
165 ἀλλὰ περὶ τοῦ δουλεύειν καὶ τῆς μεγίστης ταλαιπωρίας
ἀγωνίζοιτο.

27 Ἀκούω δ᾽ αὐτὸν λέγειν ὡς, εἴ τι ἦν ἀδίκημα τὸ μὴ
παραγενέσθαι ἐν ἐκείνῳ τῷ καιρῷ, νόμος ἂν ἔκειτο περὶ
αὐτοῦ διαρρήδην, ὥσπερ καὶ περὶ τῶν ἄλλων ἀδικημάτων.
170 οὐ γὰρ οἴεται ὑμᾶς γνώσεσθαι ὅτι διὰ τὸ μέγεθος τοῦ

26. **φρούριόν τι κτλ.**: the procedure
against one guilty of προδοσία (treason
or betrayal) was through an εἰσαγγελία (see Introd. n. 167); cf. Hyperid.
Eux. xxii *sq.*, ὑπὲρ τίνων οὖν ᾤεσθε δεῖν
τὰς εἰσαγγελίας γίγνεσθαι; ... ἐάν τις,
φησί (sc. ὁ νομοθέτης), ... πόλιν τινὰ προ-
δῷ ἢ ναῦς ἢ πεζὴν ἢ ναυτικὴν στρατιάν.
— **ἐν ᾧ ἐτύγχανε**: on the assimilation, see on xii. 29. — **ταῖς ἐσχάταις
ἂν ζημίαις**: one condemned of προδοσία was put to death, refused burial
in Attica, and his property was confiscated. Cf. Xen. *Hellen.* i. 7. 22,
ἐάν τις ἢ τὴν πόλιν προδιδῷ ... ἂν κατα-
γνωσθῇ, (sc. νόμος ἐστί) μὴ ταφῆναι ἐν τῇ
Ἀττικῇ, τὰ δὲ χρήματα αὐτοῦ δημόσια
εἶναι. Hence the bones of Themistocles, who died abroad while under
sentence of treason, were buried in
Attica secretly, Thuc. i. 138. 6. On
the whole subject of προδοσία, see
M. and S., p. 419 ff.— **ὅλην τὴν πόλιν**:
on the thought, *cf.* Lycurg. *Leocr.* 59

('he will say perhaps'), ὡς οὐκ ἔνοχός
ἐστι τῇ προδοσίᾳ· οὔτε γὰρ νεωρίων
κύριος οὔτε πυλῶν οὔτε στρατοπέδων
οὔθ᾽ ὅλως τῶν τῆς πόλεως οὐδενός. ἐγὼ
δ᾽ ἡγοῦμαι τοὺς μὲν τούτων κυρίους μέρος
ἄν τι προδοῦναι τῆς ὑμετέρας δυνάμεως,
τουτονὶ δ᾽ ὅλην ἔκδοτον ποιῆσαι τὴν
πόλιν. — **τιμήσεται**: fut. mid. as pass.
So in Xen. *Cyr.* viii. 7. 15, *Anab.* i.
4. 14; *cf.* xxii. 11, and see App. and
G. 1248; H. 496 a. — **παρασκευάζεται**:
is laying his schemes, often in a bad
sense, *cf.* xii. 60. So ἐκ παρασκευῆς,
xiii. 22, but *cf.* xxxi. 30. — **τὴν ἐλευθερίαν**: this word leads up well to
δουλεύειν. Philon has cared nothing
for the general liberty, he deserves
to lose his own. On the paronomasia
in βουλεύειν, δουλεύειν, see p. 135.

27. **λέγειν**: the tense denotes repetition. G. 1291; H. 824 a. — **νόμος**:
on Solon's law, see p. 133, note 8. —
περὶ αὐτοῦ: not, of course, about
absence on that particular occasion,

ἀδικήματος οὐδεὶς περὶ αὐτοῦ ἐγράφη νόμος. τίς γὰρ ἄν
ποτε ῥήτωρ ἐνεθυμήθη ἢ νομοθέτης ἤλπισεν ἁμαρτήσε-
28 σθαί τινα τῶν πολιτῶν τοσαύτην ἁμαρτίαν; οὐ γὰρ ἂν
δή που, εἰ μέν τις λίποι τὴν τάξιν μὴ αὐτῆς τῆς πόλεως
175 ἐν κινδύνῳ οὔσης ἀλλ᾽ ἑτέρους εἰς τοῦτο καθιστάσης,
ἐτέθη νόμος ὡς μεγάλα ἀδικοῦντος, εἰ δέ τις αὐτῆς τῆς
πόλεως ἐν κινδύνῳ οὔσης λίποι τὴν πόλιν αὐτήν, οὐκ ἂν
ἄρα ἐτέθη. σφόδρα γ᾽ ἄν, εἴ τις ᾠήθη τινὰ τῶν πολιτῶν
29 ἁμαρτήσεσθαί τι τοιοῦτόν ποτε. τίς δ᾽ οὐκ ἂν εἰκότως
180 ἐπιτιμήσειεν ὑμῖν, εἰ τοὺς μετοίκους μέν, ὅτι κατὰ τὸ προσῆκον ἑαυτοῖς ἐβοήθησαν τῷ δήμῳ, ἐτιμήσατε ἀξίως τῆς
πόλεως, τοῦτον δέ, ὅτι παρὰ τὸ προσῆκον ἑαυτῷ προὔδωκε
τὴν πόλιν, μὴ κολάσετε, εἰ μή γε ἄλλῳ τινὶ μείζονι, τῇ γε

but at any such crisis. — ῥήτωρ : thus
defined in Suidas : ῥήτωρ τὸ παλαιὸν
ἐκαλεῖτο ὁ δήμῳ συμβουλεύων καὶ ὁ ἐν
δήμῳ ἀγορεύων, εἴτε ἱκανὸς εἴη λέγειν
εἴτε καὶ ἀδύνατος, εἴτε καὶ ἀπὸ τοῦ βελ-
τίστου καὶ δικαιοτάτου συμβουλεύων εἴτ᾽
ἐπ᾽ οἰκείοις λήμμασι. Hence used like
our term *statesman* (which too often
= *politician*). Cf. xxii. 2.

28. οὐ γὰρ ἂν κτλ. : Fuhr supplies
as protasis εἰ νομοθέτης ἤλπισεν . . .
ἁμαρτίαν from the foregoing. The
thought then is : 'had the lawmaker
dreamed of the possibility of such a
crime, he would never have framed
a law against the less, and neglected
a law against the greater.' See App.
— δή που : marks the sarcasm ; see on
xii. 27. — μὴ . . . καθιστάσης : the difference here, as Markland noted, is
between defensive (αὐτῆς τῆς πόλεως
ἐν κινδύνῳ οὔσης) and offensive (ἑτέρους
εἰς τοῦτο καθιστάσης) warfare. The
letter of the current law seems to

have provided, naturally enough,
against λιποτάξιον only in the latter
case. But much later, after Chae-
ronea, the people ἐψηφίσατο ἐνόχους
εἶναι τῇ προδοσίᾳ τοὺς φεύγοντας τὸν
ὑπὲρ τῆς πατρίδος κίνδυνον, Lycurg.
Leocr. 53. — ἀδικοῦντος : gen. abs.,
sc. αὐτοῦ. — ἄρα : calls attention to
the absurdity of the idea. The influence of the first οὐ at the beginning
extends over the whole sentence and
makes this second clause practically
positive in sense. — σφόδρα γ᾽ ἄν : sc.
ἐτέθη. For the ellipse, see on xii. 34.

29. κατὰ τὸ προσῆκον : the metics
were expected to serve in war, both
in the infantry, Thuc. ii. 13. 7 ; 31. 2 ;
iv. 90. 1 ; and in the fleet, i. 143. 1 ;
iii. 16. 1 ; but not in the cavalry, Xen.
Vect. 2. 5. — ἐτιμήσατε : *e.g.* by giving
them ἰσοτέλεια (see Introd. § 15), or
to fallen metics public burial along
with citizens, [Lys.] ii. 66. — εἰ μὴ
κολάσετε : a 'minatory' condition,

30 παρούσῃ ἀτιμίᾳ; ἀναμνήσθητε δὲ δι' ὅ τι ποτὲ τοὺς ἀγα-
185 θοὺς ἄνδρας γεγενημένους περὶ τὴν πόλιν τιμᾶτε καὶ τοὺς
κακοὺς ἀτιμάζετε. παρεδείχθη γὰρ ἀμφότερα ταῦτα οὐ
τῶν γεγενημένων μᾶλλόν τι ἕνεκα ἢ τῶν γενησομένων, ἵν'
ἀγαθοὶ προθυμῶνται γίγνεσθαι ἐκ παρασκευῆς, κακοὶ δὲ
31 μηδὲ ἐξ ἑνὸς τρόπου ἐπιχειρῶσιν. ἔτι δὲ ἐνθυμήθητε
190 ποίων ἂν ὑμῖν δοκεῖ οὗτος ὅρκων φροντίσαι, ὃς ἔργῳ τοὺς
πατρίους θεοὺς προὔδωκεν; ἢ πῶς ἂν χρηστόν τι βουλεῦ-
σαι περὶ τῆς πολιτείας, ὃς οὐδὲ ἐλευθερῶσαι τὴν πατρίδα
ἐβουλήθη; ἢ ποῖα ἂν ἀπόρρητα τηρῆσαι, ὃς οὐδὲ τὰ προ-

see on XII. 11. On the moral duty
involved, see on XII. 23; and cf.
Lycurg. Leocr. 74, χρή τοίνυν, ὦ
ἄνδρες, ὥσπερ τοὺς ἀγαθοὺς ἐπαινεῖτε
καὶ τιμᾶτε, οὕτω καὶ τοὺς κακοὺς μισεῖν
τε καὶ κολάζειν. — εἰ μή γε, τῇ γε:
the repetition of γε adds much to
the emphasis, 'actually,' 'at least.'
Cf. Xen. Mem. i. 5. 3, εἴ γε μηδὲ δοῦλον ἀκρατῇ (intemperate) δεξαίμεθ' ἄν,
πῶς οὐκ ἄξιον αὐτόν γε (the master
much more) φυλάξασθαι τοιοῦτον γενέσθαι; — ἀτιμία: rejection at the δοκιμασία may have entailed some loss
in full civic rights; see App.

30. περί: for this use, common in
the orators, cf. §§ 24, 34, and Ar. Eq.
764, εἰ μὲν περὶ τὸν δῆμον τὸν Ἀθηναίων
γεγένημαι βέλτιστος ἀνήρ. — παρεδείχθη: used of things set forth or
exhibited side by side for comparison; cf. Isocr. XII. 39, ὥσπερ τὴν
πορφύραν καὶ τὸν χρυσὸν θεωροῦμεν καὶ
δοκιμάζομεν ἕτερα παραδεικνύοντες τῶν
καὶ τὴν ὄψιν ὁμοίαν ἐχόντων καὶ τῆς
τιμῆς τῆς αὐτῆς ἀξιουμένων. Here it
is used like the subst. παράδειγμα,
common in the sense of a model or

example, to be used as a copy or a
warning; cf. § 34 and XVI. 14, XXII.
20. — προθυμῶνται: sc. οἱ πολῖται;
and for the mood, see on XVI. 6.—
ἐκ παρασκευῆς: intentionally, with
fixed purpose, in a good sense, but
see on § 26. — μηδὲ ἐξ ἑνὸς τρόπου:
not by any means, by no manner of
means. The separation of ἑνός from
the negative gives much greater emphasis than μηδενός. See G. 378; H.
290 a, and cf. XIII. 33, οὐδ' ὑφ' ἑνὸς
(ne ab uno quidem) αὐτὸν προσήκει
ἐλεεῖσθαι, and VII. 28, XVI. 10, XXIV. 24.

31. ὅρκων: see on § 1. — φροντίσαι: with gen., cf. VII. 17. — ἔργῳ
... προὔδωκεν: he had abandoned
his country and its gods to the im-
pious Thirty (cf. XII. 99), yet as an
ephebus he had sworn, ἀμυνῶ δὲ καὶ
ὑπὲρ ἱερῶν ... καὶ ἱερὰ τὰ πάτρια
τιμήσω. On the oath of the ephebus
(here taken from Stob. Serm. xliii. 48),
see Hermann, Staatsalt. p. 458. —
ὅς... ἐβουλήθη: the oath also ran, καὶ
ἄν τις ἀναιρῇ τοὺς θεσμοὺς ἢ μὴ πείθηται,
οὐκ ἐπιτρέψω, ἀμυνῶ δὲ καὶ μόνος καὶ
μετὰ πάντων. — ἀπόρρητα: secret

εἰρημένα ποιῆσαι ἠξίωσε; πῶς δ᾽ εἰκός ἐστι τοῦτον, ὃς
195 οὐδὲ τελευταῖος ἐπὶ τοὺς κινδύνους ἦλθε, πρότερον τῶν
κατεργασαμένων καὶ οὕτω νῦν τιμηθῆναι; σχέτλιον δ᾽
ἂν εἴη, εἰ οὗτος μὲν ἅπαντας τοὺς πολίτας περὶ οὐδενὸς
ἡγήσατο, ὑμεῖς δὲ τοῦτον ἕνα ὄντα μὴ ἀποδοκιμάσαιτε.
32 Ὁρῶ δέ τινας οἳ νῦν μὲν τούτῳ παρασκευάζονται βοη-
200 θεῖν καὶ δεῖσθαι ὑμῶν, ἐπειδὴ ἐμὲ οὐκ ἠδύναντο πεῖσαι·
τότε δέ, ὅτε οἱ κίνδυνοι μὲν ὑμῖν καὶ οἱ μέγιστοι ἀγῶνες
ἦσαν, τὰ δὲ ἆθλα αὐτὴ ἡ πολιτεία ἔκειτο, καὶ ἔδει οὐ
μόνον περὶ τοῦ βουλεύειν ἀλλὰ καὶ περὶ τῆς ἐλευθερίας
βουλεύεσθαι, τότε οὐκ ἐδέοντο αὐτοῦ βοηθῆσαι καὶ ὑμῖν
205 καὶ κοινῇ τῇ πόλει, καὶ μὴ προδοῦναι μήτε τὴν πατρίδα

sessions of the Senate are meant ;
cf. XIII. 21, εἰσελθὼν δὲ εἰς τὴν βουλὴν
ἐν ἀπορρήτῳ Θεόκριτος μηνύει κτλ. —
κατεργασαμένων : the work referred
to was the freeing of the country, as
in § 32. — καὶ οὕτω : *even in this case.*
See App. — ἅπαντας, ἕνα ὄντα : a favourite antithesis; cf. XXIV. 13, 22.
εἰ οὗτος μὲν ... περὶ οὐδενὸς ἡγήσατο,
ὑμεῖς δὲ ... μὴ ἀποδοκιμάσαιτε: the
Greek prefers co-ordination in such
cases, where we should subordinate
the first member, using a word like
while. This first member (unlike the
one in § 24) is not really hypothetical,
but denotes a fact (hence οὐδενός),
while the real hypothesis is in the
second member, hence μή. Cf. XXII.
13, and see GMT. 386, 387, and App.
— περὶ οὐδενός : see on XII. 7.
32. ὁρῶ δέ τινας : in referring to
Philon's συνήγοροι, see on XII. 86.
Note the double chiasm in the position of τούτῳ, ὑμῶν, and ἐμέ with
regard to their verbs. — ἐμὲ ... πεῖ-

σαι : such attempts would seem to
have been common, though the
orator may sometimes have invented
them to bring out his own devotion
to the right. Cf. XXX. 34, πολλὰ
δεηθέντες τῶν κατηγόρων ἡμᾶς μὲν οὐδα-
μῶς ἔπεισαν, and [Lys.] XX. 15, ἐκπριά-
μενοι τοὺς κατηγόρους. Similarly in
Ar. *Eq.* 472 sq., the sausage-seller
says, καὶ ταῦτα μ᾽ οὔτ᾽ ἀργύριον οὔτε
χρυσίον διδοὺς ἀναπείσεις οὔτε προσπέμ-
πων φίλους, ὅπως ἐγὼ ταῦτ᾽ οὐκ Ἀθηναίοις φράσω. — τὰ δὲ ἆθλα : the art. is
used because the pred. noun is definite, ' the prize.' G. 956; H. 669 a.—
πολιτεία : not in the broad sense of
form of government (as in XII. 74, *cf.*
Plat. *Resp.* 544 D, δυναστεῖαι γὰρ καὶ
ὠνηταὶ βασιλεῖαι καὶ τοιαῦταί τινες
πολιτεῖαι), but signifying the democracy of Athens. See on XII. 6, and
cf. Harp. *s.v.*, ἰδίως εἰώθασι τῷ ὀνόματι
χρῆσθαι οἱ ῥήτορες ἐπὶ τῆς δημοκρατίας.
— ἔκειτο : technical word with ἆθλα.
So also the compound with προ-, as

μήτε τὴν βουλήν, ἧς νῦν ἀξιοῖ τυχεῖν οὐ μετὸν αὐτῷ,
33 ἄλλων γε κατεργασαμένων. μόνος δή, ὦ βουλή, δικαίως
οὐδ᾽ ἂν ἀγανακτοίη μὴ τυχών· οὐ γὰρ ὑμεῖς νῦν αὐτὸν
ἀτιμάζετε, ἀλλ᾽ αὐτὸς αὑτὸν τότε ἀπεστέρησεν, ὅτε οὐκ
210 ἠξίωσεν, ὥσπερ νῦν προθύμως κληρωσόμενος ἦλθε, καὶ
τότε διαμαχούμενος περὶ αὐτῆς καταστῆναι μεθ᾽ ὑμῶν.
34 Ἱκανά μοι νομίζω εἰρῆσθαι, καίτοι πολλά γε παραλιπών. ἀλλὰ πιστεύω ὑμᾶς καὶ ἄνευ τούτων αὐτοὺς τὰ
συμφέροντα τῇ πόλει γνώσεσθαι. οὐ γὰρ ἄλλοις τισὶν
215 ὑμᾶς δεῖ περὶ τῶν ἀξίων ὄντων βουλεύειν τεκμηρίοις χρῆσθαι ἢ ὑμῖν αὐτοῖς, ὁποῖοί τινες ὄντες αὐτοὶ περὶ τὴν
πόλιν ἐδοκιμάσθητε. ἔστι γὰρ τὰ τούτου ἐπιτηδεύματα
καινὰ παραδείγματα καὶ πάσης δημοκρατίας ἀλλότρια.

---

in I. 47, ὁρῶντες οἷα τὰ ἆθλα πρόκειται
τῶν τοιούτων ἁμαρτημάτων.— ἧς : *i.e.*
a seat in the βουλή.

33. ἀτιμάζετε : see on ἀτιμίᾳ, § 29.
— **ὥσπερ νῦν** : here νῦν means *lately*,
else the choice by lot would be still
to come and ἥκει, not ἦλθε, would be
the proper word. — **κληρωσόμενος** :
used technically of the candidate, *cf.*
XXIV. 13. Hence λαγχάνω is used of
the elect, as above in § 2, and in ἡ βουλὴ
οἱ πεντακόσιοι οἱ λαχόντες τῷ κυάμῳ,
law in And. I. 96.— **καὶ τότε** : anacolu-
thontic after ὅτε, caused by the insertion of ὥσπερ νῦν κτλ. — **περὶ** : often
used by the orators of the object or
stake of a contest; see Lutz, *Präp.*
p. 132, and Lys. XIII. 17, ἐναντιώσον-

ται περὶ τῆς ἐλευθερίας, III. 43, περὶ
ἑταίρας μαχόμενοι. — **αὐτῆς** : refers to
the Senate.

34. ἱκανά μοι κτλ.: a common way
of leading up to the conclusion (*cf.*
XXII. 22, XXIII. 16); employed also
at the end of a particular part of a
speech, VII. 9, XII. 37. — **καίτοι** :
very rare with the participle. GMT.
861. See App. — **παραλιπών** : as if
ἱκανὰ νομίζω εἰρηκέναι had preceded.—
περὶ τὴν πόλιν : see on § 30. — **καινά** :
'*unheard-of.*' — **παραδείγματα** : *bad
precedents, warnings, cf.* § 30; XXVII. 5,
ἔσται παράδειγμα τοῦ μὴ ὑμᾶς ἀδικεῖν.
— **δημοκρατίας** : on the case after a
word denoting the opposite of *possession*, see G. 1143; H. 754 c.

AGAINST DIOGITON.

INTRODUCTION.

The general functions of the modern judge of probate with regard to guardians and wards were in Athens vested in the first archon.[1] Any person who had the right to make a will might in it[2] appoint for his minor children a guardian (ἐπίτροπος) or guardians, who had to qualify before the archon.[3] In case of no provision in the will, the archon made the appointment.[4] However appointed, the guardian entered into all the rights of a father, and became the κύριος[5] of the children : it was his duty to provide for their support[6] and education,[7] and to manage their property.[8]

The statute law in many of our States directs a guardian to submit an annual account of the condition of his ward's estate. Though there seems to have been no such provision in Athens, yet there were various ways in which the ward's interests were protected. If the archon was informed or himself became cognizant of neglect or maladministration,[9] he might take up the case, and, if unable to settle it by a fine, might bring it before a court.[10] Any citizen could inform against a guardian, for any kind of ill-treatment of his ward, by means of the procedure called εἰσαγ-

---

[1] On the general subject, see M. and S. p. 551 ff., adding Arist. *Resp. Ath.* 56. 6 f.; and Hermann, *Rechtsalt.* p. 12 f.; Smith, *Dict. Antiq. s.v. Epitropus.*

[2] ἐπιτροπεῦσαι κατὰ διαθήκας, Dem. XLV. 37; καταλιπεῖν ἐπίτροπον, cf. Lys. *fragg.* 43, 75.

[3] Isaeus, VI. 36.

[4] ἐπιτροπῆς κατάστασις, Arist. *ibid.* § 6.

[5] Isaeus, I. 10, v. 10. See on Lys. XVI. 10.

[6] Dem. XXVII. 60.

[7] *Ibid.* 46; Plat. *Protag.* 320 A.

[8] M. and S. p. 558 ff.; but see on § 23.

[9] Dem. XXX. 6; Aeschin. I. 158.

[10] Arist. *ibid.* § 7; Dem. XLIII. 75. On fines levied by magistrates, ἐπιβολαί, cf. Lys. XXX. 3.

γελία ὀρφανῶν κακώσεως,[11] or in case of mismanagement of the
property, by a φάσις μισθώσεως οἴκου.[12] The ἀνάκρισις in either case
was conducted by the archon, who of course presided over the
ensuing suit in the Heliastic court.

Such were the means of protecting wards during their minority.
But at the age of eighteen, the boy, after passing his δοκιμασία,[13]
became legally capable of acting for himself. At this time the
guardian was obliged to present to him a written inventory of his
estate, and an account of receipts and expenditures.[14] If the
guardian did not present the account, or if the account submitted
was unsatisfactory, the suit called δίκη ἐπιτροπῆς might follow,[15]
being brought in the first instance before the archon. In the
charge, the ward stated the sum of which he believed that he had
been defrauded.[16] The suit was τιμητός,[17] and accuser and accused
ran the risk of *epobelia*.[18] The statute of limitations (προθεσμία[19])
confined the time within which the suit could be brought to five
years.[20]

It was for such a suit that Lysias wrote the speech *Against
Diogiton*. This man had been left as guardian of his brother's
three children, — two boys and a girl. Eight years later,[21] the

---

[11] Arist. *ibid.* § 6; *cf.* § 7, end; M.
and S. pp. 358, 562. An example is
Isaeus XI. This is of course a different
sort of εἰσαγγελία from the public im-
peachments referred to in Introd. n. 167.

[12] M. and S. p. 361; called in Arist.
ibid. § 6, οἴκου ὀρφανικοῦ κακώσεως. See
below, on § 23.

[13] See Introd. § 8.

[14] λόγος τῆς ἐπιτροπῆς. *Cf.* § 25, and
Dem. XXXVI. 20, XXXVIII. 15; see M.
and S. p. 561.

[15] M. and S. p. 562, who compare the
Roman suit de rationibus distra-
hendis or actio tutelae privata.

[16] *Cf.* [Dem.] XXIX. 31, ἔστιν οὖν τοῦ
μὲν ἐγκλήματος ἀρχή "τάδ᾽ ἐγκαλεῖ Δημο-

σθένης Ἀφόβῳ· ἔχει μοῦ χρήματ᾽ Ἄφοβος
ἀπ᾽ ἐπιτροπῆς ἐχόμενα, ὀγδοήκοντα μὲν
μνᾶς" κτλ. In the Diogiton case, the
actual claim was set forth in the young
man's charge and opening speech, and
may have been repeated in the part of
the present oration that is not preserved by Dionysius.

[17] See Introd. § 45. The penalty,
however, would be in money only,
hence the words τοὺς ἐσχάτους κινδύνους
in § 2 were mere bravado.

[18] See Introd. § 49, and M. and S.
pp. 563, 951.

[19] See p. 4.

[20] Dem. XXXVIII. 17, 27.

[21] § 9.

elder son, when he came of age, was told to his consternation that
he had nothing to receive from his father's estate. He had had
reason to suppose that it was large, amounting originally to thirteen
talents [22] at the least; he now heard that his father had left a mere
trifle.[23] Documents,[24] however, through the accidental discovery of
an account-book,[25] forced Diogiton to admit that he had received nine
talents and forty minae.[26] But the guardian asserted that it was
all spent: two talents on dowries,[27] the rest on the children during
their minority.[28] After all possible efforts at a private settlement
had been made,[29] there was nothing for the wards to do but to sue
their guardian, who was also their grandfather and their uncle.[30]
The elder son was the actual prosecutor; but, after a brief opening
speech, he left the main treatment of the case to a συνήγορος,[31] his
brother-in-law, for whom Lysias wrote the speech before us. The
somewhat complicated family relations are made clearer by the
following genealogical table:

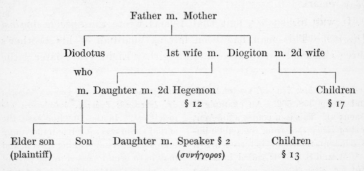

The closeness of the relationships between the parties in this
suit makes the plight of the orphans seem wretched beyond all
example; but in giving our sympathy we must remember that
in this, as in most other ancient suits, we hear only one side.

[22] §§ 4, 5, 6.

[23] Twenty minae and thirty Cyzicene
staters, § 9.

[24] § 14.

[25] § 15.

[26] 7 talents, 40 minae (§ 14) + 2 talents
(§ 15).

[27] §§ 6, 8.   [28] § 20.   [29] §§ 1–3.

[30] § 5, and see on § 4.

[31] See Introd. § 36.

Diogiton probably had some explanation to offer in his defence, though, in the face of the evidence against him, it is very hard to conjecture what his defence could have been.[32] But suits between wards and guardians were too common for the good name of the Athenians, and in no other instance does the great lack of truth and probity which we constantly have to lament in this people come out more strongly.[33] We know that at least seven of the ten famous orators were often employed in such cases,[34] among which that of Demosthenes against his own guardians is the best known. A whole class of λόγοι ἐπιτροπικοί or ὀρφανικοί once existed in the Mss. of Lysias,[35] but not one remains in them to-day.

We owe the fragment of the speech against Diogiton to the admiration it excited in Dionysius of Halicarnassus,[36] who copied it out, adding notes of his own, in the chapter on Lysias contained in his *Commentaries on the Ancient Orators*. He criticized it almost entirely from the standpoint of the rhetorician. Finding in it a remarkable example of excellence in the προοίμιον, διήγησις,[37] and main arguments, he quoted those parts only, omitting some of the arguments as well as the ἐπίλογος, a part in which Lysias, according to rhetorical rules, was not by any means strong.[38] The views of Dionysius will be found below in his own words.

---

[32] In this connexion it is a pity that the whole of the speech written by Lysias for a guardian who was accused under a δίκη ἐπιτροπῆς by his wife's brothers has not been preserved. In the fragment (43), the speaker talks as if guardians were a common mark for 'sycophantic' orphans.

[33] M. and S. p. 561. Legacies were sometimes left to the guardian to remove the temptation to steal from his wards; Dem. xxvii. 5, 45, 65. See also the case of an elder brother and guardian accused of defrauding his ward, Lys. x. 5. The judges had the reputation of siding with wards, pre-

sumably the weaker parties; *cf.* Dem. xxxviii. 20.

[34] M. and S. p. 550 f.

[35] We have the titles of at least eight; M. and S. *ibid.*

[36] The famous literary critic and rhetorician, who died about the beginning of our era. The lexicographer Photius (ninth century A.D.) also praises the speech in the highest terms (Cod. 262).

[37] These terms are explained as they occur below in Dionysius.

[38] Blass thinks that we have about two-thirds of the whole speech: *Att. Bereds.* I, p. 613.

But the speech deserves admiration for a quality more interesting to modern readers. This consists in the ἠθοποιία or delineation of the character of Diogiton and of his daughter. Diogiton is the type of heartlessness, and his utter lack of any natural feeling for his grandchildren comes out in the words with which he drives away the boy,[39] and all the more clearly for the thin pretence of affection which he has made but a moment before. Bitter irony, sarcastic play upon words, and sharp antithesis are all used to exhibit him in his true light.[40] The figure of the woman is even better drawn, and the scene in which she appears and the words she speaks are something unique in Greek prose.[41] She finds herself driven, contrary to all the prejudices of an Athenian woman in that age, to speak in a meeting of men, and, not only that, but to speak against her own father. The struggle against the power of custom is great, but the mother's heart is the stronger, and in her words we have its natural outpourings. There is nothing rhetorical nor artificial in what she says: it is not the railing complaint of a woman in a passion, but an appeal which is full of pathos and dignity.[42]

The date of this suit can be pretty closely determined. The defeat of Thrasyllus at Ephesus, where Diodotus died, was in the Spring of 409 B.C.[43] The elder son was under guardianship for eight full years.[44] Hence, allowing for the attempts at arbitration and for the necessary preliminaries, the suit cannot have been tried until late in 401 B.C.; probably it came on then or soon after.

---

[39] σκόπει αὐτὸς ἤδη πόθεν ἕξεις τὰ ἐπιτήδεια, § 9; cf. Blass, ibid. p. 614.

[40] §§ 22, 23, 25; Blass, ibid. p. 614.

[41] §§ 11–18.

[42] The asyndeton in § 16, as Blass observes, is entirely natural here; so also the mention of the gods in §§ 13, 17. Rauchenstein notes that the woman's reference to Diogiton's treatment of his other children (§ 17) is made without envy, and more in sorrow than

in anger. On the δριμύτης, or staccato effect, natural in a woman's language, see Gildersleeve, A. J. P. IX, p. 151, and Devries, Ethopoiia, p. 48.

[43] Xen. Hellen. i. 2. 9. Those who, like Jebb, set the date at 410, retain as genuine the opening section of this chapter. The date of the archon Glaucippus, mentioned in Dionysius's hypothesis, is 410–9.

[44] §§ 20, 29; see on § 9.

ΚΑΤΑ ΔΙΟΓΕΙΤΟΝΟΣ.

Ἵνα δὲ βέλτιον τῷ βουλομένῳ ἐγγένηται μαθεῖν, εἴτε ὀρθῶς ἡμεῖς ταῦτα καὶ προσηκόντως πεπείσμεθα, εἴτε καὶ διημαρτήκαμεν τὴν κρίσιν, τὴν ἐξέτασιν ἀπὸ τῶν ὑπ' ἐκείνου γραφέντων ποιήσομαι, προχειρισάμενός τε ἕνα λόγον — οὐ γὰρ ἐγχωρεῖ πολλοῖς χρῆσθαι παραδείγμασιν — ἐξ ἐκείνου τήν τε προαίρεσιν καὶ τὴν δύναμιν τοῦ ἀνδρὸς ἐπιδείξομαι, ἀποχρῆν οἰόμενος ψυχαῖς εὐπαιδεύτοις καὶ μετρίαις μικρά τε μεγάλων καὶ ὀλίγα πολλῶν γενέσθαι δείγματα. ἔστι δὲ ὁ λόγος ἐκ τῶν ἐπιτροπικῶν, ἐπιγραφόμενος Κατὰ Διογείτονος, ὑπόθεσιν δὲ ἔχων τοιάνδε ·

Διόδοτος, εἷς τῶν μετὰ Θρασύλλου καταλεγέντων ἐν τῷ Πελοποννησιακῷ πολέμῳ, μέλλων ἐκπλεῖν εἰς τὴν Ἀσίαν ἐπὶ Γλαυκίππου ἄρχοντος, ἔχων νήπια παιδία, διαθήκας ἐποιήσατο, καταλιπὼν αὐτοῖς ἐπίτροπον τὸν ἑαυτοῦ μὲν ἀδελφὸν Διογείτονα, τῶν δὲ παιδίων θεῖόν τε καὶ πάππον ἀπὸ μητρός. αὐτὸς μὲν οὖν ἐν Ἐφέσῳ μαχόμενος ἀποθνήσκει · Διογείτων δὲ πᾶσαν τὴν οὐσίαν τῶν ὀρφανῶν διαχειρισάμενος καὶ ἐκ πολλῶν πάνυ χρημάτων οὐδὲν ἀποδείξας αὐτοῖς, ἔτι περιὼν κατηγορεῖται πρὸς ἑνὸς τῶν μειρακίων δοκιμασθέντος κακῆς

On Dionysius. κρίσιν: ordinarily a legal word, but here used in the rare sense of one's *critical* judgment. Cf. γνώμῃ διαμαρτών, Dem. XXIV. 48, 110. — προχειρισάμενος: *having first treated*, a sense common in Aristotle; but cf. διεχείριζεν, § 27. — προαίρεσιν: in classical Greek often signifying a course deliberately chosen in life or politics, or a form of government; here used of Lysias's *method*. — ψυχαῖς: *persons*, cf. N. T. *Acts* ii. 41 and 43.

— μετρίαις: *reasonable*. See on XVI. 3. — ἐπιτροπικῶν: see p. 155. — Πελοποννησιακῷ: a rare adj. in Attic, used in Plat. *Legg.* 708 A. — ἀπὸ μητρός: *on the mother's side* (cf. Dem. XLV. 56), but πρός is more common in the orators in this sense. See Lutz, *Präp.* p. 155. — πρὸς ἑνός: either (1) *by one*, πρός being used sometimes in Attic for ὑπό, or (2) *in the name* or *interest of one*; on both usages, see Kühn. II, p. 447 f. — κακῆς ἐπιτροπῆς: not the

ἐπιτροπῆς. λέγει δὲ κατ᾽ αὐτοῦ τὴν δίκην ὁ τῆς ἐκείνου μὲν θυγατρι-
δῆς, τῶν δὲ μειρακίων ἀδελφῆς ἀνήρ.

προὔβαλον δὲ τὴν ὑπόθεσιν ἵνα μᾶλλον γένηται καταφανὲς εἰ
μετρίᾳ καὶ προσηκούσῃ τῇ ἀρχῇ κέχρηται. — Dion. H.,V, p. 497 ff. R.

1 Εἰ μὲν μὴ μεγάλα ἦν τὰ διαφέροντα, ὦ ἄνδρες δικασταί, οὐκ ἄν ποτε εἰς ὑμᾶς εἰσελθεῖν τούτους εἴασα, νομίζων αἴσχιστον εἶναι πρὸς τοὺς οἰκείους διαφέρεσθαι,
εἰδώς τε ὅτι οὐ μόνον οἱ ἀδικοῦντες χείρους ὑμῖν εἶναι
5 δοκοῦσιν, ἀλλὰ καὶ οἵτινες ἂν ἔλαττον ὑπὸ τῶν προσηκόντων ἔχοντες ἀνέχεσθαι μὴ δύνωνται· ἐπειδὴ μέντοι, ὦ
ἄνδρες δικασταί, πολλῶν χρημάτων ἀπεστέρηνται καὶ
πολλὰ καὶ δεινὰ πεπονθότες ὑφ᾽ ὧν ἥκιστα ἐχρῆν ἐπ᾽
ἐμὲ κηδεστὴν ὄντα κατέφυγον, ἀνάγκη μοι γεγένηται
2 εἰπεῖν ὑπὲρ αὐτῶν. ἔχω δὲ τὴν τούτων μὲν ἀδελφήν, Διογείτονος δὲ θυγατριδῆν, καὶ πολλὰ δεηθεὶς ἀμφοτέρων τὸ
μὲν πρῶτον ἔπεισα τοῖς φίλοις ἐπιτρέψαι δίαιταν, περὶ

Attic phrase, for which see p. 153. Moeris p. 143 ridicules it : τὸ γὰρ κακῆς ἐπιτροπῆς ἀνόητον· ἀγαθῆς γὰρ οὐδεὶς δικάζεται. — **λέγει τὴν δίκην**: this phrase seems to take the place of the usual συνδικεῖ or συνηγορεῖ. Cf. Dinarch. I. III, τὰς δίκας λέγοντος ὑπὲρ Κτησίππου καὶ Φορμίωνος.

1. **τὰ διαφέροντα** : the issues at stake, but see on XXXI. 5.— **εἰς ὑμᾶς** : cf. XXXI. I. — **τούτους** : although the elder son was the real plaintiff, doubt-less the younger was also in court, if only to excite pity. — **αἴσχιστον** : a public quarrel or a suit between kindred was a scandal. Cf. Isaeus, I. 6, ἐγὼ μὲν γὰρ οὐχ ὅτι ἀδίκως κινδυ-νεύω, τοῦθ᾽ ἡγοῦμαι μέγιστον εἶναι τῶν παρόντων κακῶν, ἀλλ᾽ ὅτι ἀγωνίζομαι

πρὸς οἰκείους, οὓς οὐδ᾽ ἀμύνεσθαι καλῶς ἔχει. See the long excuse at the opening of [Dem.] XLVIII. — **τέ** : a simple connective. Cf. § 22, and see on XXXI. 2. — **χείρους** : for the mean-ing, see on XVI. 3. — **ἔλαττον ἔχοντες** : 'being taken at a disadvantage,' cf. Plat. Rep. 343 D, δίκαιος ἀνὴρ ἀδίκου πανταχοῦ ἔλαττον ἔχει. Here almost = defrauded. Cf. XII. 49. — **ὑφ᾽ ὧν ἥκιστα ἐχρῆν** : a common phrase ; cf. § 10, and Cic. Fam. v. 1, video …me desertum a quibus mi-nime conveniebat. — **κηδεστήν** : the word signifies any connexion by marriage, affinis, here brother-in-law ; see the genealogy on p. 154.

2. **πολλὰ δεηθεὶς ἀμφοτέρων** : cf. XXX. 34, quoted on XXXI. 32. — **τοῖς φίλοις** : thus Demosthenes before

πολλοῦ ποιούμενος τὰ τούτων πράγματα μηδένα τῶν
ἄλλων εἰδέναι· ἐπειδὴ δὲ Διογείτων ἃ φανερῶς ἔχων ἐξ-
15 ηλέγχετο, περὶ τούτων οὐδενὶ τῶν αὐτοῦ φίλων ἐτόλμα
πείθεσθαι, ἀλλ᾽ ἐβουλήθη καὶ φεύγειν δίκας καὶ μὴ οὔσας
διώκειν καὶ ὑπομένειν τοὺς ἐσχάτους κινδύνους μᾶλλον ἢ
τὰ δίκαια ποιήσας ἀπηλλάχθαι τῶν πρὸς τούτους ἐγκλη-
3 μάτων, ὑμῶν δέομαι, ἐὰν μὲν ἀποδείξω οὕτως αἰσχρῶς
20 αὐτοὺς ἐπιτετροπευμένους ὑπὸ τοῦ πάππου ὡς οὐδεὶς πώποτε ὑπὸ τῶν οὐδὲν προσηκόντων ἐν τῇ πόλει, βοηθεῖν
αὐτοῖς τὰ δίκαια, εἰ δὲ μή, τούτῳ μὲν ἅπαντα πιστεύειν,
ἡμᾶς δὲ εἰς τὸν λοιπὸν χρόνον ἡγεῖσθαι χείρους εἶναι. ἐξ
ἀρχῆς δ᾽ ὑμᾶς περὶ αὐτῶν διδάξαι πειράσομαι.

bringing suit against his guardians would have preferred περὶ ὧν διαφερό-μεθα τοῖς οἰκείοις ἐπιτρέπειν, xxvii. 1, cf. xxx. 2, where he says the guardian ought ἐν τοῖς φίλοις διαδικάσασθαι ('settled up') τὰ πρὸς ἐμέ. —ἐπιτρέψαι δίαιταν: a standing phrase; cf. frag. 16. 2, οὐδεπώποτ᾽ ἠθέλησε συνελθεῖν ... οὐδὲ δίαιταν ἐπιτρέψαι, [Dem.] LIX. 45, συνῆγον αὐτοὺς οἱ ἐπιτήδειοι καὶ ἔπεισαν δίαιταν ἐπιτρέψαι αὐτοῖς. Private, not public (Smith, Dict. Antiq. s.v. Diae-tetae, I, p. 620, 623) arbitrators are meant. They were chosen from persons named by both sides, and arranged a meeting such as that described in § 12 ff. Ordinarily the parties bound themselves to abide by the decision given. See Schoemann, Gr. Alt. I, 501; Gilbert, Antiq. p. 391. —ἃ φανερῶς κτλ.: observe that the rel. clause stands first. See on XII. 43 and cf. XXIV. 22.—ἐτόλμα: for the meaning, cf. §§ 15, 20, and see on XII. 5.— μὴ οὔσας διώκειν: bring suit to set aside

his default. When a party to a suit in an ordinary court did not appear, he lost it by default (ἐρήμην ὀφλεῖν, sc. δίκην, Poll. VIII. 60, cf. Plat. Apol. 18 C, ἐρήμην κατηγοροῦντες). But if his absence was due to illness or other good reason, he might enter a new suit to set his default aside (τὴν δίκην ἀντι-λαχεῖν, Poll. VIII. 61). When the default occurred before the public arbitrators, this new suit was called ἡ μὴ οὖσα δίκη, and the suitor was said τὴν μὴ οὖσαν ἀντιλαχεῖν, Poll. VIII. 60; cf. M. and S. p. 974. — τοὺς ἐσχάτους κινδύνους: see p. 153, note 17.—πρός: 'on the part of.' See on XVI. 10.

3. ἐπιτετροπευμένους: reduplicated like a real compound. Cf. Thuc. i. 132, ἐπετρόπευεν, and see App. to XII. 73. — τὰ δίκαια: cogn. acc. (G. 1054; H. 716 b); cf. v. 1, δοκεῖ αἰσχρὸν εἶναι ... μὴ βοηθῆσαι Καλλίᾳ τὰ δίκαια. — Here the proem ends and the comments of Dionysius follow.

Τοῦτο τὸ προοίμιον ἁπάσας ἔχει τὰς ἀρετὰς ὅσας δεῖ τὸ προοίμιον
ἔχειν. δηλώσουσι δὲ οἱ κανόνες αὐτῷ παρατεθέντες οἱ τῶν τεχνῶν.
ἅπαντες γὰρ δή που παραγγέλλουσιν οἱ συνταξάμενοι τὰς τέχνας,
ὅταν ᾖ πρὸς οἰκείους ὁ ἀγών, σκοπεῖν ὅπως μὴ πονηροὶ μηδὲ φιλοπράγμονες οἱ κατήγοροι φανήσονται· κελεύουσί τε πρῶτον μὲν τὴν
αἰτίαν εἰς τοὺς ἀντιδίκους περιιστάναι καὶ τοῦ ἐγκλήματος καὶ τοῦ
ἀγῶνος, καὶ λέγειν ὅτι μεγάλα τἀδικήματα καὶ οὐκ ἐνῆν αὐτὰ μετρίως
ἐνεγκεῖν, καὶ ὅτι ὑπὲρ ἀναγκαιοτέρων προσώπων ὁ ἀγὼν καὶ ἐρήμων
καὶ ἧττον ὑπεροφθῆναι ἀξίων, οἷς μὴ βοηθοῦντες κακίους ἂν ἐφάνησαν,
καὶ ὅτι προκαλούμενοι τοὺς ἀντιδίκους εἰς διαλλαγὰς καὶ φίλοις τὰ
πράγματα ἐπιτρέποντες καὶ τὰ δυνατὰ ἐλαττοῦσθαι ὑπομένοντες οὐδενὸς ἠδυνήθησαν τυχεῖν τῶν μετρίων. ταῦτα μὲν δὴ παραγγέλλουσι
ποιεῖν οἱ τεχνογράφοι, ἵνα τὸ ἦθος τοῦ λέγοντος ἐπιεικέστερον εἶναι
δόξῃ. δύναται δὲ αὐτοῖς εὔνοιαν τοῦτο ποιεῖν καὶ ἔστι κράτιστον τῆς
κατασκευῆς μέρος. ταῦθ᾽ ὁρῶ πάντα διὰ τοῦ προοιμίου τοῦδε γεγο-
νότα. καὶ μὴν εἴς γε τὸ εὐμαθεῖς τοὺς ἀκροατὰς ποιῆσαι κελεύουσι
συστρέψαντας εἰπεῖν τὸ πρᾶγμα, ἵνα μὴ ἀγνοῶσι τὴν ὑπόθεσιν οἱ

ON DIONYSIUS. τεχνῶν : systems,
methods, τέχνη being the regular
name for a treatise on rhetoric from
the time of Corax and Tisias down.
See Introd. § 11, and cf. τεχνογράφοι,
below.—παραγγέλλουσιν : recommend.
— φιλοπράγμονες : generally means
meddlesome, like πολυπράγμων, XXIV.
24, but here litigious, pettifogging.
Cf. πράγματα, XII. 3, and φιλοπραγμο-
σύνη, Dem. XXXIX. 1. — τὴν αἰτίαν...
περιιστάναι : cf. [Dem.] XL. 20, περιιστάναι τὰς αὑτῶν συμφορὰς εἰς ἐμέ.
Cf. the intrans. tense περιέστηκε, XII.
64. — ἀναγκαιοτέρων : on the meaning of the comparative, see H. 649 a.
— προσώπων : persons, a late usage
in this general sense ; cf. persona.
— κακίους : for the meaning, see on
χείρους, XVI. 3. — φίλοις ... ἐπιτρέποντες : sc. for arbitration, see above,
§ 2 ; and on the force of the tense,

see G. 1255 ; H. 825. — τὰ δυνατὰ
ἐλαττοῦσθαι : the verb is used in its
idiomatic sense of exacting less than
one's due, waive one's rights. Cf.
[Lys.] II. 64 ; Thuc. i. 77, καὶ ἐλασσού-
μενοι γὰρ ἐν ταῖς ξυμβολαίαις πρὸς τοὺς
ξυμμάχους δίκαις. The acc. τὰ δυνατὰ
is cognate ; see on § 3. For the two,
cf. [Dem.] LVI. 14, ἡγούμενοι δεῖν ἐλατ-
τοῦσθαί τι καὶ συγχωρεῖν ὥστε μὴ δοκεῖν
φιλόδικοι εἶναι. — ὑπομένοντες : having
the patience, with inf. GMT. 903, 2.
— οὐδενὸς ... μετρίων : so Dem. XXX.
I, οὐδενὸς ἐδυνήθην τυχεῖν τῶν μετρίων.
— αὐτοῖς : i.e. for speakers. — ποιεῖν :
i.e. παρέχειν. Cf. Plat. Apol. 20 D,
κἀγὼ ὑμῖν πειράσομαι ἀποδεῖξαι τί ποτ᾽
ἐστὶ τοῦτο ὃ ἐμοὶ πεποίηκε τό τε ὄνομα
καὶ τὴν διαβολήν. — κατασκευῆς : a
rhetorical term for the constructive
reasoning in an argument as opposed
to the destructive, ἀνασκευή. — συστρέ-

δικασταί, καὶ οἷά περ ἂν ᾖ τὰ μέλλοντα λέγεσθαι, τοιοῦτο καὶ τὸ
προοίμιον ὑποτίθεσθαι ἀπ᾽ ἀρχῆς, καὶ δεῖγμα τοῦ πράγματος ποιουμένους εὐθὺς ἀπ᾽ ἐνθυμημάτων πειρᾶσθαι ἄρχεσθαι. ἔχει δὴ καὶ
ταῦτα τὸ προοίμιον. ἔτι περὶ τῆς προσοχῆς ὧδέ πως τεχνολογοῦσιν,
ὅτι δεῖ τὸν προσεκτικοὺς μέλλοντα ποιεῖν τοὺς ἀκροατὰς καὶ λέγειν
θαυμαστὰ καὶ παράδοξα καὶ δεῖσθαι τῶν δικαστῶν ἀκοῦσαι. φαίνεται
δὴ καὶ ταῦτα πεποιηκὼς ὁ Λυσίας. καὶ πρόσεστι τούτοις τὸ λεῖον
τῆς ἑρμηνείας καὶ τὸ ἀφελὲς τῆς κατασκευῆς, ὧν μάλιστα δεῖ τοῖς
ὑπὲρ ἐκείνων προοιμιαζομένοις.

    Ἄξιον δὲ καὶ τὴν διήγησιν ὡς ᾠκονόμηται καταμαθεῖν. ἔχει δὲ
οὕτως ·

4   Ἀδελφοὶ ἦσαν, ὦ ἄνδρες δικασταί, Διόδοτος καὶ Διογείτων ὁμοπάτριοι καὶ ὁμομήτριοι, καὶ τὴν μὲν ἀφανῆ
οὐσίαν ἐνείμαντο, τῆς δὲ φανερᾶς ἐκοινώνουν. ἐργασαμένου δὲ Διοδότου κατ᾽ ἐμπορίαν πολλὰ χρήματα πείθει
αὐτὸν Διογείτων λαβεῖν τὴν ἑαυτοῦ θυγατέρα, ἥπερ ἦν

ψαντας : a military term used of solid
formations (cf. Xen. Hellen. vi. 4. 12,
ἐπὶ πεντήκοντα ἀσπίδων συνεστραμμένοι
ἦσαν), employed by rhetoricians to
signify conciseness and brevity. Cf.
Aeschin. III. 100, συστρέψας γράφει. —
ἐνθυμημάτων: arguments.—προσοχῆς:
we aim at three points in a προοίμιον
(exordium), says the Auct. ad
Herenn. I. 6, ut attentos, ut do-
cilis, ut benevolos auditores
habere possimus. Of the historian, Lucian says (Hist. Conscr. 53):
ὁπόταν δὲ καὶ φροιμιάζηται, ἀπὸ δυοῖν
μόνον ἄρξεται, οὐχ ὥσπερ οἱ ῥήτορες ἀπὸ
τριῶν, ἀλλὰ τὸ τῆς εὐνοίας παρεὶς προσ-
οχὴν καὶ εὐμάθειαν εὐπορήσει τοῖς ἀκούουσι. — τεχνολογοῦσιν : another rhetorical word. — παράδοξα : see on
XVI. I. — τὸ λεῖον : the use of the
neut. of the adj. for the correspond-
ing abstract, so common in Thucy-

dides.—ἐκείνων : sc. τῶν ἀναγκαιοτέρων
προσώπων. — διήγησιν : the regular
rhetorical term for the narrative
part of a speech, 'statement of the
case.'

    4. ἀφανῆ οὐσίαν : Harpocration
says, ἀφανὴς οὐσία καὶ φανερά · ἀφανὴς
μὲν ἡ ἐν χρήμασι καὶ σώμασι καὶ σκεύεσι,
φανερὰ δὲ ἡ ἔγγειος. This is the general distinction like our personal and
real estate, but frequently slaves,
cattle, valuable house-furnishings, and
money in the bank were classed under
φανερά. Cf. XII. 83. See Hermann,
Privatalt. p. 96 f. — ἐνείμαντο : the
regular word used of the division
of an inheritance ; cf. XVI. 10. —
ἐργασαμένου : cf. [Dem.] LVI. 34,
πολλὰ χρήματ᾽ εἰργασμένοι παρὰ τὴν
σιτηγίαν τὴν εἰς Ῥόδον. — πείθει αὐτὸν
κτλ. : marriages between kinsfolk

30 αὐτῷ μόνη· καὶ γίγνονται αὐτῷ ὑεῖ δύο καὶ θυγάτηρ.
5 χρόνῳ δὲ ὕστερον καταλεγεὶς Διόδοτος μετὰ Θρασύλλου
τῶν ὁπλιτῶν, καλέσας τὴν ἑαυτοῦ γυναῖκα, ἀδελφιδῆν
οὖσαν, καὶ τὸν ἐκείνης μὲν πατέρα, αὑτοῦ δὲ κηδεστὴν καὶ
ἀδελφόν, πάππον δὲ τῶν παιδίων καὶ θεῖον, ἡγούμενος διὰ
35 ταύτας τὰς ἀναγκαιότητας οὐδενὶ μᾶλλον προσήκειν
δικαίῳ περὶ τοὺς αὑτοῦ παῖδας γενέσθαι, διαθήκην αὐτῷ
δίδωσι καὶ πέντε τάλαντα ἀργυρίου παρακαταθήκην·
6 ναυτικὰ δὲ ἀπέδειξεν ἐκδεδομένα ἑπτὰ τάλαντα καὶ τετταράκοντα μνᾶς, . . . δισχιλίας δὲ ὀφειλομένας ἐν Χερρο-

were not forbidden in Athens, and were sometimes all but directed by law (see on XXIV. 14), the object being to keep property in the family. Even a half-brother (not a full-brother) and sister by the same father might marry. Lysias himself married his sister's daughter (see Introd. § 23). A marriage like that of Diodotus with his *brother's* daughter, though allowed in Athens, was unheard of in Rome before the Emperor Claudius married Agrippina (Tac. *Ann.* xii. 5). — ὑεῖ : see App.

5. χρόνῳ δὲ ὕστερον : on the date, see p. 156. — καταλεγείς : the regular word, see on XVI. 13. For the part. gen., *cf.* xxx. 8, οὐδὲ τῶν πεντα-κισχιλίων κατελέγην, and XXIV. 13. — Θρασύλλου : a noted general in the Peloponnesian war, an opponent of the Four Hundred (Thuc. viii. 73), esp. at Samos (*ibid.* 75), where he was general with Thrasybulus (*ibid.* 76) and defeated the Peloponnesians off Cynossema (*ibid.* 104 f.). See also on § 7. Having been one of the generals at Arginusae (Xen. *Hellen.* i. 7. 29),

he was put to death. *Cf.* Paus. vi. 7. — ἀναγκαιότητας : a word found only here in Attic Greek, but used in Polyb. xviii. 51. 10 ; see App. Thalheim compares Dem. XLV. 54, τὰ τῆς συγγενείας ἀναγκαῖα.

6. ναυτικά : *sc.* χρήματα, § 7. Money lent on ' bottomry ' (*i.e.* the security being the ship and her cargo) is meant. As the risk was apt to be great, the interest charged was often very high, running up to 30 per cent or thereabouts ; see Boeckh, *Staatsh.* I, p. 166 ff. — ἐκδεδομένα : used as a mercantile word (for a different use, see § 8). *Cf.* Bekker, *Anec.* p. 247, 21 : ἔκδοσις· τὸ ἔξωθεν τῆς πόλεως δά-νεισμα, τὸ ἐπὶ ναυσὶ καὶ φορτίοις διδό-μενον. ἦν δὲ τὰ τοιαῦτα ἐπισφαλῆ μέν, πολύτοκα δέ. — μνᾶς . . . : see App. — δισχιλίας : the word δραχμάς is here, as often, purposely omitted. A sum as large as 2000 *minae* was expressed in talents. A man like Diodotus could not have possessed it. — Χερρονήσῳ : there were many Athenian settlers in the Thracian Chersonese. *Cf.* And. III. 13 ff., τίνος

40 νήσῳ. ἐπέσκηψε δέ, ἐάν τι πάθῃ, τάλαντον μὲν ἐπιδοῦναι
τῇ γυναικὶ καὶ τὰ ἐν τῷ δωματίῳ δοῦναι, τάλαντον δὲ τῇ
θυγατρί. κατέλιπε δὲ καὶ εἴκοσι μνᾶς τῇ γυναικὶ καὶ
7 τριάκοντα στατῆρας κυζικηνούς. ταῦτα δὲ πράξας καὶ
οἴκοι ἀντίγραφα καταλιπὼν ᾤχετο στρατευσόμενος μετὰ
45 Θρασύλλου. ἀποθανόντος δὲ ἐκείνου ἐν Ἐφέσῳ Διογείτων τὴν μὲν θυγατέρα ἔκρυπτε τὸν θάνατον τοῦ ἀνδρός,
καὶ τὰ γράμματα λαμβάνει ἃ κατέλιπε σεσημασμένα,
φάσκων τὰ ναυτικὰ χρήματα δεῖν ἐκ τούτων τῶν γραμμα-
8 τείων κομίσασθαι. ἐπειδὴ δὲ χρόνῳ ἐδήλωσε τὸν θάνα-
50 τον αὐτοῖς καὶ ἐποίησαν τὰ νομιζόμενα, τὸν μὲν πρῶτον
ἐνιαυτὸν ἐν Πειραιεῖ διῃτῶντο· ἅπαντα γὰρ αὐτοῦ κατελέλειπτο τὰ ἐπιτήδεια· ἐκείνων δ᾽ ἐπιλειπόντων τοὺς μὲν
παῖδας εἰς ἄστυ ἀναπέμπει, τὴν δὲ μητέρα αὐτῶν ἐκδίδωσιν ἐπιδοὺς πεντακισχιλίας δραχμάς, χιλίαις ἔλαττον ὧν

ἕνεκα πολεμήσωμεν; . . . Χερρόνησον καὶ
τὰς ἀποικίας καὶ τὰ ἐγκτήματα καὶ τὰ
χρέα ἵνα ἀπολάβωμεν; — ἐπέσκηψε: a
common word in describing a man's
parting or dying wishes. — ἐάν τι
πάθῃ: a euphemism, like si quid
humani accidisset. — ἐπιδοῦναι:
for the meaning, see on XVI. 10.—
δωματίῳ: cf. XII. 10. — δοῦναι: see
App. — κυζικηνούς: see p. 206.

7. ἀντίγραφα: copies of the will
(the original given to Diogiton, § 5).
On the practice of leaving copies
with friends, see Becker, Charicles
(Engl. trans.), p. 171, M. and S.,
p. 597.— ἐν Ἐφέσῳ: where Thrasyllus
was defeated in the spring of 409 B.C.
by Tissaphernes and the Syracusans;
Xen. Hellen. i. 2. 9. — ἔκρυπτε: with
two accs. G. 1069; H. 724. Cf. Xen.
Anab. i. 9. 19, ὅσα ἐπέπατό τις, ἥκιστα

Κῦρον ἔκρυπτεν. — τὰ γράμματα: the
papers. — ἐκ: a somewhat rare use,
but cf. Isocr. XVII. 21, τὰ χρήματ᾽
ἐκ τῶν συγγεγραμμένων . . . ἀποδώσει,
and Lutz, Präp. p. 51.

8. τὰ νομιζόμενα: as the bones
were evidently not brought home in
this case, the 'last honours' (see on
XII. 18, 21, 96) here means the building of a cenotaph (cf. § 21) at which
yearly libations would be made. —
ἐν Πειραιεῖ: as Diodotus had been
engaged in commerce. — εἰς ἄστυ:
Diodotus and Diogiton may have
owned together (cf. § 4, τῆς δὲ φανερᾶς
ἐκοινώνουν) a house there; cf. § 16,
τῆς οἰκίας τῆς αὐτῶν. — ἐκδίδωσιν ἐπιδούς: Diogiton, becoming again her
κύριος, married her to Hegemon, § 12.
On the technical terms, see on XVI. 10.

—χιλίαις ἔλαττον: though it fell short

9 ὁ ἀνὴρ αὐτῆς ἔδωκεν. ὀγδόῳ δ᾽ ἔτει δοκιμασθέντος μετὰ
ταῦτα τοῦ πρεσβυτέρου τοῖν μειρακίοιν, καλέσας αὐτοὺς
εἶπε Διογείτων ὅτι καταλίποι αὐτοῖς ὁ πατὴρ εἴκοσι μνᾶς
ἀργυρίου καὶ τριάκοντα στατῆρας. "ἐγὼ οὖν πολλὰ τῶν
ἐμαυτοῦ δεδαπάνηκα εἰς τὴν ὑμετέραν τροφήν. καὶ ἕως
60 μὲν εἶχον, οὐδέν μοι διέφερεν· νυνὶ δὲ καὶ αὐτὸς ἀπόρως
διάκειμαι. σὺ οὖν, ἐπειδὴ δεδοκίμασαι καὶ ἀνὴρ γεγένη-
10 σαι, σκόπει αὐτὸς ἤδη πόθεν ἕξεις τὰ ἐπιτήδεια." ταῦτ᾽
ἀκούσαντες ἐκπεπληγμένοι καὶ δακρύοντες ᾤχοντο πρὸς
τὴν μητέρα, καὶ παραλαβόντες ἐκείνην ἧκον πρὸς ἐμέ,
65 οἰκτρῶς ὑπὸ τοῦ πάθους διακείμενοι καὶ ἀθλίως ἐκπεπτωκότες, κλάοντες καὶ παρακαλοῦντές με μὴ περιιδεῖν αὐτοὺς
ἀποστερηθέντας τῶν πατρῴων μηδ᾽ εἰς πτωχείαν κατα-
στάντας, ὑβρισμένους ὑφ᾽ ὧν ἥκιστα ἐχρῆν, ἀλλὰ βοηθῆ-
11 σαι καὶ τῆς ἀδελφῆς ἕνεκα καὶ σφῶν αὐτῶν. πολλὰ ἂν
70 εἴη λέγειν, ὅσον πένθος ἐν τῇ ἐμῇ οἰκίᾳ ἦν ἐν ἐκείνῳ τῷ
χρόνῳ. τελευτῶσα δὲ ἡ μήτηρ αὐτῶν ἠντεβόλει με καὶ
ἱκέτευε συναγαγεῖν αὐτῆς τὸν πατέρα καὶ τοὺς φίλους,
εἰποῦσα ὅτι, εἰ καὶ μὴ πρότερον εἴθισται λέγειν ἐν ἀν-

by one fifth (§ 6), the balance was
not a mean dowry ; see on XVI. 10.
It was the same as that of the mother
of Demosthenes, Dem. XXVII. 4.

9. **δοκιμασθέντος** : see p. 154. —
ὀγδόῳ δ᾽ ἔτει μετὰ ταῦτα : referring
to the removal εἰς ἄστυ, *in the eighth
year after this*, but eight full years
after the death of Diodotus ; *cf.* §§ 20,
29. — **εἴκοσι ... στατῆρας** : hence he
acknowledged only the sum which
Diogiton had given to his wife, § 6.
She had turned it over to Diogiton,
§ 15. — **εἶχον** : see on XVI. 14.

10. **ὑπό** : causal, see on VII. 21. —

ἐκπεπτωκότες : as pass. of ἐκβάλλω,
cf. § 16, and see on XII. 57. — **ἀποστερηθέντας** : on the use of the partic.,
see G. 1585 ; H. 982.

11. **πολλὰ ἂν εἴη** : *cf.* Dem. IX. 60,
ὡς ὑβρίζετο ... πόλλ᾽ ἂν εἴη λέγειν,
[Plat.] *Theag.* 121 C, τὰ μὲν οὖν ἄλλα
πολλὰ ἂν εἴη λέγειν. — **τελευτῶσα** : as
adv., see on XII. 60. — **ἠντεβόλει καὶ
ἱκέτευε** : these words are often used
together, like 'begged and besought.'
Cf. XXII. 21 and I. 25, ἠντεβόλει δὲ καὶ
ἱκέτευε μὴ ἀποκτεῖναι. For the augment of ἠντεβόλει, see App. to XII. 73.
— **λέγειν ἐν ἀνδράσι** : on the confined

δράσι, τὸ μέγεθος αὐτὴν ἀναγκάσει τῶν συμφορῶν περὶ
12 τῶν σφετέρων κακῶν δηλῶσαι πάντα πρὸς ἡμᾶς. ἐλθὼν
δ᾽ ἐγὼ ἠγανάκτουν μὲν πρὸς Ἡγήμονα τὸν ἔχοντα τὴν
τούτου θυγατέρα, λόγους δ᾽ ἐποιούμην πρὸς τοὺς ἄλλους
ἐπιτηδείους, ἠξίουν δὲ τοῦτον εἰς ἔλεγχον ἰέναι περὶ τῶν
πραγμάτων. Διογείτων δὲ τὸ μὲν πρῶτον οὐκ ἤθελε,
80 τελευτῶν δὲ ὑπὸ τῶν φίλων ἠναγκάσθη. ἐπειδὴ δὲ συν-
ήλθομεν, ἤρετο αὐτὸν ἡ γυνή, τίνα ποτὲ ψυχὴν ἔχων ἀξιοῖ
περὶ τῶν παίδων τοιαύτῃ γνώμῃ χρῆσθαι, "ἀδελφὸς μὲν
ὢν τοῦ πατρὸς αὐτῶν, πατὴρ δ᾽ ἐμός, θεῖος δὲ αὐτοῖς καὶ
13 πάππος. καὶ εἰ μηδένα ἀνθρώπων ᾐσχύνου, τοὺς θεοὺς
85 ἐχρῆν σε" φησί "δεδιέναι· ὃς ἔλαβες μέν, ὅτ᾽ ἐκεῖνος
ἐξέπλει, πέντε τάλαντα παρ᾽ αὐτοῦ παρακαταθήκην. καὶ
περὶ τούτων ἐγὼ ἐθέλω τοὺς παῖδας παραστησαμένη καὶ
τούτους καὶ τοὺς ὕστερον ἐμαυτῇ γενομένους ὀμόσαι ὅπου

life of Athenian women, at least of the
higher classes, see Hermann, *Privatalt.* § 10, and Becker, *Charicles* (Engl.
trans.), p. 462 ff. They rarely met
any men save their near relatives;
cf. III. 6, εἰσῆλθεν εἰς τὴν γυναικωνῖτιν,
ἔνδον οὐσῶν τῆς τε ἀδελφῆς τῆς ἐμῆς καὶ
τῶν ἀδελφιδῶν, αἳ οὕτω κοσμίως βεβιώ-
κασιν ὥστε καὶ ὑπὸ τῶν οἰκείων ὁρώμεναι
αἰσχύνεσθαι.

12. εἰς ἔλεγχον ἰέναι: see on XVI. 1.
—οὐκ ἤθελε: see on XII. 58. — ψυχὴν:
heart, cf. [Lys.] VI. 23, τίνα αὐτὸν
δοκεῖτε ψυχὴν ἔχειν, ὁπότε τὰ μὲν
ἔσχατα καὶ τὰ αἴσχιστα ἐποίει μηνύων
κατὰ τῶν ἑαυτοῦ φίλων; For a different sense, see on XXII. 20.

13. ᾐσχύνου, δεδιέναι: for these
two verbs used as here, the one of
men, the other of gods, cf. § 17, and
XXIV. 10. — ὅς: for the meaning,

see on XII. 40. — ἔλαβες μέν: in § 14
the construction changes, where we
might have had the woman's original words κεκόμισαι δέ κτλ. — τοὺς
παῖδας παραστησαμένη: this, the
ὅρκος κατὰ τῶν παίδων, was one of
the most binding of oaths, from its
solemn form and because the punishment for perjury might extend to the
children. Cf. XII. 10, Dem. XXIX. 33,
ἡ μήτηρ πίστιν ἤθελησ᾽ ἐπιθεῖναι κατ᾽
ἐμοῦ καὶ τῆς ἀδελφῆς παραστησαμένη
κτλ. As women could not give evidence in courts, the oath was really
their only means of testifying. On
its uses, see Smith, *Dict. Antiq.* s.v.
Diaetetae, I, p. 622; M. and S. p.
898 ff. — τοὺς ὕστερον: i.e. those by
her marriage with Hegemon. — ὅπου
ἄν: as for instance in one of the
temples. Cf. Dem. XXXVI. 15, Isocr.

ἂν οὗτος λέγῃ. καίτοι οὐχ οὕτως ἐγώ εἰμι ἀθλία οὐδ'
90 οὕτω περὶ πολλοῦ ποιοῦμαι χρήματα, ὥστ' ἐπιορκήσασα
κατὰ τῶν παίδων τῶν ἐμαυτῆς τὸν βίον ἐκλιπεῖν, ἀδίκως
14 δὲ ἀφελέσθαι τὴν τοῦ πατρὸς οὐσίαν." ἔτι τοίνυν ἐξήλεγχεν αὐτὸν ἑπτὰ τάλαντα κεκομισμένον ναυτικὰ καὶ τετρακισχιλίας δραχμάς, καὶ τούτων τὰ γράμματα ἀπέδειξεν·
95 ἐν γὰρ τῇ διοικίσει, ὅτ' ἐκ Κολλυτοῦ διῳκίζετο εἰς τὴν
Φαίδρου οἰκίαν, τοὺς παῖδας ἐπιτυχόντας ἐκβεβλημένῳ τῷ
15 βιβλίῳ ἐνεγκεῖν πρὸς αὐτήν. ἀπέφηνε δ' αὐτὸν ἑκατὸν
μνᾶς κεκομισμένον ἐγγείῳ ἐπὶ τόκῳ δεδανεισμένας καὶ
ἑτέρας δισχιλίας δραχμὰς καὶ ἔπιπλα πολλοῦ ἄξια· φοι-
100 τᾶν δὲ καὶ σῖτον αὐτοῖς ἐκ Χερρονήσου καθ' ἕκαστον
ἐνιαυτόν. "ἔπειτα σὺ ἐτόλμησας" ἔφη "εἰπεῖν, ἔχων
τοσαῦτα χρήματα, ὡς δισχιλίας δραχμὰς ὁ τούτων πατὴρ

XVII. 20, And. I. 42. — **κατὰ τῶν παίδων**: so Dem. XIX. 292, and see Dem.
XXIX. 33 quoted above. In taking
oaths, one often laid the hand on the
object by which he swore, as in And.
I. 126, λαβόμενος τοῦ βωμοῦ ὤμοσεν,
Isaeus VII. 17, καθ' ἱερῶν.

14. διοικίσει and **διῳκίζετο**: only
here in this sense, see App. The
usual word is ἐξοικίζομαι (or ἐξοικέω,
cf. XXXI. 9, and the lexicon. But cf.
δια- in διέπλευσα, XII. 17, διαπεράω, δια-
πέτομαι, διαβιβάσαι [Lys.] II. 28, δια-
βαίνω. On the repetition of the same
idea in subst. and verb, cf. Aeschin. I.
147, τὰς διατριβὰς ... ἃς μετ' ἀλλήλων
ζῶντες διέτριβον. — **Κολλυτοῦ**: a deme
lying north of the Acropolis, see Curtius, *Stadtgeschichte von Athen*, p. 21.
It was a favourite quarter for resi-
dences. *Cf.* Plut. *de Exil.* p. 601 C,
τὸ δέ σε μὴ κατοικεῖν Σάρδεις οὐδέν

ἐστιν· οὐδὲ γὰρ Ἀθηναῖοι πάντες κατοι-
κοῦσι Κολλυτόν.— **Φαίδρου**: unknown,
but possibly he was Diogiton's new
father-in-law. The boys, however,
seem to have stayed on for a time in
the house owned jointly by themselves
(as their father's heirs) and Diogiton;
cf. §§ 16 and 10.— **τῷ**: see App.— **ἐνεγκεῖν**: depends on the idea of *saying*
implied in ἐξήλεγχεν κτλ. G. 1525.

15. ἐγγείῳ ἐπὶ τόκῳ: *on a real
estate mortgage. Cf.* [Dem.] XXXIV.
23, 24. For the use of ἐπί denoting
the security, *cf.* XIX. 25, λαβὼν ἐκκαί-
δεκα μνᾶς ἐπ' αὐτῇ (*i.e.* φιάλῃ χρυσῇ),
and Lutz, *Präp.* p. 112 f.— **σῖτον**
κτλ.: possibly as interest on the debt
mentioned in § 6. On the corn dealings with the Chersonese, see p. 90.
— **ἔπειτα**: used like εἶτα, XII. 26.—
ἅπερ: for the meaning, *cf.* ὅσονπερ,
§ 27, and see on VII. 22.

κατέλιπε καὶ τριάκοντα στατῆρας, ἅπερ ἐμοὶ καταλει-
16 φθέντα ἐκείνου τελευτήσαντος ἐγώ σοι ἔδωκα· καὶ ἐκβα-
105 λεῖν τούτους ἠξίωσας θυγατριδοῦς ὄντας ἐκ τῆς οἰκίας τῆς
αὐτῶν ἐν τριβωνίοις, ἀνυποδήτους, οὐ μετὰ ἀκολούθου, οὐ
μετὰ στρωμάτων, οὐ μετὰ ἱματίων, οὐ μετὰ τῶν ἐπίπλων
ἃ ὁ πατὴρ αὐτοῖς κατέλιπεν, οὐδὲ μετὰ τῶν παρακαταθη-
17 κῶν ἃς ἐκεῖνος παρὰ σοὶ κατέθετο. καὶ νῦν τοὺς μὲν ἐκ
110 τῆς μητρυιᾶς τῆς ἐμῆς παιδεύεις ἐν πολλοῖς χρήμασιν
εὐδαίμονας ὄντας· καὶ ταῦτα μὲν καλῶς ποιεῖς· τοὺς δ᾽
ἐμοὺς ἀδικεῖς, οὓς ἀτίμους ἐκ τῆς οἰκίας ἐκβαλὼν ἀντὶ
πλουσίων πτωχοὺς ἀποδεῖξαι προθυμεῖ. καὶ ἐπὶ τοιούτοις
ἔργοις οὔτε τοὺς θεοὺς φοβεῖ, οὔτε ἐμὲ τὴν συνειδυῖαν
115 αἰσχύνει, οὔτε τοῦ ἀδελφοῦ μέμνησαι, ἀλλὰ πάντας ἡμᾶς
18 περὶ ἐλάττονος ποιεῖ χρημάτων." τότε μὲν οὖν, ὦ ἄνδρες
δικασταί, πολλῶν καὶ δεινῶν ὑπὸ τῆς γυναικὸς ῥηθέντων
οὕτω διετέθημεν πάντες οἱ παρόντες ὑπὸ τῶν τούτῳ πεπραγμένων καὶ τῶν λόγων τῶν ἐκείνης, ὁρῶντες μὲν τοὺς
120 παῖδας οἷα ἦσαν πεπονθότες, ἀναμιμνησκόμενοι δὲ τοῦ
ἀποθανόντος ὡς ἀνάξιον τῆς οὐσίας τὸν ἐπίτροπον κατέ-

---

16. **οἰκίας τῆς αὐτῶν**: see on §§ 8,
14. — **ἐν τριβωνίοις** : coarse or worn
ἱμάτια (Suidas says ἱμάτιον παλαιὸν).
Cf. Ar. *Vesp.* 117. A guardian treats
his ward in much the same fashion
in Isaeus, v. 11.—**οὐ μετὰ ἀκολούθου**·
none but the poorest Greeks ever went
out unattended, and the younger boy
should have had a παιδαγωγός. See
Becker, *Charicles* (Engl. trans.), pp.
3 and 226 ; Hermann, *Privatalt.* p. 85.
On the asyndeton here, see p. 156,
note 42. — **στρωμάτων** : see Becker,
p. 3 ; Hermann, p. 160.

17. **ἐν πολλοῖς χρήμασιν**: *cf.* Xen.

Anab. iii. 2. 25, ἐν ἀφθόνοις βιοτεύειν,
'live in clover.' — **ἀποδεῖξαι** : often
nearly equiv. to ποιῆσαι (cf. XXVIII.
4, ἐπηγγέλλετο . . . ὑμᾶς μὲν διὰ τὰς
εἰσφορὰς πενεστέρους ἀποδείξειν, *frag.*
I. 5, τοὺς ὑεῖς πτωχοὺς ἐποίησεν, αὐτὸν
δὲ ἀντὶ καπήλου μυροπώλην ἀπέδειξεν), but used here, like ἀποφήνειε,
§ 22, with the idea of *representing*.
— **ἐπί** : a common usage with verbs
of feeling to denote the ground ; *cf.*
XIV. 42, ἐπὶ μὲν τοῖς καλοῖς αἰσχύνεσθαι,
ἐπὶ δὲ τοῖς κακοῖς φιλοτιμεῖσθαι.

18. **διετέθημεν**: *affected.* — **ὑπό**: see
on VII. 21. — **τῆς οὐσίας** : does not

λιπεν, ἐνθυμούμενοι δὲ ὡς χαλεπὸν ἐξευρεῖν ὅτῳ χρὴ περὶ
τῶν ἑαυτοῦ πιστεῦσαι, ὥστε, ὦ ἄνδρες δικασταί, μηδένα
τῶν παρόντων δύνασθαι φθέγξασθαι, ἀλλὰ καὶ δακρύον-
125 τας μὴ ἧττον τῶν πεπονθότων ἀπιόντας οἴχεσθαι σιωπῇ.

Ἵνα δὲ καὶ ὁ τῶν ἀποδείξεων χαρακτὴρ καταφανὴς γένηται, θήσω
καὶ τὰ ἐπὶ τούτοις λεγόμενα. τὰς μὲν οὖν ἰδίας πίστεις ὡς οὐ
πολλῶν ἔτι λόγων δεομένας δι᾽ αὐτῶν βεβαιοῦται τῶν μαρτύρων,
οὐδὲν ἕτερον ἢ τοῦτο εἰπών·

Πρῶτον μὲν οὖν τούτων ἀνάβητέ μοι μάρτυρες.

Τὰ δὲ τοῦ ἀντιδίκου δίκαια διχῇ νείμας ὡς τὰ μὲν ὁμολογήσαντος
αὐτοῦ λαβεῖν καὶ εἰς τὰς τροφὰς τῶν ὀρφανῶν ἀνηλωκέναι σκηψα-
μένου, τὰ δὲ ἐξάρνου γενηθέντος εἰληφέναι κἄπειτα ἐλεγχθέντος ὑπὲρ
ἀμφοτέρων ποιεῖται τὸν λόγον, τάς τε δαπάνας οὐχ ἃς ἐκεῖνος ἀπέφηνε
γενέσθαι λέγων καὶ περὶ τῶν ἀμφιβόλων τὰς πίστεις ἀποδιδούς.

19 Ἀξιῶ τοίνυν, ὦ ἄνδρες δικασταί, τῷ λογισμῷ προσέχειν
τὸν νοῦν, ἵνα τοὺς μὲν νεανίσκους διὰ τὸ μέγεθος τῶν συμφορῶν ἐλεήσητε, τοῦτον δ᾽ ἅπασι τοῖς πολίταις ἄξιον ὀργῆς
130 ἡγήσησθε. εἰς τοσαύτην γὰρ ὑποψίαν Διογείτων πάντας
ἀνθρώπους πρὸς ἀλλήλους καθίστησιν, ὥστε μήτε ζῶντας

depend on ἀνάξιον, which is put first
for emphasis. — τῶν ἑαυτοῦ: refers to
the first person in διετέθημεν. G. 995;
H. 686 a. In such cases the pronoun
expresses mere reflex action in general without denoting any particular
person, and sometimes, as here,
means one's own. Kühn. § 455, 7.
— τῶν παρόντων: in effect a repetition
of οἱ παρόντες, allowed because so
much intervenes. — δακρύοντας: sc.
πάντας from μηδένα, cf. Lycurg. Leocr.
133, οὐδεμία πόλις αὐτὸν εἴασε παρ᾽ αὑτῇ
μετοικεῖν, ἀλλὰ (sc. πᾶσα) μᾶλλον τῶν
ἀνδροφόνων ἤλαυνεν.

On Dionysius. ἰδίας πίστεις: his
own (the speaker's) proofs, as distinguished from δίκαια (four lines
below), the claims of Diogiton; (cf.
Dem. XVIII. 7, εἰ μὴ τῶν δικαζόντων
ἕκαστος ὑμῶν τὰ τοῦ λέγοντος ὑστέρου
δίκαια εὐνοϊκῶς προσδέξεται.) — γενηθέντος: post-classical for γενομένου. —
τῶν ἀμφιβόλων: 'the disputed items.'

19. ἀξιῶ: the acc. ὑμᾶς might have
followed; see App. — τῷ λογισμῷ:
the guardian's accounts, see on λόγος,
§ 25. — πάντας ἀνθρώπους: see on
XVI. 15.

μήτε ἀποθνήσκοντας μηδὲν μᾶλλον τοῖς οἰκειοτάτοις ἢ τοῖς
20 ἐχθίστοις πιστεύειν · ὃς ἐτόλμησε τὰ μὲν ἔξαρνος γενέσθαι, τὰ δὲ τελευτῶν ὁμολογήσας ἔχειν, εἰς δύο παῖδας καὶ
135 ἀδελφὴν λῆμμα καὶ ἀνάλωμα ἐν ὀκτὼ ἔτεσιν ἑπτὰ τάλαντα
ἀργυρίου καὶ τετρακισχιλίας δραχμὰς ἀποδεῖξαι. καὶ εἰς
τοῦτο ἦλθεν ἀναισχυντίας, ὥστε οὐκ ἔχων ὅποι τρέψειε τὰ
χρήματα, εἰς ὄψον μὲν δυοῖν παιδίοιν καὶ ἀδελφῇ πέντε
ὀβολοὺς τῆς ἡμέρας ἐλογίζετο, εἰς ὑποδήματα δὲ καὶ εἰς
140 ἱμάτια καὶ εἰς γναφεῖον καὶ εἰς κουρέως κατὰ μῆνα οὐκ
ἦν αὐτῷ οὐδὲ κατ᾽ ἐνιαυτὸν γεγραμμένα, συλλήβδην δὲ
21 παντὸς τοῦ χρόνου πλεῖν ἢ τάλαντον ἀργυρίου. εἰς δὲ τὸ
μνῆμα τοῦ πατρὸς οὐκ ἀναλώσας πέντε καὶ εἴκοσι μνᾶς
ἐκ πεντακισχιλίων δραχμῶν, τὸ μὲν ἥμισυ αὐτῷ τίθησι,
145 τὸ δὲ τούτοις λελόγισται. εἰς Διονύσια τοίνυν, ὦ ἄνδρες

20. ὅς : for the meaning, see on
οἵτινες, XII. 40. — ἐτόλμησε : for the
meaning, see on XII. 5. — τὰ δὲ κτλ. :
this was an admission forced upon
Diogiton by the βιβλίον, § 14, cf.
§ 28. But he proceeded to assert that
he had expended the whole amount
thus acknowledged. — λῆμμα καὶ ἀνάλωμα : technical terms, as in Dem.
XXVII. 24, XXVIII. 12. — ὅποι τρέψειε
τὰ χρήματα : 'under what head to set
the sums.' Cf. Isaeus VI. 41, ἠρώτων
... ὅποι τετραμμένα εἴη τὰ χρήματα,
'what had been done with the money,'
and ὅποι, below, § 25. For the mood
of τρέψειε, representing an interroga-
tive or deliberative subj., see G. 1490.
— ὄψον : this term means a relish
eaten with bread, or sometimes, as
here, everything edible except bread.
See Hermann, Privatalt. p. 223. —
πέντε ὀβολούς : comparisons show

that this was a large sum for the
purpose. See Boeckh, Staatsh. I,
p. 128. — γναφεῖον : see on XXIII. 2.
— εἰς κουρέως : probably a colloquial-
ism (cf. XII. 12), with which Frohberger compares Ar. Eq. 467, σὺ δ᾽
οὐδὲν ἐξ ἁμαξουργοῦ λέγεις; The barber was the manicure and pedicure
of antiquity. He also sold perfumes,
oil for anointing, etc. See also p. 107.
— πλεῖν : on the form, see App.

21. μνῆμα : in this case a cenotaph. On the forms and cost of
monuments, see Becker, Charicles
(Engl. trans.), p. 393 ff.; Hermann,
Privatalt. p. 383. — αὐτῷ : as if he
had undertaken to share the cost. —
τίθησι : cf. θήσω, § 28, and ponere.
— Διονύσια : the art. is regularly
omitted in Lysias with names of festivals (Frohberger). — τοίνυν : here a
particle of transition, not, as usually,

δικασταί, (οὐκ ἄτοπον γάρ μοι δοκεῖ καὶ περὶ τούτου
μνησθῆναι) ἑκκαίδεκα δραχμῶν ἀπέφηνεν ἐωνημένον
ἀρνίον, καὶ τούτων τὰς ὀκτὼ δραχμὰς ἐλογίζετο τοῖς παι-
σίν· ἐφ' ᾧ ἡμεῖς οὐχ ἥκιστα ὠργίσθημεν. οὕτως, ὦ
150 ἄνδρες, ἐν ταῖς μεγάλαις ζημίαις ἐνίοτε οὐχ ἧττον τὰ
μικρὰ λυπεῖ τοὺς ἀδικουμένους· λίαν γὰρ φανερὰν τὴν
22 πονηρίαν τῶν ἀδικούντων ἐπιδείκνυσιν. εἰς τοίνυν τὰς
ἄλλας ἑορτὰς καὶ θυσίας ἐλογίσατο αὐτοῖς πλεῖν ἢ τετρακισχιλίας δραχμὰς ἀνηλωμένας, ἕτερά τε παμπληθῆ, ἃ
155 πρὸς τὸ κεφάλαιον συνελογίζετο, ὥσπερ διὰ τοῦτο ἐπίτροπος τῶν παιδίων καταλειφθείς, ἵνα γράμματ' αὐτοῖς ἀντὶ
τῶν χρημάτων ἀποδείξειεν καὶ πενεστάτους ἀντὶ πλουσίων
ἀποφήνειε, καὶ ἵνα, εἰ μέν τις αὐτοῖς πατρικὸς ἐχθρὸς ἦν,
ἐκείνου μὲν ἐπιλάθωνται, τῷ δ' ἐπιτρόπῳ, τῶν πατρῴων
23 ἀπεστερημένοι, πολεμῶσι. καίτοι εἰ ἐβούλετο δίκαιος
εἶναι περὶ τοὺς παῖδας, ἐξῆν αὐτῷ, κατὰ τοὺς νόμους οἳ
κεῖνται περὶ τῶν ὀρφανῶν καὶ τοῖς ἀδυνάτοις τῶν ἐπιτρό-

of inference. — ἑκκαίδεκα: about a third too much; see Boeckh, Staatsh. I, p. 96. — ἀρνίον: the usual sacrifice at this festival. — τὰς ὀκτώ: on the article, cf. XXII. 8, and see G. 948; H. 664 a. — ἐφ' ᾧ: for the syntax, see on XXXI. 11. — οὕτως: belongs to the whole sentence, not to any one word. See on τοσοῦτον, XII. 84, and cf. adeo. — ζημίαις: losses; cf. §§ 25, 29, and see on VII. 12.

22. τέ: see on XXXI. 2. — παμπληθῆ: 'to a vast amount.' — πρὸς τὸ κεφάλαιον: 'to complete the tale,' where κεφάλαιον means the total amount of 7⅔ talents acknowledged by Diogiton, § 20. So Froh-

berger, who compares Cic. Verr. II. 5. 73, ad eorum numerum (sc. explendum) cives Romani necati. See App. — συνελογίζετο: summed up. — ὥσπερ καταλειφθείς: see App. to XII. 7. — ἀποδείξειεν and ἀποφήνειε: see on § 17. — πατρικὸς ἐχθρός: hereditary foes as well as friends were recognized by Greek morals. See on XII. 2. — ἐπιλάθωνται and πολεμῶσι: on the difference in tense, see App. to XVI. 6, and on the change of mood from the opt. above, GMT. 321.

23. ἐξῆν: without ἄν, see on XII. 32. — κεῖνται: as pass. of τίθημι, see on § 10, and cf. XXII. 3. — ἀδυνάτοις: on the meaning, see oration XXIV.

πων καὶ τοῖς δυναμένοις, μισθῶσαι τὸν οἶκον ἀπηλλαγμέ-
νον πολλῶν πραγμάτων, ἢ γῆν πριάμενον ἐκ τῶν προσ-
165 ιόντων τοὺς παῖδας τρέφειν· καὶ ὁπότερα τούτων ἐποίησεν, οὐδενὸς ἂν ἧττον Ἀθηναίων πλούσιοι ἦσαν. νῦν δέ
μοι δοκεῖ οὐδεπώποτε διανοηθῆναι ὡς φανερὰν καταστήσων τὴν οὐσίαν, ἀλλ᾽ ὡς αὐτὸς ἕξων τὰ τούτων, ἡγούμενος
δεῖν τὴν αὑτοῦ πονηρίαν κληρονόμον εἶναι τῶν τοῦ τεθνεῶ-
24 τος χρημάτων. ὁ δὲ πάντων δεινότατον, ὦ δικασταί·
οὗτος γὰρ συντριηραρχῶν Ἀλέξιδι τῷ Ἀριστοδίκου,
φάσκων δυοῖν δεούσας πεντήκοντα μνᾶς ἐκείνῳ συμβαλέσθαι, τὸ ἥμισυ τούτοις ὀρφανοῖς οὖσι λελόγισται, οὓς ἡ
πόλις οὐ μόνον παῖδας ὄντας ἀτελεῖς ἐποίησεν, ἀλλὰ καὶ
175 ἐπειδὰν δοκιμασθῶσιν ἐνιαυτὸν ἀφῆκεν ἁπασῶν τῶν

— τοῖς δυναμένοις : on this subst. use,
cf. xxiv. 12, and see G. 1560; H. 966.
— μισθῶσαι τὸν οἶκον : a guardian
who was unable, for any reason, or
merely disinclined to manage his
ward's estate (οἶκος, see on xii. 93)
himself, might let it, by an auction
held before the archon, to the highest
bidder. The lessee (ὁ μισθούμενος) had
to give security (ἀποτίμημα) for the
rent. If this security was land, on
it was set a ὅρος with an inscription,
as ὅρος χωρίου καὶ οἰκίας ἀποτίμημα παιδὶ
ὀρφανῷ Διογείτονος, CIA. II, 1135. The
rent was often more than twelve per
cent. See M. and S. pp. 362, 559;
Smith, Dict. Antiq. s.v. Misthoseos
Phasis; and Sandys on Arist. Resp.
Ath. 56. 7. — ὡς καταστήσων : for the
syntax, see on xii. 73. — φανερὰν :
i.e. by turning it into land or mort-
gages. See on § 4. But here the
whole phrase suggests that Diogiton
did just the opposite, for the counter-

word ἀφανίζειν has the double sense
of turn into cash and make away
with. — πονηρίαν : personified; cf.
xii. 78.

24. ὁ δὲ κτλ. : an introductory rel.
clause. See H. 1009 a, and cf. xxiv.
11. — ὦ δικασταί : a rare omission
of ἄνδρες. See App. — συντριηραρχῶν : the custom by which two men
shared a trierarchy (see on xii. 38)
arose in the hard times in the latter
part of the Peloponnesian war.
Boeckh (Staatsh. I, p. 638) calls the
present the earliest known instance,
but as we cannot be sure of the exact
year of it, Gilbert (Antiq. p. 370)
quotes Isocr. xviii. 59 f. (405–404 b.c.)
as the earliest certainly known. —
δυοῖν δεούσας : on the phrase, see G.
382, 3 ; H. 292. — ἀτελεῖς : this immunity did not include the εἰσφορά
(see on xii. 20). Boeckh, Staatsh. I,
p. 534. — ἐποίησεν : not a gnomic
aor., but referring to the time of

λητουργιῶν. οὗτος δὲ πάππος ὢν παρὰ τοὺς νόμους τῆς
ἑαυτοῦ τριηραρχίας παρὰ τῶν θυγατριδῶν τὸ ἥμισυ πράτ-
25 τεται. καὶ ἀποπέμψας εἰς τὸν Ἀδρίαν ὁλκάδα δυοῖν
ταλάντοιν, ὅτε μὲν ἀπέστελλεν, ἔλεγε πρὸς τὴν μητέρα
180 αὐτῶν ὅτι τῶν παίδων ὁ κίνδυνος εἴη, ἐπειδὴ δὲ ἐσώθη
καὶ ἐδιπλασίασεν, αὑτοῦ τὴν ἐμπορίαν φάσκει εἶναι.
καίτοι εἰ μὲν τὰς ζημίας τούτων ἀποδείξει, τὰ δὲ σωθέντα
τῶν χρημάτων αὐτὸς ἕξει, ὅποι μὲν ἀνήλωται τὰ χρήματα
οὐ χαλεπῶς εἰς τὸν λόγον ἐγγράψει, ῥᾳδίως δὲ ἐκ τῶν ἀλλο-
26 τρίων αὐτὸς πλουτήσει. καθ᾽ ἕκαστον μὲν οὖν, ὦ δικασταί, πολὺ ἂν ἔργον εἴη πρὸς ὑμᾶς λογίζεσθαι· ἐπειδὴ δὲ
μόλις παρ᾽ αὐτοῦ παρέλαβον τὰ γράμματα, μάρτυρας
ἔχων ἠρώτων Ἀριστόδικον τὸν ἀδελφὸν τὸν Ἀλέξιδος
(αὐτὸς γὰρ ἐτύγχανε τετελευτηκώς) εἰ ὁ λόγος αὐτῷ εἴη ὁ
190 τῆς τριηραρχίας· ὁ δὲ ἔφασκεν εἶναι, καὶ ἐλθόντες οἴκαδε
ηὕρομεν Διογείτονα τέτταρας καὶ εἴκοσι μνᾶς ἐκείνῳ συμ-
27 βεβλημένον εἰς τὴν τριηραρχίαν. οὗτος δὲ ἐπέδειξε δυοῖν
δεούσας πεντήκοντα μνᾶς ἀνηλωκέναι, ὥστε τούτοις λελογίσθαι ὅσονπερ ὅλον τὸ ἀνάλωμα αὐτῷ γεγένηται. καίτοι
195 τί αὐτὸν οἴεσθε πεποιηκέναι περὶ ὧν οὐδεὶς αὐτῷ σύνοιδεν,

the enactment.—**πράττεται**: *exacted.*
Cf. ἀργύριον πράξασθαι, I. 25.
25. Ἀδρίαν: sc. κόλπον, omitted
as usual. — **ὁλκάδα**: a general term
for the merchant-ship as opposed
to ναῦς μακρά. Torr, *Ancient Ships*,
p. 23, with note 59.— **κίνδυνος**: *risk.*
This would be an extra one in that
sea; cf. *frag.* I. 4, ὥστε πολὺ ἀσφαλέστερον εἶναι δοκεῖν εἰς τὸν Ἀδρίαν
πλεῖν ἢ τούτῳ συμβάλλειν (lend money),
and Hor. III. 9. 23, improbo
iracundior Hadria. — **ἐσώθη**:
frequently used of a safe return,

as in XVI. 16.— **ὅποι**: see on § 20.
— **λόγον**: the regular term for the
guardian's account; see p. 153. It is
called λογισμός in § 19, γράμματα in § 26.
26. τετελευτηκώς: see on VII. 10,
and for the tense, on XII. 27.—
τέτταρας καὶ εἴκοσι: the trierarchy
cost almost fifty minae on the aver-
age. Boeckh, *Staatsh.* I, p. 671.
27. ἀνηλωκέναι: the infin. with
ἀποδείκνυμι is very rare. See App.
λελογίσθαι: on the tense, see GMT.
590.— **ὅσονπερ**: see on § 15.— **περὶ**
ὧν ... ἀλλ᾽ αὐτὸς κτλ.: English re-

ἀλλ᾽ αὐτὸς μόνος διεχείριζεν, ὃς ἃ δι᾽ ἑτέρων ἐπράχθη καὶ
οὐ χαλεπὸν ἦν περὶ τούτων πυθέσθαι, ἐτόλμησε ψευσά-
μενος τέτταρσι καὶ εἴκοσι μναῖς τοὺς αὑτοῦ θυγατριδοῦς
ζημιῶσαι; καί μοι ἀνάβητε τούτων μάρτυρες.

ΜΑΡΤΥΡΕΣ.

28   Τῶν μὲν μαρτύρων ἀκηκόατε, ὦ δικασταί· ἐγὼ δ᾽ ὅσα
τελευτῶν ὡμολόγησεν ἔχειν αὐτὸς χρήματα, ἑπτὰ τάλαντα
καὶ τετταράκοντα μνᾶς, ἐκ τούτων αὐτῷ λογιοῦμαι, πρόσ-
οδον μὲν οὐδεμίαν ἀποφαίνων, ἀπὸ δὲ τῶν ὑπαρχόντων
ἀναλίσκων, καὶ θήσω ὅσον οὐδεὶς πώποτ᾽ ἐν τῇ πόλει, εἰς
205 δύο παῖδας καὶ ἀδελφὴν καὶ παιδαγωγὸν καὶ θεράπαιναν
χιλίας δραχμὰς ἑκάστου ἐνιαυτοῦ, μικρῷ ἔλαττον ἢ τρεῖς
29 δραχμὰς τῆς ἡμέρας. ἐν ὀκτὼ ἔτεσιν αὗται γίγνονται
ὀκτακισχίλιαι δραχμαί, καὶ ἀποδείκνυνται ἐξ τάλαντι
περιόντα καὶ εἴκοσι μναῖ. οὐ γὰρ ἂν δύναιτο ἀποδεῖξαι
210 οὔθ᾽ ὑπὸ λῃστῶν ἀπολωλεκὼς οὔτε ζημίαν εἰληφὼς οὔτε
χρήσταις ἀποδεδωκώς. . . .

quires *which* (ἅ) in the second clause,
but Greek avoids the repetition of
the relative in a new case by omitting
it or by using a pers. or dem. pron.
Cf. περὶ τούτων, below, and VII. 40,
XXII. 13, 21, and see G. 1040, 1041;
H. 1005. — **αὐτὸς μόνος** : for the contrast, see on XXXI. 17. — **ζημιῶσαι** :
mulct, see on ζημίαις, § 21.

28. **ὡμολόγησεν** : for the fact, *cf.*
§ 20. — **ὑπαρχόντων** : *principal*, see
on XXXI. 15. — **θήσω** : see on § 21. —
παιδαγωγόν : see on § 16. — **χιλίας
δραχμάς** : a liberal allowance for the
time of Lysias. Even later, seven
minae a year was the allowance of
Demosthenes in his minority, his

sister and his mother. Boeckh calculated that a family of four grown
persons could obtain the mere necessaries of life for 360 drachmae a year.
Staatsh. I, 142 ff.

29. **καὶ ἀποδείκνυνται** : see App. —
ἀπολωλεκώς : used absolutely ; *cf.*
ἀποδεδωκώς, below. — **ζημίαν εἰληφώς** :
probably a commercial phrase, in
which λαμβάνω takes the place of the
somewhat legal word ὀφλισκάνω. *Cf.*
κέρδος λαβεῖν, Ar. *Ach.* 906, *Nub.* 1064,
κακὸν λαβεῖν, *Nub.* 1310, Xen. *Symp.*
iv. 50, and ζημίαν λαβεῖν ἄμεινόν ἐστιν
ἢ κέρδος κακόν, Soph. *frag.* 738 Nauck.²
For ζημίαν, see on § 21. — Dionysius
quotes no more of this speech.

APPENDIX.

I. — MANUSCRIPTS AND EDITIONS.

A. — MANUSCRIPTS.

THE CODEX PALATINUS X (Heidelbergensis 88) is the sole early authority for the text of all but one[1] of the orations of Lysias printed in the present edition. All the other manuscripts of these orations were copied from X, as Hermann Sauppe showed in his *Epistola Critica ad Godofredum Hermannum scripta*, Lipsiae, 1841, p. 7 ff. This manuscript, written in the twelfth century, was brought from Nicaea to the west; from Italy it passed to Heidelberg; in 1622 it was carried off to Rome by Leo Allatius and in 1797 by Napoleon to Paris; finally in 1815 it was returned to Heidelberg. It is on parchment, consists of 142 leaves, and was written throughout by one hand, but contains a few corrections by a second; most of the corrections were made by the first writer himself. In many cases he found a choice of readings even in his archetype, either variants or emendations, which he wrote in, without deciding which were the better.[2] The manuscript on the whole has a low reputation for correctness. Aside from this, it had suffered greatly before it reached Italy for the first time, having lost one whole quaternion and three leaves of another. The former contained the end of oration xxv, a whole speech κατὰ Νικίδου ἀργίας (as the index on folio 1 of the Ms. shows), and the beginning of xxvi; the latter included the end of v and the beginning and part of the middle of vi. Further, folio 9 (in oration ii) is stained by some black liquid so that most of both sides of the leaf is, and was before the Ms. came to Italy, illegible. Sauppe was the first to prove that all the other Mss. were copied from this after its mutilation and defacement, as they exhibit the same lacunae and make sad

---

[1] Oration xxxii; see Appendix to it. Further, orations i and ii (not here printed), though they are found in X, also come from a different family; see M. Erdmann, *de Pseudolysiae Epitaphii codd.*, Strassburg, 1881.

[2] On the history of the Ms., Sauppe, *ibid.*, Schöll, *Hermes*, XI, p. 202 ff.

work of the passage written on the soiled leaf. The first printed edition, that of Aldus, shows the same deficiencies. It is evident, therefore, that the readings of the copies are of no more critical importance than the conjectures of the learned of to-day. It was natural that many of these readings should be happy, correcting as they did manifest errors in X. This is especially true of those of

CODEX LAURENTIANUS C (pl. 57, 4), which Bekker (who preceded Sauppe) held to be the best Ms. of Lysias. The other principal copies will be found cited in Bekker's edition. I mention here only the two to which I have had occasion to refer in the following notes : —

CODEX VATICANUS M (66).
CODEX URBINAS O (117).

The latter gets its name from the *Bibliotheca Urbinas,* added to the library of the Vatican in 1657.

B. — PRINCIPAL EDITIONS.

EDITIO PRINCEPS : ALDUS, *Venice,* 1513. In his *Oratores Graeci* (generally so called, though Aldus speaks of them as *Rhetores*), I, pp. 86–197 (including the Life and Estimate by Dionysius of Halicarnassus). Aldus used either X or a copy; see Sauppe, *Epist. Crit.* p. 9 ; Schöll, *Hermes,* XI, p. 204 note.

Stephanus, Geneva, 1575. In his *Oratorum Veterum Orationes.* The citations of Lysias in Liddell and Scott's Lexicon are made by its pages. Professor Seymour kindly lent me his copy of this book, but I have used my own copy (formerly W. H. Thompson's) of the Aldine.

Taylor, London, 1739. *Lysiae Orationes et Fragmenta.* With his own notes and those of Markland.

Reiske, Leipzig, 1772. In Vols. V and VI of his *Oratores Graeci.*

Bekker, Berlin (also *Oxford*), 1823. In Vol. I of his *Oratores Attici.*

Dobson, London, 1828. In Vol. II of his *Oratores Attici* with variorum notes including those of Dobree.

Baiter and Sauppe, Zurich, 1839–1843. In their *Oratores Attici.*

Scheibe, Leipzig, 1852, and (in 1855) *Lysiae Orationes ad codicem Palatinum nunc denuo collatum.* Often reprinted.

Westermann, Leipzig, 1854. *Lysiae Orationes.*

Cobet, Amsterdam, 1863. *Lysiae Orationes.*

SELECTED ORATIONS WITH COMMENTARY.

Rauchenstein, Berlin, 1848. *Ausgewählte Reden des Lysias.* Revised seven times by him and now (for Orations XII, XIII, XVI, XXV, XXXI) in its tenth, 1889, and (for VII, XIX, XXII, XXIII, XXIV, XXX, XXXII) ninth, 1886, edition as revised by *Fuhr.* With critical and explanatory notes.

Van Herwerden, Groningen, 1863. *Lysiae Orationes Selectae* (I, XII, XIII, XVI, XXV, XXXII). With critical notes.

Frohberger, Leipzig, 1865–1870. *Ausgewählte Reden von Lysias.* Vol. I, Or. XII, XIII, XXV, 1865; revised by *Gebauer,* 1880. Vol. II, Or. I, X, XIV, XV, XXXII, 1868. Vol. III, Or. XVI, XIX, XXIV, XXX, XXXI (with a grammatical and a subject index), 1870. Explanatory and (extremely long) critical notes.

The same, Leipzig, 1873–1875. *Kleine Ausgabe.* Vol. I, Or. XII, XIII, XVI, XXV, XXXI, 1873; revised by *Gebauer,* 1882. Vol. II, Or. VII, X, XIV, XV, XIX, XXII, XXIV, XXX, XXXII, 1875; revised by *Thalheim,* 1892.

Stevens, Chicago, 1876. *Select Orations of Lysias with introductions and explanatory notes* (Or. II, VII, XII, XIII, XXII). Several times reprinted.

Shuckburgh, London, 1882. *Lysiae Orationes XVI with analysis, notes, appendices and indices* (Or. V, VII, IX, X, XII, XIII, XIV, XVI, XVII, XIX, XXII, XXIII, XXIV, XXVIII, XXX, XXXII). Now in its fourth edition, 1890.

Kocks, Gotha, 1885–1887. *Ausgewählte Reden des Lysias.* Vol. I, Or. VII, XII, XIII, XVI, XIX, 1885. Vol. II, Or. XXI, XXII, XXIII, XXIV, XXV, XXVIII, XXX, XXXI, XXXII, XXXIII, 1887. With short explanatory notes.

Weidner, Leipzig, 1888. *Lysiae Orationes Selectae, mit Einleitungen, erklärendem Index und einem Anhang aus Xenophons Griechischer Geschichte.* Contains Or. I, VII, X, XII, XIII, XVI, XIX, XXII, XXIII, XXIV, XXV, XXX, XXXI, XXXII, with a brief collation of X.

Bristol, Boston, 1892. *Ten Selected Orations of Lysias* (VII, XII, XVI, XVII, XIX, XXII, XXIII, XXIV, XXXII, XXXIII). With explanatory notes and appendices.

II. — CRITICAL NOTES.

For the Ms. readings I have depended on Kayser's collation of X in Scheibe's second edition (using a reprint of 1871); on the additions and corrections of Lampros (in *Hermes,* X, p. 257 ff.) and of Schöll (*ibid.,* XI, p. 202 ff.); and on Weidner's critical appendix. I have printed the text of X everywhere unless the contrary is indicated in the following notes, except that I have felt with Schöll (*l.c.*) that there was no need (especially in an edition of this grade) of cataloguing mere orthographical variants of a sort that contribute nothing whatever to our knowledge of the text of Lysias, being errors with which all Mss. of the time abound. I do not mean cases in which the spelling of words is or has been in dispute, but blunders like οὐχ᾽ ὡς, ὑφῶν, μεταταῦτα, ἐπειδ᾽ ἄν, obvious mistakes in breathings, the omission of ι subscript and points like μηδεμία. Those who need to study such matters will find the material in the articles of Lampros and Schöll. Further, my text agrees with that of Fuhr (in his tenth edition of XII, XVI, XXXI, and his ninth of VII, XXII, XXIII, XXIV, XXXII), unless the contrary is stated. It will be seen that I have drawn freely from his critical appendix, as well as from that of Frohberger-Gebauer-Thalheim. The following abbreviations are used in the notes (besides the letters X, C, cod. M, O, referring to the Mss.): —

B., Bekker; Cob., Cobet; F., Fuhr; Fr., Frohberger; Herw., Van Herwerden; M., Markland (the Vatican Ms. is rarely cited and always as cod. M.); R., Reiske; Rn., Rauchenstein; S., Sauppe; Sch., Scheibe; T., Taylor; Turr., Turicenses Editores; W., Weidner. Some of these abbreviations are avoided in the App. to XXXII to prevent confusion with the signs for the special Mss. of that speech. By 'Meisterhans' is meant his *Grammatik der Attischen Inschriften,* and by '*Bl.-Kühn. Gr.*', the *Ausführliche Grammatik* of Kühner, revised by Blass, 1890 ff.

VII.

Title. περὶ: Harp., Phot. ὑπὲρ, X.

1. ἀπροσδοκήτοις: T. ἀπροσδοκήτως, X. — κοινοὶ: Stephanus. οἱ κοινοί, X.

2. ἐλάαν: Cobet, *cf.* Meisterhans, p. 24. ἐλαίαν, X. So throughout the speech. — προσῆσαν: Rn. προσῄεσαν, X. — φασιν: M., omitted in X. — ἡγού-
ηγού
μενοι: οἰόμενοι, X. Either might stand (*cf.* Schöll, *Hermes,* XI, p. 210), but F. quotes XII. 25, 36, 54, 85, 96, 100, to show that ἡγούμενοι is the commoner; οἰόμενοι occurs in XIII. 86. — ἀπορωτάτην: X, vulg. ἀπορωτέραν, Tournier, Graux, F. — ψευδῆ ἀποδεῖξαι: Dobree, Francken. ἀποδεῖξαι, X. ἀπελέγξαι, Westermann, Sch., F., Fr., but this word is not found, except in Antiphon, until late. ἀπολύσασθαι, Dobree, W. — αὐτοῖς: S. αὐτοῖς, X.

3. ἄμ᾽... ἀκούσαντα: S. ἀλλ᾽... ἀκούσαντας, X. This, according to Lutz (*die Casus-adverbien bei den attischen Rednern,* p. 33), is the only place where Lysias uses ἅμα joined with a person. With things, ἅμα τούτῳ κραυγὴ γίγνεται, XIII. 71; ἅμα τῇ ἡμέρᾳ, frag. I. 4.

4. **δημευθέντων δ' ἐκείνου τῶν ὄντων**: Meutzner, Thalheim. *δημευθέντων τῶν ὄντων δ' ἐκείνου*, X, Sch. *δημευθέντων δὲ τῶν ἐκείνου*, Rn., F. — **δωρειάν**: Morgan, *cf.* Meisterhans, p. 31 f., Bl.-Kühn. *Gr.* I, p. 139. *δωρεάν*, X, edd. — **ὠνοῦμαι**: Emperius. *ὠνούμην*, X. *ἐωνούμην*, Sch., Fr., but the impf. has not an aoristic sense here nor in the passages usually cited to support it, XXII. 11, Aesch. III. 91, Andoc. I. 134. — **'Ἀπολλόδωρος**: there was a long discussion and investigation in the matter of the rewards to be given to the murderers. We have a contemporary document bearing upon it in an inscription, *CIA*. I, 59, discussed in Hicks, *Greek Historical Inscriptions*, p. 105 ff.

5. **μυρίαι**: O. *μορίαι*, X.

6. **ὁ πόλεμος**, Dobree. *πόλεμος*, X. — **τότε τῇ**: R. *τῇ*, X. — **καὶ ὅτι τοῦτο**: Röhl, F. *καὶ τοῦτο*, X. After *ἄλλως τε καὶ* we generally have a participle or a causal, rarely a conditional or temporal conj. It stands with a finite verb only in late authors (Fuhr). — **πλεῖν**: Franke, F., Geb., W. *πλεῖον̮*, X. On the form *πλεῖν*, see Bl.-Kühn., *Gr.* I, p. 216, where it is explained not as a contraction but as a shortened form ('hyphaeresis') of *πλεῖον*, *cf.* *οἶμαι* and *οἴομαι*. In Attic classical inscriptions *πλεῖν* is not found, but only *πλέον*, not *πλεῖον*, Meisterhans, p. 120, but the language of some of them contradicts Moeris, p. 294, *πλεῖν ἢ μύριοι*, *Ἀττικῶς*, *cf.* Schwab, *Hist. Syntax der Griechischen Comparativen*, pp. 197, 202, 211.

7. **θαυμαστὸν δ'**: C. *δ'* om. X. — **ἠδυνάμεθα**: see App. to XII. 99. — **ὅσῳ**: Meutzner. *ὅσοι*, X.

10. **ὃς δύο**: Harp., Suid., Phot. *s.v. σηκός*. *δύο δ'*, X. — **τρίτῳ δὲ ἔτει**: vulg. *τρίτῳ δὲ*, X. — **εἰργάσατο**: S. *εἰργάσατο ἐνιαυτόν*, X. — **ὃς τέθνηκε· κᾆτα τρία ἔτη**: S. after Meutzner. *ὃς τέθνηκε ταῦτα τρία ἔτη*, X. But the point of interest to the speaker is the length of the leases, not the date of the death of Alcias. — **Πρωτέας**: X has *Πρωτέως*.

11. **σηκὸν**: vulg. *οἶκον*, X. — **φανερώτερον**: schedae Brulart. (notes on the margin of Stephanus's edition in the *Bibl. Nationale*), M., T. *φανερῶς*, X.

12. **αἱρούμενος**: S. *ἡγούμενος*, X. — **σκοπεῖν**: X, vulg. *σκοπεῖν ἄν*, Fr., F., W. But the pres. inf. alone here represents the impf. of the judges' thought and the following impf. *ἐπεχείρουν* is unchanged in tense from their direct thought, although it is changed in person, from the third to the first. The condition is a simple one, not contrary to fact: 'if he made this attempt, he was considering,' etc. — **ἐγίγνετό μοι**: Rn. *ἐγίνετο τῷ*, X. On the tense, F. and Fr. compare *ἐκέρδαινον*, § 32, but they miss the point that *ἐγίγνετο* is an indir. question. — **περιποιήσαντι**: Kayser. *τῷ* (del. Dobree) *ποιήσαντι*, X.

13. **καὶ ὑμᾶς**: *καὶ ὑ̮μᾶς*, X. — **ἐγίγνετο**: *ἐγίνετο*, X.

14. **ἐνόντος**: Cob. *ὄντος*, X. — **παρ' ὑμῖν**: X, Sch. *παρ' ὑμῶν*, Meutzner, F., Fr., W. I have returned to the reading of X, influenced by the passages quoted in the note and by Dem. XIX. 137, LIV. 39, quoted by Lutz, *Präpositionen*, p. 147. So Thalheim. — **ἐγὼ δέ**: inserted by Frei as a contrast to *οὗτος μέντοι*.

— τοιοῦτον : Hertlein. τούτων, X. — γιγνομένας : Gildersleeve in a private letter. γενομένας, X, edd. If γενομένας stands, it can only be indir. disc. after ἀποφήναιμι; and as it must refer to past time, it makes nonsense. Fr. takes ἄν with both γενομένας (representing an aor. indic.) and ἀποφήναιμι, a potential opt.; but this is impossible, and nothing like it can be found, for in Dem. xxxxv. 71, quoted by Fr., μαθών is equiv. to a protasis. Hamaker conjectured ἀποφήναιμ' ἄν. But Gildersleeve's is the neater emendation, and involves the slightest possible change, from γενομένας to γινομένας. On the sense of the impf. partic. here, see the note on ἐγίγνετο in § 13, the suggestion for which comes from the same scholar.

16. ἄν ᾖ : Morgan, cf. §§ 18, 20, 28, and see Rutherford, *New Phrynichus,* p. 243. ἄν ἦν, X, edd. — οὐκ ἄν οἷόν τε ἦν δίκην με : X, Sch., Fr. οὐκ ἄν οἷός τε ἦν δίκην, Cob., F., W. — ἤδη : W. ᾔδειν, Emperius, Fr., F. εἰδείην, X, Sch.

17. οἰκετῶν : Palmer. εἰκότων, X. — σῶν : Cob. σῶον, X. — ἀνενεγκεῖν : C. ἂν ἐνεγκεῖν, X.

18. ᾖ : Cob. ἦν, X, cett. — τοὺς παριόντας ἤ : X, Rn., Fr. Omitted after Dobree by Sch., F., on the ground that the danger the speaker ran from the passers-by had been mentioned in § 15; for he treats of 1) παριόντες (§ 15); 2) οἰκέται (§ 16); 3) his tenants (§ 17); 4) his neighbours (§ 18). But, as Thalheim remarks, *die παριόντες werden hier in anderem Zusammenhang erwähnt als* § 15. The τοὺς περιοικοῦντας γείτονας of Hamaker, W., is attractive, but not necessary. — ἀποκρυπτόμεθα : X. ἀποκρυπτόμενοι οἰόμεθα, Sch.

19. ὅς φησιν ὡς : X, edd. except W., who omits ὅς φησιν, probably rightly. No exact parallels for φησιν ὡς are quoted, except Xen. *Hellen.* vi. 3. 7, Theoph. *Char.* 29. — παρειστήκη : Cob. παρειστήκει, X, cett.

20. ὑπέλιπες : Franz. ἀπέλιπες, X. — ᾖ : Morgan. ἦν, X, cett.

21. σοι : Aldus. μοι, X.

22. ὡς φῂς μ' ἰδών : after φῄς of Blass; but for the ι subscript (so Thalheim), see Bl.-Kühn. *Gr.* § 289, Anm. 3. φῂσ · μὴ δεῖν, X. εὐθύς μ' ἰδών, F. ὅτε φῇς μ' ἰδεῖν, M., Thalheim. φήσας μ' ἰδεῖν, R., Sch. εἰ φῂς μέν μ' ἰδεῖν ... τοὺς δ' ἄρχοντας, W. — οὗτοι : Muretus. οὕτω, X, Sch., Fr.

23. ὅτ' εἰ μὲν : Rn., Thalheim. ὃς εἰ μὲν, X, but the rel. in such a usage should refer to the subject of πάσχω. ὅσῳ εἰ μὲν, Sch., F., but in this usage a comp. or sup. commonly stands with ὅσῳ, cf. § 7. — ταύτην ζημίαν : B. ταύτην τὴν ζημίαν, X. — τούτου μὲν : Auger. τοῦτο μὲν, X. — ἅμα : B. ἀλλα, X. — τε λόγων : B. γε λόγων, X.

24. πυρκαϊὰς : the word πυρκαϊά regularly means *fire* or, in law, arson. Here it is to be interpreted either as in the note or as a burnt stump which has grown up again into a wild olive (see introd. to this speech, p. 3). But either interpretation is unique for this word, and the ancient lexicographers take no notice of it. It may be corrupt. Sandys suggests πυκνάς, cf. Xen. *Anab.* iv. 8. 2. — καὶ ἐκκόψαι : bracketed by F., following Halbertsma and Fr.

25. **καὶ τὴν πατρίδα** : added by Kayser, except καὶ added by Sch. — **ἐπιγνώμονας**: M., after Harpocration. γνώμονας, X. — **παρέχομαι**: W. So xii. 74, where F.¹⁰ follows him, but cf. xxii. 12. παρέξομαι, X, F.⁹ — **ἐζημίωσέ μ᾽ ὡς**: Meutzner. Without μ᾽, X. — **ἐργαζόμενον**: C. ἐργαζομένους, X.

26. **οὕτω**: inserted before περὶ by Dobree. — **μίαν μορίαν**: Herw., Fr. μορίαν, X. μίαν, Blass, Thalheim.

27. **τῶν τριάκοντα**: X has τῶν 'λ. — **τοιοῦτον**: B. τοιοῦτο, X, but see Bl.-Kühn. Gr. I, p. 606.

28. **ἦ**: Morgan. ἦν, X, cett.

29. **μορίων**: Fr. μοριῶν, cett. See p. 3, note 25. — **ἐπεργαζόμενον**: R. ἀπεργαζόμενον, X. — **ζημιῶσαί με**: Meutzner, Fr. cf. § 25. ζημιῶσαι, X. με before πώποτε, R. — **ἀπογράψαι**: in X stands ἀπέγραψέ. — **με**: T. με ἐγγὺς, X.

31. **ἢ ὡς**: T., Fr. ὡς, X. ὧν, R., W., but see Bohlmann, de attractionis usu, p. 34. — **τἄλλα**: in the much debated state of the question of accent, I have with F. followed X. τᾶλλα, Fr., W., Sch. See G. 119; H. 106; Bl.-Kühn. Gr. I, p. 331, Anm. 4. — **λητουργῶν**: F., Thalheim, after Meisterhans, § 15, 3; Bl.-Kühn. Gr. I, pp. 185, 252. λειτουργῶν, X, W.

34. **γὰρ ἔχων**: R. παρέχων, X. — **ἔτι εἰσὶν**: Westermann, Fr., Rn., W. εἰσὶν, X, F. — **ἕτοιμός εἰμι**: Sch. ἕτοιμος ἤμην, X. Possibly ἕτοιμος stood here without a verb (as often, see Kühn. Gr. § 354 c), and ἤμην (see Bl.-Kühn, Gr. II, p. 222) was a late addition. — **ἰσχυρότατον**: B. ἰσχυρότερον, X, Fr., W.

35. **δοκεῖ δεινὸν εἶναι**: cod. Venetus acc. to T. δοκεῖν εἶναι, X. — **περὶ αὐτῶν**: in X περὶ αὐτῶν. — **ἔλοιντο**: Rn. εἵλοντο, X.

36. **οἶμαι εἶναι**: T., from a Ms. εἶναι εἰπεῖν, X.

37. **ἔλεγον ἃ οὗτος ἐβούλετο**: B. The last three words stand after ὡμολόγουν in X. εἰ ἤλεγχον, Sch. — **προσῆκεν**: T., M. προσήκει, X. — **μετ᾽ ἐμοῦ**: Stephanus, Sched. Brul. with the note V.C. (vetus codex according to Reiske). This usage of μετά seems to be unique in the orators, for Isocr. iv. 53, quoted by Rn., is not a parallel; see Lutz, pp. 84, 82. μητ᾽ ἐμοῦ, X. πρὸς ἐμοῦ, C; see Lutz, p. 155.

38. **τοῦτον**: T. τούτῳ, X.

39. **γὰρ**: suggested by F. and inserted by Thalheim. — **εἰδέναι**: F., after Bartelt. ἐγνωκέναι, Hamaker, Sch., Thalheim, W. In X a verb is lacking. — **ἐπαιτιώτατοι**: for a full consideration of this passage, see my note in Harvard Classical Studies, Vol. V, 1894.

40. **ἕνεκα**: C. οὕνεκα, X, see on xxii. 3. — **ἥδιον**: T. ἤδη, X. — **ἐμὲ αὐτῶν**: Schott. ἐμὲ αὐτὸν, X.

42. **παρὰ**: C. ἢ ἄρα, X.

43. **παραδιδόντος**: Fr. διδόντος, X.

XII.

1. τοιαῦτα: X. τοιαῦτα γὰρ, Contius, W., but the asyndeton is more striking; cf. 84, and οὕτως, XXXII. 21, XIII. 31. — **ἀνάγκη:** Krüger's remark (*Spr.* 62, 1, Anm. 3), that ἐστί very rarely occurs with this word, holds good for Lysias. ἀνάγκη occurs twelve times: with ἐστί, twice, XIII. 92 and 44 (but in the latter there is no inf.); without ἐστί, seven times, IV. 8, X. 5, XII. 1, XIX. 1, 3, XXII. 7, XXVI. 6; with ἦν, twice, XIII. 79, XXXIII. 4; with γεγένηται, once, XXXII. 1. Only in the last passage is the dat. used with the phrase, and it is inserted between ἀνάγκη and its verb. For the usage of Andoc., see *Harvard Stud. in Class. Phil.* II, 57. *Cf.* App. to XVI. 7.

2. πρὸ τοῦ: Lysias uses πρό only seven times, always temporally; see Lutz, *Präp.* pp. 3, 60. — **ὑπὲρ τῶν ἰδίων ἤ:** om. F., following Herw.

3. ποιήσομαι: X, F., W., Fr. ποιήσωμαι, vulg. Weber, *Entwick. der Absichts-sätze*, p. 161, counts this case among subjvs.; but for examples in prose of this fut., see GMT. 367, and the note in Gebauer's large edition of Lysias. This is the only case of the construction in Lysias. — **δι' ἐλαχίστων:** the only occurrence, according to Lutz, *Präp.* p. 66, of this phrase in the orators.

5. πονηροί: R. πονηροὶ μὲν, X. — **προτρέψαι:** W. τραπέσθαι, X, to which τοὺς λοιποὺς πολίτας must be taken as subj.; but this changed subj. is awkward, especially in view of οὐ τοιαῦτα ποιεῖν ἐτόλμων. F. prefers but does not print W.'s conjecture; cf. Isocr. II. 8, εἰ δέ τις τοὺς κρατοῦντας τοῦ πλήθους ἐπ' ἀρετὴν προτρέψειεν. — **τοιαῦτα λέγοντες:** M. καὶ τοιαῦτα λέγοντες, X.

6. πένεσθαι: M. γενέσθαι, X. — **τὴν δ' ἀρχὴν:** Scaliger. τὴν ἀρχὴν, X.

7. περὶ οὐδενὸς ἡγοῦντο: F. and Fr. speak of this phrase as used for the common παρ' οὐδέν, and Fr. considers it due to parallelism with the following περὶ πολλοῦ. But from Lutz, *Präp.* (p. 152 f.) it would seem that παρ' οὐδέν is not used in this sense in the orators, and Lysias uses περὶ οὐδενὸς in VII. 26 and XXXI. 31, being the first orator to use the phrase with this verb (Lutz, p. 133). — **ἕνεκα:** C. οὕνεκα, X. — **ὥσπερ ... πεποιηκότες:** in such sentences the translation *as if* may be used for convenience, but the partic. is not really conditional, as the neg. in such cases is οὐ. *Cf.* VII. 15 and GMT. 867. For examples in Lysias, see XXV. 31, οἴονται χρῆναι ὃν ἂν βούλωνται κακῶς ποιεῖν, ὥσπερ τῶν μὲν ἄλλων ἀδικούντων, ἄριστοι δὲ ἄνδρες αὐτοὶ γεγενημένοι, and XXIV. 18, XXXII. 22. In all these, the clause with ὥσπερ has an ironical tone. See also XXII. 12.

9. θεοὺς ... νομίζει: translate, *he didn't believe in gods or in men either;* or else, with Sauppe, cf. the Homeric οὐδέ τι τίει ἀνέρας οὐδὲ θεούς, *Il.* ix. 238. For νομίζω in this latter sense examples are scarce, but see Plat. *Gorg.* 466 B, Ar. *Nub.* 962, both passive.

11. ἐπειδὴ: F. ἐπεί, X. See App. to XXXII. 2. — **ὡμολόγητο:** Fritzsche, since the agreement was on both sides. ὡμολο̄γ̣, X. ὡμολόγησα, vulg. — **φιάλας**
ἀργυρᾶς: C. φιάλας Γρ ατ̣ρ̣ X, the correction being by the first hand (Schöll). — **τέτταρας:** Pertz. τέσσαρας, vulg.

12. πρός: rare in Lysias in this local sense, occurring besides in x. 28, xiii. 81, frg. 94 (Lutz, *Präp.* p. 156). — **ὅποι**: cod. Vindobonensis, S. **ὅπῃ**, X. — **τἀδελφοῦ**: Cob. τὰ τοῦ ἀδελφοῦ, X.

14. πρόθυμον: X, F., Fr. πρόθυμος, W.

15. ἤδη: Morgan, see App. to vii. 16. ἤδειν, cett. — **ταύτῃ**: originally a real dat. of the instrument (*sc.* ὁδῷ), and not an 'instrumental'; see Brugmann, *Gr. Gram.*² §§ 83, 187; Bl.-Kühn. *Gr.* § 336, η. So εἰκῇ, vii. 12. For the other view, see G. Meyer, *Gr. Gram.*² p. 364 f.

16. τριῶν θυρῶν: it is impossible to identify these doors with certainty. We do not know how elaborate was the interior of the house of Damnippus, although we know that it ran from one street to another. Nor do we know just where Lysias and Damnippus had their hurried talk. On this subject, see my note in *Harvard Stud. in Class. Phil.* V, p. 52.

17. ἐγὼ μὲν: Ad. Müller. ἐγώ, X. — **πεπυσμένος**: corr. from πεπεισμένος by first hand, X. — **ἐπ' ἐκείνων**: Aldus. ὑπ' ἐκείνων, X.

18. ἐξ οὐδεμιᾶς: Cob. οὐδὲ μιᾶς, X. — **κλεισίον**: S. κλίσιον, X. See Meisterhans, Anm. 172, 328.

19. κτήσεσθαι: Dobree. κτήσασθαι, X. See Madvig, *Adv. Crit.* I, p. 156 ff.; GMT. 127; and my note on δοῦναι, § 26. — **καὶ τοῦ τρόπου**: according to Fr., the clause τῆς γὰρ κτλ. takes the place of a ὥστε clause, as in xiii. 80; *cf.* vi. 17. So Jebb, *Select. from the Attic Orators*, p. 253, comparing Andoc. iii. 33. — **τοῦ αὐτῶν**: vulg. τοῦ αὑτῶν, X. — **ὅτε τὸ πρῶτον**: X, Sch., Gebauer (who cites Xen. *Anab.* vii. 8. 14, Plut. *Arat.* 2, Thuc. iv. 94, Hom. *Od.* xxiii. 213 f.). ὅτε πρῶτον, Hertlein, F.; *cf.* xiv. 16. ὅτε περ πρῶτον, W.; *cf.* xvii. 3.

20. ὥσπερ οὐδ' ἂν: Westermann. ὥσπερ ἂν, X. "Omit the 'not,' the statement remains intelligible, but ceases to be effective." Jebb, *ibid.* — **γ' ὄντας**: vulg. ὄντας, X. — **πάσας μὲν**: R. πάσας, X. — **εἰσενεγκόντας**: M. ἐνεγκόντας, X.

21. εἰς τοὺς πολεμίους: see note. Lutz (*Präp.* p. 9) quotes only this example from Lysias. Of his others, the greater part are military, many being this very phrase. — **ἀτίμους**: M. ἀτίμους τῆς πόλεως, X.

22. τοσοῦτον: vulg. τοιοῦτον, X.

24. ὅσιον: vulg. ὅσον, X. — **ὅ τι**: Brunck. εἴ τι, X.

25. ἦ: Morgan, see App. to vii. 16. ἦν, cett. — **ἵνα ⟨ἀποθάνωμεν ἢ ἵνα μὴ⟩ ἀποθάνωμεν**: the words in brackets are not in X, but were inserted by R.; so Fr., Gebauer. Thus there are two single and three double questions put to Eratosthenes. ἀντέλεγον ἵνα μὴ ἀποθάνητε, F., following Usener, *Rhein. Mus.* XXV, 590; *cf.* Spengel, *Rhet.* I, 165 f. But S. and W. follow X; others insert μὴ from C.

26. ἀποκτείνειας: Kayser. ἀποκτείνῃς, X. — **φῇς**: X, edd., except F., W., φής. So below. But see App. to vii. 22. — **οὐκ ἐμοί**: Madvig, *Adv. Crit.* I, 175. οὐκ οἴει ἐμοί, X, Sch. δεῖν is inserted after τουτοισὶ by Cob. and Gebauer after an earlier conjecture of Madvig, but οἴει χρῆναι, W., is more probable than this; *cf.* § 89, VII. 23, XXX. 8. The reading in the text, however, is the most difficult, and perhaps gives the best cadence.

27. προσετάχθη: R. ἐτάχθη, X. — ἔπειτα: X. ἐπεί τοι, T., Sch. — τῷ **ἧττον:** Canter. τῷ πίστιν, X. — **γνώμην:** X. ἐναντίαν γνώμην, R., Sch., but the preceding ἀντειπών makes this unnecessary.

28. ἐὰν: Cob., following inscriptions; *cf.* Meisterhans, Anm. 262, and p. 213, 38. ἂν, X, vulg.

29. ἰσχυροτέρα: Dobree. ἰσχυροτέρα αὐτῆς, X. — **παρὰ τοῦ:** Canter. παρ' αὐτοῦ, X.

30. μὲν δὴ: C. μηδὲν δη, X. — σώζειν... **παρόν:** S., Sch. σώζοντα αὐτὸν καὶ τὰ τούτοις ἐψηφισμένα ὄν, X. — **πᾶσιν:** R. πάντες, X. — **ὀργίζεσθε:** X. ὠργίζεσθε, M., W., but *cf.* § 31, συγγνώμην ἂν ἔχοιτε.

31. τοῖς διὰ: R. τούτοις διὰ, X.

33. παρ' αὐτοῖς: vulg. παρ' αὐτοῖς, X. — **περὶ αὐτῶν:** vulg. περὶ αὐτῶν, X.

34. ἐτυγχάνετε and **ἀπεψηφίζεσθε:** Kayser. ἐτύχετε and ἀπεψηφίσασθε, X. — **ὑεῖς:** F. υἱεῖς, X, vulg. On the usage of the forms, see Meisterhans, p. 47, § 17, and Bl.-Kühn. *Gr.* I, p. 508; *cf.* App. to XXXII. 4. — **'Ερατοσθένη:** C, B. 'Ερατο-σθένην, X.

35. ὑμέτεροι: R. ἡμέτεροι, X. — **σφᾶς γ αὐτοὺς:** F. σφᾶς αὐτούς, X, Sch. Lysias says either ἢ που... γε, or ἢ που... σφόδρα (so W.). See examples in Gebauer, *De arg. ex contr. form.* p. 71 f. — **περιέργους:** X. περιέργως, T., Sch., but the following partic. shows the reason why they would be περίεργοι. — **ὑπὲρ ὑμῶν:** vulg. ὑπὲρ ἡμῶν, X. — **τιμωρουμένους:** M. τηρουμένους, X, W. Although the middle of τιμωρέομαι generally denotes revenge in *one's own* interest, yet F. cites I. 40 as parallel to the present case. Hence διατεινομένους (Fr.) and κηδομένους (Rn.) are unnecessary. The former is too far from X, the latter too weak for contrast with ἀφήσουσιν.

36. τεθνεώτων: R. τεθνειώτων, X. — **ἀκρίτους:** vulg. ἀκρίτως, X. — **ὑφ':** C. ἀφ', X.

37. οὐδ' ἂν: W. οὐδ', X, F., vulg. — **δύναιντ' ἀξίαν:** W. δύναιντ' ἂν, X, F., vulg. But F. inserts with M. ἀξίαν before δύναιντο.

38. κατηγορούμενα: κατηγορουμένα, X. κατηγορημένα, C, Sch. — **λέγοντες:** corr. from λέγοντας by first hand of X. — **ὑμᾶς:** Bake. ὑμῖν, X, Sch. A possibility would be ἀποδεικνύοντες ὑμῖν. The verb ἐξαπατᾶν is used absolutely in XXXI. 16. — **ἢ ὡς πόλεις:** Meutzner. ἢ πόλεις, M., Sch. πόλεις, X. The conjecture ἢ ὡς πρεσβεύσαντες πόλεις of W. (*cf.* Isocr. XVI. 21, quoted in the note) is attractive but unnecessary.

39. ὑμετέραν: R. ἡμετέραν, X.

40. τοσαῦτα ἐσκύλευσαν: R. ἐσκύλευσαν τοσαῦτα, Sch. τοσαῦτα, om. X. — **εἷλον:** by erasure from εἷχον, first hand of X. — **οἷα τὰ:** Cob. οἷα, X. — **ὅτι ἑαυτοῖς:** after T., Sluiter, Sch. οἷς αὐτοῖς, X. ἑαυτοῖς, Classen.

41. αὐτοῦ: Dobree, Francken, p. 85. αὐτῶν, X, Sch. This may be kept by supposing with Kayser (so W.) that there is a lacuna before § 42, or by inserting οὗτος somewhere after ὅτε πρῶτον in § 42.

42. ἔπραξεν: vulg. ἔπραξαν, X.

43. ὑμετέρῳ: vulg. ἡμετέρῳ, X.

44. φυλὰς: T. φυλακὰς, X, Sch. But the latter would refer to the cavalry, and 1) the ephors had no constitutional powers, and hence could not appoint cavalry officers; 2) if the regular phylarchs were meant, the phrase would be τοὺς φυλάρχους. —**χρείη**: vulg. χρὴ, X. —**μόνον**: changed from μόνων in X by first hand. —**ψηφιεῖσθε**: Cob. ψηφίσαισθε, B., Sch. ψηφίσησθε, X. The fut. indic. here, according to Weber, *ibid.*, p. 163, is in a final, not an object clause, and hence falls under GMT. 324. But *cf.* Aeschin. III. 64 f., where we certainly have object clauses.

45. καλῶς: Fr. καί, X, vulg. —**ὑμᾶς**: M., T. ἡμᾶς, X.

47. κἀκεῖνοι: Hertlein. Om. X.

48. ἐχρῆν ἂν: X, Sch. ἐχρῆν αὐτὸν, B., F., Fr., W. On the use of ἄν here, see GMT. 423, and p. 410. —**ἀλλὰ τὰ**: C. ἀλλὰ τἀληθῆ, X.

50. ἕν τῳ λόγῳ: Lipsius. ἐν τῷ λόγῳ, X, vulg. —**τ' αὐτῷ**: F. τε αὐτῷ, Sch. τ' αὐτὰ ὦ, X.

51. καὶ τὰς: Rn. suggested ἀποδείξω after καί. W. inserts ἑώρα after διαφοράς. Hamaker inserted τε after ἀμφότερα, but this leaves the change still too harsh. —**μόνοι**: R. μοι, X.

52. εἰ: Schott. καί, X. —**κάλλιον**: C, Cob. κάλλιον ἂν, X, vulg. —**κατειληφότος**: vulg. κατειληφότες, X. —**αὐτοῦ**: vulg. αὐτοῦ, X. —**εὔνοιαν**: M. συνουσίαν, X. —**ἐπὶ Φυλῇ**: on the note, *cf.* Vischer in *Rhein. Mus.* IX, 388, who quotes, from an inscription, ἐν Ἐλευσῖνι καὶ Πανάκτῳ καὶ ἐπὶ Φυλῇ (*CIA.* II, part 3, 1217). On the situation and remains of the fortress, see Baedeker's *Greece*, p. 115. —**Ἐλευσῖνάδε**: vulg. ἐλευσίναδε, X.

53. ἐδείξαμεν: Geel. ἔδοξαν, X. —**Πειραιῶς**: T. Πειραιέως, X. —**αὐτοὺς**: W. conjectures τούτους, which is attractive.

55. Φείδων: X has, after this word, ὁ τῶν τριάκοντα, which Herw. struck out. —**Λαμπτρεὺς**: T. Λαμπρεὺς, X. —**καὶ**: om. X. —**αὐτοὶ**: M. αὐτοὺς, X. —τοῖς: R. ἢ τοῖς, X. —**ἄστεως**: see on § 92. ἄστεος, X.

56. ᾦ: Rn., S. οἶ, X. οἶς, Sch. —**τεθνεῶτες**: C. τεθνειότες, X. —**θᾶττον**: Pertz. θᾶσσον, X.

57. εἰ δ' ὑμεῖς δικαίως, οἱ τριάκοντα ἀδίκως: R. εἰ δ' ὑμεῖς ἀδίκως, οἱ τριάκοντα δικαίως, X, Sch. —**δὴ ἑτέρων**: vulg. δι' ἑτέρων, X.

58. κρείττους αὐτῶν: vulg. κρείττους αὐτῶν, X.

59. ἐδανείσατο: vulg. ἐδανείσαντο, X.

60. ὅλας: Fritzsche. Cob. sets it after πόλεις. Om. X. —**οἶς**: T. οὓς, X. — Arist. *Resp. Ath.* 38 throws light on some of the statements of Lysias here. Hitherto, it has been supposed that πόλεις referred to the cities of the Spartan allies, who (except the Boeotians and Corinthians) followed Pausanias when his jealousy of Lysander led him to Athens (Xen. *Hellen.* ii. 4. 30). But Aristotle says that the Ten who succeeded the Thirty had already fallen before the arrival of Pausanias, and that they were succeeded by a Second Ten, who had begun negotiations for peace with the patriots in Piraeus before Pausanias came. (Lysias and the other authors do not mention this Second Ten, see above, p. 26.) The forces, therefore, that aided the First Ten were Lysander, with his mercenaries (Xen. *Hellen.* ii. 4. 28 f., in number one thousand, according to Diod. xiv. 33), and his brother Libys with a fleet (Xen. *ibid.;* of forty ships, Diod. *ibid.*). Aristotle does not here mention either of these by name, but says only that the First Ten were helped by Callibius and the Peloponnesians then at hand, together with some of the knights. Callibius was the harmost, sent with a garrison (of seven hundred, according to Arist. 37) to maintain the Thirty. By Πελοποννησίων τῶν παρόντων Aristotle may mean what was left of this garrison, or he may mean Lysander and Libys with their forces, or both. Lysias is evidently speaking loosely of what was done under the two Tens. For μισθω-σάμενοι cannot truthfully be used of the Second, nor πόλεις ἐπάγοντες of the First; while the words Λακεδαιμονίους καὶ τῶν συμμάχων ... πεῖσαι belong properly to the expedition of Pausanias, who was not summoned by either Ten so far as we know (least of all by the First!). Finally, the following words, οὐ διαλλάξαι ἀλλ' ἀπολέσαι παρεσκευάζοντο can refer only to the First Ten, the Second having actually begun to negotiate before Pausanias arrived. Hence the Second may well be included under the ἄνδρες ἀγαθοί (παρεσκευάζοντο τὴν πόλιν εἰ μὴ δι' ἄνδρας ἀγαθούς).

61. οἶδ᾽ ὅτι οὐ: vulg., Sch. οὐ, om. X. οὐκ οἶδ᾽ ὅτι, F., after W., who however prints ὥστ᾽ οὐκ οἶδ᾽ ὅτι. — πλείστων: R. πλεῖστον, X.

62. Θηραμένους: see above, p. 29. Neither Xenophon nor Thucydides had a very high opinion of this much discussed man, but Aristotle (*Resp. Ath.* 28) eulogizes him highly, and says: "Men of more than superficial judgment do not believe that he was a professional destroyer of all governments, as his detractors say, but rather that he supported all so long as they did not outrage the law; for he was a man who could live under any form of government, — and this is behaving like a good citizen, — but who was the foe, not the tool, of governments that went beyond the laws." — ὡς ἂν: C. ὡς, X. — παραστῇ κτλ.: the explanation in the note, which I owe to Professor Seymour, shows that the text is not defective here, as most editors think. According to them, the idea must be something like 'let nobody *think it strange* (or *wrong*) that I accuse Theramenes.' Gebauer conjectures καὶ μηδενὶ τοῦτο ἐπαχθὲς παραστῇ. W. prints ἀδικῶ Θηραμένους κατηγορῶν. — ἀπολογήσεσθαι: M. ἀπολογήσασθαι, X. — ἐκείνῳ: T. ἐκείνοις, X.

64. γὰρ ἦν: R. γὰρ, X. — τοὺς Θηραμένους: Sch. τοῦ Θηραμένους, X. The article is not used with this name in this speech. — αἰτίου ... γεγενημένου: B. αἰτίους ... γεγενημένους, X.

65. ὑπ᾽ αὐτῶν: S. ὑπ αὐτοῦ, X, W. It does not appear from any other author that the πρόβουλοι had power to fill any of the offices. Theramenes, one of the Four Hundred, was nominated and chosen general by the Four Hundred themselves; see Arist. *Resp. Ath.* 30. Cf. Thuc. viii. 89. 2. But perhaps

Lysias is speaking loosely and does not mean αὐτῶν to refer to the πρόβουλοι but to the Four Hundred, understood in τοῖς πράγμασι.

66. ἑαυτὸν παρεῖχεν: Dobree. ἑαυτὸν τῇ πόλει παρεῖχεν, X. — Κάλλαισχρον: vulg. Κάλαισχρον, X. — προτέρους: Canter. πραοτέρους, X. — αὐτοῦ: Sch. αὐτοῦ, X, vulg.

67. Ἀρχεπτόλεμον: vulg. Ἀρχιπτόλεμον, X. — αὐτῷ: vulg., Sch. αὐτῷ, X, W.

68. ηὑρηκέναι: F., see Meisterhans, p. 136. εὑρηκέναι, X. — αὐτῷ: S., Sch. αὐτῷ, X, vulg.

69. σωτήρια: M. σωτηρίαν, X. — ἕνεκα: Westermann; cf. Meisterhans, p. 177, and see App. to XXII. 3. οὕνεκεν, X. ἕνεκεν, Sch. — ἐν τοῖς αὐτοῦ: vulg. ἐν τοῖς αὐτοῦ, X.

70. αὐτὸς ἐκείνοις: Canter. αὐτοῖς ἐκείνοις, X. — Πειραιῶς: vulg. *Πειραιέως, X. — περιελεῖν: vulg. περιαιρεῖν, X. — καταλῦσαι: vulg. καταλύσαι, X. — ἀποστερήσεσθε: Cob. ἀποστερηθήσεσθε, X.

71. ὡμολογημένος: Westermann. λεγόμενος, X. — ὑπ' ἐκείνων: M. ὑπ' ἐκείνου, X. — ἐκ Σάμου: the exact chronological order of events here is an extremely vexed question. For the latest consideration of it, see Boerner, De rebus a Graecis inde ab a. 410 usque ad a. 403 gestis, Göttingen, 1894, p. 49 ff.

72. παρόντος: Boblenz. παρόντων, X. Either is possible (Schöll). — διαπειλοῖτο: Cob. ἀπειλοῖτο, X. ἀπειλοῖ, Sch. The Greeks used διαπειλοῦμαι and ἀπειλῶ, like διακελεύομαι and κελεύω, διόμνυμαι and ὄμνυμι. — ψηφίσαισθε: vulg. ψηφίσοισθε, X.

73. ὑμᾶς: Contius. ἡμᾶς, X. — ἐξεκλησιάζετε: S., Sch.; so X in XIII. 73 and 76, and cf. Xen. Hellen. v. 3. 16. So the aor. in Thuc. viii. 93; cf. Bl.-Kühn. Gr. II, p. 415. ἐκκλησιάζετε, X, but the present, though in indir. disc., can hardly be retained on account of ἐν ἐκείνῃ τῇ ἡμέρᾳ. ἠκκλησιάζετε, Fr., F., W. after Dind. Dem.[3] praef. xxvii f., and so in Lysias XIII. But the principle of false analogy in augment and reduplication of denominative verbs (Bl.-Kühn. Gr. II, p. 34) appears often in Lysias, e.g. ἐπεδήμησε, XII. 71, cf. XVI. 4; ἐνετεθύμητο, XII. 70; ἐπεθυμοῦμεν, XVI. 11; ἡνειχόμην, III. 9; ἐπιτετροπευμένος, XXXII. 3; ἐπιτετήδευται, XIII. 65; [ἐπηνώρθωσαν, II. 70]; and in I. 25 and XXXII. 11 we should probably emend to ἠντεβόλει.

74. παρέχομαι: R., W. παρέξομαι, X. Cf. VII. 25, XXII. 12. — μέλοι: T. μέλλοι, X. — ποιήσαισθ'... κελεύοι: X, vulg. before Sch. ποιήσετε... κελεύει, Cob., Sch., F. But see GMT. 690.

75. γοῦν: vulg. γ' οὖν, X.

76. παρήγγελτο: Cob., Kayser, on account of the following πρότερον ᾔδεσαν. Cf. Thuc. viii. 66. 1, 69. 2; Dem. XXIII. 14. παρηγγέλλετο, X. — δέκα δ': B., Sch. δέκα δὲ, Aldus. δέκα, X. — τὴν αἰτῶν: vulg. τὴν αὐτῶν, X.

77. ἐν τῇ βουλῇ: the truth of Xenophon's description of this whole scene with its dramatic ending is now open to the gravest doubts. See Aristotle's account of it (Resp. Ath. 37), evidently in part, at least, based on documentary

evidence; *cf.* Bauer, *Lit. und hist. Forschungen zu Arist. Ath. Pol.*, p. 163 f. —
δι' αὐτὸν: S. *δι' αὐτόν*, X, vulg. — **φροντιζόντων**: Dobree, Sch. *φροντίζων δὲ*
(*ἐ*, W.) *τῶν*, X. *φροντιζόντων αὐτῶν*, W. — **τοῖς εἰρημένοις τρόποις ὑπ' ἐμοῦ**: on
this order, *cf.* Dem. XIX. 174, *τὴν μὲν γραφεῖσαν ἐπιστολὴν ὑπ' ἐμοῦ*, and see
Frohberger's critical note in his large edition. Lysias has the noun following
the partic. in XIII. 43, *τὰς γεγενημένας συμφορὰς τῇ πόλει*. But in our passage
I think that the unusual order need not be defended on any general principle,
since it is necessary for clearness in order to separate *αὐτοῖς* which follows
from *τρόποις*. — **αὐτοῖς αἴτιος**: Kayser. *αὐτὸς αἴτιος*, X. — **αὐτοῖς ἔργῳ**: M.,
after C. *αὐτῷ ἔργῳ*, X. *αὐτὸς ἔργῳ*, M., Sch. *αὐτῷ τῷ ἔργῳ*, Fr., W.

78. **αἰτίῳ γεγενημένῳ**: W. *αἰτίου γεγενημένου*, R., Sch. *αἴτιοι γεγενημένοι*, X.
— **αὐτοὺς φίλους**: Stephanus, vulg. *αὐτοὺς φίλους*, X. — **τῆς αὐτοῦ**: B. *τῆς αὐτοῦ*
changed from *αὐτῶν* (vulg. before B.) by the first hand of X. — **ἤδη . . . κατέλυσε**: X, Sch., W. *δὶς . . . κατέλυσε*, S., F., in the belief that it is improbable
that Lysias would not have referred to Theramenes's attempt to overthrow the
Thirty, and for parallelism with the following *δίς*. But Lysias is careful
scarcely to refer at all to any opposition by Theramenes to the Thirty (only
in § 77), for this was what won Theramenes favour with the people.

79. **τῶν τούτου**: Rn. *τῶν τουτουΐ*, X. — **μὲν**: added by R.

80. **μέλλειν**: vulg. *μέλειν*, X. — **ὑμεῖς ὑμῖν**: F.; *cf.* Dem. XXIV. 157. *ὑμῖν
αὐτοῖς*, X.

81. **κατηγόρηται**: Bake, Sch., W. *κατάγνωτε*, Emperius, F. *κατηγορεῖτε*, X.
— **μὲν**: I have adopted this from Fuhr's suggestion in his critical note. For
confusion of *μέν* and *δέ* in the Mss., *cf.* Gebauer to XIII. 30 (smaller edition);
for *μέν*, *μέντοι*, *cf.* Plat. *Protag.* 247 A, Xen. *Anab.* ii. 1. 13. *δή*, Sch. *μὲν
δή*, W. *δὲ*, X. — **αὐτὸς ἦν**: M. *αὐτὸς ἦν*, X. — **κρινομένων**: R. *γινομένων*, X.

82. **καὶ οὗτοι**: Dobree. *καίτοι οὗτοι*, X. — **ἀκρίτους**: X has *ἀκρίτως*; so in
§§ 36 and 83.

83. **ἀποκτείναιτε**: B. *ἀποκτείνοιτε*, vulg., Sch. *ἀπεκτείνοιτο*, X. — **δημεύσαιτε**: R. *δημεύσετε*, X. — **τὰς οἰκίας**: Sch. *οἰκίας*, X.

84. **ἱκανὴν οὐκ**: Sintenis. *οὐκ*, X. Reiske inserted *ἱκανὴν* after *λαβεῖν.
αὐτῶν ἀξίαν*, Rn., W. — **δύναισθε**: B. *δύνησθε*, X. — **δοκεῖ**: vulg. *δοκῇ*, X. —
τοσοῦτον ἤ: R. *τοσοῦτον δ'*, X.

85. **ἐδύναντο**: M. *δύναιντο*, X. — **ἐλθεῖν**: C. *ἐλεῖν*, X. — **ἔσεσθαι καὶ**: Cob.,
Fritzsche; *cf.* XXII. 19, XXX. 34. *ἔσεσθαι τῶν πεπραγμένων*, X. *ἔσεσθαι τῶν
τε πεπραγμένων*, R., S., Sch., F., Fr., W.

86. **συνερούντων**: R. *συνεργούντων*, X. — **κἀγαθοὶ**: T. *ἢ ἀγαθοί*, X. — **τῆς
τούτων**: M. *τῆς*, X. — **ἀπολλύναι**: M. *ἀποδοῦναι*, X. — **οὐδὲ τὰ**: R. *οὔτε τά*, X.

87. **Ἐρατοσθένη**: X has *Ἐρατοσθένην*. — **τεθνεώτων**: C. *τεθνειώτων*, X.

88. **τῶν ἐχθρῶν**: Gebauer. *παρὰ τῶν ἐχθρῶν*, X. — **δεινὸν εἰ**: *δεινὸν οἱ*, X. —
ἀπολέσασιν ἐπ': C, B. *ἀπολέσασιν δήπου ἐπ'*, S., Sch. *ἀπολέσασιν ἦπου ἐπ'*, R.
ἀπολέσασιν ἦπου, X, with a marginal note signifying corruption. — **βοηθεῖν**: vulg.
Νοηθεῖεν, X.

ХII.   189

89. πολλῷ: R.   πολλοί, X. — **ῥᾷον:** Contius.   ῥᾴδιον, X. — **τῶν ἄλλων Ἑλλή-νων:** for the latest and fullest consideration of this class of genitives, see Schwab, *Hist. Syntax der gr. Comparation*, pp. 38 ff., 162 ff., 289 ff.

90. δείξετε: M.   δείξατε, X.

91. τούτων: X, vulg.   τούτου, F.   But see p. 28, note 25. — **κρύβδην εἶναι:** Sch.   κρύβδην, X.

92. Πειραιῶς: vulg.   Πειραιέως, X; also in §§ 94, 95. — **διὰ τοῦτον:** X, B., W. (*Jahrb.* CXXXVIII, p. 312).   διὰ τούτων, C, Sch., F. — **ἄστεως:** F.   ἄστεος, X, vulg.   But see Bl.-Kühn. *Gr.* I, p. 441; Meisterhans, p. 108.

93. μὲν ἐκ: Baiter, Sch.   μὲν ἂν ἐκ, X. — **ὀνειδῶν:** vulg.   ὀνειδιῶν, X.

94. πονηροτάτων: R.   πονηροτέρων, X. — **σφετέρας:** M.   ὑμετέρας, X.

96. ἀπέκτειναν: R.   ἀπέκτεινον, X. — **ἀφέλκοντες:** R.   ἀφελόντες, X. — **αὐτῶν** (in both places): vulg.   αὑτῶν, X.

98. ὠφέλησεν: Boblenz.   ὠφέλησαν, X, Sch. — **σωτήρια:** R.   So X, corrected from σωτηρία by first hand.   σωτηρία, cett. codd.

99. οὐδέν: inserted by Canter. — **ὑπέρ τε τῶν ἱερῶν:** τε inserted by S. — **ἠδύνασθε:** the Ms. gives the augment in ἠ- both here and in VII. 7.   In § 36 and other places generally it gives ἐ-.   In the uncertain state of the question (see Bl.-Kühn. *Gr.* II, p. 404; Meisterhans, p. 134) I have with F. followed the Ms. in all cases.   See G. 517; H. 355 b.

100. ἡμῶν: Auger.   ὑμῶν, X. — **κατεψηφισμένους ἔσεσθαι:** Kayser.   καταψηφιεῖσθαι, X.— There is a full treatment of the popular belief in this period on the state after death by H. Meuss in the *Jahrbücher für Philologie*, CXXXIX, p. 801 ff., *die Vorstellungen vom Dasein nach dem Tode bei den attischen Rednern.*   In the popular speech the dead were called neither body nor soul (σῶμα, ψυχή), but simply 'the dead' (οἱ ἀποθανόντες, οἱ τετελευτηκότες).   Of their physical condition nothing is clearly formulated.   But it was the general view that they still existed.   Death did not mean annihilation, but only the end of life on earth; *cf.* Lys. XII. 88; II. 70.   The dead were supposed to know what went on in the world, as is clear from our passage, although the idea is put more strongly here than anywhere else in the orators.   Elsewhere it is conditioned; *cf.* Isocr. IX. 2, εἴ τις ἐστὶν αἴσθησις τοῖς τετελευκόσι περὶ τῶν ἐνθάδε γιγνομένων (the same in XIX. 42, *cf.* 44; Lycurg. *Leocr.* 136; Dem. XIX. 66, XX. 87, XXIII. 40).   It was believed that one should act so as to please them, and should avoid what would displease them; *cf.* the above passages, Aeschines III. 259; Isaeus IX. 4, 19; Lys. *Frag.* 74, Sch.   Their friends should punish their enemies and murderers (Lys. XIII. 41, 42, 92), for they themselves were helpless (XII. 36, 88).   It is clear that the Homeric idea of a consciousless ψυχή (the ἀμενηνὰ κάρηνα of Od. xi) is gone, although what replaces it is still quite undefined in conception.

XVI.

1. συνῄδη : Morgan. See App. to VII. 16. συνῄδειν, cett.

2. ἀηδῶς : R. ἀηδῶς ἢ κακῶς, X, but R. rightly explained ἢ κακῶς as a gloss.

3. ἐπιδείξω : X, Sch. ἀποδείξω, Herw., F., Fr., W., and so in XXXII. 27, ἐπέδειξε, X, Sch., but ἀπέδειξε, Pluygers, F., Fr. W. In both places the reason for the change seems to be a wish to make Lysias use the same compound throughout a given speech, for in XVI. 7 and 12 the compound of ἀπό is used and also in XXXII. 3, 6, 20, 22, 25. But the task of establishing such conformity in the authors would be endless and useless. *E.g.*, in Lys. XXIX. 13, we have the compound of ἐπί (emended by nobody), but in § 5, ἀπό, in XXX. 15, ἐπί, in § 9, ἀπό. In Dem. XVIII. 95 and 142 ἐπί, in §§ 131, 250 ἀπό, in XXVII. 47, 48, 50, 51, 52 ἐπί, in §§ 19, 26, 62 ἀπό. The subst. ἐπίδειξις occurs in Lys. XXXIII. 2, Dem. XVIII. 280, but ἀπόδειξις, Lys. XII. 19, Dem. XVIII. 300, 310, all in practically the same sense. A different principle seems to govern Herwerden's emendation in Lys. I. 4 where he changed ἐπιδεῖξαι (followed by τοῦτο ὡς) to ἀποδεῖξαι because in § 5 ἐπιδεῖξαι is used with the simple accusative. This is exactly contrary to what he did in XVI. 3, where he changed ἐπιδείξω (followed by τοῦτο ὡς) to ἀποδείξω, although the latter occurs with the simple acc. in § 7 and with the partic. there and in § 12. And if the choice depended on a difference of constructions, we should certainly keep ἐπιδείκνυμι with the strange inf. in XXXII. 27 (*cf.* Xen. *Mem.* ii. 3. 17), since none of the constructions used with ἀποδείκνυμι in the same speech are like this. The fact is, that though properly there was a distinction between the two verbs, they were synonyms in common usage, in the general sense of *show, prove*, and it mattered not which an author wrote. A look over the examples in Demosthenes (see Preuss's Index) is enough to convince one of this ; see also the lexicon. From Lysias, I quote the following constructions : ἐπιδείκνυμι with simple acc., I. 5 ; 21 ; III. 44 ; with partic., XXIV. 1 ; XXX. 15 ; ὅτι, XXVIII. 9 ; XXIX. 13 ; πότερον, XXVIII. 10 ; τοῦτο ὅτι or ὡς, I. 4 ; XVI. 3 ; inf., XXXII. 27 ; mid., XII. 52 ; pass., IV. 12. — ἀποδείκνυμι, with simple acc., XIII. 51 ; XVI. 7 ; XXVIII. 4 ; XXX. 11 ; 13 ; XXXII. 17 ; 20, 22, 25 ; with partic., VII. 39, 43 ; XVI. 12 ; XXIX. 5 ; XXX. 9 ; XXXII. 3 ; 6 ; ὡς, III. 4 ; VII. 14 ; XII. 38 ; XIII. 33 ; 83 ; XIV. 22 ; XXII. 6 ; τοῦτο ὡς, XXIII. 1, *cf.* XII. 34 ; ὅπου, XII. 39 ; περὶ τούτων, XXXI. 16 (corrected by first hand from ἐπι-) ; pass., III. 40 ; XVII. 10 ; XXXII. 29. The conclusion is that we should follow the best codices in all such cases. — φαίνωμαι καί : R. φαίνωμαι, X. — ἵππευον : M. ἵππευον οὔτ᾽ ἐπεδήμουν, X, but the position of the last two words is suspicious, and ἐπεδήμουν may have been suggested by the occurrence below of ἐπεδημοῦμεν.

4. ἐπεδημοῦμεν : M.'s conjecture for the verb of this clause om. in X. — μεθισταμένης τῆς πολιτείας : Aldus, vulg. μεθισταμένῃ τῇ πολιτείᾳ, X.

5. καὶ μηδέν : Halbertsma. καὶ τοῖς μηδέν, X. But there is no distinction intended between the two classes.

6. ἐγγεγραμμένοι : M.   ἐπιγεγραμμένοι, X, wrong on account of the preceding ἐν and dative. — ἀναπράττητε : vulg. before Scheibe. ἀναπράττηται, X. Of recent editors only Jebb and Shuckburgh retain the vulg., but this seems right to me, for it is near the reading of X, and in its tense (GMT. 87) it denotes the repeated number of cases which would arise after the report of the phylarchs had *once for all* (ἀπενεγκεῖν, aor., *cf.* App. to xxxii. 2) been made. Lysias is very careful in observing this distinction between the pres. and aor. subjv. or opt. All the final clauses cited from him by Weber (*Entwick. der Absichtssätze*, p. 160 ff.) bear out the rule in GMT. (save the only apparent exceptions in which εἰδῆτε and ἐπίστησθε appear). This is particularly well illustrated in xii. 72, xxii. 15, and xxxii. 22, where both tenses are used in the same sentence. Fuhr and Sch. read ἀναπράξητε (Schedae Brulart., T., *cf.* Harp. *s.v.* κατάστασις), so Weber himself, p. 162 ; S. and W. read ἀναπράξαιτε.

7. συνδίκοις : followed in X by οὔτε κατάστασιν παραλαβόντα : del. Halbertsma, see Fuhr *ad loc.* — γνῶναι ὅτι : Kayser. γνῶναι διότι X. — ἀποδείξειαν : Cob. ἀποδείξαιεν, X. — αὐτοῖς : dat., in spite of its nearness to the inf., because of φυλάρχοις which belongs closely to the impers. phrase ἀναγκαῖον ἦν. *Cf.* And. ii. 7 and my note in *Harvard Studies in Class. Phil.* II, p. 58. Below, ἱππεύσαντας could not be dat., in spite of its nearness to the impersonal, on account of the preceding ἐκείνοις. The other instances of this impersonal in Lys. are ἀναγκαῖόν μοί ἐστι λέγειν, xvii. 1, and ἀναγκαιότατον ff. in xii. 9, where the μοι belongs to ἐδόκει. See App. to xii. 1.

8. ὥστε μηδὲν δι᾽ ἄλλο με ἡγεῖσθε : T.   ὥστ᾽ εἰ μηδὲν διαβάλλομαι ἡγεῖσθε, X. — ἤ : Morgan, see App. to vii. 16. ἦν, X, edd.

9. ταύτης : X, W. αὐτῆς, Fr., F., but W. notes ' αἰτίαι latius patent quam τὰ κατηγορημένα.' — μόνων : vulg. μόνων̆ (ων above), X. Either form might stand.

10. μηδεπώποτε . . . γενέσθαι : for a full consideration of the syntax of this passage, see my note in *Harvard Studies in Class. Phil.* III, p. 191 f. Add xxxii. 2 to the passages there quoted. For ἔγκλημα in the sense of *ground of complaint*, not the mere written accusation, *cf.* xxxii. 2, and see M. and S., p. 195.

11. διῴκηκα : S. διῴκησα, X. — τὰς : Rn. περὶ τὰς, X, but *cf.* Theopomp. apud Athen. 261 B, 527 A, 532 D. ἑτέρας, Cob., W.

13. Βοιωτούς, Pertz, because Lys. did not use the article with proper names. τοὺς Βοιωτούς, X. — ἔφην : vulg. ἔτι, X. So in Plat. *Protag.* 360 E, ἔφη, B, ἔτι, T. "This use of φάναι is rare enough (see the note), but if it is to be altered it is better to write εἶπον with Dobree, *cf.* i. 23, than to strike out ἔτι with W. and write μ᾽ ἐκέλευον ἐκ τοῦ." F. Still, see W. on this whole passage in *Jahrbücher*, CXXXVIII, p. 318. — παρασκευάσαντα : margin of the Leyden and Hamburg Aldines, R., Fr. παρασκευάσαντι, X.

15. ἐναποθανόντων : M. ἐνθανόντων, X. — ὕστερος : Contius. ὕστερον, X. — Στειριῶς : Cob. Στειριέως, X. Contraction may occur in gen. and acc. of -ευ-stems when -ευ- follows a vowel. G. 267 ; H. 208 D. This regularly happened in

the fifth century and first part of the fourth; Meisterhans, § 55, 9. See on
XXIII. 5. — ἀνθρώποις : vulg. ἀνοῖς, X.

16. παριέναι : Herbst. προσιέναι, X. The object was to get by, not to
attack. — ἀποκληρῶσαι : M.,W., on account of ἀκληρωτί below, so that ἀποχωρίσαι, X, F., would be due to a gloss. *Cf.* Thuc. iv. 8. 9; Hdt. ii. 32; iii. 25.
With ἀποχωρίσαι the phrase ἀπὸ τοῦ λοιποῦ στρατοπέδου must be understood. —
σεσωμένους: W., *cf.* H. 461 a; Veitch, *s.v.*; Bl.-Kühn., II, p. 544; Meisterhans,
§ 69, 3. σεσωσμένους, X, F., vulg.

18. κομᾷ : Hamaker. τολμᾷ, X. But ἀπ’ ὄψεως is pointless without κομᾷ,
and if ἐπιτηδεύματα refers to τολμᾷ, then ἐκ . . . ἐθελόντων has no antithesis.
With ὠφελεῖσθαι Lys. has elsewhere ἐκ and the gen. of *things; cf.* XXI. 18; XXII.
20; XXVII. 7; but of *persons* ὑπό, IX. 14, and ἀπό, XVIII. 20.

19. ἀμπεχόμενοι : Dobree. ἀπερχόμενοι, X.

20. τὰ τῆς πόλεως : R. τῶν τῆς πόλεως, X.

21. τοὺς τοιούτους : Francken. τούτους, X. — ἀξίους τινὸς : Gebauer after
Dobree's τινὸς ἀξίους. In X, τινὸς is omitted, but ἄξιος seems not to occur absolutely in Attic. On the other hand, as τις in this pregnant sense is used (acc.
to Fr., but see XIX. 58 ?) in only one other place in Lys. (XVII. 1), R. was perhaps right in suggesting λόγου, *cf.* [Lys.] IX. 13; better Cobet's πολλοῦ, *cf.*
x. 3, XXXIII. 3. — W. with Francken supposes that the end of the speech is lost,
but see Blass, *Att. Bereds.* I, p. 520 f.

XXII.

1. ὅτι : X, vulg., Thalheim. ὅτε, S., F., Fr., W., unnecessarily, for in the
sense here there is no actual difference between θαυμάζοντες ὅτε and ὅτι, and ὅτε
could not well belong to the *perfect* προσεληλύθασιν. — τοὺς λόγους : Hirschig, F.,
W., approved by Sch., *cf.* XII. 2, XXIV. 26. λόγους, X. ποιουμένους λόγους, Fr.,
Thalheim.

2. ὡς ἀκρίτους : Aldus. ὡς ἀκρίτως, X, C. — γνώσεσθαι : Aldus. γνώσεσθε, X.
— ἀκρίτους ἀπολωλέναι : X, vulg. Röhl considered ἀκρίτους a gloss, and F.
conjectures ἀδίκως. But ἀκρίτους, though an unnecessary addition, is a natural
one from the speaker's point of view; *cf.* Xen. *Anab.* v. 7. 29.

3. ἕνεκα : Sch. here and in §§ 12, 20 (*bis*); *cf.* on VII. 40, XXXII. 10. οὕνεκα, X.
— βουλήν : X. διαβολήν, Halbertsma, Fr., but this leaves μέν without meaning,
and αὐτοῖς and τῶν ἄλλων obscure.

4. αἰσχρὸν δ’ : Dobree, who transferred the δέ from δεδιὼς δὲ, X, C.

5. ἀνάβητε. εἰπὲ σὺ ἐμοί : Fr., on account of σύ, which shows that the first
imv. is addressed to the whole company of dealers. ἀνάβηθι εἰπὲ σὺ ἐμοί, X, C.
ἀνάβηθι καὶ εἰπὲ σὺ ἐμοί, R., Sch.—ἀξιοῖς: S. ἀξιοῖς ᾖ, X, B. ᾖ ἀξιοῖς, Francken,
F., W., Fr. But the ᾖ is more likely to be an interpolation than to have been
transferred in position, and it is not necessary in the formula with ἄλλο τι ;

cf. Plat. *Gorg.* 467 D, 470 B, *Euthyphro* 10 D, and Kr. *Spr.* 62, 3, 8, Kühn. § 587, 18. Yet for ἄλλο τι οὖν ἤ, *cf.* And. I. 95.

6. πλείω σῖτον: M., after σῖτον πλείω, Stephanus.   πλείω om. X, which, acc. to W., has πόλειωιτον corrected to πόλει σῖτον.

7. χρῆν: R.   χρή, X. — καὶ μακρότερον: X, vulg., F.   διὰ μακροτέρων, P. R. Mueller, Fr., W., as the usual phrase, *cf.* Isocr. xiv. 3. Cobet wrote μακρότερα, on the ground that not μακρῶς but μακρὰ εἰπεῖν (*cf.* Isocr. iv. 73) is proper; but *cf.* λεγόμενον μακρῶς, Antiph. *Incert.* 268 Kock.   And for μακρότερον (= *a longer speech*) F. compares Hyper. iii. xlviii. 20, βραχὺ δ᾽ ἔτι εἰπών.

8. τέτταρες: Bergk.   δύο, X, *i.e.* in archetype δ΄ (= τέτταρες) which was taken for δύο.   *Cf.* Kaibel on And. I. 17 in *Hermes* XVII, p. 414, Droysen, *Sitzungsber. d. Berl. Akad.*, 1882, p. 218.   νῦν, Thalheim. — φιλονεικοῦσιν: X. φιλονικοῦσιν, F., W. — κἂν ὀβολῷ: Graux, F., W. (who omits αὐτούς).   ὀβολῷ X, vulg.   See p. 90, note 18.

9. δὲ τῆτες: Emperius, Thalheim.   δὲ ἐπίτηδες, X.   δ᾽ ἔτι τῆτες, R., W. δ᾽ ἐπὶ τῆς τῆτες, Fr.   δ᾽ ἐπὶ τῆσδε, B., Sch., F. — καὶ ὡς ... φαίνονται: F. considers this an interpolation, as Lysias does not elsewhere add anything after παρέξομαι but at once produces the witness (in X a lacuna here follows that word with μρα in the margin), and because of the somewhat awkward repetition of οὗτος, τούτους, οὗτοι.   It may be added that the words from οὗτοι δέ seem scarcely to depend strictly upon ὡς, for Anytus would be called merely as a witness to what he had said the year before. Wilamowitz, *Aristoteles und Athen*, I, p. 377, would omit ὡς and set a colon or period before καί.

10. ἀπολογήσεσθαι: Stephanus.   ἀπολογήσασθαι, X, Aldus.

11. ἀλλὰ γὰρ: Aldus, R., edd.   ἀλλὰ μὲν γὰρ, X. — τούτῳ τῷ λόγῳ οὐκ ἐλεήσεσθαι: W., Thalheim; for ἐλεέω similarly used *cf.* § 21, xxvii. 12, xxviii. 14, Plat. *Apol.* 34 C, Dem. xxvii. 53, and see on § 21.   τοῦτον τὸν λόγον οὐκ ἐλεύσεσθαι, X, vulg.   καταφεύξεσθαι, Rn.   τρέψεσθαι, Cob.   πορεύεσθαι, Fr.   On ἐλεύσεσθαι, only here in Attic prose, see Lobeck, *Phryn.*, p. 37 f.   Rutherford (*New Phrynichus*, p. 110) defends it here, believing that the inf. ἰέναι never has a fut. sense.   But see GMT. 30, and for two excellent examples of a future sense in -ιέναι, *cf.* xxv. 22.   It may be that ἐλεύσεσθαι was a gloss on some rare word of similar meaning. — ὑμῖν: C.   ἡμῖν, S.

12. ἕνεκα: see App. to § 3. — νῦν: Hofmeister, *Iota Demonstr.* p. 45.   νυνί, X, vulg. — ὑμᾶς μάρτυρας παρέχομαι: X, Thalheim, vulg. before Sch., who followed M.'s ὑμῖν μάρτυρας παρέξομαι.   ΜΑΡΤΥΡΕΣ, so F., W.   It is true that one might expect αὐτούς with ὑμᾶς (*cf.* vii. 25, xii. 74, Plat. *Apol.* 19 D), yet the change is unnecessary.

14. αὐτοὶ: M.   οὗτοι, X. — κεκλῆσθαι: S.   κεκλεῖσθαι, X, Sch.

15. ἐν τοῖς αὐτοῖς: Rn., Cob., Fr., F.   ἐν τούτοις τοῖς, X, Sch., W.   ἐν τοῖς καιροῖς, Thalheim. — ἐν οἷσπερ: X.   ὥσπερ, Thalheim.   ἐν οἷς περιγίγνονται, W. ἐν οἷσπερ οὐδ᾽, R.   Observe that the clause ὅταν γὰρ κτλ. is not so narrow in sense as not to include war times.

17. ἐστιν: X, F., Fr., Thalheim. ἐστίν, Sch., W., after Hermann's theory, see Göttling, *Accentl.*, p. 404.

18. ἀρνουμένων: a wholly uncertain restoration which, in order to give an antithesis to τοὺς ὁμολογοῦντας, I write after καὶ ἀρνουμένων, Dobree. ἀλλ᾽ ἀρνου-μένων, S., F., W. (where the conjunctions seem unlikely). *Cf.* ἀλλ᾽ ἀμφισβη-τούντων, Fr., ἀμφισβητούντων, Thalheim. λαμβάνειν, X, which M. and Sch. merely omit as dittography from below; but F. suggests that ἁμαρτάνειν may have somehow stood here. πειρωμένων λανθάνειν, R. — ἐπιθυμεῖτε: X, F., Thal-heim, *cf.* GMT. 503, Gebauer, *Arg. ex contr.* p. 50. ἐπεθυμεῖτε, R., Sch. ἐπιθυ-μοῖτε, Dobree, Fr., W. — τῶν ἀρνουμένων: after these words R. and W. add ἢ παρὰ τῶν ὁμολογούντων, unnecessarily, *cf.* xxxii. 21, Xen. *Anab.* vi. 1. 23, both cited by F.

19. τούτων: Kayser. αὐτῶν, X.

20. ἕνεκα: see on § 3. — παραδείγματος: X; om. Dobree, but *cf.* [Isocr.] i. 34, παραδείγματα ποιοῦ τὰ παρεληλυθότα τῶν μελλόντων. — οὕτω γὰρ: X. οὗτοι γάρ, T., W. — μόγις: X, edd. μόνως, P. R. Müller, *cf.* Aeschin. i. 34, μόνως γὰρ ἂν οὕτως ἄνεκτοι γένοιντο, and Dinarch. i. 27. But for μόγις F. cites the use of μόλις in Isocr. viii. 27, [i]. 52, Dem. *Proem.* xxx. — αἱροῦνται: T. αἰτοῦνται, X. — παύσασθαι: Aldus, vulg. before Sch., who with later edd. wrote παύεσθαι for παύσεσθαι, X. But the aor. is the proper tense here as in § 8. *Cf.* GMT. 87, and see App. to xvi. 6.

21. ἀπέθνησκον: *cf.* Meisterhans, p. 50. ἀπέθνῃσκον, X. — ἐφ᾽ οὕς: R. ἐφ᾽ οἷς, X, but *cf.* § 5. — παρὰ τούτων: T. παρ᾽ αὐτῶν, X. — τίν᾽ αὐτοὺς: R. τίνα αὐτοὺς, C. τὴν αὐτὴν, X. — εἰσπλέουσιν: R. ἐκπλέουσιν, X.

22. ὅτου: S. ὅτε, X, Sch. This emendation removes one of the rare uses of the indic. in a general condition cited in GMT. 535.

XXIII.

1. τουτῳὶ: Sch. τούτῳ, X, vulg. On the omission of the article, see Rn. on xiii. 16, xxiv. 6, and Hofmeister, *Ueber Gebr. und Bedeut. des Jota demonstr.*, p. 33 f.

2. ὁπόθεν: M. ὁπότε, X. — Ἱπποθωντίδι: S. from inscriptions, *cf.* Meister-hans, p. 17. ἱπποθοωντίδι, X.

3. τοὺς Ἑρμᾶς, ἵνα οἱ: vulg. τοὺς ἑρμασινᾶ. οἱ, X. τοὺς Ἑρμᾶς οἱ, W. On the position and nature of 'the Hermae' see Milchhöfer in Baumeister's *Denk-mäler*, p. 166, and the passages collected by him in Curtius, *Stadtgeschichte von Athen*, p. XXXIII, 90 ff., and p. XCI, 40 ff. The old view (still defended by Curtius *ibid.* p. 170) that they were a double row running east and west and dividing the market into halves, the 'political agora' lying to the south, is not supported by these passages. These show only that 'the Hermae' began at the

Stoa Poecile (situation doubtful) and the Stoa τοῦ βασιλέως, that they were many, that the place where they stood was called simply οἱ Ἑρμαῖ, that they were a good starting point for making the circuit of that part of the market where were the ἱερὰ καὶ ἀγάλματα, that they were near shops, that they were probably not in a stoa, and that they were in the market. (I owe this note to Professor White.) — γιγνώσκοιεν : γινώσκοιεν, X. — φεύγοι : R. φύγοι, X.

5. Πλαταιῶν : Cobet on Hyperid. *Epitaph.* p. 44 ; *cf.* Meisterhans, p. 37, and see App. to XVI. 15. So Πλαταιαῖς and Πλαταιᾶ throughout this speech. Πλαταιέων, *etc.*, X, vulg. — ὑόν : Morgan, and so below. *Cf.* App. to XII. 34. υἱόν, X, edd.

6. γιγνώσκοι : γινώσκοι, X. — ὑὸν : see on § 5. — ἤδη : Morgan. See App. to XII. 15. — ἕνη : Rn., *cf.* Meisterhans, pp. 66, 130. ἔνη, X, vulg.

9. ὑπὸ τοῦ Heldmann, F., W. ὑπὸ, X, Sch. — ἐμαρτύρησεν : X, which Sch. defends against Westermann's ἐμαρτύρετο. — εἰς αὔριον : Wilamowitz, *Arist. und Athen*, II, p. 371, note 6. εἰς ἀγορὰν, X, edd.

10. ἀντιγραφῆς : edd. before and since B. ἀντιγρᾶ, X. ἀντιγράψεως, C, B. — λέγων : after it Rn.[7] inserted ὁ ἕτερος, believing that there was a difference in meaning between ἐξαιρεῖσθαι and ἀφαιρεῖσθαι here ; but *cf.* F.'s critical note, and M. and S. p. 659.

11. τοῦτον ἐξαιροῖτο ἢ ἄγοι φάσκων : Sch. after R. who conjectured τοῦτον ἐξαιροῖτο ἢ εἰς δουλείαν ἄγοι φάσκων. τοῦτον ἄγοι ἢ φάσκων, X.

13. γιγνώσκειν : γινώσκειν, X. — αὐτὸς : Hertlein. οὗτος, X. — Ἀριστόδικος : C, corrected. ἀριστόδημος, X, C 1.

14. ἐπισκηψάμενος : T. ἐπισκεψάμενος, X. — αὐτοῦ : C. αὐτὸν, X. — ἐπειδὴ : ἐπεί, X. See on XXXII. 2. — ἐξέτεισε : F., *cf.* Meisterhans, p. 144. ἐξέτισε, X, vulg. — καθ' ὅ τι : Morgan. καθότι, X, edd.

15. ἐκεῖ ᾤκει : Rn. after M.'s ᾤκει ἐκεῖ, the adverb being omitted in X.

16. ἃ καὶ : Wilamowitz, *ibid.* p. 372, note 9. καὶ ἃ, X, edd.

XXIV.

1. οὐ πολλοῦ : C, D'Orville, B. πολλοῦ, X, Aldus, R. ὀλίγου, Contius, Cob. πολλὴν ὀλίγου, W. — γὰρ : M., om. X. — ἐφ' ἧς : X, edd. ἐφ' ᾗ, Dobree ; but for the gen., *cf.* Hdt. vii. 150, Isocr. xx. 13 (where, however, his avoidance of hiatus may account for it), and Dem. xxi. 180, τὴν ἐπὶ τῆς πομπῆς καὶ τοῦ μεθύειν πρόφασιν. See Lutz, *Präp.* p. 102. — δοίην : for the fullest consideration of the construction, see Hale in *Transactions Am. Phil. Assoc.* 1893, p. 156 ff. — ἄξιον : as βεβίωκα ἄξιος does not seem to be Greek, we must emend with R. to ἀξίως, or else, as Rn. suggests, insert βίον, unless indeed the distance of ἄξιον from βεβιωκότα accounts for the solecism.

2. δοκεῖ: Aldus.   δοκῇ, X. — εἰ μὲν κτλ.: X, explained, as in the note, by Guttentag, F., Thalheim.   οὐ μὲν γὰρ ἕνεκα χρημάτων με (C) συκοφαντεῖ, S., Sch., and οὐδ᾽ ὡς . . . τιμωρεῖται (omitting ψεύδεται), Cob., Kayser, Sch.

3. ἰᾶσθαι: Cob.   ἰᾶσθαι καλῶς, X.   ἰᾶσθαι, εἰκότως, P. R. Müller, Thalheim.

4. οἷός τ᾽ ὦ: P. R. Müller, W.; cf. Dem. xxxvii. 3.   οἷον, X.   οἷόν τε, Aldus, vulg.   But the subjv. of εἰμί is not elsewhere omitted in this formula in the orators (Schulze, Quaest. Gramm. p. 17, who conjectured οἷόν τ᾽ ᾖ), and in it the personal construction prevails, as Schulze's examples show.   Cf. ὡς ἂν δύνωμαι, xii. 3, 62, xvi. 9, xix. 1.   The omission of the subjv. in Antiphon, v. 32, vi. 8 (if genuine) does not affect the usage in our formula.

5. τὴν . . . εὐπορίαν . . . τὸν ἄλλον: Aldus, C.   τῆς . . . εὐπορίας . . . τῶν ἄλλων, X, Stephanus. — τυγχάνει: X.   τυγχάνω, Aldus.   τυγχάνει ὤν, R., B.

6. ἦν ἂν: T., cf. Bohlmann, de attractionis usu, p. 28.   ἦς ἂν, X.

7. τοὺς καὶ: R.   καὶ τοὺς, X.

8. ἐπόμενα: C, R.   ἐχόμενα, X. — τότε ἀφαιρεθείην: X.   τοῦτο ἀφαιρεθείην, Rosenberg, Fr., W.; but cf. the passages quoted in the note, and Gebauer, de Arg. ex contr. formis, p. 112.

9. κατασταθεὶς: for the occurrence of this aor. pass., see Gebauer, App. to xii. 35 (larger edition), and Bl.-Kühn. Gr. II, pp. 197, 588.   In our passage, F. and Fr. think that it is employed to give a comical rhythmical effect, which they indicate by εἰ γὰρ ἐγὼ | κατασταθεὶς | χορηγὸς | τραγῳδοῖς. — προκαλεσαίμην: R.   προσκαλεσαίμην, X. — καὶ: X.   εἶτα, C, B.   καίτοι, Cob., F., W.   κᾆτα, Gebauer. — τύχοι τι: Emperius.   τύχοι τις, X. — γενόμενον: X.   γενόμενος, C, B. — ὁμολογεῖν ἂν ἐμὲ: inserted by Rn., F., Thalheim, after Kayser's ὁμολογεῖν ἂν, following εἶναι. — καὶ ἔτι πονηρότερον: X, F., Fr.   καὶ τί ἔτι πονηρότερον; S., Cob.   καὶ ἔστι τι πονηρότερον; Sch.

10. ἐγὼ γὰρ οἶμαι: F., after C, which has πάντας οἶμαι, and so B., Turr., Thalheim.   ἐγὼ γὰρ, X.   ἔγνων γὰρ, Sch.   εἰκὸς γὰρ, Kayser, Fr. — τοῦτο ζητεῖν: F. (see his Animad. in Or. Att. p. 37), Thalheim.   τοιοῦτο ζητεῖν, X.   τοιοῦτόν τι ζητεῖν, Sch.   τοιοῦτον ῥᾳστώνην τινὰ ζητεῖν, C, B., Turr. — ἐγώ, καὶ: X, Sch., W.   ἐγὼ ὢν καὶ, R.   ἐγὼ ὢν, Herw., F., Fr., Thalheim, but unnecessarily; see my note. — ἐξηῦρον: ἐξεῦρον, X. — τῶν ἀναγκαίων: this, according to Rademacher (Jahrb. für Philol. CLI, p. 241), is a spurca iocatio.   He compares Xen. Cyr. i. 6. 36, and concludes that the cripple means that he uses a horse for all journeys longer than those εἰς τἀναγκαῖα.

11. ἀναβαίνω: in X follow the words ῥᾴδιόν ἐστι μαθεῖν, del. Sch.

12. τοῦτον ἂν: Kayser.   τοῦτον, X.   σιωπᾶν ἂν, Sch.   Yet the ἂν may be unnecessary if σιωπᾶν represents such an impf. as ἐκέρδαινον in vii. 32; so Kocks. — δυνατός εἰμι: Kayser.   δυνατὸς εἴην, X.

13. πάντας: X, vulg.   As Suid. s.v. ἀνάπηρον has ἐάσαντας, Fr. conjectured ἐλεήσαντας and Rn. πεισθέντας. — θεσμοθέται: inserted by Fr.   Om. X, Sch.

14. οὔθ᾽ οὗτος . . . εὖ ποιῶν: I have indicated a lacuna, being unconvinced by any of the emendations proposed for εὖ ποιῶν of X.   The words εὖ ποιῶν may mean *happily, fortunately* (see Fr., Thalheim), or *and he is right* (*cf.* XXXII. 17, XXVIII. 8); or some word like φαίνεται may be lost. At any rate, we need something to lead up to the following γάρ, which cannot refer back to § 13, as the train of thought is changed at § 14 with ἀλλὰ γάρ, 'enough of this nonsense, for ——' (see on XII. 99). Jebb conjectures οὔθ' οὗτος εὔλογα δοκεῖ ποιεῖν, which seems to me too violent, though it is in the right direction. εὖ φρονῶν, *if he is in his senses*, Rn., F., after ὅστις εὖ φρονῶν, M. οὔθ' ὑμῖν οὗτος (οὗτος ὑμῖν, R., Fr., Thalheim) εὖ ποιῶν, Contius. εὖ νοῶν, S. —ἐπικλήρου: Stephanus. ἐπὶ κλήρου, X.

15. λέγει: C. λέγω, X. —ὀνομάσειε: Rn. ὀνομάσαι, X. —μέλλων: X. μέλλων δόξειν, Herw., Cob., F. —πραόνως, ταῦτα: Kayser, F., Thalheim (Emperius had conjectured πραόνως μηδὲν). πρᾷον ὡς μηδὲ ψεύδηται ταῦτα, X. πραόνως, μηδὲ ψεύδηται, ταῦτα, Sch.

16. τοὺς πενομένους: R. πενομένους, X.

17. πρεσβυτέροις: Fr. ἑτέροις, X, Sch.

18. οὓς ἂν: B. οὓς ἐὰν, X. —ὑπάρξαντας: Stephanus. συνάρξαντας, X.

20. μυροπώλιον: X; *cf.* Dem. xxv. 52, xxxiv. 13, and ἀρτοπώλιον, Ar. *Ran.* 112, *frag.* 1, Kock; also Bl.-Kühn. *Gr.* II, p. 276. μυροπωλεῖον, C, Sch. In C, ὁ δὲ follows this word; in X, οἱ δὲ. —ὅποι: B. ὅπη, X. —τύχῃ: Stephanus (τύχη, Aldus). τύχοι, X. —τοὺς ἐγγυτάτω: M. ἐγγυτάτω, X. —τοὺς πλεῖστον: M. οὐ πλεῖστον, X. —ἀμουγέπου: Morgan; *cf.* Bl.-Kühn. *Gr.* I, p. 614. ἀμοῦ γέ που, edd. since Bekker, who emended ἄλλου γέ που of X.

21. ὑπὲρ: X, edd. except F., Fr., Thalheim (who read περὶ without a note). —ὁμοίως τούτῳ φαύλων: X, Aldus, Sch., Fr.; *cf.* Blass, *Att. Ber.* I, p. 639. φαύλων ὁμοίως τούτῳ, Dobree, F., Thalheim, W.

22. μηδ' οὖ: vulg., where X has μὴ δ' οὖ. Fuhr notes that, if μηδ' οὖ is right, a lacuna must be supposed before it; see his App. to XIX. 49. μὴ τοίνυν οὖ, W. —μόνου: M. μόνον, X. —ἀρχῶν: X. Om. Kayser, Fr., Thalheim, W., *cf.* τῶν καλλίστων καὶ μεγίστων in § 23; but τῶν μεγίστων has just been used in § 21 in a very different sense. Hence I think ἀρχῶν necessary here.

23. δειλαιότατος: M. δικαιότατος, X. —ἀπεστερημένος εἴην: X. For εἴην here Hertlein read ἦν, and Fr. εἰμί, but see note, and *cf.* Gebauer, *de Arg. ex contr. formis*, p. 204. —θῆσθε: B. θέσθε, X. —τὴν ψῆφον: Contius, T. τῇ ψήφῳ, X.

24. φιλαπεχθήμων: after this word F. sets ἀλλ' οὐδ' ἂν ... ὁμοίως (§ 25), and puts ἀλλ' οὐ τοιαύταις ... χρώμενος after βίαιος. But, as Thalheim remarks, the two questions are much alike, ὑβριστής = φιλαπεχθήμων, βίαιος = θρασύς. And as the answer οὐδ' ἂν φήσειε κτλ. evidently refers to § 15, it belongs to the question ἀλλ' ὅτι ... βίαιος, which merely repeats the expression of § 15. —βίου: followed in X by πρὸς τὰ τοιαῦτα, del. Francken and later editors.

25. ἀλλ' οὐδ' ἂν: C. οὐδ' ἂν, X. —Χαλκίδα: Fr. and later editors. Χαλκίδα τὴν ἐπ' Εὐρίπῳ, X. —ἀπάντων: X, F., Sch. περὶ ἁπάντων, Dobree, Fr., W., thinking that κινδυνεύειν needed an adverbial modifier to correspond to ἀδεῶς πολιτεύεσθαι; but F. compares XXXI. 7. ἐνδεὴς ἁπάντων, R. ἀπελθών, Bäker,

Thalheim. A word or two may have been lost, but ἁπάντων alone makes sense; see the note.

26. ὁμοίων: Contius, Cobet, Francken, recent editors. ὁμοίως, X, Sch. — αὐτῆς: corr. in X from αὐτῶν.

27. περιγίγνεσθαι: περιγίνεσθαι, X.

XXXI.

1. εἰς ὑμᾶς: Cob. and later edd. ὡς ὑμᾶς, X, Sch. In his critical note to I. 10, Frohberger cites twelve other passages in Lysias (besides three in spurious orations) in which ὡς appears as a preposition (as, *e.g.*, in § 13). But none are cases of this legal phrase. Still, from Lutz, *die Casus-Adverbien bei den attischen Rednern*, p. 8, it appears that Lysias was rather fond of using ὡς as a prep., and it may be the right reading here. — εἰς τὸ βουλευτήριον: B. εἰς τὸ δικαστήριον, X; *cf.* xxx. 34. Halbertsma and W. omit the words, but they are necessary for the sense; *cf.* [Lys.] xx. 1, 14, 17. — βουλεύσειν: Fr. συμβουλεύσειν, X, Sch., W. The latter word is used properly in Plat. *Apol.* 31 C, but not here.

2. ἀποφανεῖν: Cob. ἀποφαίνειν, X, Sch. — τῷ δυνάσθαι: the only causal usage of the articular inf. in Lysias. Birklein, *Entwickel. der subst. Infin.* p. 60.

3. ἐγώ τε: M. ἔγωγε, X. — ὅμως δ': M. ὅμως, X, Sch.

4. περὶ αὐτὸν: Lutz, *Präp.* p. 136, cites half a dozen other examples of this use of περί, but no other from Lysias. It is common in Plato and Plutarch. — εἰσι λέγειν: R. εἰσι λόγῳ, X. εἰσι τῷ λόγῳ, Sch. — ἐμοῦ μόνου: Fr. μόνου, X. — ὁποῖός: F. suggests ὁποῖός τις, as the simple ὁποῖος is not found elsewhere in Lysias. See his note.

5. πρὸς τῷ εἶναι: the earliest occurrence of πρός with the dat. of the art. infin., and the only one in Lysias. Birklein, *ibid.* p. 60. — μετέχουσι: X, edd. before B., W. μετέχουσιν, B. (after C?), F., Fr.

6. ὅσοι δὲ: C, B. οἱ δὲ, Fr., W. καὶ γὰρ οἱ, Aldus, R., Sch. καὶ γὰρ, X. — κἂν: Dryander, W.; *cf.* § 22. ῥᾳδίως ἂν, Rn., F. ἂν, X, Sch.

8. κατὰ τοσοῦτον: C, R., B. κατὰ τοσοῦτο, Fr.; but in Lysias the form in ν prevails even before consonants, Bl.-Kühn. *Gr.* I, p. 606. κατὰ τοῦτο, X, Sch. — ἀστέως: see App. to XII. 92. ἄστεος, X. — τἀναντία: C, B. τὰ ἐναντία, X.

9. ἐνθένδε: B. ἐνθάδε, X. — μετεβάλλοντο: W., F. μετεβάλοντο, X, vulg. — κατειργασμένοις: C, R., vulg. κατεργασαμένῳ, X. — οὐ γὰρ: W., F. οὐδ', X, vulg. — παρέσχεν: R., after παρέσχε of Stephanus. παρασχεῖν, X, Sch.

10. καίτοιγε: Sch. καὶ γὰρ, X. — ἡμᾶς: T. ὑμᾶς, X. — μὴ ἐβουλόμεθα: M. μὴ βουλόμεθα, X.

12. ἦν ταλαιπωρεῖν: T. ἢ ταλαιπωρεῖ, X. — ὁρᾶτε: Aldus. ὁρᾶται, X. — λῃτουργεῖν: F.; *cf.* Meisterhans, p. 28. λειτουργεῖν, X, vulg.

13. ὃς οὔ τι : S.   οὔτ᾽ εἰ, X. — συγκατελθεῖν : after this word, X has φῇ δὲ
καὶ ταῦτα καὶ αὐτὸς γενόμενος, which I have merely omitted, not being satisfied
with any emendation which I have seen proposed for this place.   καὶ ταῦτα, ὡς
φησί, καὶ ἀστὸς γενόμενος, C, B.   φησὶ δὲ ταῦτα καὶ αὐτὸς παραγενόμενος, Sluiter, who
took the words as a gloss referring to Lysias.   οὐκοῦν μετ᾽ οὐδετέρων ἂν βουλεύσειεν
ὁ τοιοῦτος γενόμενος, F., with Rn., who meant these words as a transition to εἰ
μέντοι κτλ., not pretending that they were what Lysias wrote.   φαίνεται δὲ κατὰ
πάντα κακὸς γενόμενος, W.

15. ἐπιγενομένην : Herw.   γενομένην, X, Sch. — λῃτουργεῖν : see App. to § 12.

16. ἀποδείξω : corr. by first hand from ἐπιδείξω in X.   See App. to xvi. 3. —
ἐνθάδ᾽ : Aldus.   ἔνθα, X, om. C. — Διότιμον : Fr.   αὐτὸν Διότιμον, X, Sch.

17. ὠφελήσει, κερδανεῖ : C, vulg.   ὠφελήσοι, κερδαίνοι, X.   ὠφελῆσαι, κερδαίνοι,
Aldus.   Lysias has no sure case of the rare fut. opt. in an object clause ; see
Weber, *Entwickel. der Absichts-Sätze*, p. 164. — ὁρμώμενος : Aldus.   ὁρώμενος, X.

18. πρεσβυτέροις : Naber, Halbertsma.   πρεσβυτάτοις, X, Sch. — τἀναγκαῖα :
Dobree.   ἀναγκαῖα, X, Sch. — αὐτόν : the dative seemed necessary to R., and
W. amends to αὐτοί, both being changes to avoid the somewhat rare acc. with
ἐπεξελθεῖν.   But αὐτοί, as F. remarks, leaves the verb absolute.   This might be
supported by such a place as Xen. *Anab.* v. 2. 7, μάχονται γὰρ ἐπεξεληλυθότες
καὶ ἡ ἄφοδος χαλεπή, but no change is required in view of Antiphon I. 11; II. a. 2;
IV. γ. 6; Dem. xxi. 107, xxxvii. 59 (passages cited by Baiter and Sauppe);
Eur. *Androm.* 735 (cited by Maetzner).

19. τότε τ᾽ ἀφελόμενον : R.   τό τε, ἀφελόμενον, X. — οἰκτίραντες : W., F.
οἰκτείραντες, X, Sch.   See Meisterhans, p. 142.

20. οἶδα : Contius, T.   ἤδη, X. — γιγνώσκειν : B.   γινώσκειν, X. — οἱ οἰκεῖοι : T., M.
οἰκεῖοι, X. — τοιαῦτα : the explanation in the note is Rn.'s.   But Fr. thought that
something was missing after ἐστίν, as, *e.g.*, τὰ περὶ τούτους αὐτῷ ἠσεβημένα.
Heldmann set οἷα μὲν . . . παρήσω before τοιαῦτα. — δίκαιον : Emp.   ἱκανόν, X.

21. ὑὸν : see App. to xii. 34. — ἂν ποιήσαντα : Dobree, Cob.   ἂν ποιήσοντα,
X, Turr., Sch.   ποιήσοντα, Dobree, Francken, Fr., W.   In deference to the
present prevailing opinion, I have not left ἂν with the fut. partic. in the text,
though far from persuaded that it cannot stand here as well as in other passages
in Attic prose with fut. indic., opt., and partic., as a survival of the usage
actually found in Homer, even though its syntax is much disputed there.   See
Humphreys in *Amer. Jour. Phil.* III, p. 114 ; GMT. 197, 208, 216.

22. μίκρ᾽ : Emperius.   μηδ᾽, X.

24. ἂν : B., om. X. — ὡς ἔσται : in xxx. 26 f. we have a question similar to
τί ἂν δοκιμάσαιτε, followed by similar constructions, *viz.* : διὰ τί δ᾽ ἄν τις ἀποψη-
φίσαιτο τούτου; πότερον ὡς . . . παραγεγενημένου; (ὡς causal and subjective) . . . ἀλλ᾽
ὅτι . . . εἰσενήνοχεν; (causal) . . . ἀλλ᾽ ὡς, ἐὰν νῦν αὐτοῦ φείσησθε, αὖθις ἀποδώσει τὰς
χάριτας; Cf. Plat. *Gorg.* 509 E, δεῖ δύναμίν τινα καὶ τέχνην παρασκευάσασθαι, ὡς,
ἐὰν μὴ μάθῃ αὐτὰ καὶ ἀσκήσῃ, ἀδικήσει; where *cf.* οὐ γὰρ ἀδικήσει just above.   Weber,
ibid. p. 163, classes our clause as final.   Gildersleeve (*A. J. P.* VI, p. 57) says:

'One would have expected ἀλλ' ὡς ἐσόμενον βελτίω, but possibly some such notion as ἐλπίζετε (xiv. 2) was floating through the mind of the orator. A slight anacoluthon is preferable to Weber's harsh construction.' But the explanation given in the note, with the examples (cited by F.) just quoted and others in Krüger, seems to me satisfactory.— τότε κακὸν: C. τότε ἀγαθὸν, X.— πᾶσι: X, Rn., Fr. τοῖς πράξασι, Francken, W. But the emendation is as weak as the Ms. reading, for the gnome does not require application to a special person or a class. Herwerden suggested φασι, supposing that we have here a proverb, ὕστερον τῶν ἔργων κτλ. F. suggests ἀεί.

25. τοὺς πονηροὺς: vir celeberrimus apud Taylorum. τοῖς πονηροῖς, X.

26. ναῦς: F., Animadversiones in Oratores Atticos, p. 46, from the law quoted in the note; cf. Poll. viii. 52. ναῦν, X. — ὅπως μὴ: R. ὅπως, X. — ἀλλ' ὅπως τιμήσεται: lacking in X, inserted by Rn. after M.'s ἀλλ' ὅπως τιμηθήσεται. For the use of the fut. mid. as pass., see La Roche, Beiträge zur Gr. Gram. I, p. 227 ff.; Bl.-Kühn, Gr. II, p. 112. — γ': Stephanus. τ', X. — ταλαιπωρίας: S., F., W. τιμωρίας, Dobree, Sch. ἀτιμίας, Kayser, Fr. ἀπορίας, X. But perhaps it would be best to omit, with Hundeck (Quaest. Lys. p. 6), the words καὶ τῆς μεγίστης ἀπορίας as due to a gloss on τοῦ δουλεύειν. — ἀγωνίζοιτο: Rn., and it is now generally adopted as a pis aller, for the place is still in need of a better emendation, and ἀγωνίσαιτο (R.) would be the better tense. ἐκκλησιάζεται, X. ἐκκλησιάζοιτο, C.

28. ποτε: vulg. τοτε, X.

29. κατὰ τὸ προσῆκον: Rn. οὐ κατὰ κτλ., X. But it was the duty of metics to do service in war; see note and Gilbert, Antiq. p. 178. — ἀτιμίᾳ: F. and Fr. seem to think that this refers only to the disgrace of rejection. But the term is strong (and repeated in ἀτιμάζετε, § 33), and is hardly, if ever, used in the orators except in the technical sense. Meier and Schoemann, p. 245 f., quoting this passage with Dem. xxv. 30, and believing that Harp. s.v. παλιναίρετος does not prove conclusively that a rejected candidate could stand again (the view of Fr.), hold that, in certain cases of ἀποδοκιμασία, disability to hold office followed. But they admit (p. 1028) that Theramenes was chosen ambassador only a year after he failed to pass the δοκιμασία for στρατηγός (Lys. xiii. 10).

30. δι' ὅ τι ποτὲ: Sch. διότι ποτὲ, B. διότι ποτε, X, Aldus. — γεγενημένους: Gebauer, F. γιγνομένους, X, Sch., Fr., W. γενομένους, R. — παρεδείχθη: Rn. ἐδείχθη, X. κατεδείχθη, Fr., Gebauer.

31. πατρίους: van der Es, Fr., W. πατρῴους, X, Sch. — καὶ οὕτω νῦν: so I have emended, after Gebauer's (de arg. ex contr. formis, p. 31) πρότερον καὶ τῶν κατεργασαμένων οὕτω νῦν τιμηθῆναι. For a similar, though not exactly the same usage, cf. ὅμως δὲ φαίνεται καὶ οὕτως ἐνδεεστέρα, Thuc. i. 10. 3. καὶ οὕτω συντιμηθῆναι, X, where the συν- is inconsistent with πρότερον. καὶ οὕτωσί γε τιμηθῆναι, R. καὶ αὐτῶν κινδυνευσάντων, Rn., F. αὐτῷ σωτήρια τιμηθῆναι, W. — εἰ οὗτος κτλ.: on the varying uses of the negatives in this sort of co-ordination after verbs of

wonder, *etc.*, *cf.* Morris on Thuc. i. 121. 5; F. on Lysias xxx. 32; Fr. on our passage; Kühn. *Gr.* § 513, 5; and Goodwin, cited in my note. Our passage is the only one known to me in which the negatives in the two clauses are of different sorts. For a large collection of these sentences, see Gebauer, *de arg. ex contr. formis*, p. 154 ff.

32. ἠδύναντο : see App. to XII. 99.—βουλεύεσθαι : C, B., Turr., Sch. βούλεσθαι, X (μούλεσθαι acc. to W.). ἀγωνίζεσθαι, Fr., F. διαμάχεσθαι, W. — ἄλλων γε : Stephanus. ἄλλων τ᾽, X (acc. to W.). ἄλλων, C. ἄλλων τῶν, W.

33. ἀτιμάζετε : X, vulg. ἀτιμάσετε, Fr., F., W. — διαμαχούμενος : M. διαμαχόμενος, X.

34. ἱκανά μοι : R. (*cf.* XII. 79). ἱκανὰ μέν, X. — καίτοι : X, Sch., Turr. καίπερ, Fr., F., W. The use of καίτοι with the partic. is very rare in Attic, yet see Ar. *Eccl.* 159, Xen. *Mem.* i. 7. 2, Plat. *Rep.* 511 D; *cf.* also Simon. ap. Plat. *Prot.* 339 C. In late authors it is common; *cf.* Strabo, pp. 37, 70, 812; Plut. *Pericles*, 13; Arrian, *Anab.* i. 5. 7; iii. 26. 2; iv. 21. 4; vii. 6. 2, 16. 3, 20. 8; Luc. *Nigr.* 8; 20; *Tim.* 34; *Alex.* 3; *de Salt.* 64; 79; *Hist. Conscr.* 40; 57; *V. H.* i. 28. The usage is natural enough and emendation seems unnecessary.— τούτων αὐτοὺς : R. τούτων αὐτῶν, X. — ὄντες αὐτοί : Aldus. ὄντες αὐτῷ, X.— καινὰ : anon. apud T. κοινὰ, X.

XXXII.

This speech is not found in the Mss. of Lysias. It is preserved (see p. 155) in Dion. H. *De Lysia iudicium* (Reiske, V, p. 497 ff.). The best manuscripts are M = cod. Ambrosianus D 119, of the fifteenth century, and F = cod. Laurentianus or Florentinus 59, 15, of the twelfth century. I have used L. Sadée's collation of them, in his dissertation *De Dionysii Hal. scriptis rhetoricis*, Argentorati, 1878, p. 112 ff., employing also Desrousseaux's edition of Dionysius, *Jugement sur Lysias*, Paris, 1890, and on the Mss. in general, Usener in the *Jahrbb. für Phil.* CVII, p. 145, and his *De Dion. Hal. libris manuscriptis*, Index Schol. Bonn, 1878 ; also for §§ 1–4 the scholia (Pl.) of Maximus Planudes to Hermogenes (in Walz, *Rhet. Graec.*, p. 546 f.), which are found, too, in cod. S (Par. 1983) of Bekker. For the inferior Mss. I have relied mainly upon the apparatus of Desrousseaux. They are T (of Bekker, called D by Desrousseaux) = cod. Par. 2944, and C = cod. Par. 2131, both belonging to the family of F ; also P = cod. Pal. 58, B = cod. Par. 1742, and A = cod. Par. 1657 (copied from P and hence rarely cited), all three belonging to the family of M. In the following notes I have not used the abbreviations M., T., B., F., and S., to denote the scholars mentioned on p. 178, but have printed their names in full to avoid confusion with the signs used here for the Mss. The critical notes in the editions of Fuhr, Weidner and Frohberger (revised by Thalheim) have been of great use. Unless the contrary is noted, my text of the oration itself agrees with the text of Fuhr. I have, however, quoted more at length from the remarks of Dionysius himself than is usual in editing this oration.

ON THE TEXT OF DIONYSIUS. ἐγγένηται: Sadée. γένηται, codd., vulg. — ποιήσομαι: TC. ποιοῦμαι, cett. codd. — τε ἔνα: Sadée. τινα, codd., vulg. — ἐπιδείξομαι: A, Sadée. ἐπιδείξομεν, cett. codd., vulg. — οἰόμενος: MPBF, Sadée. οἰόμενοι, TC, vulg. — Γλαυκίππου: γλαυσίππου, TC. — παιδίων: παίδων, MPB. — μητρός: μητερος, TC. — ἐν: om. F. — αὐτοῖς: αὐτὸς, TC. — κατ᾽ αὐτοῦ: Stephanus. καὶ αὐτοῦ, codd. — προὔβαλον: PB, Desrousseaux. Cf. Polyb. iii. 113. 6. προὔλαβον, cett. codd., vulg. — τῇ: Desrousseaux after Rademacher. Om. codd., vulg.

1. τὰ διαφέροντα, ἅ: codd., W. δικασταί, τὰ διαφέροντα, S, Pl., vulg., Fr., Thalheim. — εἰδώς τε: Pl., S. εἰδὼς, codd., which may possibly stand, cf. XIII. 11. — πεπονθότες: F, Pl. παθόντες, M.

2. τὴν τούτων: Desrousseaux, cf. § 5 and hypothesis. τούτων, codd., edd. — τοῖς φίλοις: Sylburg, R., Thalheim, W. αὐτοὺς τοῖς φίλοις, Pl., S., Fr., Fuhr. τοὺς φίλους, MF. — δίαιταν: S. τὴν δίαιταν, Pl. διαιτᾶν, MF. Aldus and Desrousseaux give with MF τοὺς φίλους ἐπιτρέψαι διαιτᾶν, the latter comparing the inf. with ἐπιτρέπω in Lys. XIII. 15, Xen. Anab. vii. 7. 8 (add And. I. 21, [Dem.] XL. 16, Isaeus, II. 29, Plat. Apol. 35 D); but the construction of τοὺς φίλους would be obscure to the ear after ἔπεισα, and this same error of διαιτᾶν for δίαιταν occurs in cod. F1 in Dionys. De Isaeo iudic., p. 602, 13 R., and in a fragment of Lys., 16.2 Sch. — τούτων: F, Pl., vulg. τούτου, M, Desrousseaux. — ἐπειδή: Pl., Fuhr, W. ἐπεὶ, codd., vulg. But on ἐπεί in this sense, see Fuhr's critical note, and cf. App. to §§ 8 and 25, and to XII. 11, XXIII. 14. — Διογείτων: codd. ὁ Διογείτων, Pl., vulg. — ἐξηλέγχετο: Pl., vulg. ἐξηλέγκτο, codd., Aldus, R. ἐξεληλέγκτο, conjecture of Fuhr. — ἐβουλήθη: MS, vulg., cf. Meisterhans, p. 134. ἠβουλήθη, F, Pl., R., Aldus, Fuhr (9th ed.; but see his critical note to XIII. 6, 10th ed.). — ὑπομένειν: Fuhr, after καθυπομένειν, S, and as the probable reading of the first hand of F; see G. 1272 and App. to XVI. 6. ὑπομεῖναι, M., vulg., ει and αι of this word in rasura, F. καὶ ὑπομεῖναι ... μᾶλλον, add. in marg., F.

ON DIONYSIUS. ἀρετὰς: om. TC. — ᾖ: om. MPBF. — ὁ: om TC. — φανήσονται: φανήσωνται, F. — κελεύουσί: κελεύουσιν, M. — τἀδικήματα: Markland. ἀδικήματα, codd. — τοῦδε: om. MPB. — λέγεσθαι: γενέσθαι, F. — εὐθὺς: Sylburg. καὶ εὐθὺς, codd. — δὴ: δὲ, TC, vulg. — προσεκτικοὺς: προτρεπτικούς, TC. — πρόσεστι: van der Vliet, Desrousseaux. προσέτι, codd., vulg. — ὑπὲρ ἐκείνων: MPB, Desrousseaux after Sadée. ὑπεκείνων, cett. codd., vulg.

4. Διογείτων λαβεῖν : FM. λαβεῖν Διογείτων, Pl., S, Bekker, Fr., W. — ὑεῖ : Morgan. υἱοί, codd., vulg., a form impossible for Lysias; see App. to XII. 34. The dual υἱεῖ occurs in cod. X of XIX. 46 (omitted by Keck, *Ueber den Dual*) where we should read ὑεῖ. It is true that with δύο we generally find a plural (Keck, p. 42 ff.), but the dual occurs in *frag.* 4 Sch., and the change to ὑεῖ is easier than to ὑεῖς. υἱώ, Fuhr. υἱέε, W. υἱοί, Thalheim.

5. τῶν ὁπλιτῶν : FM. See Meier and Schöm., *Att. Process*, p. 120. τοῦ ἐπὶ τῶν ὁπλιτῶν, T, R., Bekker, Sch., but Desrousseaux cites Hauvette-Besnoult, *Les Stratèges Athéniens*, p. 150. — τὸν : FM.; om. T, *cf.* on § 2. — ἀδελφόν : the codd. add ὁμοπάτριον (so vulg.), which was struck out by Herw. (so Fuhr, W., Fr., Thalheim) on the ground that Lysias would have added καὶ ὁμομήτριον, hence that it was a mere late interpolation from § 4. — ἀναγκαιότητας : MF. ἀνάγκας, T, Bekker, Sch., Fr. οἰκειότητας, W. — δικαίῳ περὶ τοὺς αὑτοῦ : Sauppe (*cf.* § 23) and recent editors. καὶ ὥσπερ τοῦ αὑτοῦ, FMPB. ἑτέρῳ εἰς τοὺς (τὰς T) αὑτοῦ παῖδας ἐπιτρόπῳ, TC., Bekker. The word ἐπιτρόπῳ, printed by Sauppe and Sch., is not necessary ; *cf.* § 23 (Herw., Fr.).

6. ναυτικὰ : T, Markland, edd. αὐτίκα, cett. codd., Aldus. — μνᾶς, ... δισχιλίας : something seems lost here, as noted by Sauppe, who would supply ἐγγείου δὲ δισχιλίας δραχμὰς δεδανεισμένας. *Cf.* § 15. Fuhr's suggestion, ἑκατὸν δ' ἐγγείῳ ἐπὶ τόκῳ δεδανεισμένας, *cf.* § 15, is better. — Χερρονήσῳ : Χερονήσῳ, F. — δοῦναι : this word may be interpolated, *cf.* Markland's and Frohberger's note. Fuhr cites in support Isaeus, II. 9, but see Thalheim's note. — κατέλιπε δὲ : R. κατέλιπε, F. κατέλιπεν, M.

7. ἔκρυπτε : ἔκρυπτεν, M. — ἀνδρός : after this word a lacuna is noted by Fuhr, since μὲν has nothing to answer it. Thalheim suggests the loss of τὰ δ' ἀντίγραφα. — τῶν : in F inserted by F 1.

8. ἐπειδὴ : Fuhr ; see App. to § 2. ἐπεί, codd. — χρόνῳ : FM. τῷ χρόνῳ, TC., Bekker, Sch. — ἐν : superscribed in F 1. — κατελέλειπτο : καταλέλειπτο, MF. — ἐπιλειπόντων : R. ὑπολειπόντων, codd. — αὐτῆς : codd. αὐτῇ, Sylburg, Sch., W., but, as Thalheim notes, Diodotus had not given the money *to* the woman ; *cf.* § 6.

9. εἶπε : F. εἶπεν, M. — καταλίποι : Stephanus. καταλείποι, codd. — διέφερεν : Rn. after διέφερε, Aldus, vulg. διέφερον, codd.

10. κλάοντες : Cob., Herw., see Bl.-Kühn. *Gr.* I, p. 133. κλαίοντες, codd. — περιιδεῖν : ὑπεριδεῖν, F 1 pr., corr. — ἀποστερηθέντας : ἀποστερρηθεντας, F. — ἕνεκα : Dobson. οὕνεκα, codd., but see App. to XXII. 3, and Bl.-Kühn. *Gr.* II, p. 251.

11. ἠντεβόλει : Cob., Fr., W. See App. to XII. 73. ἠντιβόλει, codd. — ἱκέτευε : T, edd. ἱκέτευσε, FM. — εἰ καὶ μὴ πρότερον : F, W., Thalheim. εἰ καὶ πρότερον μὴ, TC., vulg. εἰ μὴ καὶ πρότερον, MAB.

12. Ἡγήμονα : TC, edd. ἡγεμόνα, cett. codd. — εἰς : εἰ, M. — ἰέναι : TC, edd. εἶναι, cett. codd. — πραγμάτων : codd., vulg. χρημάτων, Halbertsma, Fuhr, Thalheim, W.; attractive but unnecessary.— ὑπὸ : TC, edd. ἀπὸ, cett. codd.

13. τοὺς θεοὺς : codd.   τούς γε θεοὺς, Herw., W., Fuhr. — ἐξέπλει : Taylor. ἐξέλιπε, codd. — παρ' αὐτοῦ παρακαταθήκην : παρ' αὐτοῦ καταθήκην, TC. — ἐθέλω : Rn. θέλω, codd. — τοὺς ὕστερον : καὶ ὕστερον, TC. — οὗτος λέγῃ : MFAPB, Fuhr, W., Thalheim.   αὐτὸς λέγῃς, TC, vulg. — ἐκλιπεῖν: Sch.   καταλιπεῖν, codd.

14. αὐτὸν : TC, edd.   αὐτὴ, F 2, M.   αὐτῇ, F 1. — κεκομισμένον : F 2.   κεκο- σμημένον, F 1, T.   κεκοσμισμένον, M. — ναυτικὰ : Markland.   αὐτίκα, codd., Aldus. — διοικίσει : Matthaei.   διοικήσει, codd. — διῳκίζετο : διοικίζετο, M.   For this and διοικίσει, Cobet, *Var. Lect.* p. 68, would read ἐξῳκίζετο and ἐξοικίσει. — Κολλυτοῦ : Turr., *cf.* Meisterhans, p. 73.   Κολυττοῦ, codd. — τῷ: TC, acc. to Desrousseaux, but T has τῳ acc. to Bekker ; the other codd. omit the word and so Aldus and R. Modern editors vary between τῷ (Sch., Fuhr, Fr., W.) and τῳ (Bekker, Turr.). Either might stand, as Fr. remarks, the former from the point of view of the mother, the latter from that of the boys. — αὐτὴν : R.   ταύτην, codd.

15. κεκομισμένον : κεκοσμημένον, F 1. — ἐγγείῳ : Naber.   ἐγγείους, MPBF. ἐγγύους, TC.

16. ἐκβαλεῖν : TC, Bekker, Sch.   ἐκβάλλειν, FPB, Fuhr, Fr., W., Thalheim, λλ *in rasura* M.   But on the distinction in the tenses of the inf. in Lysias see App. to § 2 and xvi. 6. — ἠξίωκας: codd., vulg., Turr.   ἠξίωσας, Pluygers, Fuhr, Fr., W. — αὐτῶν : PB.   αὐτῶν, cett. codd. — οὐ μετὰ ἀκολούθου : om. TC., add. in marg. M 1. — τῶν : om. FTC. — ὁ : om. MPBF. — κατέλιπεν : κατέλιπε, F.

17. ἀτίμους : ἀτίμως, TC. — προθυμεῖ : Herw., Cob., and so φοβεῖ, αἰσχύνει, ποιεῖ below.   προθυμῇ, codd., vulg. — φοβεῖ : φοβῇ, codd. — τὴν συνειδυῖαν : MPBF.   τὴν σὴν θυγατέρα τὴν συνειδυῖαν, TC. — αἰσχύνει : αἰσχύνῃ, codd. — ποιεῖ : ποιεῖς, MPBF.   ποιῇ, TC.

18. πάντες : om. TC. — πιστεῦσαι : πιστεῦσαί τινα, TC. — μὴ ἧττον : MPBF, Fuhr, Thalheim, *cf.* οὐχ ἧττον, § 21, though μηδὲν ἧττον, TC, vulg., Fr., W., is commoner.

19. ἀξιῶ : Rn. added ὑμᾶς after τοίνυν (*cf.* i. 36, iv. 12), unnecessarily ; *cf.* xiv. 20, 22, xvii. 10, cited by Fuhr, who conjectures ἄξιον without ὑμᾶς.   But the occurrence of this in a different gender just below would then be awkward. — ἐλεήσητε : ἐλεήσετε, M. — τοσαύτην γὰρ : τοσαύτην δ', TC. — πρὸς ἀλλήλους : MPB, Fuhr, W., Fr.   εἰς ἀλλήλους, F, vulg., which may be defended (*cf.* And. i. 68, Thuc. iv. 27. 3, and see Lutz, *Präp.* pp. 11, 17), though πρός is commoner (*cf.* xxv. 30), and εἰς may here be a mere repetition from the foregoing. The words are omitted in TC. — μήτε ... μήτε : Bekker and modern edd.   μηδὲ ... μηδὲ, codd.

20. τὰ μὲν : this is in F 1 corr. from τῶν μὲν which might stand. — ἔχειν : R. ἐλεῖν, codd.   ἐλθεῖν, Aldus. — λῆμμα : Aldus.   λῆμα, codd. — τετρακισχιλίας : Herw., Van der Es ; *cf.* §§ 14, 28.   ἐπτακισχιλίας, codd., Sch. — ὅποι : Dobree. ὅπου, codd. — τρέψειε : Dobree, Contius.   στρέψειε, codd., except στρέψειεν, F, whence Fuhr τρέψειεν. — καὶ εἰς ἱμάτια : inserted by Fr., so Fuhr, W.   εἰς γναφεῖον (γναφίον M) ἱμάτια, codd., Ald.   ἱμάτια is omitted by R., Bekker, Sch.,

though Scaliger conjectured εἰς γναφείαν καὶ εἰς ἱμάτια, and Markland γναφεῖον
ἱμάτιά τε. Desrousseaux reads ὑποδήματα δὲ καὶ ἱμάτια. — κουρέως: FMPB, Fuhr,
W., Thalheim. κουρέον, TC, whence κουρεῖον, vulg. — κατὰ μῆνα: in TC these
words follow αὐτῷ, so the older edd. and Fr. — πλεῖν: Rn. and later edd.; the
Attic form, see App. to VII. 6. πλεῖον, codd., vulg.

21. αὐτῷ τίθησι, τὸ δὲ τούτοις λελόγισται: R. αὐτῶν τίθησι τούτοις λελόγισθαι
(λελογίσθαι, M), codd. — ἐφ' ᾧ: Sylburg. ἐφ' ὧν, codd. — ὦ ἄνδρες: codd.; cf.
Rockel, de allocutionis usu, pp. 18, 21. Fuhr added δικασταί after a marginal
note in M.

22. πλεῖν: Rn. and later edd., cf. § 20. πλέον, codd., vulg. — πρὸς τὸ κεφάλαιον: Lutz (Präp. p. 174) follows here the old explanation of summatim
recensere, but then the preposition should be ἐν or ἐπί (pp. 38, 104). The
usage seems to resemble rather that of relation (cf. Plat. Theaet. 186 A), not that
of manner; cf. Isaeus, VI. 45 (quoted by Fr.), Lutz, p. 173. — παιδίων: MPBF.
παίδων, TC. — καταλειφθείς: καταληφθείς, FC. — τῶν χρημάτων: MPBF. χρημάτων, TC. — τῷ δ' ἐπιτρόπῳ: Fr. and later editors. τῷ δ' ἐπί (ἐπι, F), FM.
τὸν δ' ἐπί, T. τὸν δ' ἐπεί, C1. τῷ δ' ἐπεί, C2. After πατρῴων TC have εἰσὶν,
and the vulg. before Fr. was τῷ δ' ἐπεὶ τῶν πατρῴων εἰσὶν ἀπεστερημένοι.

23. ἐβούλετο: edd. ἠβούλετο, codd., Fuhr; but see App. to § 2. — ἀπηλ-
λαγμένον: Dobree, Fuhr, W., Thalheim. ἀπηλλαγμένοις, FMPB. ἀπηλλαγμένος,
TC, Fr., Sch. — πριάμενον: FMPB, Fuhr, W., Thalheim. πριάμενος, TC, Fr.,
Sch. — ὁπότερα: FMPB, Fuhr; cf. Isaeus, I. 22. ὁπότερον, TC, edd. — κατά-
στήσων: TC, edd. καταστήσονται, FMPB.

24. ὦ δικασταί: codd., vulg. ὦ ἄνδρες δικασταί, Herw., Fuhr, Fr., W.
So in §§ 26, 28, XIX. 34. But see Rockel, ibid. p. 21. — Ἀλέξιδι: ἀλεξίδη, F. —
δεούσας: Aldus. δέουσαν, codd. — συμβαλέσθαι: Aldus. συμβάλλεσθαι, codd.
— τούτοις: Dobree, Fr., Fuhr. τούτων, MPB. τούτων τοῖς, FTC, Aldus, Bekker,
Turr. τούτων τούτοις, R., W. αὐτοῖς, Sch., Rn. — θυγατριδῶν: FMPB. θυγα-
τριδῶν αὐτοῦ, TC, Bekker. αὐτοῦ θυγατριδῶν, cod. Guelf., Fr., Sch. — λῃτουργιῶν:
Fuhr, Thalheim. λειτουργιῶν, codd., edd.; but see Meisterhans, p. 29, and
App. to VII. 31.

25. τὸν Ἀδρίαν: TC. τὴν ἀνδρίαν, MPBF1. τὴν ἀ·δρίαν, F corr. — ἀπέστελλεν: ἐπέστελλεν, F. — ἐπειδὴ δὲ: Rn., W., Fr. ἐπεὶ δὲ, codd., vulg. — αὐτοῦ:
F2. αὐτοῦ, cett. codd. — φάσκει: Rademacher, Desrousseaux. φάσκων, MPBF,
whence Fuhr conjectured with likelihood that something like αὐτὸς τὴν ὠφέλειαν
ἔλαβε had fallen out before αὐτοῦ. ἔφασκεν, TC, edd. — ὅποι μὲν: MPBF, Sch.,
Turr., and later edd. ὅπη μὲν, C, Aldus. ὅπη μὴ, T. ὅπη δὲ μὴ, R. ὅπῃ μὲν,
Bekker.

26. ὦ δικασταί: see on § 24. — ἔργον εἴη: MPB, Fuhr, W. εἴη ἔργον, FTC,
vulg. — δὲ: om. M. — τὸν Ἀλέξιδος: MPBF, Sch., and recent editors. τοῦ
Ἀλέξιδος, TC. — ἐτύγχανε: ἐτύγχανεν, M. — ὁ τῆς: Herw., Fr., Fuhr, W. τῆς,
codd., vulg. — ηὕρομεν: Desrousseaux; cf. Meisterhans, p. 136; Bl.-Kühn. Gr.
II, p. 11. — τέτταρας: MPBF. τετταράκοντα, TC.

27. ἐπέδειξε : codd., vulg. ἀπέδειξε, Pluygers, Fr., and later edd., but see App. to XVI. 3. — δεούσας : δέουσαν, TC, *cf.* § 24. — ἀνηλωκέναι : codd., edd. Fuhr conjectures ἀνηλωμένας on account of the rarity of the infin. in this construction, but though rare it occurs with verbs of this general meaning of *showing ;* see Kühn. § 484, 15 ; GMT. 915, 5. — ὥστε : F. ὥs γε, cett. codd. — ὅσονπερ : ὅσον ὅπερ, TC. — οἴεσθε : οἴεσθαι, FTC. — οὐδεὶς αὐτῷ : MPB, Rn., Thalheim. αὐτῷ οὐδεὶς, FTC, vulg. — διεχείριζεν : codd., edd., except Fuhr, who has διεχείρισεν. — μναῖς : μνᾶς, TC. — ΜΑΡΤΥΡΕΣ : om. in codd., except in margin of T.

28. ὦ δικασταί : see on § 24. — ἔχειν αὐτὸς : MPBF, recent edd. αὐτὸς ἔχειν, TC, vulg. — αὐτῷ : MPBF, Fuhr, W. αὐτῶν, TC, vulg. — ἑκάστου : ἑκάστω, M.

29. ἔτεσιν αὗται : MPB, Aldus, Stephanus, R., Desrousseaux. αὗται ἔτεσι, TC, cett. edd. αὗται ἔτεσιν, F. — γίγνονται : MPB. γίνονται, cett. codd. — καὶ ἀποδείκνυνται : TC, omitted in other codd. For convenience I follow the vulgate in the insertion of these words, though agreeing with Fuhr that the lacuna more probably contained something like the thought in Dem. XXVII. 37. — περιόντα : the words τῶν ἑπτὰ ταλάντων follow περιόντα in all codd. and all edd. except Westermann's and Thalheim's, who strike them out after Mark-land. If they are kept we should insert τῶν τετταράκοντα μνῶν after Markland ; so Sch., Fuhr. — λῃστῶν : τῶν λῃστῶν, TC.

III. — ATTIC MONEY.

TABLE.

1 obol	= about	$0.03
6 obols = 1 drachma =	"	$0.18
100 drachmae = 1 mina =	"	$18.00
60 minae = 1 talent =	"	$1080.00

Attic coins were made of silver.[1] In calculating their values, one may conveniently begin with the drachma. This contained 4.366 grams or 67.376 grains of pure silver. In one United States silver dollar there are 371.25 grains of pure silver, so that the grain has the legal value of .269 + cents. The drachma, therefore, estimated in U.S. silver money at its legal value (in the ratio to gold of 1 : 16), would be worth a fraction over 18 cents. On this basis the above table is calculated. In English money the drachma may be estimated at about 9 pence ; in French, at about a franc.

[1] The chalcus, a copper coin of the value of ⅛ of an obol, was introduced just before the Peloponnesian War and got into common use. There were probably even smaller denominations in copper after that time.

The talent and the mina were not coins but weights. When used of money, the term talent signifies, for the time of Lysias, the equivalent of 57.75 lbs. of silver (avoirdupois weight), and it was worth 6000 drachmae. The actual Attic coins in use were the drachma and its multiples (the commonest being the four-drachma piece), and the obol with its multiples (such as the three-obol piece) and fractions (the $\frac{1}{2}$ and $\frac{1}{4}$ obol).

Two other coins are mentioned in the selections from Lysias contained in this volume, — the daric and the Cyzicene stater.[2] The daric was a Persian gold coin of great purity. It contained about 125.5 grains of gold, and was therefore equivalent to about $5.40 in American gold (one dollar containing 23.22 grains). It passed current among Athenians as the equivalent of 20 Attic drachmae. The Cyzicene stater was a coin of the town of Cyzicus. It was made of electrum, a mixture of gold and silver, and it passed current as the equivalent of 28 Attic drachmae.

Reckoned by the above figures, the sum of which Lysias was robbed by the Thirty,[3] — 3 silver talents, 400 Cyzicene staters, and 100 darics, — amounted to the equivalent of $5616 (taking the Cyzicene stater at 28 drachmae and the daric at 20 drachmae). This seems small, as the bulk of a man's fortune, but the value of money may best be appreciated by a consideration of what may be bought with it. From the Thirty-second oration[4] it appears that a liberal allowance for the support of two boys, their sister, a παιδαγωγός, and a maid-servant was 1000 drachmae ($180) a year, or a little less than 3 drachmae (54 cents) a day. This means that these five persons could have been supported on the annual income of the equivalent of $3000 at 6 per cent. That this sum was generous for the purpose is clear enough from what the orator says in that passage, and his estimate is supported by other passages in the authors. Thus, even later, when prices were higher, Demosthenes (during his minority), together with his mother and sister and their necessary slaves, had an annual allowance of 7 minae[5] ($126), together with the house in which they lived. Boeckh calculated[6] that in the time of Socrates a family of four grown persons could have lived comfortably on about five-sevenths of this sum.

[2] Cf. XII. 11, XXXII. 6.
[3] Cf. XII. 11.
[4] § 28.
[5] Cf. Dem. XXVII. 36.

[6] See Staatsh. p. 142 ff. For prices of houses, slaves, food-stuffs, clothing, etc., see the same work, p. 82 ff.

IV. — CHRONOLOGY.

B.C. 459.   Birth of Lysias.[1]

456.   Death of Aeschylus.

455.   Euripides appears as a tragic poet.

449.   Death of Cimon.   Predominance of Pericles begins.

445.   Thirty years' truce.

444.   Foundation of Thurii.   Herodotus and Lysias (later ?) among the colonists.[2]

436.   Birth of Isocrates.

434.   The Parthenon finished.

431.   The Peloponnesian War begins.

429.   Death of Pericles.

428.   Siege of Plataea.[3]

427.   Fall of Plataea.
      Gorgias in Athens.[4]
      Birth of Plato.

421.   Peace of Nicias.

418.   Tisias in Athens.[5]

415.   Sicilian expedition sails.

413.   Athenian defeat in Sicily.

412.   Revolution in Thurii.   Lysias banished.[6]

411.   Lysias in Athens again.
      Establishment and overthrow of the Four Hundred.
      Death of Antiphon.[7]

409.   Thrasyllus defeated at Ephesus.[8]

406.   Arginusae.   Condemnation of the generals.
      Dionysius becomes master of Syracuse.[9]
      Deaths of Euripides and Sophocles.

405.   About August : Aegos Potami.
      Late autumn or in winter : Siege of Athens begins.

404.   Embassies to the Spartans.[10]

[1] The traditional date ; but see Introd. § 15.

[2] See Introd. § 16.

[3] See p. 105, note 10.

[4] See Introd. § 12.

[5] See Introd. note 42.

[6] See Introd. § 17.

[7] See Introd. § 14, and on XII. 65 ; cf. 67.   [8] See p. 156, note 43.

[9] See Introd. § 23.

[10] See on XII. 69 ff. In arranging the order of the events of this and the next year I have chiefly followed Boerner ; see above, p. 25, note 5. According to the common view the Thirty were in power for eight instead of three months, and the death of Theramenes and the occupation of Phyle by Thrasybulus happened early in the year 403.

B.C. 404. April: ἡ περὶ εἰρήνης ἐκκλησία.[11]
Surrender of Athens.   Return of the exiles.[12]
Lysander returns to Samos, reduces it, and comes back to Athens.[13]
About September: ἡ περὶ πολιτείας ἐκκλησία.[14]   The Thirty established.
Lysias in exile.
Death of Theramenes.
Winter: Thrasybulus occupies Phyle.
Disarming of οἱ ἔξω τοῦ καταλόγου.[15]
Slaughter at Eleusis.[16]
Thrasybulus occupies Munychia.   Death of Critias.
The Thirty expelled.   The First Ten.[17]

403. First Ten's government.[18]
Spring: Second Ten.[19]
Pausanias in Athens.
The reconciliation.
Early Autumn: Return of the Patriots.[20]
Citizenship given to Lysias and others and withdrawn.
Lysias *Against Eratosthenes*.[21]
Lysias Or. XXXIV.[22]

401. Expedition of Cyrus (the *Anabasis*).
Overthrow of the Thirty in Eleusis.[23]
Lysias Or. XXXII?[24]

399. Return of the Ten Thousand Greeks.
Death of Socrates.

398. Lysias Or. XXXI?[25]

395. Corinthian War.   Haliartus.[26]   Death of Lysander.
Lysias Or. VII?[27]

394. Battle of Nemea.[28]
Agesilaus (accompanied by Xenophon) returns to Greece.[29]
Xenophon exiled.

390. Death of Thrasybulus.

389. Birth of Aeschines.

387. Peace of Antalcidas.[30]

---

[11] See on XII. 70.   [12] See *ibid*.
[13] See on XII. 71.
[14] See on XII. 70.
[15] See on XII. 40.
[16] See on XII. 52.
[17] See p. 26.
[18] See p. 26.
[19] See App. to XII. 60.
[20] See p. 27.

[21] See p. 26 f.   [22] See Introd. § 39.
[23] See p. 27, note 19.
[24] See p. 156.
[25] See p. 135.
[26] See on XVI. 13.
[27] See p. 6.
[28] See on XVI. 15.
[29] See on XVI. 16.
[30] See p. 93.

B.C. 384.   Birth of Aristotle.
     383.   Birth of Demosthenes.
     380.   Last known work of Lysias.[31]
     378.   Traditional date of the death of Lysias.[32]

[31] See Introd. § 24.   [32] See *ibid.*

LIST OF ABBREVIATIONS OF BOOKS OF REFERENCE.

Blass, *Att. Bereds.* = *Die Attische Beredsamkeit* von F. Blass. Zweite Auflage. 1887.

Bl.-Kühn. *Gr.* = Blass's revision of Kühner's grammar (see Kühn. below). Vol. I, 1890 ; Vol. II, 1892.

Boeckh, *Staatsh.* = *Die Staatshaushaltung der Athener* von A. Boeckh. Dritte Auflage, von M. Fränkel. 1886.

CIA. = *Corpus Inscriptionum Atticarum.*

G. = Goodwin's *Greek Grammar.* Revised edition. 1893.

GMT. = Goodwin's *Syntax of the Greek Moods and Tenses.* Rewritten and enlarged. 1890.

Gilbert, *Antiq.* = *The Constitutional Antiquities of Sparta and Athens* by G. Gilbert. English translation of the second German edition of Vol. I of the following-named work. 1895.

Gilbert, *Staatsalt.* = *Handbuch der Griechischen Staatsalterthümer* von G. Gilbert. Vol. II. 1885.

Gow = *A Companion to School Classics* by J. Gow. 1889.

H. = Hadley's *Greek Grammar.* Revised by Allen. 1885.

Hermann, *Privatalt.* = *Lehrbuch der Griechischen Privatalterthümer* von K. F. Hermann. Dritte Auflage von H. Blümner. 1882.

Hermann, *Rechtsalt.* = *Lehrbuch der Griechischen Rechtsalterthümer* von K. F. Hermann. Dritte Auflage von Th. Thalheim. 1884.

Hermann, *Staatsalt.* = *Lehrbuch der Griechischen Staatsaltertümer* von K. F. Hermann. Sechste Auflage von V. Thumser. Zweite Abteilung. 1892.

Jebb, *Att. Or.* = *The Attic Orators from Antiphon to Isaeos* by R. C. Jebb. 1876.

Kr. *Spr.* = *Griechische Sprachlehre für Schüler* von K. W. Krüger, Erster Theil. Fünfte Auflage. 1875.

Kühn. = *Ausführliche Grammatik der Griechischen Sprache* von R. Kühner. Zweite Auflage. 1869.

Lutz, *Präp.* = *Die Präpositionem bei den Attischen Rednern* von L. Lutz. 1887.

M. and S. = *Der Attische Process* von Meier and Schömann. Neu bearbeitet von J. H. Lipsius. 1883–1887.

Meisterhans = *Grammatik der Attischen Inschriften* von K. Meisterhans. Zweite Auflage. 1888.

Schoemann, *Gr. Alt.* = *Griechische Alterthümer* von G. F. Schoemann. Dritte Auflage. 1871–1873.

Smith, *Dict. Antiq.* = *Dictionary of Greek and Roman Antiquities* by W. Smith, W. Wayte, and G. E. Marindin. Third Edition. 1890–1891.

GREEK INDEX.

[Roman numerals followed by old style Arabic (as XXII. 2) refer to orations and sections, generally to the notes thereon or to the Appendix (App.). The sign § followed by a numeral (as § 12) refers to the sections of the Introduction. A few references are made by pages (as p. 106). Neither the Greek nor the English Index is intended to be exhaustive.]

ἀγαπήσειν, XII. 11.

ἀγαπητῶς, XVI. 16.

ἄγειν εἰς δούλειαν, XXIII. 9.

ἀγορά, p. 106; XII. 96.

ἀγορανόμοι, XXII. 16.

ἀγὼν ἀτίμητος, § 45; δημόσιος and ἴδιος, § 36; τιμητός, § 45.

ἄδεια, XII. 85; XXII. 19.

ἀδικέω, constrs. with, XXXI. 24; as pf., VII. 1; XII. 14.

Ἀδρίας, XXXII. 25.

ἀδύνατοι, p. 117; XXIV. 4.

Ἀθήνη Σκιράς, p. 2.

αἰκία, XXIII. 2.

Αἰσχυλίδης, XII. 48.

αἰτίαν ἔχω, XXII. 18.

ἀκόλουθος, XXXII. 16.

ἄκυρος καδίσκος, § 49.

Ἄλεξις, XXXII. 24.

Ἁλίαρτος, XVI. 13.

Ἀλκίας, VII. 10.

ἀλλά, in questions, XXIV. 24.

ἀλλὰ γάρ, VII. 9; XII. 40; XII. 99.

ἄλλος, besides, VII. 25; τῶν ἄλλων after sup., XII. 89.

ἄλλο τι, XXII. 5.

ἀλλότριος, with gen., XXXI. 34.

ἄλλως τε καί, VII. 6 App.

ἅμα, VII. 3 App.

ἀμουγέπου, XXIV. 20.

ἀμφίθυρος, XII. 15.

ἀμφισβητέω, XXIII. 10; XXIV. 14.

ἄν, iterative, VII. 12.

omission of, XII. 34; 47; XVI. 8; XXIV. 11.

omitted with verbs of necessity, etc., XII. 32.

omitted with μέλλω, XII. 99.

position of, VII. 6; XII. 1; 37; 63; 82.

with ἔδει, VII. 22; ἐχρῆν, XII. 48.

with fut., XXXI. 21 App.

without a verb, XII. 78.

ἀνάβηθι, XII. 24.

ἀναβιβασάμενος, XII. 24.

ἀναγκαῖον ἦν, XVI. 7 and App.

ἀναγκαιότητας, XXXII. 5.

ἀνάγκη, XII. 1 App.

ἀναθέμενος, VII. 19.

ἀνάκρισις, §§ 46; 47; p. 104.

ἀνάλωμα, XXXII. 20.

ἀναρπάζουσιν, XXII. 15.

ἀναφέρω, constructions with, VII. 17; XII. 81.

ἀνθ᾽ ὅτου, XII. 2.

ἀνθ᾽ ὧν, XII. 94.

ἀντεγράψατο, XXIII. 5.

ἀντιβολεῖν, XXXII. 11.

ἀντίγραφα, XXXII. 7.

ἀντιγραφή, § 46; p. 104.

ἀντίδοσις, XXIV. 9.

Ἀντικλῆς, VII. 4.

Ἀντισθένης, VII. 10.

ἀντιτιμᾶσθαι, § 45.

Ἀντιφῶν, XII. 67.

ἀντωμοσία, § 47; XXIII. 13.

Ἄνυτος, XXII. 8.

ἄξιον ἦν, XII. 32; 64.

ἄξιος, cheap, XXII. 8.

ἀπέδοσαν, XXII. 2.

ἀπετόλμησε, VII. 28.

ἀπέφαινεν, XII. 73.

ἀπό, causal, XVI. 19; ἀπὸ ἴσης παρασκευῆς, XXXI. 3; ἀφ᾽ ὑμῶν, VII. 8.

ἀπογραφή, § 46, n. 169; VII. 29.

ENGLISH INDEX.

COLLEGE SERIES OF GREEK AUTHORS

Edited under the supervision of

JOHN WILLIAMS WHITE,

Professor of Greek in Harvard University,

AND

THOMAS D. SEYMOUR,

Professor of the Greek Language and Literature in Yale University,

With the coöperation of eminent scholars, each of whom is responsible for the details of the work in the volume which he edits.

GINN & COMPANY, Publishers,

Boston.   New York.   Chicago.   Atlanta.   Dallas.

GREEK TEXT-BOOKS

GINN & COMPANY, Publishers,

Boston.   New York.   Chicago.   Atlanta.   Dallas.